PMI-ACP^{SM} Exam Prep

Rapid Learning to Pass the

PMI Agile Certified Practitioner (PMI-ACP)^{SM} Exam—

On Your FIRST Try!

By Mike Griffiths, PMI-ACP, PMP, CSM

RMC
Publications, Inc.

PMI-ACP^{*SM*} *Exam Prep*
By Mike Griffiths, PMI-ACP, PMP, CSM

Printed in the United States of America

First Printing

ISBN: 978-1-932735-58-1

Library of Congress Control Number: 2012936159

Figures 3.29, 3.39, 3.40, 3.41, 3.42, 4.5, 4.6, 4.7, 4.8, 4.9, 4.13, 4.14, 4.26, 4.31, 5.6, 5.7, Umbrella Man, Shovel Man, Vision Man, and Cart Man were adapted from images originally published by Leading Answers, Inc., original image copyright © 2012 Leading Answers, Inc. Images reproduced and adapted with permission from Leading Answers, Inc., www.leadinganswers.com.

"PMI-ACP," "PMI Agile Certified Practitioner (PMI-ACP)," "PMBOK," "PMI," "PMP," and "SeminarsWorld" are either marks or registered marks of the Project Management Institute, Inc.

"Tricks of the Trade" and "PM FASTrack" are registered trademarks of RMC Project Management, Inc.

RMC Publications, Inc.

Phone: 952.846.4484
Fax: 952.846.4844
E-mail: info@rmcproject.com
Web: www.rmcproject.com

Dedication

I would like to dedicate this book to my son, Jake, and my best friend and wife, Sam. Sam has little interest in agile project management but knows it inside and out because of her ongoing support, which includes listening to me rehearse presentations and proofreading articles.

Thank you for once again doing more than your fair share of the hard work in our lives while I was off writing this book.

Author's Acknowledgments

I would like to recognize David Anderson for encouraging me to start blogging about agile project management in 2005 when we were working on the APLN board together. He helped me overcome my feeling of it being a vain pursuit to instead see it as a way of helping people and connecting with like-minded professionals. Thanks, it has opened many doors for me.

I am grateful, too, to Doug DeCarlo, who got me started writing articles for Gantthead.com magazine and put me in touch with RMC and the discussions for this book.

From RMC, Laurie Diethelm has been a superstar without whom this book would not have happened. She was a fast learner of agile concepts and recognized them as descriptions of how people actually work. Instead of this book being a big writing task, it was an incremental process of iterating through chapters, fleshing out ideas, then adding exercises and questions. Her input was beyond editorial and more a collaborative development. She transformed my disjointed ramblings into a consistent voice and steered my rants toward useful exam preparation advice. However, the biggest thing she did was to provide consistent encouragement and a rational voice when competing demands for my time threatened the timeline.

Rose Brandt did a great job on fact checking, often reconciling multiple different views of the same term into some degree of clarity—when I would have been tempted to dismiss them as contradictory.

Jason Craft transformed my scribbles into comprehendible diagrams, and this book's consistent appearance is in large part due to his hard work.

Thanks are due to the reviewers, too, who provided valuable feedback on sometimes incomplete chapters, making adaptation and improvement possible.

Finally thanks to the indexers, typesetters, and publishers whose roles and work often go unrecognized, but without whom, quite literally, there would be no book.

To these people and those I have not directly mentioned here, but still helped, thank you. My name may be on the cover, but your work and influence are in these pages and I am grateful.

Mike Griffiths

Publisher's Acknowledgments

RMC would like to thank the following people for their invaluable contributions to this book:

Editors	Production/Layout	Graphics
Laurie Diethelm	Jason Craft	Jason Craft
Rose Brandt	Whitney Thulin	
Deborah Kaufman	Dave Pedersen	

Reviewers

Dr. Alistair Cockburn
Co-author of the Manifesto for Agile Software Development, co-founder of the International Consortium for Agile, PMI-ACP Steering Committee Member

Dennis Stevens
PMI-ACP Steering Committe Member, PMI® Agile Community of Practice Council Leader
Enterprise Agility Coach, Leading Agile

Michele Sliger
PMI-ACP Steering Committee Member, co-author of The Software Project Manager's Bridge to Agility
Sliger Consulting

Theofanis C. Giotis, MSc, Ph.D. C., PMP, MCT, PRINCE2
12PM Consulting

Ursula Kusay, PMP
CSC Deutschland Akademie GmbH

Anton Josef Müller PMP, CBAP
CSC Deutschland Akademie GmbH

Andreas Buzzi, PMP, CSM and OpenGroup certified Architect & IT Specialist

Carlos Sánchez-Sicilia, PMP, CBAP, CGEIT, CRISC

Jeffrey S. Nielsen, PgMp, PMP

Margo Kirwin, PMP, CPLP

Additional Contributors

Eric Rudolf
Barbara A. Carkenord

We'd also like to offer a special note of appreciation for the author, Mike Griffiths, who truly practices what he preaches. Throughout this project, Mike maintained his focus on delivering tremendous value to his readers, regardless of how overwhelming the endeavor seemed at times. This was by no means a small effort, and the timeline was extremely demanding. Mike stayed steady throughout the project, delivering chapter after chapter of insightful content, with a clear voice and vision and, not least, a sense of humor.

Table of Contents

About Mike Griffiths

 Mike Griffiths is a world-renowned project manager, trainer, consultant, and writer, holding multiple project management and agile-related certifications. Mike was on the original PMI-ACP Steering Committee, which defined the agile-related knowledge, skills, tools, and techniques to be tested on the PMI-ACP exam. He is also currently helping to create the new *A Guide to the Project Management Body of Knowledge (PMBOK® Guide)—Fifth Edition*, as well as the upcoming Software Extension to the *PMBOK® Guide*.

Mike frequently presents at PMI® Global Congress conferences, and teaches a two-day Agile Project Management course for the Project Management Institute (PMI) as part of their traveling SeminarsWorld® program. He also helped start the PMI® Agile Community of Practice, which is now the largest PMI community in existence.

Mike helped create the agile method DSDM (Dynamic Systems Development Method) and has been using agile methods including FDD, Scrum, and XP for the last 17 years. Mike also served on the Board of Directors for the Agile Alliance and the Agile Project Leadership Network (APLN). In addition to extensive agile methods experience, Mike is very active in traditional project management, holding both the PMP® and PRINCE2 certifications.

About RMC Project Management, Inc., and RMC Publications, Inc.

Founded in 1991 by Rita Mulcahy, RMC Project Management is the innovator in project management training and professional development. Over the last 20-plus years, hundreds of thousands of project managers in over 50 countries have utilized one of our professional development resources, classes, or e-Learning courses to expand their project management knowledge and further their careers. Today, RMC offers a wide range of innovative classes and products for beginning and advanced project managers—as well as those seeking a project management or business analysis certification.

When people ask what makes RMC different than other companies, our answer is threefold: 1) we minimize the number of hours needed to learn, 2) we maximize knowledge delivery and retention in everything we do, and 3) we communicate knowledge that is immediately applicable by project managers in the real-world. This simple, yet powerful philosophy has turned RMC into one of the fastest-growing training organizations in the world.

Free Updates

Purchase of this book includes access to updates regarding the PMI-ACP exam, as well as additional tips and information to help you prepare for the exam. Access this information at **www.rmcproject.com/agileprep**. Have this book with you when you go to the website.

We Need You to Help Us Stop Copyright Infringement

As the publisher of some of the best-selling exam prep books on the market, RMC is also, unfortunately, one of the most illegally copied. It is true that many people use our materials legally and with our permission to teach exam preparation. However, from time to time, we are made aware of others who copy our exam questions, Tricks of the Trade®, and other content illegally and use them for their own financial gain.

If you recognize any of RMC's proprietary content being used in other exam prep materials or courses, please notify us at copyright@rmcproject.com immediately. We will do the investigation. Please also contact us at the e-mail address above for clarification on how to use our materials in your class or study group without violating any laws.

Contact Us

We love to hear your feedback. Is there anything in this book that you wish was expanded? Is there anything we focus on too much, or is there anything not covered that you think should be here? We would love to hear from you. Send us an e-mail at **agileprep@rmcproject.com**.

INTRODUCTION

Chapter One

Why the PMI-ACP℠ Certification Is Important

What? The Project Management Institute is creating an agile certification? I was skeptical myself. After all, PMI already had a well-recognized methodology in place, as documented in the *PMBOK® Guide*, and there were several other established approaches to agile project management already out there.[1] So what value could this new certification bring to the industry?

Skepticism and all, I made the choice to get involved with the PMI-ACP Steering Committee for two key reasons:

1. PMI had a large elephant in the room. Many IT projects were using agile methods, and PMI could offer project managers little guidance on how to help manage those projects.
2. PMI had made the decision to create a knowledge base and a certification program, and I could either be on the outside wondering if the program would be effective, or on the inside helping to steer it in the right direction.

The ironic thing was that I had initially been drawn to agile out of rebellion against what I thought PMI and the *PMBOK® Guide* represented.[2] As I learned more about agile and about PMI and the *PMBOK® Guide*, however, it became clear that what I was really rebelling against was the blind, unreasoned application of project management principles in a domain (IT projects) in which concepts like unchanging plans and low execution risk are invalid.

Despite this realization, my early skepticism of PMI creating an agile certification was hard to overcome. I worried the program would fail and quietly fade away or that PMI might simply create a light version of the *PMBOK® Guide* or develop a multiple waterfall approach that project managers would think was agile and then try to force onto their teams.

My fears were soon put to rest when I found out who else was on the PMI-ACP Steering Committee. Luminaries like Alistair Cockburn (pronounced Co-burn) and industry experts like Michele Sliger, Dennis Stevens, Mike Cottmeyer, Jesse Fewell, and Ahmed Sidkey were all contributing to the development of the certification. As a group, we would not let the program be compromised or diluted.

No matter how much integrity a program has, however, no certification can truly guarantee that someone has a particular level of knowledge or competence. The fact that someone has letters behind their name does not override the need for hiring managers to interview, assess, and get references for candidates before they trust them with projects. But achieving the PMI-ACP certification does contribute to an overall measure of a project manager's qualifications. Applicants are required to pass a three-hour exam that is more rigorous than many other agile certifications, and the exam prerequisites of 2,000 hours of general project experience and 1,500 hours of agile project or methodology experience help ensure they have real-world experience.

At the end of the day, a large part of the value of a certification is in the credibility of the organization offering it. This is where PMI has an advantage over other programs. Its certifications are well structured, the test is professionally designed and administered, and the results are recognized within the project management community, with over 400,000 registered PMP-certified project managers and more than 3 million copies of the *PMBOK® Guide* in circulation.

So the value of the PMI-ACP certification lies in two points. First, it comes from PMI, an entity that is well known and trusted by organizations and their hiring managers for their credential standards. Second, despite PMI being a somewhat unlikely parent for an agile certification, the PMI-ACP exam is created by agile experts for agile practitioners, and it is not tied to a single agile methodology. As a result, the PMI-ACP certification is well positioned to become the new standard for agile professionals.

About the PMI-ACP Exam

In this first chapter of the book, we'll discuss the scope of the exam at a high level. Just like on a project, you need to know what is in scope, what is out of scope, and whether there are any particular hoops you will have to jump through to be successful. Let's start by addressing the qualification requirements, some key exam assumptions, and the exam content.

Qualifying to Take the Exam

Passing the PMI-ACP exam is just one component of achieving your PMI-ACP certification. The other components are related to education, experience, and training. In order to qualify to take the exam, you need to have all of the following:

Education	General Project Experience	Agile Project Experience	Training in Agile Practices
High school diploma or equivalent	2,000 hours (about 12 months) of project team experience within the last five years	1,500 hours (about 8 months) of agile project team or Agile methodology experience within the last three years	21 hours

> *PMI may make changes to aspects of the exam, including the qualification requirements, the application process, the passing score, and the breakdown of questions in each process group. For the latest information, please visit www.pmi.org and read your authorization notice carefully. Any differences between what is listed here and what is communicated by PMI should be resolved in favor of PMI's information.*

Having 1,500 hours of agile experience means you probably have been exposed to many of the concepts the exam will test you on, but since there are several different agile methods (e.g., Scrum, feature-driven development (FDD), extreme programming (XP), etc.), the terminology used on the exam might be different from what you have used on your projects. As you go through this book, identify any such terms or concepts and note how they differ from your real-world experience so you will be prepared when you see them on the exam.

 Exam Assumptions

The following are key points to note about the exam. Understanding these assumptions can be extremely helpful when answering questions on the exam, especially difficult situational questions.

1. Despite the amount of project experience and training required, this exam is focused on basic agile projects. Complex topics such as scaling agile practices or using an agile methodology outside of standard small project implementations are not covered on the PMI-ACP exam. Keep this in mind when you take the exam and use this knowledge to frame how you understand the context of the questions presented. In essence, the exam is testing you on plain-vanilla agile.
2. Each agile method has a unique vocabulary. The PMI-ACP exam attempts to be methodology agnostic. In other words, Scrum or FDD terminology is not used throughout. Instead, the exam uses terms that are thought to be universal, such as "iteration" (not "sprint"). If you find yourself unsure about the meaning of a word in a question, think in general agile terms, not specific methodology terms.

Exam Content

The Project Management Institute provides the "PMI Agile Certified Practitioner (PMI-ACP)^{SM} Examination Content Outline" on its website (www.pmi.org). This document describes what topics the exam covers. It breaks the content down into tools and techniques (T&Ts), knowledge and skills (K&Ss), and domains.

This breakdown can seem overwhelming at first, but remember, if you have the required agile training and project experience, you have likely been exposed to most of the concepts the exam will test you on. How the concepts are divided into categories is somewhat arbitrary, and in terms of what you need to understand to pass the exam, the categories are of little consequence. Understanding the basic principles is much more important.

That said, the breakdown is valuable in creating a logical framework to group the concepts, so it is easier to understand the principles and how the topics are related to each other. It also provides useful insight into how the marks are awarded on the exam.

Let's explore this breakdown in more detail:

» **Tools and Techniques (T&Ts)**—These are things you should *be able to do*. As a result, the exam attempts to test your *ability to apply them*, often through "do," "calculate," or "identify what happens next" types of questions. Questions about tools and techniques make up 50 percent of the exam.

» **Knowledge and Skills (K&Ss)**—These are things you should *know*. Therefore, the exam attempts to test your *understanding and recall* of them, often through questions that asses whether you remember the "how" and "why" of the topics being tested. Questions about knowledge and skills make up the remaining 50 percent of the exam.

» **Domains**—The exam content outline defines six groupings or clusters of T&Ts and K&Ss.[3] While you will not be specifically tested on the domains, these groupings define how PMI intends the topics to be understood and taught. The domains are *useful uniting bonds*.

Chapters 3 through 8 of this book are organized in alignment with the exam domains, describing all the T&Ts and K&Ss that are part of each domain.

So to summarize the breakdown, the exam will test you on things you should be able to do (tools and techniques) and what you should know (knowledge and skills). These concepts can be grouped into six domains. The following table is my interpretation of how the tools and techniques and knowledge and skills fall into the different domains. It also provides a preview of the topics we will cover in this book.

Exam Content and Domain Breakdown		
Domain	**Tools and Techniques** (50% of Exam Questions)	**Knowledge and Skills** (50% of Exam Questions)
Value-Driven Delivery (*Chapter 3*)	» ROI, NPV, IRR » Agile earned value management (EVM) » Product roadmap » Value stream mapping » WIP limits » Relative prioritization » Risk-adjusted backlog » Cumulative flow diagrams » Task/Kanban boards » Chartering » Customer-valued prioritization » Risk burn down graphs	» Prototypes, simulations, demonstrations » Incremental delivery » Prioritization » Project and quality standards » Agile contracting » Agile accounting » Systems thinking » Variations in agile methods » Value-based analysis
Stakeholder Engagement (*Chapter 4*)	» Wireframes » Servant leadership » User stories/ backlog » Conflict resolution » Agile modeling » Velocity » Information radiators » Distributed teams » Personas » Burn down/up charts » Story maps » Negotiation	» Incorporating stakeholder values » Communications management » Leadership tools and techniques » Stakeholder management » Active listening » Facilitation methods » Globalization, culture, and team diversity » Vendor management » Participatory decision models
Boosting Team Performance Practices (*Chapter 5*)	» Daily stand-ups » Co-located teams » Team space » Agile tooling » Adaptive leadership » Emotional intelligence	» Brainstorming techniques » Building empowered teams » Coaching and mentoring » Building high-performance teams » Team motivation » Co-location and geographically dispersed teams
Adaptive Planning (*Chapter 6*)	» Process tailoring » Iteration and release planning » Wide band delphi and planning poker » Progressive elaboration » Timeboxing » Minimally marketable feature (MMF) » Ideal time » Affinity estimating » Relative sizing/ story points	» Time, budget, and cost estimation » Value-based decomposition and prioritization » Agile charters » Business case development » Innovation games

Exam Content and Domain Breakdown				
Domain	**Tools and Techniques** (50% of Exam Questions)		**Knowledge and Skills** (50% of Exam Questions)	
Problem Detection and Resolution *(Chapter 7)*	» Cycle time » Escaped defects » Continuous integration » Risk-based spike » Frequent verification and validation	» Test–driven development/ test-first development » Acceptance test-driven development	» Problem solving » Control limits » Failure modes and alternatives	» Variance and trend analysis
Continuous Improvement *(Chapter 8)*	» Retrospectives		» Knowledge sharing » Process analysis » Applying new agile practices	» PMI's Code of Ethics and Professional Conduct » Continuous improvement » Self-assessment

In addition, I've included an Agile Framework chapter in this book (chapter 2). This chapter focuses on foundational concepts such as the Agile Manifesto and agile methods and terminology, which are also listed as knowledge and skills on the exam content outline.[4]

As noted earlier, 50 percent of the marks on the exam are awarded for tools and techniques questions and 50 percent are awarded for knowledge and skills questions. The knowledge and skills section is further broken down into three tiers:

» **Level 1**: There are 18 knowledge and skills in level 1. These are deemed the most important knowledge and skills concepts to know. Therefore, 33 percent of the overall exam questions will test you on these topics.
» **Level 2**: There are 12 knowledge and skills in level 2. Questions about these concepts make up 12 percent of the exam.
» **Level 3**: There are 13 knowledge and skills in level 3. These concepts are given the least amount of emphasis on the exam, making up just 5 percent of the total exam questions.

Figure 1.1: Exam Score Breakdown

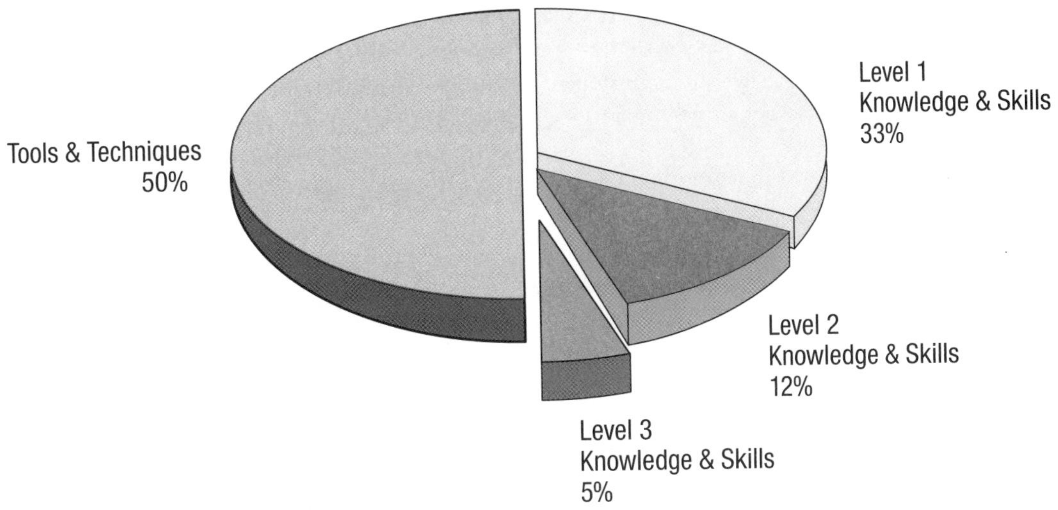

Tools & Techniques 50%

Level 1 Knowledge & Skills 33%

Level 2 Knowledge & Skills 12%

Level 3 Knowledge & Skills 5%

Therefore, to maximize your scoring potential on the knowledge and skills questions, you should give the most attention to mastering the level 1 topics, as they account for most of the K&S marks. Level 2 and level 3 knowledge and skills are still important on the exam, but together, they only represent 17 percent of the questions. The following table provides an overview of the knowledge and skills in each level in alphabetical order. As we discuss each K&S in later chapters of this book, you will see indicators of what their level is for the exam.

Level	Knowledge and Skills	
Level 1	» Active listening » Agile Manifesto values and principles » Assessing and incorporating community and stakeholder values » Brainstorming techniques » Building empowered teams » Coaching and mentoring within teams » Communications management » Feedback techniques for product » Incremental delivery	» Knowledge sharing » Leadership » Prioritization » Problem solving » Project and quality standards for agile projects » Stakeholder management » Team motivation » Time, budget, and cost estimation » Value-based decomposition and prioritization
Level 2	» Agile frameworks and terminology » Building high-performance teams » Business case development » Co-location and geographically dispersed teams » Continuous improvement processes » Elements of a project charter for an agile project	» Facilitation methods » Participatory decision models » PMI's Code of Ethics and Professional Conduct » Process analysis » Self-assessment » Value-based analysis
Level 3	» Agile contracting methods » Agile project accounting principles » Applying new agile practices » Compliance (organization) » Control limits for agile projects » Failure modes and alternatives » Globalization, culture, and team diversity	» Agile games » Principles of systems thinking » Regulatory compliance » Variance and trend analysis » Variation in agile methods and approaches » Vendor management

Remember, you won't be tested on what these categories, breakdowns, or percentage splits are. You will not see questions about what knowledge and skills fall into level 2 or be asked to list the six domains. The purpose of this information is to help you understand what is in scope and what is out of scope for the exam. Knowing this allows you to focus your studies and not spend time on concepts that aren't tested on the exam, such as multiproject enterprise agile.

Now let's spend a little more time exploring the domains (i.e., the groupings or suggested learning modules for the exam materials). Again, you will not be tested on which K&Ss and T&Ts fall under which domain, but understanding these concepts in the context of the domain will help you more easily organize the information and pull the concepts together in your mind.

Domain 1—Value-Driven Delivery

This domain focuses on maximizing business value through prioritization, iterative delivery, and risk management. The following is a summary of the efforts included in the Value-Driven Delivery domain:

- » Prioritize based on value
- » Perform retrospectives and adaptation
- » Define acceptance criteria
- » Create situationally specific processes
- » Chunk work to maximize value and gain feedback
- » Reduce risks early
- » Deliver incrementally and get feedback
- » Examine value and early termination
- » Reduce cost of changes
- » Proactively reduce risk
- » Keep stakeholders informed of dependencies
- » Do demos and get feedback
- » Consider value and risk in prioritization
- » Actively reprioritize
- » Consider nonfunctional requirements

We will discuss the T&Ts and K&Ss associated with these activities in more detail in chapter 3 of this book.

Domain 2—Stakeholder Engagement

This domain deals with understanding stakeholder needs, getting stakeholders involved, and keeping them informed. The following is a summary of the efforts included in the Stakeholder Engagement domain:

- » Get the right stakeholders
- » Continuously engage the stakeholders
- » Cement stakeholder involvement
- » Actively manage stakeholder interest
- » Frequently discuss what "done" looks like
- » Show progress and capabilities
- » Candidly discuss estimates and projections

We will discuss the T&Ts and K&Ss associated with these activities in more detail in chapter 4 of this book.

Domain 3—Boosting Team Performance Practices

This domain links team-related topics, including forming teams, empowering them, building team commitment, and promoting collaboration. The following is a summary of the efforts included in the Boosting Team Performance Practices domain:

- » Create team norms collectively
- » Build cross-functional teams
- » Promote generalizing specialists
- » Spread agile values, principles, and terms
- » Promote self-organization
- » Create a safe team environment
- » Research team and personal motivators
- » Promote team consensus-making

» Reduce communication costs
» Shield the team from outside interruptions
» Create a uniting vision
» Work with the team to track velocity

We will discuss the T&Ts and K&Ss associated with these activities in more detail in chapter 5 of this book.

Domain 4—Adaptive Planning

This domain deals with estimating, creating different levels of plans, getting feedback on progress, and updating plans. The following is a summary of the efforts included in the Adaptive Planning domain:

» Plan at multiple levels
» Involve the team and customer to engage them in planning
» Manage expectations via actual results
» Tailor the process to project characteristics
» Update the plan based on project priorities
» Ensure encompassing estimates
» Use appropriate estimate ranges
» Base projections on completion rates
» Factor in diversions and outside work

We will discuss the T&Ts and K&Ss associated with these activities in more detail in chapter 6 of this book.

Domain 5—Problem Detection and Resolution

This domain is concerned with encouraging whole-team tracking and resolution of risks. The following is a summary of the efforts included in the Problem Detection and Resolution domain:

» Promote open team communications
» Manage risks and problems as a team
» Factor in impediments
» Track risks visually
» Communicate risks

We will discuss the T&Ts and K&Ss associated with these activities in more detail in chapter 7 of this book.

Domain 6—Continuous Improvement (Product, Processes, People)

The final domain deals with how to improve various aspects of the project—including its product, processes, and people—via retrospectives and experiments. The following is a summary of the efforts included in the Continuous Improvement domain:

» Tailor the process to the project
» Improve based on retrospectives
» Make team adjustments
» Eliminate waste
» Communicate lessons learned
» Work in pairs to spread knowledge and skills
» Test out improvement suggestions

We will discuss the T&Ts and K&Ss associated with these activities in more detail in chapter 8 of this book.

Using This Book to Pass the PMI-ACP Exam

Now that we've talked about the high-level scope of the exam, let's explore the approach and structure of this book and how you can use this resource to pass the PMI-ACP exam.

This Book's Approach

To explain my approach to this book, let's first go over a little history about how the exam content was chosen in the first place. When designing the PMI-ACP exam, the steering committee needed to base the content outline on existing books and resources so that candidates would understand what the exam would test them on. When choosing the books, we went back and forth on our decisions of which resources to include, since there are so many good resources available. And while we recommend that people learn as much as they can, we also had to recognize the need for keeping the exam content—and the preparation process for the exam—reasonable. In the end, we selected the following 11 books:

1. *Agile Estimating and Planning,* by Mike Cohn
2. *Agile Project Management: Creating Innovative Products,* 2nd ed., by Jim Highsmith
3. *Agile Project Management with Scrum,* by Ken Schwaber
4. *Agile Retrospectives: Making Good Teams Great,* by Esther Derby and Diana Larsen
5. *Agile Software Development: The Cooperative Game,* 2nd ed., by Alistair Cockburn
6. *Becoming Agile...in an Imperfect World,* by Greg Smith and Ahmed Sidky
7. *Coaching Agile Teams: A Companion for ScrumMasters, Agile Coaches, and Project Managers in Transition,* by Lyssa Adkins
8. *Lean-Agile Software Development: Achieving Enterprise Agility,* by Alan Shalloway, Guy Beaver, and James R. Trott
9. *The Software Project Manager's Bridge to Agility,* by Michele Sliger and Stacia Broderick
10. *The Art of Agile Development,* by James Shore and Shane Warden
11. *User Stories Applied: For Agile Software Development,* by Mike Cohn

Reading all of these books takes some time, since the 11 books add up to more than 4,000 pages. The books also cover a lot more material than you need to know for the exam. From each book, we extracted the portions that best covered the exam content outline topics, and the exam questions were then targeted at those specific sections.[5]

Figure 1.2 illustrates which of the main exam topics are covered in each book and then what subsections of the book's coverage are tested on the exam:

Figure 1.2: The Relationship Between the Main Exam Topics and the Resource Books

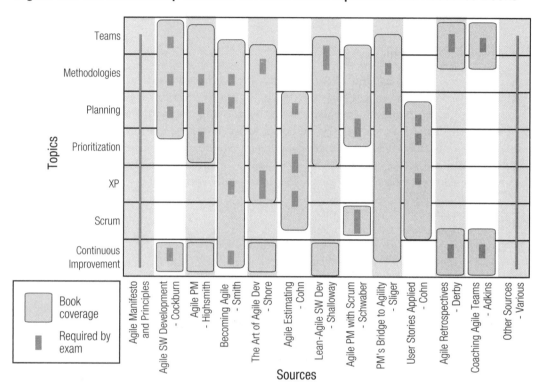

In the diagram, the vertical columns represent the Agile Manifesto, the 11 books chosen by the steering committee, and other sources we used to create the exam content outline.[6] The general exam topics (teams, methodologies, planning, prioritization, XP, Scrum, and continuous improvement) are represented in the horizontal rows. Within the diagram, the light green boxes represent what general exam topics are covered by each book, and the darker green boxes represent the portions of each book that are required knowledge for the exam.

This depiction is for discussion purposes only; I had to simplify the topics to make the diagram legible, so the resulting image is not a complete picture of the exam content outline.[7] The purpose of the diagram is to show that the books cover a lot of content that is not actually tested on the exam. The resources were chosen in the first place because they best reflected the content in the exam, and reading all of the books would certainly help you expand your knowledge. However, the exam will test you on just a small subset of the information contained in these books.

The approach I took to creating this *PMI-ACP^SM Exam Prep* book was to collect all the dark green "Required by exam" topics and explain them with a common voice. In addition, I have included supporting material, some of which is also discussed in the 11 books and some of which is discussed in other sources, along with my own insights, to create the appropriate context for the topics and explain how the tools and techniques would be used in practice.

Figure 1.3: *PMI-ACP*^{*SM*} *Exam Prep* Book Content

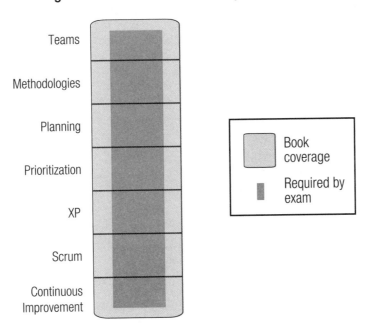

So this book covers all the required content, plus some extra information that helps make the exam content relevant and useful. At over 300 pages, the book isn't small, but it is considerably shorter than the more than 4,000 pages contained within the source books.

When creating this book, I had to balance just covering the topics in the exam in a bare-bones format, or writing a primer for agile and everything in the exam. In the end, after asking myself what kind of a guide I would like to read and talking to several candidates taking the pilot PMI-ACP exam, I ended up taking the approach of covering all the topics and writing a fair amount of "glue" and "how-you-would-use-this" material, which together will best prepare readers for the exam.

How This Book Is Organized

As noted earlier, this book is structured around the domains. You do not have to read it in sequence, but tackling complete chapters at a time will provide the most comprehensive coverage of a topic.

Some of the exam topics fit in multiple domains. For example, agile games could be covered in Domain 2: Stakeholder Engagement or Domain 4: Adaptive Planning. I will describe most concepts in detail in just one domain, but I may also briefly mention some topics in other domains in which they may be used. As noted earlier, the particular category a concept falls into is much less important than understanding what the T&T or K&S is, and how it is used.

Each domain chapter is organized the same way: a list of Quicktest topics, an introductory discussion, an "In This Chapter" breakdown, review materials, a Professional Responsibility and Ethics discussion, and a practice exam. The *PMI-ACP*^{*SM*} *Exam Prep* book can be used alone, but it is also designed to be part of an exam prep system with RMC's *PM FASTrack*® exam simulation software and *Hot Topics* flashcards (see the discussion at the end of this chapter about other resources to use in preparing for the exam).

Quicktest

The quicktest list at the beginning of each chapter highlights the "required by exam" content. Refer back to this list when you are finished reading the chapter to test your knowledge. See if you can recall what each concept means, how it's used, and its relevance on agile projects. The concepts are listed in the Quicktest in the order they appear within the chapter.

Introduction to Each Chapter

The introductory discussion provides an overview of the chapter and key information for understanding the material covered in the chapter.

"In This Chapter" Breakdown

You will first see this breakdown in chapter 3, Value-Driven Delivery. The table shows how each chapter is broken into sections or practices, and indicates which T&Ts and K&Ss are covered in each section. It also indicates the different levels (1, 2, or 3) of the K&Ss discussed. Remember, the majority of the exam questions will test you on T&Ts (50 percent) and level 1 K&Ss (33 percent). The exam gives less focus to level 2 K&Ss (12 percent) and level 3 K&Ss (5 percent).

When the concepts are discussed within the chapter, the tools and techniques and knowledge and skills are identified with the following icons:

Review Materials and Exercises

In addition to explaining the topics in a direct and practical way, I've included several exercises in each chapter to help you work through and understand the concepts. I encourage you to actually do the exercises, rather than jump right to the answers, even if the value of the exercise does not seem evident to you. If you work through the exercises, you will find the concepts stick with you better than if you simply read the explanations.

The answers are listed immediately following the exercises. Although some readers may wish the answers were shown later in the book, it is more effective to place them right after the exercise. If you want to keep yourself from seeing the answers, simply have a blank piece of paper handy to cover the answers until you have completed the exercise and are ready to review it.

 I've also included tips in each chapter, which are identified by this Tricks of the Trade® symbol. The tips will give you some extra insight on what you need to know about the exam, offer suggestions for studying for the exam, or provide tips for the real-world application of the concepts.

Professional Responsibility and Ethics Discussion

At the end of each chapter, I've included a brief discussion with examples of how some of the T&Ts and K&Ss discussed in the chapter relate to PMI's Code of Ethics and Professional Responsibility.[8] Although the Code is a level 2 K&S and would not otherwise warrant this much focus in the book, it is important for us to understand. Each person who applies to take the exam agrees to abide by the Code as part of the application process, and it affects us daily, in all aspects of our projects.

Practice Exam

The practice exam at the end of each chapter allows you to review the material and test your understanding. On the following page, you will find a score sheet to use as you take the practice exams. Make a copy of it for each practice exam.

Note: You cannot simply practice answering questions to prepare for this exam. The questions in this book (and in *PM FASTrack*®) are provided to help you assess your knowledge and to get you familiar with the types of questions that are on the exam. So focus most of your study efforts on reading this book, doing the exercises, and filling gaps in your knowledge about agile practices.

Score Sheet

Make a copy of the score sheet on the following page for each chapter's practice exam. (Note: If you are using RMC's full PMI-ACP℠ Exam Prep System, please see the study plan instructions on page 15.)

Question Number	First Time	Why I Got the Question Wrong	Second Time	Why I Got the Question Wrong
1.				
2.				
3.				
4.				
5.				
6.				
7.				
8.				
9.				
10.				
11.				
12.				
13.				
14.				
15.				
16.				
17.				
18.				
19.				
20.				
Total Score	First Time		Second Time	

How will I improve how I take the exam next time?

How to Study for the PMI-ACP Exam

Studies have shown that if you review a topic three times, you will remember it. Therefore, you should thoroughly read this book once and then go through it two more times, focusing most on the areas you had trouble understanding or where you have gaps in your knowledge or real-world experience.

Step-by-Step Study Plan

I recommend that you use one of the following study plans. Follow Plan A if you own RMC's complete PMI-ACP^{SM} Exam Prep System (see the discussion at the end of this chapter about other resources to use in preparing for the exam). Follow Plan B if you do not own the entire system.

Plan A: Using This Book with the PMI-ACP^{SM} Exam Prep System (*PMI-ACP^{SM} Exam Prep* book, *PM FASTrack*®, and *Hot Topics*)

1. Read this book for the first time and complete all the exercises, focusing more time on the chapters where you have the most gaps in your agile knowledge or experience. Focus most on items you did not know or did not do prior to beginning this course of study. Do not take the practice exams as part of your initial read-through of the book. Instead, wait until step 4 to answer practice questions, using *PM FASTrack*® instead.
2. As you finish each chapter, review the Quicktest terms listed on the first page of the chapter to make sure you know the meaning of each term or concept and its use on agile projects. Use the *Hot Topics* flashcards to improve your recall and test your understanding of that chapter.
3. If at all possible, form a study group any time after you have read the book for the first time on your own. This can actually make your study time shorter and more effective. You will be able to ask someone questions, and the studying (and celebrating afterward) will be more fun. A study group should consist of only three or four people. (See the following discussion of "How to Use This Book in a Study Group.")
4. Once you feel confident about the material, test yourself with the first 10 questions from each domain in *PM FASTrack*®. This will help you determine how much more study time you need and which chapters to read more carefully. This step will also give you a baseline against which to track your progress as you continue to study.
5. Using the score sheet provided in this book, review each question you got wrong in *PM FASTrack*®, writing down the specific reasons for each wrong answer. Assess why the correct choice is correct and why the other answers are wrong. Continue to study this book, focusing in detail on the areas in which you have gaps in your knowledge and skimming the sections or chapters in which you did well. Correct any errors in your understanding of the concepts discussed in this book.
6. Make sure you really know the material, and then take a full PMI-ACP exam simulation on *PM FASTrack*®. WARNING: You should limit yourself to two full PMI-ACP exam simulations before you take the actual exam. Otherwise, you diminish the value of *PM FASTrack*® and will see too many of the questions repeated between exams.
7. Review the questions you got wrong on the *PM FASTrack*® simulation. As with step 5, use the score sheet provided in this book and make sure you identify in writing the specific, not general, reason you got each question wrong on the simulation.
8. Use your list of why you got each question wrong (from step 7) to determine which material to study further, and then study this material.
9. Take your final PMI-ACP simulation exam.
10. Use the *Hot Topics* flashcards and other materials to retain the information you have learned until you take the exam.
11. PASS THE EXAM!

Plan B: Using This Book as a Stand-Alone

1. Read this book for the first time and complete all the exercises, focusing more time on the chapters where you have the most gaps in your agile knowledge or experience. Focus most on items you did not know or did not do prior to beginning this course of study. Do not take the practice exams as part of your initial read-through of the book.

2. As you finish each chapter, look at the Quicktest terms listed on the first page of the chapter and make sure you know the meaning of each term or concept. Review any terms you are unsure of to improve your recall and test your understanding of that chapter.

3. If it is at all possible, form a study group any time after you have read the book for the first time on your own. This can actually make your study time shorter and more effective. You will be able to ask someone questions, and the studying (and celebrating afterward) will be more fun. A study group should consist of only three or four people. (See the following discussion of "How to Use This Book in a Study Group.")

4. Once you feel confident about the material, take all the practice exams at the end of each chapter in one sitting. This will give you a baseline against which to track your progress as you continue to study. It will also help you determine how much additional study time you need and which chapters to read more carefully.

5. Review each question you got wrong in the chapter practice exams, writing down the specific reasons for each wrong answer on the score sheet that is provided in this book. Assess why the correct choice is correct and why the other answers are wrong. Continue to study this book, focusing in detail on the areas in which you have gaps in your knowledge and skimming the sections or chapters in which you did well. Correct any errors in your understanding of the concepts discussed in this book.

6. Make sure you really know the material, and then retake the practice exams in the book. As with step 5, use the score sheet to identify in writing the specific, not general, reason you got each question wrong.

7. Use your list of why you got each question wrong (from step 6) to determine which material to study further, and then study this material. Make sure you are confident you have filled your gaps before taking the exam.

8. PASS THE EXAM!

How to Use This Book in a Study Group

To get started, pick someone to lead the discussion of each chapter (preferably someone who is not comfortable with the chapter, because the presenter often learns and retains the most in the group). Each time you meet, go over questions about topics you do not understand and review key concepts on the exam using the *Hot Topics* flashcards, if you have them. Most groups meet for one hour per chapter. Either independently or with your study group, do further research on questions you do not understand or that you answered incorrectly.

Each member of the study group should have his or her own copy of the book. (Please note that it is a violation of international copyright laws to make copies of the material in this book or to create derivative works from this copyrighted book.)

Those leading a PMI-ACP exam preparation course using RMC's products may want to contact RMC for information on our Corporate Partnership program. Partners may be allowed to create slides or other materials using content from this book. Also, ask about other tools for study groups and independent instructors and how to receive quantity discounts on this book, *PM FASTrack®*, or *Hot Topics*.

Other Resources to Use in Studying for the Exam

In addition to this book, RMC offers a complete PMI-ACP^{SM} Exam Prep system, including:

***PM FASTrack*® Exam Simulation Software for the PMI-ACP Exam.** This software contains 500 practice questions to help you prepare for the exam. You can sort questions by domain, keyword, and PMI-ACP simulation. The software automatically scores and keeps records of your exams with its comprehensive grading and reporting capability. All questions are cross-referenced with this book, making it easy to go back and study your weak areas.

Hot Topics **Flashcards**, in audio, flip book, or mobile format. These flashcards feature the most important and difficult-to-recall PMI-ACP-related terms and definitions. They are an excellent study tool for people with busy schedules. You can use them at the office, on a plane, or in your car, adding instant mobility to your study routine.

To achieve the PMI-ACP certification, however, you will need more than exam prep materials. As noted earlier in this chapter, passing the PMI-ACP exam is only one component of the certification program. You also need training and experience. A good course in the fundamentals of agile project management and real-world experience working on an agile project will give you the foundation you need. Theories are much easier to understand—and in turn apply to your real-world projects—when you have experience to relate back to.

Now let's move on to the Agile Framework chapter, where we'll discuss key agile concepts that will establish a basis for understanding much of the rest of this book. We'll then begin the discussion of the domains in the later chapters of the book.

AGILE FRAMEWORK

Chapter Two

Before we launch into the exam domain chapters, let's define and clarify some key concepts that will impact your understanding of the material presented in the rest of this book. In essence, this chapter sets the scene for agile project management. It explores some of the differences between agile and traditional project management approaches, including why using agile methods is often the best choice for certain projects, and it summarizes foundational agile ideas.[1]

While many of the PMI-ACP exam questions are about specific tools and techniques, an understanding of the agile framework concepts is still relevant to answering the questions correctly. This is especially true if you are faced with a question that appears to have two or more reasonable answers. In such cases, think about the underlying agile framework to help you make the right selection.

Why Agile Methods?

Why do we need another approach to managing projects? Isn't the method that is already extensively documented in the *PMBOK® Guide* sufficient?

The answer is simple: different types of projects require different methods. In our everyday lives, we see the value of customizing our approach to different situations, often in small ways. For example, we choose what information to communicate and how to present it based on our audience. We don't resolve every issue the exact same way; instead, we adjust our approach to be effective for the unique situation. This same concept applies to how we manage our projects. Some projects, especially knowledge worker projects occurring in fast-moving or time-constrained environments, call for an agile approach.

Knowledge Worker Projects Are Different

First let's discuss a little history that is not tested on the exam but does help set the scene. Initially humans wandered the earth as hunter-gatherers. When people started planting crops and herding animals, it changed society and work. This was the Agricultural Revolution. As a result, people wandered less, and they lived and worked in one place.

The next big revolution came with the development of machines and factories, when people left their farms and villages to move to cities. This was the Industrial Revolution, which eventually led to the development of many of today's project management ideas, including Gantt charts, functional decomposition, and localized labor. In turn, these developments led to the creation of tools like the work breakdown structure (WBS).

The latest major revolution—which we are in now—is known as the Information Revolution. This revolution is focused on information and collaboration, rather than manufacturing. It places value on the ownership of knowledge and the ability to use that knowledge to create or improve goods and services.

The Information Revolution relies on knowledge workers. These are people with subject matter expertise who communicate their knowledge and take part in analysis and/or development efforts. Knowledge workers are not only found in the IT industry; they are also engineers, teachers, scientists, lawyers, doctors, and many others employed today. In fact, knowledge workers have become the largest segment of the North American workforce.

So what makes knowledge worker projects different from manufacturing projects? The following table presents a comparison of industrial work versus knowledge work:[2]

Characteristics of Industrial Work	Characteristics of Knowledge Work
Work is visible	Work is invisible
Work is stable	Work is changing
Emphasis is on running things	Emphasis is on changing things
More structure with fewer decisions	Less structure with more decisions
Focus on the right answers	Focus on the right questions
Define the task	Understand the task
Command and control	Give autonomy
Strict standards	Continuous innovation
Focus on quantity	Focus on quality
Measure performance to strict standards	Continuously learn and teach
Minimize cost of workers for a task	Treat workers as assets, not as costs

EXERCISE

Review the items in each column of the following table and place a check mark next to any that describe your job. When you are finished, look at the pattern of the check marks. Are they mostly on the left (industrial work) or mostly on the right (knowledge work)?

Characteristics of Industrial Work	Characteristics of Knowledge Work
☐ Work is visible	☐ Work is invisible
☐ Work is stable	☐ Work is changing
☐ Emphasis is on running things	☐ Emphasis is on changing things
☐ More structure with fewer decisions	☐ Less structure with more decisions
☐ Focus on the right answers	☐ Focus on the right questions
☐ Define the task	☐ Understand the task
☐ Command and control	☐ Give autonomy
☐ Strict standards	☐ Continuous innovation
☐ Focus on quantity	☐ Focus on quality
☐ Measure performance to strict standards	☐ Continuously learn and teach
☐ Minimize cost of workers for a task	☐ Treat workers as assets, not as costs

The communication and collaboration required for knowledge worker projects are often more uncertain and less defined than in industrial work. As people applied industrial work techniques to knowledge worker projects, frustration—and project failures—increased, and agile methods were developed in response. These methods collected knowledge worker techniques and adapted them for use on projects, starting with software development initiatives but then later applying them to other knowledge worker projects.

This development of agile methods took place over many years and was done by different people. As a result, we have inconsistencies in terminology and multiple methodologies. For example, Scrum calls its timeboxed development efforts "sprints," while Extreme Programming (XP) calls them "iterations." The rest of this chapter will help establish a framework for understanding what agile project management is and explain some of the key concepts you need to know, starting with the Agile Manifesto.

K&S Level 1 — The Agile Manifesto

The PMI-ACP exam will not test you on details like dates or the names of the Agile Manifesto creators. We have included this information here for your reference, but you do not need to know it for the exam.

The Agile Manifesto came about as the result of a meeting in February 2001 that brought together a number of software and methodology experts, who then defined the Agile Manifesto and Agile Principles. The experts in attendance were:

- » Kent Beck
- » Mike Beedle
- » Arie van Bennekum
- » Alistair Cockburn
- » Ward Cunningham
- » Martin Fowler
- » James Grenning
- » Jim Highsmith
- » Andrew Hunt
- » Ron Jeffries
- » Jon Kern
- » Brian Marick
- » Robert C. Martin
- » Steve Mellor
- » Ken Schwaber
- » Jeff Sutherland
- » Dave Thomas

The Agile Manifesto reads as follows:[3]

Manifesto for Agile Software Development

We are uncovering better ways of developing software by doing it and helping others do it. Through this work we have come to value:

Individuals and interactions *over processes and tools*
Working software *over comprehensive documentation*
Customer collaboration *over contract negotiation*
Responding to change *over following a plan*

That is, while there is value in the items on the right, we value the items on the left more.

While the Agile Manifesto is simple in structure and sparse in words, there is a lot of good stuff in the four values stated here. Understanding the ideas that are being conveyed is important not just for the exam, but also for the application of any agile methodology on real-world knowledge worker projects, even if they are not software development projects.

First, the format of "**A** over B," such as "**Individuals and interactions** over processes and tools," addresses intention, focus, and effort. It is not as black and white or as simple as "Do **A** instead of B." Instead, it is acknowledging that **A** and B will likely both exist on projects, but that we should apply our focus, emphasis, and intention to **A** more than B. With this in mind, let's look at these four statements in more detail. (Note: Although the Agile Manifesto uses software development terms, think about how the concepts also apply to other types of knowledge worker projects as you read this section.)

1. **Individuals and interactions** over processes and tools:

   The message here is that while processes and tools will likely be necessary on our projects, we should try to focus the team's attention on the individuals and interactions involved. This is because projects are undertaken by people, not tools, and problems get solved by people, not processes. Likewise, projects are accepted by people, scope is debated by people, and the definition of a successfully "done" project is negotiated by people. Focusing early on developing the individuals involved in the project and emphasizing productive and effective interactions help set up a project for success.

© 2012 RMC Publications, Inc • 952.846.4484 • info@rmcproject.com • www.rmcproject.com

This is not to say that processes and tools cannot help in successfully completing a project. They are certainly important assets, and for those of us who have an engineering background, we may naturally tend toward the logic and predictability of processes and tools. Yet projects are ultimately about people, so to be successful, we need to spend the majority of our time in what may be the less comfortable, messy, and unpredictable world of people. If you tend toward processes rather than people, the first value of "individuals and interactions over processes and tools" is a great reminder of where to focus your time, energy, and passion.

2. **Working software** over comprehensive documentation:

   This value speaks to the need to deliver. Software projects are typically initiated with the goal of creating valuable, high-quality software, yet they often get caught up on interim deliverables such as extensive documentation that does not support the ultimate goal of working software. Software without documentation is certainly problematic and hampers support and maintenance. But comprehensive documentation without software is next to valueless to most organizations.

   With the move to make software development more of an engineering discipline in the 1980s and 1990s, there was a heightened demand for documentation. And because this period was also the advent of increasingly large teams, complex software systems, and a legacy of undocumented, unsupportable applications, such documentation was essential. Many software developers are detail-oriented and process-driven; although these characteristics are often highly beneficial, they can also mean the developers' focus can easily be distracted from the real reason they are undertaking software projects—to write valuable software. So the Agile Manifesto's emphasis on valuing working software over comprehensive documentation acts as a necessary and useful reminder of why these projects are commissioned in the first place—to build something useful. Documentation by itself, or at the expense of working software, is not useful.

3. **Customer collaboration** over contract negotiation:

   This value reminds us to be flexible and accommodating, rather than fixed and uncooperative. It is similar to the difference between "being right" and "doing the right thing." We could build the product exactly as originally specified, but if the customer changes their mind or priority, it would be better to be flexible and work toward the new goal, as opposed to the goal that was originally stated.

   It is notoriously difficult to define an upfront, unchanging view of what should be built. This challenge stems from the dynamic nature of knowledge worker products, especially software systems; software is intangible and difficult to reference, companies rarely build the same systems twice, business needs change quickly, and technology changes rapidly. Rather than beat up the client with a change management process that is really more of a change suppression process, we should recognize at the start that things are going to change, and we should work with the customer throughout the project toward a shared definition of "done." This requires a more trusting relationship and more flexible contract models than we often see on projects, but it again moves the emphasis from nonvalue-adding activities (like arguing about scope) to productive work. (See chapter 3, Value-Driven Delivery, for more on agile contracting.)

4. **Responding to change** over following a plan:
   As we just discussed, initial plans are sometimes inadequate. Instead of investing effort in trying to bring the project back in line with the original plan, we should spend more of our effort and energy responding to the inevitable changes on the project. But this doesn't mean the Agile Manifesto is suggesting we abandon planning and just react to changes. We still need to plan,

but we also need to acknowledge that the initial plans were made when we knew least about the project (at the beginning), and as the work progresses, we will need to update the plan.

The importance of responding to change over following a plan is particularly true for software projects, where high rates of change are common. Again, instead of suppressing changes and spending a lot of time managing and tracking a largely static plan, we need to acknowledge that things will change. Agile projects have highly visible queues of work and plans in the form of backlogs and task boards. The intent of this agile value is to broaden the number of people who can be readily engaged in the planning process, adjust plans, and discuss the impacts of changes.

The Agile Manifesto is not a set of rules telling us to do one thing instead of another. It is more subtle, and more powerful—it guides us to consider projects from a value-based perspective. Yes, we will need processes, tools, documentation, and plans on our projects; yet while dealing with these assets, we should remember that our focus must be on the people engaged, the product we are building, cooperation, and flexibility. Agility is the capacity to execute projects while focusing our efforts on the items on the left side of these value statements, rather than those on the right.

EXERCISE: MATCH THE AGILE MANIFESTO VALUES

Draw arrows matching the Agile Manifesto value beginnings on the left to their corresponding endings on the right. Note: You may want to have a sheet of paper handy to cover up the exercise answers as you go through this book

Start		End
Working software	Over	Processes and tools
Responding to change	Over	Comprehensive documentation
Individuals and interactions	Over	Contract negotiation
Customer collaboration	Over	Following a plan

ANSWER

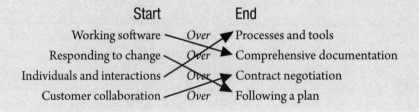

Guiding Principles

In addition to the four agile values, the authors of the Manifesto created twelve guiding principles for agile methods. These are:[4]

Principles behind the Agile Manifesto

We follow these principles:

Our highest priority is to satisfy the customer through early and continuous delivery of valuable software.

Welcome changing requirements, even late in development. Agile processes harness change for the customer's competitive advantage.

Deliver working software frequently, from a couple of weeks to a couple of months, with a preference to the shorter timescale.

Business people and developers must work together daily throughout the project.

Build projects around motivated individuals. Give them the environment and support they need, and trust them to get the job done.

The most efficient and effective method of conveying information to and within a development team is face-to-face conversation.

Working software is the primary measure of progress.

Agile processes promote sustainable development. The sponsors, developers, and users should be able to maintain a constant pace indefinitely.

Continuous attention to technical excellence and good design enhances agility.

Simplicity—the art of maximizing the amount of work not done—is essential.

The best architectures, requirements, and designs emerge from self-organizing teams.

At regular intervals, the team reflects on how to become more effective, then tunes and adjusts its behavior accordingly.

 These values and principles are key to understanding agile, and they can help you when you are faced with two seemingly correct options on the exam. In such instances, look for the answer that best matches the agile values or principles.

Let's take a closer look at each of the 12 principles. Again, although software development terms may be used, think about how the concepts apply to other types of knowledge worker projects as you read this section.

1. **Our highest priority is to satisfy the customer through early and continuous delivery of valuable software.**

   There are three main points in this principle. The first is to satisfy the *customer*. If we produce perfect plans and documentation and only delight the project management office (PMO) or the quality assurance (QA) group, we have failed; the focus should be on the customer.

The second point is *early and continuous delivery*. We must structure the project and the project team to deliver early and then deliver frequently. This can be a struggle if people are reluctant to share incomplete work, and it takes courage and support for everyone to become comfortable with this idea. We must achieve this point if we are to learn of problems while we still have time to fix them, however. It is better to get something wrong up front and have time to correct it than to discover the issue much later when so much more has been built on top of a faulty foundation.

The final point is that what we are delivering is *valuable software*, not completed work products, WBS items, documentation, or plans. The focus is on the end goal. For software projects, this is the software; for other types of projects, the end goal will be the product or service that the project was undertaken to deliver or enhance.

2. **Welcome changing requirements, even late in development. Agile processes harness change for the customer's competitive advantage.**

   Changes can be great for a project if they allow us to deliver some late-breaking, high-priority feature. Yet from a traditional project management point of view, changes are often seen in a negative light; they are designated as scope creep and considered to be the reason the project deviated from the plan. Many traditional projects have such rigorous change control procedures that only the highest priorities make it through. On such projects, much of the time and effort is spent logging and managing change requests.

   This kind of rigorous change management approach is problematic for software projects or for any type of project that experiences high rates of change. In contrast, agile project management accepts that changes will occur. In fact, the XP methodology advocates that we "embrace change." Instead of creating a high-overhead mechanism for processing changes, agile methods use a lightweight, high-visibility approach for prioritizing the changes into the backlog of work to be done.

   By accepting that changes will happen and by setting up an efficient way to deal with them, a team can spend more time developing the project's end product. Rather than suppressing changes, agile methods work to create a well-understood, high-visibility way of handling changes that keeps the project adaptive and flexible as long as possible.

3. **Deliver working software frequently, from a couple of weeks to a couple of months, with a preference to the shorter timescale.**

   Despite our best intentions and knowledge that early feedback is valuable, it is human nature to want to create something good before sharing it. However, we are doing ourselves a disservice by holding on to our work for so long. It is better to get feedback early and often to avoid going too far down the wrong track.

   This principle emphasizes the importance of releasing work to a test environment and getting feedback. Frequent testing and feedback are so important that continuous integration tools have been created to provide feedback to developers about any code they have written that breaks the build. (See chapter 7, Problem Detection and Resolution, for more on continuous integration.) Agile teams need feedback on what they have created thus far to see if they can proceed, or if a change of course is needed.

   Delivering within a short timeframe also has the benefit of keeping the business engaged and keeping dialogue about the project going. With frequent deliveries, the project team regularly has results to show the business and has opportunities to get feedback. Often at these demos, the team learns of new requirements or changes in business priorities that are valuable planning inputs.

4. **Business people and developers must work together daily throughout the project.**

The frequent demos I mentioned in the previous paragraph are an example of business representatives and developers working together throughout the project. Daily face-to-face engagement with business representatives is one of the most difficult principles to ensure from a practical standpoint, but it is really worth pushing for. Written documents, e-mails, and even telephone calls are often inefficient ways of transferring information when compared to face-to-face interactions.

By working with business representatives daily, the development team learns about the business in a way that is far beyond what a collection of requirements-gathering meetings can ever achieve. As a result, the development team is better able to suggest solutions and alternatives to business requests. The business representatives also learn what types of solutions are expensive or slow to develop, and what features are cheap. They can then begin to fine-tune their requests in response.

When it isn't possible to have daily interactions between the business representatives and the development team, agile methods try to get the two groups working together regularly in some way, perhaps every two days or whatever type of frequent involvement will work. Some teams use a "proxy customer," in which an experienced business analyst (BA) who is familiar with the business interests serves as a substitute, but this is not an ideal option.

5. **Build projects around motivated individuals. Give them the environment and support they need, and trust them to get the job done.**

In software estimation models like COCOMO (discussed in more detail in chapter 5, Boosting Team Performance Practices), the difference having the best people makes compared to having the best processes and tools is a factor of 10:1. This means that having motivated and smart people on the team can make the biggest difference in whether a project will be delivered successfully and efficiently.

While we may not always be able to pick our dream team, we can do our part to try to motivate our team members. Since the team is such an important factor on the project, agile methods promote empowered teams. People work better when they are given the autonomy to organize and plan their own work. Agile methods advocate freeing the team from the micromanagement of completing tasks on a Gantt chart. Instead, the emphasis is on craftsmanship, peer collaboration, and teamwork, which result in higher rates of productivity.

Knowledge worker projects involve team members who have unique areas of expertise. Such development teams are best served when they are allowed to make many of the day-to-day decisions and handle local planning for the project. As project managers, this does not mean that we abdicate involvement or abandon our team; instead, we recognize the team members as experts in what they do and provide the support they need to ensure they are successful.

6. **The most efficient and effective method of conveying information to and within a development team is face-to-face conversation.**

Written documents are great for creating a lasting record of events and decisions, but they are slow and costly to produce. In contrast, face-to-face communications allow us to quickly transfer a lot of information and also convey emotion and body language.

With face-to-face conversations, questions can be immediately answered instead of "parked" with the hope that there will be a follow-up explanation or the answer will become clear later. As an example of this concept, if instead of reading this book, you were talking to me directly, we could quickly skip all the stuff you already know and focus on the areas you want to learn more about. Written documents have to assume a lower starting point so as not to confuse the general audience.

Of course, this recommendation for face-to-face conversations cannot be applied to all communications, but it should be followed whenever possible. This is one example of how agile methods need to be customized or scaled for each project, and such scaling does take skill. As team sizes grow, face-to-face communications are harder to organize, and we have to introduce an appropriate level of written documentation.

7. **Working software is the primary measure of progress.**

By adopting "working software" as the primary measure of progress, we immediately promote working software as the project focus, and efforts to create documentation and designs become a supporting rather than primary activity. Expressions like "What gets measured gets done" and "You get what you measure" apply here, since measurement reinforces activity. If a feature cannot be measured or tested—in other words, if it does not "work"—it is not considered complete. This emphasis on "working" software helps ensure the team gets acceptance of features, rather than marking items as "completed development" when they have not yet been accepted.

This definition of progress and the binary nature of "working software" create a results-oriented view of the project. Interim deliverables and partially completed work get no external recognition. Instead, the end goal of the project—a product that can be used by the business—remains the project focus.

8. **Agile processes promote sustainable development. The sponsors, developers, and users should be able to maintain a constant pace indefinitely.**

Agile methods strive to maximize value over the long term. Some of the rapid application development (RAD) techniques that preceded agile promoted—or at least accepted—long, intense periods of prototyping prior to demos. The trouble with the RAD approach of working teams for long hours over an extended period of time is that people burn out and start to make mistakes. It is not a sustainable practice.

So instead of long, intense development periods, agile methods recognize the value of maintaining a sustainable pace that allows team members to have a work-life balance. Not only is a sustainable pace better for the team, but it benefits the organization as well. Long workdays lead to people resigning, and then the organization loses talent and domain knowledge. Hiring and integrating new members into a team is a slow and expensive process.

Therefore, working at a pace that can be maintained indefinitely creates a happier and more productive team. Happy teams also get along with the business representatives better than overworked teams. There is less tension, and work relationships improve. Some agile methods like XP previously recommended maintaining a 40-hour workweek as a guiding principle. Today most methods do not establish specific limits, but they do recommend paying close attention to the level of effort the team is putting forth to ensure a sustainable pace.

9. **Continuous attention to technical excellence and good design enhances agility.**

   While we want the development team to work hard and deliver a lot of value, we also have to be mindful of keeping the design clean, efficient, and open to changes. Technical excellence and good design allow the product or development team to understand and update the design easily.

   In the software world, once the code base becomes tangled, the organization loses its ability to respond to changing needs. In other words, it loses its agility. So we need to give the development team enough time to undertake refactoring. Refactoring is the housekeeping, cleanup, and simplifications that need to be made to code to ensure it's stable and can be maintained over the long term.

   A project needs to balance its efforts of delivering high-value features with giving continuous attention to the design of the solutions. This balance allows a system to deliver long-term value without becoming difficult to maintain, change, or extend.

10. **Simplicity—the art of maximizing the amount of work not done—is essential.**

    The most reliable features are those we do not build—since there is nothing that could go wrong with them. And, in the software world, up to 60 percent of features that are built are either infrequently used or never used.[5]

    Because so many features that are built are never actually used, and because complex systems have an increased potential to be unreliable, agile methods focus on simplicity. This means boiling down requirements to the essential elements only.

    Complex projects take longer to complete, are exposed to a longer horizon of risk, and have more potential failure points and opportunities for cost overruns. Therefore, agile methods seek the "simplest thing that could possibly work" and recommend that this solution be built first. This approach is not intended to preclude further extension and elaboration of a product—instead, it is simply saying, "Let's get the plain-vanilla version built first." This approach not only mitigates risk but also helps boost sponsor confidence.

11. **The best architectures, requirements, and designs emerge from self-organizing teams.**

    This principle may sound odd, depending on how literally you read it. Essentially it is saying that to get the best out of people, we have to let them self-organize. People like self-organizing; it allows them to find an approach that works best for their methods, their relationships, and their environment. They thoroughly understand and support the approach, because they helped create it. As a result, they produce better work.

    If you take a more literal approach to this statement, however, you may ask why the best architectures, requirements, and designs come from the project team, rather than from the organization's best architects, business analysts, and designers, who may not be on the team. In my experience, the answer to this question is that architectures, requirements, and designs are best when they are implemented by those who originate them. Although external recommendations may have more technical merit on paper, if they are implemented differently than originally envisioned or without conviction by the team, they will ultimately be less successful.

    Self-organizing teams with the autonomy to make decisions have a higher level of ownership and pride in the architectures, requirements, and designs they create than in those that are forced on them or "suggested" from external sources. Internally created approaches go through the team vetting process for alignment and approval. Simply put, ideas created by the team do not need to be sold to the team since they have already been vetted. In contrast, ideas coming from outside the team do need to be sold to the team for the implementation to be successful, and this is sometimes a challenging task.

Another factor that supports this principle is that the self-organizing project team is closest to the technical details of the project. As a result, they are best able to spot implementation issues, along with opportunities for improvements. So instead of trying to educate external resources about the evolving structure of the project, agile methods leverage the capacity of the team to best diagnose and improve the architectures, requirements, and designs. After all, the team members are the most informed about the project and have the most vested in it.

12. **At regular intervals, the team reflects on how to become more effective, then tunes and adjusts its behavior accordingly.**

Gathering lessons learned at the end of a project is, frankly, too little, too late. Instead, we need to gather lessons learned while they are still applicable and actionable. This means we need to gather them *during* the project and—most importantly—make sure we do something about what we've learned to adjust how we complete work on the remainder of the project.

Agile projects employ frequent reviews or "lookbacks," called retrospectives, to reflect on how things are working on the project and to identify opportunities for improvements. These retrospectives are typically done at the end of each iteration. This means there are many retrospectives on each project. One advantage of doing retrospectives so frequently is that the details do not get forgotten. Compare this to conducting a single lessons learned review at the end of a project, when team members are asked to think back a year or more to recall what went well and where there were issues.

Another disadvantage of only gathering lessons learned at the end of a project is that the lessons will not be really helpful to the organization until another project with similar business or technical domains or team dynamics comes along. And at that point, it is often easy to dismiss lessons learned from another project as not applicable to the current situation. On an agile project, the lessons learned are captured from the team as the project progresses, so no one can claim they do not apply. Instead, the team knows they are relevant and is pushed to tune and adjust their behavior accordingly.

EXERCISE: SEVERE SUMMARIES

To make sure you understand the intent behind each of the Agile Manifesto principles, shorten them to just five words or less that describe the essence of the idea. These shortened descriptions can then serve as a memory aid to help you recall the whole principle when you take the exam. The first two have been done for you as an example.

	Principle	Shortened Version
1	Our highest priority is to satisfy the customer through early and continuous delivery of valuable software.	*Satisfy customer with great software*
2	Welcome changing requirements, even late in development. Agile processes harness change for the customer's competitive advantage.	*Welcome change*
3	Deliver working software frequently, from a couple of weeks to a couple of months, with a preference to the shorter timescale.	
4	Business people and developers must work together daily throughout the project.	
5	Build projects around motivated individuals. Give them the environment and support they need, and trust them to get the job done.	
6	The most efficient and effective method of conveying information to and within a development team is face-to-face conversation.	
7	Working software is the primary measure of progress.	
8	Agile processes promote sustainable development. The sponsors, developers, and users should be able to maintain a constant pace indefinitely.	

	Principle	Shortened Version
9	Continuous attention to technical excellence and good design enhances agility.	
10	Simplicity—the art of maximizing the amount of work not done—is essential.	
11	The best architectures, requirements, and designs emerge from self-organizing teams.	
12	At regular intervals, the team reflects on how to become more effective, then tunes and adjusts its behavior accordingly.	

ANSWER

Your description may vary, depending on what part of the principle stands out most for you, but the following are possible abbreviations.

	Principle	Shortened Version
1	Our highest priority is to satisfy the customer through early and continuous delivery of valuable software.	*Satisfy customer with great software*
2	Welcome changing requirements, even late in development. Agile processes harness change for the customer's competitive advantage.	*Welcome change*
3	Deliver working software frequently, from a couple of weeks to a couple of months, with a preference to the shorter timescale.	*Deliver frequently*
4	Business people and developers must work together daily throughout the project.	*Work with business*
5	Build projects around motivated individuals. Give them the environment and support they need, and trust them to get the job done.	*Motivate people*
6	The most efficient and effective method of conveying information to and within a development team is face-to-face conversation.	*Face-to-face communications*
7	Working software is the primary measure of progress.	*Measure software done*

	Principle	Shortened Version
8	Agile processes promote sustainable development. The sponsors, developers, and users should be able to maintain a constant pace indefinitely.	*Maintain sustainable pace*
9	Continuous attention to technical excellence and good design enhances agility.	*Maintain design*
10	Simplicity—the art of maximizing the amount of work not done—is essential.	*Keep it simple*
11	The best architectures, requirements, and designs emerge from self-organizing teams.	*Team creates architecture*
12	At regular intervals, the team reflects on how to become more effective, then tunes and adjusts its behavior accordingly.	*Reflect and adjust*

The Declaration of Interdependence (DOI)

> The DOI is not tested on the exam, but it does highlight important ideas for the agile community.

In 2005, the cofounders of the Agile Project Leadership Network (APLN), now known as the Agile Leadership Network (ALN), created the Declaration of Interdependence for agile project management. This declaration reads:[6]

Declaration of Interdependence

Agile and adaptive approaches for linking people, projects and value

We are a community of project leaders that are highly successful at delivering results. To achieve these results:

» *We **increase return on investment** by making continuous flow of value our focus.*
» *We **deliver reliable results** by engaging customers in frequent interactions and shared ownership.*
» *We **expect uncertainty** and manage for it through iterations, anticipation, and adaptation.*
» *We **unleash creativity and innovation** by recognizing that individuals are the ultimate source of value, and creating an environment where they can make a difference.*
» *We **boost performance** through group accountability for results and shared responsibility for team effectiveness.*
» *We **improve effectiveness and reliability** through situationally specific strategies, processes and practices.*

The Declaration of Interdependence (DOI) focuses on the project management side of agile projects. While the Agile Manifesto and agile methods offer whole-project guidance, the DOI is aimed at leaders. With this focus in mind, let's explore some of the thinking behind each principle:

1. **We increase return on investment by making continuous flow of value our focus.**

   This statement means agile projects concentrate their efforts on developing features that the business asks for. Through this focus, the project can benefit the business the most and gain a high level of support for the process. When your projects consistently deliver business results, they are hard to ignore or cancel, and the business is more likely to approve requests from your projects.

2. **We deliver reliable results by engaging customers in frequent interactions and shared ownership.**

When planning interactions with the business, try to be more like the good neighbor whom you see frequently and can easily call on, rather than the intrusive relative who moves in for a while and then disappears for a year. Work toward having regular and engaging business interactions, instead of a huge upfront requirements-gathering phase followed by no interaction with the business until you deliver the project's result. Frequently show the business representatives how the system is evolving and make it clear that the business is driving the design by listening to and acting on their feedback.

3. **We expect uncertainty and manage for it through iterations, anticipation, and adaptation.**

Since software functionality is hard to describe, and since technology and business needs change quickly, software projects typically have a lot of unanticipated changes, as do other knowledge worker projects. This DOI statement means that instead of trying to create and follow a rigid plan that is likely to break, it is better to plan and develop in short chunks (iterations) and adapt to changing requirements.

4. **We unleash creativity and innovation by recognizing that individuals are the ultimate source of value, and creating an environment where they can make a difference.**

The saying "We manage property and lead people; if you try to manage people, they feel like property" recognizes that we need to motivate people, not simply tell them what to do. Projects are completed by living, breathing people, not tools or processes. To get the best out of a team, we must treat the team members as individuals, provide for their needs, and support them in their job. Paying people a wage might guarantee that they show up, but how they contribute once they are there is governed by a wide variety of factors. If you want the best results from people, provide the best environment.

5. **We boost performance through group accountability for results and shared responsibility for team effectiveness.**

Empowered teams are not only happier and more productive, they are also more likely to take ownership of problems and try hard to solve them. Assuming a command-and-control style to delegate work tasks often has an unrecognized side effect: if a workaround or solution is not on a team member's task list, what is the motivation for the team member to solve it? In contrast, if the team members have made a social commitment to each other to deliver working functionality and they encounter a problem, they will rally together to deliver solutions. Everyone needs to share the responsibility for making the project—and the team as a whole—successful.

6. **We improve effectiveness and reliability through situationally specific strategies, processes, and practices.**

Real projects are complex and messy. Rarely do all the ideal conditions for agile development present themselves. Instead, we have to interpret the project situation and make the best use of the techniques, people, and tools available to us. There is no single cookbook for how to run successful projects; instead, we need to adjust our approach to best fit the project ingredients and the environment we are presented with.

Agile Methods

There are over a dozen actively used agile methodologies. The common ones are Scrum, Extreme Programming (XP), Feature-Driven Development (FDD), Dynamic Systems Development Method (DSDM), and the Crystal family of methods (i.e., Crystal Clear, Crystal Yellow, Crystal Orange, etc.). Other related methods include lean software development and Kanban development.

The two most widely used agile methods are Scrum and XP, which are prominently featured on the PMI-ACP exam, though you may see some test questions about the other methodologies as well. In this section, we will explore the main concepts, roles, activities, and deliverables of the Scrum and XP methods, and we'll briefly discuss the other common agile methods to give you a sense of what they are. To reflect the focus of the exam, however, we won't go into detail for these other methods.

Scrum

Scrum is a popular agile model that is lightweight and easy to understand, but like all agile methods, it is difficult to truly master. The methodology documented in the "Scrum framework" is a set of team guidance practices, roles, events, artifacts, and rules to execute projects by. The theory behind Scrum is based on the three pillars of Transparency, Inspection, and Adaptation:

- » **Transparency**: This pillar involves giving visibility to those responsible for the outcome. An example of transparency would be creating a common definition of what "done" means, to ensure that all stakeholders are in agreement.
- » **Inspection**: This pillar involves timely checks on how well a project is progressing toward its goals, looking for problematic deviations or differences from the goals.
- » **Adaptation**: This pillar involves adjusting a process to minimize further issues if an inspection shows a problem or undesirable trend.

These three pillars guide all aspects of Scrum projects, but there are also four planned opportunities for Inspection and Adaptation within the Scrum framework:

- » Sprint retrospective
- » Daily Scrum meeting
- » Sprint review meeting
- » Sprint planning meeting

These opportunities are indicated in the following diagram and are explained in more detail later in this section.

Figure 2.1: Scrum Process

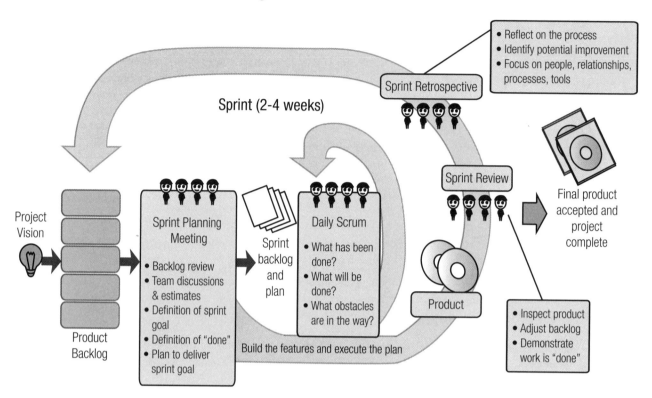

Now let's discuss the Scrum methodology in terms of the different roles on a Scrum team, the activities or events that occur within this methodology, and its deliverables or artifacts.

Scrum Teams

Scrum teams are made up of the development team, a product owner, and a ScrumMaster.

Development Team   The development team is the group of professionals who build the product increments in each iteration, or "sprint" as it is termed in the Scrum methodology. The development team is empowered to manage its own work, and its members are self-organizing and cross-functional. In other words, the development team consists of people who can fulfill all the roles needed to complete the work (e.g., analysis, build, and test).

Product Owner   The product owner is responsible for maximizing the value of the product. This person has the sole responsibility for managing the product backlog, including its prioritization, accuracy, shared understanding, value, and visibility.

ScrumMaster   The ScrumMaster is responsible for ensuring that Scrum is understood and used. The ScrumMaster is a servant leader to the development team, removing impediments to progress, facilitating events as needed, and providing coaching. The ScrumMaster also assists the product owner with managing the backlog and communicating the vision, goals, and backlog items to the development team.

Events

The Scrum methodology refers to several different types of activities or events—sprints, sprint planning meetings, daily scrums, sprint review meetings, and sprint retrospectives.

Sprints   A sprint is a timeboxed (time-limited) iteration of one month or less to build a potentially releasable product. Most Scrum sprints are either two weeks or one month long. Each sprint includes a sprint planning meeting, daily scrums, the development work, a sprint review meeting, and the sprint retrospective.

Each sprint is like a miniproject. During the sprint, no changes are made that would affect the sprint goal, although the scope may be clarified or renegotiated as new information becomes available. The development team members are kept the same throughout the sprint.

Sprint Planning Meeting   A sprint planning meeting is used to determine what will be delivered in that sprint and how the work will be achieved. The product owner presents the backlog items, and the whole team discusses them to create a shared understanding. The development team forecasts what can be delivered based on estimates, projected capacity, and past performance to define the sprint goal. The development team then determines how this functionality will be built and how the team will organize to deliver the sprint goal.

Daily Scrum   The daily scrum is a 15-minute timeboxed daily meeting. During this meeting, the development team synchronizes activities, communicates, and raises issues. It is held at the same place and time, and each development team member provides answers to the following three questions about the work he or she is doing during the sprint:

1. What has been achieved since the last meeting?
2. What will be done before the next meeting?
3. What obstacles are in the way?

The daily scrum is used to assess progress toward the sprint goal. The ScrumMaster makes sure these meetings happen and helps remove any identified obstacles.

Sprint Review   A sprint review is a meeting held at the end of the sprint to inspect the increment, or evolving product, that was built and to change the backlog if necessary. The development team demonstrates the work that is "done" and answers any questions about the increment. The product owner decides what is done and what is not yet done. The product owner and the team discuss the remaining product backlog and determine what to do next.

Sprint Retrospective   At the end of the sprint, the team holds a sprint retrospective to reflect on the process and look for opportunities for improvement. The retrospective occurs after the sprint review and before the next sprint planning meeting. This timing allows the team to incorporate the product owner's feedback from the sprint review and also allows them to factor improvements identified during the retrospective into the next plan. The team focuses their inspection on people, relationships, processes, and tools. They explore what went well, in addition to identifying opportunities for improvement that they can implement in the next sprint.

Artifacts

Now that we've discussed the roles and activities that are part of the Scrum framework, let's look at the deliverables of the product backlog and sprint backlog, as well as the definition of "done" for these deliverables.

Product Backlog   The product backlog is the ordered list of everything that might be needed for the product. It serves as the single source for requirements. This backlog is dynamic and evolves as the product evolves. It contains features to be built, functions, requirements, quality attributes (often referred to as nonfunctional requirements), enhancements, and fixes. Higher-ranked items are more detailed, and therefore, the estimates for these items are more precise. Low-priority items may not get developed, or they may be deferred in favor of higher-priority work.

"Grooming" the product backlog is the process of adding more detail and order to the backlog and refining the estimates of the backlog items. This effort is done by the development team and the product owner. For example, the development team may update its estimates, and based on that new information, the product owner may change the priority of the items in the backlog.

Sprint Backlog   The sprint backlog is the set of items from the product backlog that were selected for a specific sprint. The sprint backlog is accompanied by a plan of how to achieve the sprint goal, so it serves as the development team's forecast for the functionality that will be part of the sprint. It is a highly visible view of the work being undertaken and may only be updated by the development team.

Definition of Done   Now let's look at the definition of "done" for the artifacts. When a backlog item is described as done, everyone must be in agreement about what "done" means. To remove any ambiguity, the team should collectively create the definition of done for the items before they begin work on them.

Using these roles, events, artifacts, and collective definitions, the Scrum team iteratively builds increments of the solution, involving the customer frequently to ensure they are creating the right product.

EXERCISE: SCRUM OWNERSHIP/RESPONSIBILITY

In the following table, place a check mark in the appropriate column(s) for the development team, product owner, or ScrumMaster to indicate who owns or is responsible for each item.

Item	Development Team	Product Owner	ScrumMaster
Estimates			
Backlog priorities			
Agile coaching			
Velocity predictions			
The definition of "done"			
Process adherence			
Technical decisions			
Sprint planning			

© 2012 RMC Publications, Inc • 952.846.4484 • info@rmcproject.com • www.rmcproject.com

ANSWER:

Item	Development Team	Product Owner	ScrumMaster
Estimates	✓		
Backlog priorities		✓	
Agile coaching			✓
Velocity predictions	✓		
The definition of "done"	✓	✓	✓
Process adherence			✓
Technical decisions	✓		
Sprint planning	✓	✓	✓

Extreme Programming (XP)

Extreme Programming is a software-development-centric agile method. While Scrum at the project management level focuses on prioritizing work and getting feedback, XP focuses on software development good practices. Therefore, expect to see a lot of software references in the following discussion. As with the Agile Manifesto values and principles, see if you can think of ways the XP values and the ideas behind the practices can be applied to nonsoftware knowledge worker projects.

The core values of this methodology are simplicity, communication, feedback, courage, and respect, and these values manifest themselves in the practices undertaken throughout the XP life cycle.

- » **Simplicity**: This value focuses on reducing complexity, extra features, and waste. The team should keep the phrase "Find the simplest thing that could possibly work" in mind and build that solution first.
- » **Communication**: This value focuses on making sure all the team members know what is expected of them and what other people are working on. The daily stand-up meeting is a key communication component.
- » **Feedback**: The team should get impressions of suitability early. Failing fast can be useful, especially if in doing so we get new information while we still have time to improve the product.
- » **Courage**: It takes courage to allow our work to be entirely visible to others. In pair programming, team members share code and often need to make bold simplifications and changes to that code. Backed up by automated builds and unit tests, developers need to have the confidence to make important changes.
- » **Respect**: Respect is essential on XP projects where people work together as a team and everyone is accountable for the success or failure of the project. This value also relates to pair programming; team members need to recognize that people work differently, and respect those differences.

Figure 2.2 shows an illustration of the XP life cycle:

Figure 2.2: Extreme Programming

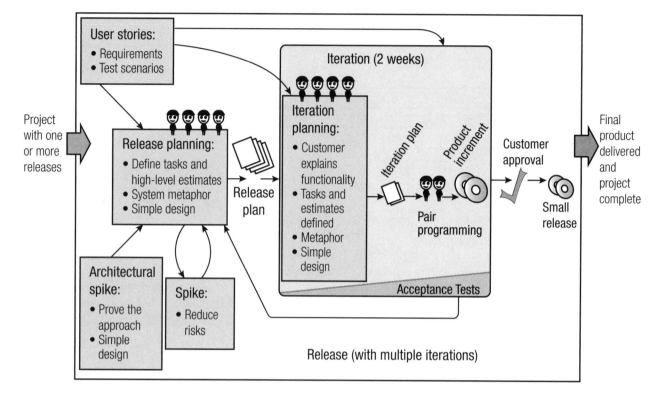

In XP, lightweight requirements known as "user stories" (indicated in figure 2.2) are used in planning releases and iterations. Iterations are typically two weeks long, and developers work in pairs to write code during these iterations. All software developed is subjected to rigorous and frequent testing. Then, upon approval by the on-site customer, the software is delivered as small releases.

"Architectural spikes" are iterations used to prove a technological approach, and "spikes" are periods of work undertaken to reduce risks. The spikes are blended into the release planning processes.

XP Practices

The XP method exercises a number of simple but powerful core practices, which are indicated in figure 2.3. We'll discuss these practices in more detail, beginning with the outer ring and working our way in.

Figure 2.3: XP Core Practices

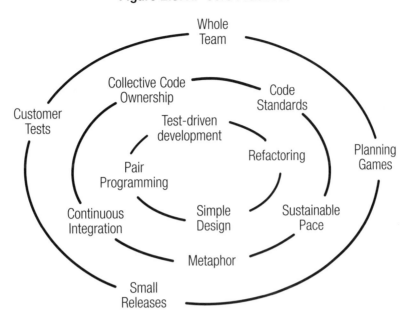

Whole Team   The whole team practice is the idea that all the contributors to an XP project sit together in the same location, as members of a single team.

This team includes a "customer"—a business representative who provides the requirements, priorities, and business direction for the project. The team is also comprised of developers and usually quality assurance (QA) and business analysis (BA) people, although the QA and BA roles may be fulfilled by developers if they have the required skills. In addition, there is sometimes a coach who helps keep the team on track and guides the process, and there may be a manager who facilitates external communications and coordinates the team's activities.

XP emphasizes the notion of generalizing specialists, as opposed to role specialists. In other words, anyone who is qualified for a role can undertake it—the roles are not reserved for people who specialize in just one particular area. This practice helps optimize the use of resources, since people who can perform multiple jobs are able to switch from one role to another as the demand arises. The practice also allows for more efficient sharing of information and helps eliminate circumstances where people in certain roles are idle or overstretched at points in the project.

Planning Games   XP has two primary planning activities, or planning games—release planning and iteration planning.

A release is a push of new functionality all the way to the production user. A project typically has one or more releases, with no more than one or two releases happening in a single year. During release planning, the customer outlines the functionality required, and the developers estimate how difficult the functionality will be to build. Armed with these estimates and priorities, the customer lays out the plan for the project delivery. The initial attempts at estimating will likely be imprecise, so this process is revisited frequently and improved as the priorities and estimates evolve.

Iterations are the short development cycles within a release that Scrum calls "sprints." Iteration planning is done at the start of every iteration, or every two weeks. The customer explains what functionality they would like to see in the next two weeks, and then the developers break this functionality into tasks and estimate the work. Based on these estimates (which are more refined than the release planning estimates) and the amount of work accomplished in the previous iteration, the team commits to what work they think they can complete in the two-week period.

Small Releases
Frequent, small releases to test environments are encouraged in XP, both at the iteration level to demonstrate progress and increase visibility for the customer, and at the release level to rapidly deploy working software to the target audience. Quality is maintained in these short delivery timeframes by rigorous testing and through practices like continuous integration, in which suites of tests are run as frequently as possible (see the description of continuous integration later in this section and again in chapter 7, Problem Detection and Resolution).

Customer Tests
As part of defining the required functionality, the customer describes one or more tests to show that the software is working. The team then builds automated tests to prove to themselves and the customer that the software is working.

Collective Code Ownership
In XP, any pair of developers can improve or amend any code. This means multiple people work on all the code, which results in increased visibility and knowledge of the code base. This practice leads to a higher level of quality; with more people looking at the code, there is a greater chance defects will be discovered. There is also less of an impact to the project if one of the programmers leaves, since the knowledge is shared.

Code Standards
Although collective code ownership has its advantages, allowing anyone to amend any code can result in issues if the team members take different approaches to coding. To address this risk, XP teams follow a consistent coding standard so that all the code looks as if it has been written by a single, knowledgeable programmer. The specifics of the standard each team uses are not important; what matters is that the team takes a consistent approach to writing the code.

Sustainable Pace
XP recognizes that the highest level of productivity is achieved by a team operating at a sustainable pace. While periods of overtime might be necessary, repeated long hours of work are unsustainable and counterproductive. The practice of maintaining a sustainable pace of development optimizes the delivery of long-term value.

Metaphor
XP uses metaphors and similes to explain designs and create a shared technical vision. These descriptions establish comparisons that all the stakeholders can understand to help explain how the system should work. For example, "The billing module is an accountant that makes sure transactions are entered into the appropriate accounts and balances are created."

Even if the team cannot come up with a single, poetic metaphor to describe something, they can use a common set of names for different elements to ensure everyone understands where and why changes should be applied.

Continuous Integration
Integration involves bringing the code together and making sure it all compiles and works together. This practice is critical, because it brings problems to the surface before more code is built on top of faulty or incompatible designs.

XP employs continuous integration, which means every time a programmer checks in code to the code repository (typically several times a day), integration tests are run automatically. Such tests highlight broken builds or problems with integration, so that the problems can be addressed immediately.

Test-Driven Development   As we've discussed, testing is a critical part of the XP methodology. To ensure good test coverage so that problems can be highlighted early in development, XP teams often use the practice of test-driven development. With this approach, the team writes tests prior to developing the new code.

If the tests are working correctly, the initial code that is entered will fail the tests, since the required functionality has not yet been developed. The code will pass the test once it is written correctly. The test-driven development process strives to shorten the test-feedback cycle as much as possible to get the benefits of early feedback.

Refactoring   Refactoring is the process of improving the design of existing code without altering the external behavior or adding new functionality. By keeping the design efficient, changes and new functionality can easily be applied to the code. Refactoring focuses on removing duplicated code, lowering coupling (dependent connections between code modules), and increasing cohesion.

Simple Design   By focusing on keeping the design simple but adequate, XP teams can develop code quickly and adapt it as necessary. The design is kept appropriate for what the project currently requires. It is then revisited iteratively and incrementally to ensure it remains appropriate.

XP follows a deliberate design philosophy that leans toward, "What is the simplest thing that could work?" as opposed to complex structures that attempt to accommodate possible future flexibility. Since code bloat and complexity are linked to many failed projects, simple design is also a risk mitigation strategy.

Pair Programming   In XP, production code is written by two developers working as a pair to write and provide real-time reviews of the software as it emerges. This practice may seem inefficient, but XP advocates assert that it saves time because the pairs catch issues early and there is a benefit in having the larger knowledge base of two people. Working in pairs also helps spread knowledge about the system through the team.

By taking a disciplined and rigorous approach to applying these practices, XP teams succeed in delivering high-quality software systems.

EXERCISE: XP CHUNK OR MADE-UP JUNK?

Separate the real XP elements (the XP Chunks) from the made-up terms (Made-up Junk) in the following table by placing a check mark in the appropriate column.

Item	XP Chunk	Made-up Junk
Sample design		
Small revisions		
Courage		
Passion		
Execution game		
Complexity		
Refactoring		
Remarketing		
Simplicity		
Architectural spoke		
Iteration		
Sustainable pace		
Continuous interpretation		

ANSWER

Item	XP Chunk	Made-up Junk
Sample design		✓
Small revisions		✓
Courage	✓	
Passion		✓
Execution game		✓
Complexity		✓
Refactoring	✓	
Remarketing		✓
Simplicity	✓	
Architectural spoke		✓
Iteration	✓	
Sustainable pace	✓	
Continuous interpretation		✓

Feature-Driven Development (FDD)

Feature-Driven Development (FDD) is a simple-to-understand yet powerful approach to building products or solutions. A project team following the FDD method will first develop an overall model for the product, build a feature list, and plan the work. The team then moves through design and build iterations to develop the features.

Figure 2.4: Feature-Driven Development

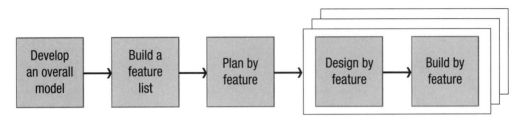

FDD recommends a set of good practices, derived from software engineering. These practices include:

» **Domain object modeling**: In this practice, teams explore and explain the domain (or business environment) of the problem to be solved.
» **Developing by feature**: This practice involves breaking functions down into two-week or shorter chunks and calling them features.
» **Individual class (code) ownership**: With this practice, areas of code have a single owner for consistency, performance, and conceptual integrity. (Note that this is quite different from XP's collective code ownership idea that aims to spread the knowledge to other team members.)
» **Feature teams**: These are small, dynamically formed teams that vet designs and allow multiple design options to be evaluated before a design is chosen. Feature teams help mitigate the risks associated with individual ownership.
» **Inspections**: These are reviews that help ensure good-quality design and code.
» **Configuration management**: This practice involves labeling code, tracking changes, and managing the source code.
» **Regular builds**: Through regular builds, the team makes sure the new code integrates with existing code. This practice also allows them to easily create a demo.
» **Visibility of progress and results**: This practice tracks progress based on completed work.

Feature-Driven Development is the agile methodology that popularized cumulative flow diagrams (discussed in chapter 3, Value-Driven Delivery) and parking lot diagrams (one-page summaries of project progress). Both are useful tracking and diagnostic tools that are now used by other agile approaches.

Dynamic Systems Development Method (DSDM)

DSDM was one of the earlier agile methods, and it started out quite prescriptive and detailed. Its coverage of the project life cycle is broad, encompassing aspects of an agile project ranging from feasibility and the business case to implementation. Figure 2.5 is an illustration of the DSDM life cycle.

Figure 2.5: DSDM

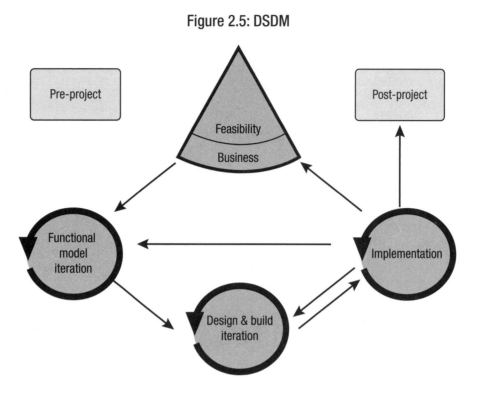

DSDM is centered on eight principles. Although these principles were created before the Agile Manifesto was written, they are closely aligned to the Manifesto. The eight principles are:

1. Focus on the business need
2. Deliver on time
3. Collaborate
4. Never compromise quality
5. Build incrementally from firm foundations
6. Develop iteratively
7. Communicate continuously and clearly
8. Demonstrate control

DSDM helped to popularize early architectural considerations, agile suitability filters, and agile contracts.

Crystal

Crystal is a family of methodologies designed for projects ranging from those run by small teams developing low-criticality systems (Crystal Clear) to those run by large teams building high-criticality systems (Crystal Magenta). The Crystal framework provides a great example of how we can tailor a

© 2012 RMC Publications, Inc • 952.846.4484 • info@rmcproject.com • www.rmcproject.com

method to match a project's and an organization's characteristics. Figure 2.6 outlines the more basic Crystal methods (Clear, Yellow, Orange, and Red).

Figure 2.6: Crystal Clear, Yellow, Orange, and Red Methods

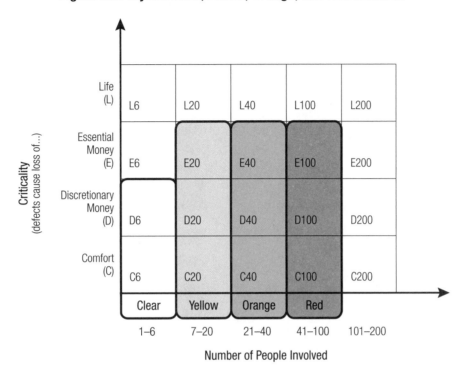

In figure 2.6, team size is represented on the X (horizontal) axis and the level of project criticality is indicated on the Y (vertical) axis. Crystal Clear is aimed at small projects with core team sizes of one to six people. Crystal Clear projects develop systems in which a failure could result in a loss of comfort (e.g., a video game crash) or a low-level financial loss (e.g., a word processor crash resulting in lost business time). As projects engage more people and develop increasingly critical applications, we need to scale the processes beyond face-to-face communications and introduce additional validation and traceability measures.

For the exam, you don't need to understand how the different Crystal methods work, but the approach this family of methodologies takes to scaling methods to fit the project has significantly influenced agile thinking. The Crystal methodologies embrace and promote many other agile principles as well, including:

» **Frequent delivery**: Crystal methodologies build increments of a solution and check these incremental builds for acceptance.
» **Reflective improvement**: This practice involves regularly checking for ways to improve and then implementing the new methods.
» **Osmotic communication**: This means team members are co-located to allow them to efficiently share information.
» **Personal safety**: Crystal methods emphasize the need to create an environment where people can safely raise issues or questions.
» **Focus**: This means team members know what to work on and have the time and peace of mind to work on it.

» **Easy access to expert users**: Through such access, the team can get up-to-date requirements and rapid feedback.
» **Technical environment**: Crystal methods rely on automated tests, configuration management, and frequent integration.

Lean Software Development

Strictly speaking, lean software development is not an agile methodology, but lean and agile values are closely aligned. Lean is a set of principles that have been taken from lean manufacturing approaches and applied to software development. These principles focus on seven core concepts, as indicated in figure 2.7.

Figure 2.7: Lean Software Development

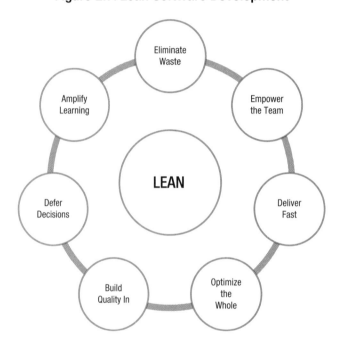

Now let's look at these seven core concepts in more detail:

» **Eliminate waste**: To maximize value, we must minimize waste. For software systems, waste can take the form of partially done work, delays, handoffs, unnecessary features, etc. Therefore, to increase the value we are getting from projects, we must develop ways to identify and then remove waste.
» **Empower the team**: Rather than taking a micromanagement approach, we should respect team members' superior knowledge of the technical steps required on the project and let them make local decisions to be productive and successful.
» **Deliver fast**: We can maximize the project's return on investment (ROI) by quickly delivering valuable software and iterating through designs. We find the best solution through the rapid evolution of options.
» **Optimize the whole**: We aim to see the system as more than the sum of its parts. We go beyond the pieces of the project and look for how it aligns with the organization. As part of optimizing the whole, we also focus on forming better intergroup relations.
» **Build quality in**: Lean development doesn't try to "test-in" quality at the end; instead, we build quality into the product and continually assure quality throughout the development process, using techniques like refactoring, continuous integration, and unit testing.

» **Defer decisions**: We balance early planning with making decisions and committing to things as late as possible. For example, this may mean reprioritizing the backlog right up until it is time to plan an iteration, or avoiding being tied to an early technology-bounded solution.

» **Amplify learning**: This concept involves facilitating communication early and often, getting feedback as soon as possible, and building on what we learn. Software projects are business and technology learning experiences, so we should start soon and keep learning.

Lean gives us techniques and concepts such as value stream mapping, the seven forms of waste, pull systems, and work in progress (WIP) (see chapter 3, Value-Driven Delivery, for more on these concepts).

EXERCISE: MATCH AGILE PRACTICES TO LEAN PRINCIPLES

In the following table, match the everyday agile practice to the most relevant lean principle.

Agile Practice	Lean Principle						
	Eliminate waste	Empower the team	Deliver fast	Optimize the whole	Build quality in	Defer decisions	Amplify learning
Teams make their own decisions							
Just-in-time iteration planning							
Team retrospectives							
Two-week iterations							
Unit test as we go							
Shadow the business to learn what they do							
The evolving prototype is the specification							

ANSWER

Some of these agile practices map to multiple lean principles, but the most direct matches are indicated below:

Agile Practice	Lean Principle						
	Eliminate waste	Empower the team	Deliver fast	Optimize the whole	Build quality in	Defer decisions	Amplify learning
Teams make their own decisions		✓					
Just-in-time iteration planning						✓	
Team retrospectives							✓
Two-week iterations			✓				
Unit test as we go					✓		
Shadow the business to learn what they do				✓			
The evolving prototype is the specification	✓						

Kanban Development

Kanban development is derived from the lean production system used at Toyota. "Kanban" is a Japanese word meaning "signboard." The signboard, or Kanban task board as it is also called, plays an important role in the Kanban development methodology.

The Kanban development methodology limits work in progress (WIP) to help identify issues and minimize the waste and cost associated with changes during development. It uses a pull system to take work, within the WIP limits, through the stages of development.

Figure 2.8: Task/Kanban Board

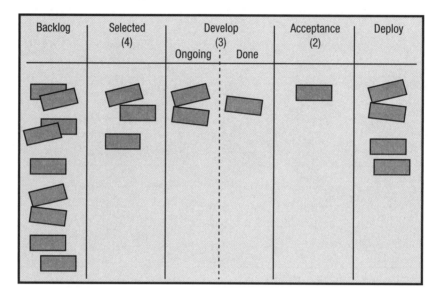

In figure 2.8, we can see the project's backlog in the first column. The second column indicates that there are three user stories currently selected for development. The project has a WIP limit of four selected user stories. The WIP limit is the maximum number of items that may be in that column, or state of progress. If the limit is reached, no new items may be moved into the column until other items are moved out. The Develop and Acceptance columns also have WIP limits; in this case, they are three and two, respectively.

Kanban development operates on five core principles:

» **Visualize the workflow**: Knowledge worker projects, by definition, manipulate knowledge, which is intangible and invisible. Therefore, having some way to visualize the workflow is very important for organizing, optimizing, and tracking it.
» **Limit WIP**: Keeping the amount of work in progress low increases the visibility of issues and bottlenecks and in turn facilitates continuous improvement. It creates a pull system of work through the development effort, reduces costs associated with changes, and minimizes sunk costs.
» **Manage flow**: By tracking the flow of work through a system, issues can be identified and changes can be measured for effectiveness.
» **Make process policies explicit**: It is important to clearly explain how things work so the team can have open discussions about improvements in an objective, rather than an emotional or subjective, way.
» **Improve collaboratively**: Through scientific measurement and experimentation, the team should collectively own and improve the processes it uses.

The Kanban development methodology has helped popularize task boards with WIP limits and pull systems created by limiting WIP (see chapter 3, Value-Driven Delivery, for more on these concepts). It also gives permission and encourages team members to try new approaches and change processes. With a continuous pull model, iterations may not be required, and activities like creating estimates can be considered waste and reduced or eliminated entirely.

T&T Process Tailoring

The DOI talks about situationally specific processes. This theme also underlies several of the agile methodologies. For example, DSDM offers suitability filters for assessing how well an approach fits a project. Crystal offers a family of methodologies in order to best serve different project sizes and complexities. Kanban development encourages modification and adaptation.

As a side note, this framework flexibility presents an examination dilemma for PMI, since there is no single "right" approach to test people on. When the PMI-ACP Steering Committee developed the exam content outline, we had to make an assumption about team size, composition, and project complexity.[7] The consensus was to test certification seekers on the practices commonly used on small- to medium-sized projects (e.g., business projects conducted by teams of 5 to 50 people using discretionary and essential funds). We recognized the irony of creating a necessarily prescriptive exam outline for a scalable, adaptive process. In the end, we selected the project characteristics that are most commonly encountered on agile projects.

Process Tailoring Guidelines

Just like do-it-yourself electrical work in your home, it can be dangerous to tailor agile processes if you do not fully understand why things are the way they are in the first place. As a general recommendation, organizations and teams that are new to agile should use the methods "out-of-the-box" for a few projects before attempting to change them. The reason to take such an approach is that the problems a new team encounters with a standard technique or practice may be due to the team's lack of skill or experience using that technique, rather than issues with the technique itself. By discarding or changing a practice before its value is recognized, the team risks losing the benefit the practice was originally designed to bring to the project.

Also, the different techniques and practices are created in balance with each other. Removing or augmenting some of these elements without understanding the relationship between them can lead to problems. For example, in XP, ruthless testing allows for courageous refactoring, and having frequent user conversations allows the project to have light requirements. If a team removes one practice without understanding its counterbalance, the project may be headed for trouble.

To put it simply, people must really know how the "plain-vanilla" process works before removing things or inventing new flavors. Alistair Cockburn's Shu-Ha-Ri model, which originated in Japanese Noh theater, supports this concept. This model's progression moves from obeying the rules (*shu*, which means to keep, protect, or maintain), consciously moving away from the rules (*ha*, which means to detach or break free), and finally unconsciously finding an individual path (*ri*, which means to go beyond or transcend).

TRICKS OF THE TRADE® In this book, we address the Shu-Ha-Ri model here to illustrate the appropriate approach to method tailoring, but this model will not be specifically tested on the exam. The exam is focused at the *shu*, or obeying the rules, level. So if you are faced with a question when taking the exam and your answer is "It depends on a whole bunch of other circumstances the question has not told me," think back to the *shu* level, following a basic process model. To help choose the correct answer, ask yourself, "What does plain-vanilla XP or Scrum recommend?"

We'll discuss process tailoring again in more detail in chapter 8, Continuous Improvement

Agile Process Overview Chart

The remaining chapters explain specific agile tools and techniques and knowledge and skills that are covered on the exam, beyond the foundational concepts we've discussed here. The following graphic, figure 2.9, is a high-level, timeline-oriented view of when many of these activities and elements may occur on a simple project implementation and shows which portions are commonly repeated. Revisit this diagram as you go through the book to get a high-level overview of the agile process and how the different concepts fit into this big-picture view.

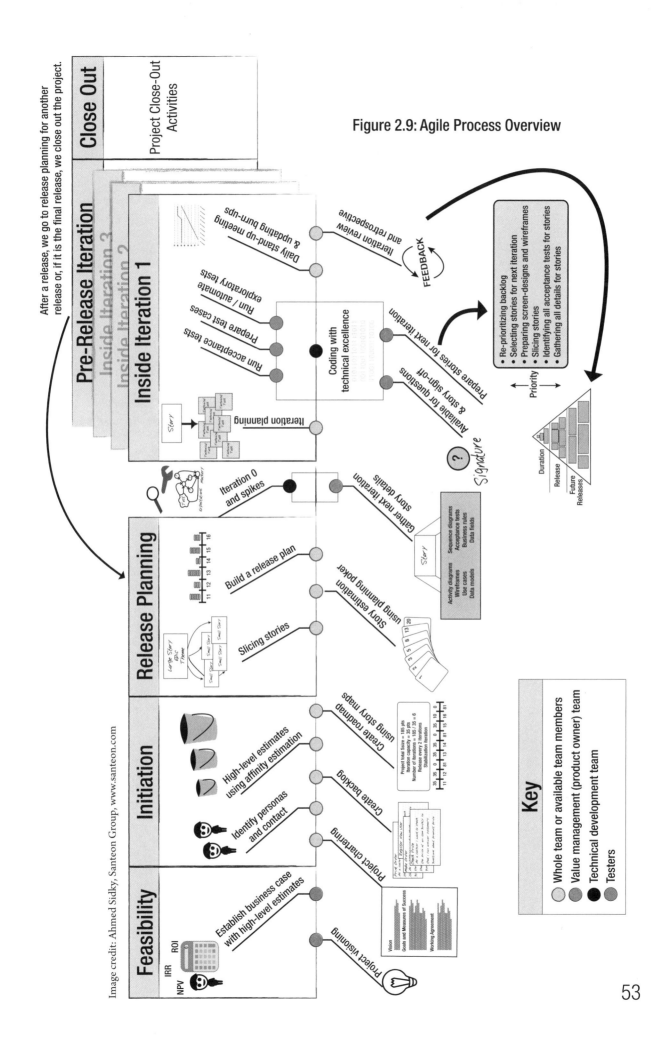

Figure 2.9: Agile Process Overview

Image credit: Ahmed Sidky, Santeon Group, www.santeon.com

53

Professional Responsibility and Ethics

Before we move on to the next chapter, let's look at how PMI's Code of Ethics and Professional Conduct (available on PMI's website: www.pmi.org) applies to agile framework concepts.[8] There are four main areas of this code—Responsibility, Respect, Fairness, and Honesty—and we'll cover each in turn, looking at examples of how they relate to the concepts discussed in this chapter. As you read this section, think about your real-world projects and how they are impacted by these different aspects of professional responsibility and ethics.

Responsibility

» **Make decisions based on the best interests of the company**: Agile practices strongly support this area of professional and social responsibility. Establishing a group definition of what done looks like and having high levels of sponsor and user involvement help ensure that the best interests of the company remain at the forefront of agile projects.

» **Report unethical behavior and violations**: Extreme Programming's core values of Respect and Courage apply here. We need to have respect for doing the right thing and courage to speak up if we spot unethical behavior.

Respect

» **Maintain an attitude of mutual cooperation**: The Kanban concept of "improve collaboratively" fits well with this mutual cooperation goal. Concepts like the joint definition of "done" and the integral role of the business in release and iteration planning also apply here.

» **Respect cultural differences**: Again, we can look to Extreme Programming's core value of Respect, which is directly aligned with this goal. We must respect each other and our differences in order to have a healthy and successful project environment.

» **Negotiate in good faith**: The Agile Manifesto value of "Customer collaboration over contract negotiation" focuses us more on the good-faith element of negotiations than on the paper contract. Negotiations and contracts should result in win-win situations, in which the contractor is paid a fair price to create a product that is truly useful to the customer.

» **Deal with conflict directly**: Creating a healthy environment for discussion and debate is a core aspect of empowering teams. Conflict can be positive if it helps us create better solutions, but it can be damaging and corrosive if it occurs without respect and fair mediation. Creating an environment where conflict is productive rather than destructive is part of the coach and facilitator role of a ScrumMaster and any servant leader.

» **Do not use your position to influence others**: Agile projects emphasize the servant leadership role, which helps reduce the likelihood of a person in authority using positional power to influence team decisions. It is still something we have to be wary of, however. Much of the value of agile methods lies in empowered teams that make their own decisions and create their own estimates. This value is lost if people in authority override the team decisions or intimidate team members into not speaking up or voicing their ideas.

Fairness

» **Do not discriminate**: The XP value of Respect and Scrum's approach of placing the ScrumMaster in a facilitator role help guard against discrimination. The guidelines for retrospectives, which we will discuss in more detail in chapter 8, Continuous Improvement, talk about creating a safe environment for everyone to contribute to the discussion and warn against the dangers of discrimination.

Honesty

» **Understand the truth**: Many of the agile scheduled events, including sprint demos and retrospectives, are focused on transparency and understanding the truth. The goal of such events is to quickly surface misunderstandings so the appropriate action can be taken.
» **Be truthful in all communications**: Scrum includes transparency as one of its core values. Transparency means we honestly and openly report velocity, demonstrate work, and graph project status. We also report work based on features implemented, rather than those remaining to be built, to further remove any confusion and lack of clarity in status communications.

Practice Exam

1. The Extreme Programming (XP) core values include:

   A. Solutions, communication, feedback
   B. Simplicity, control, feedback
   C. Simplicity, communication, feedback
   D. Solutions, control, feedback

2. The three pillars of Scrum are:

   A. Transparency, Communication, Adaptation
   B. Inspection, Adaptation, Evolution
   C. Adaptation, Inspection, Communication
   D. Transparency, Inspection, Adaptation

3. In the daily Scrum meeting, what three questions are asked?

   A. What has been achieved since the last meeting? What will be done before the next meeting? What obstacles are in the way?
   B. What has been started since the last meeting? What might get done before the next meeting? What obstacles are in the way?
   C. What has been started since the last meeting? What will be done before the next meeting? What obstacles are in the way?
   D. What has been achieved since the last meeting? What might be done before the next meeting? What obstacles are in the way?

4. What are the names of the backlogs maintained in Scrum?

   A. Product backlog, iteration backlog
   B. Product backlog, sprint backlog
   C. Project backlog, sprint backlog
   D. Project backlog, iteration backlog

5. In Scrum, the definition of "done" is created by everyone EXCEPT:

   A. Development team
   B. Product owner
   C. ScrumMaster
   D. Process owner

6. In Extreme Programming (XP), the core practices include:

   A. Whole team, planning games, small releases
   B. One team, process game, small releases
   C. Whole team, planning games, quick releases
   D. One team, process game, quick releases

7. Select the correct combination of lean principles:

   A. Eliminate waste, empower the team, build quality in, deter decisions, amplify learning
   B. Exterminate waste, empower the team, build quality in, deter decisions, optimize learning
   C. Eliminate waste, empower the team, build quality in, defer decisions, amplify learning
   D. Eliminate waste, empower the team, build quality in, defer decisions, optimize learning

8. Which of the following are some of the planned opportunities for Inspection and Adaptation in the Scrum method?

    A. Sprint retrospective, velocity review meeting, daily scrum meeting
    B. Sprint planning meeting, sprint retrospective, sprint risk meeting
    C. Sprint retrospective, daily scrum meeting, sprint review meeting
    D. Sprint planning meeting, daily scrum meeting, retrospective planning meeting

9. When using Kanban development, the acronym WIP stands for:

    A. Waste in progress
    B. Work in progress
    C. Waste in process
    D. Work is progressing

10. Which of the following is an Agile Manifesto value?

    A. Working solutions over complete documentation
    B. Working software over comprehensive documentation
    C. Working solutions over comprehensive documentation
    D. Working software over complete documentation

11. In the Agile Manifesto, what is valued more than processes and tools?

    A. Customer collaboration
    B. Individuals and interactions
    C. Working software
    D. Responding to change

12. Which of the following Agile Manifesto values deals most closely with WIP?

    A. Customer collaboration over contract negotiation
    B. Individuals and interactions over processes and tools
    C. Working software over comprehensive documentation
    D. Responding to change over following a plan

13. When agile teams use the term "timeboxed," what do they mean?

    A. Work shall take a minimum amount of time
    B. Work can take no more than a maximum amount of time
    C. Work must be done by a given time, plus or minus 20 percent
    D. Work must happen at a set time

14. Which Agile Manifesto value is concerned with team empowerment?

    A. Customer collaboration over contract negotiation
    B. Individuals and interactions over processes and tools
    C. Working software over comprehensive documentation
    D. Responding to change over following a plan

15. The five core principles of Kanban development include:

   A.   Minimize the workflow, pull flow, make process policies explicit, improve collaboratively
   B.   Visualize the workflow, manage flow, make process policies explicit, improve collaboratively
   C.   Minimize the workflow, manage flow, make process policies explicit, improve collaboratively
   D.   Visualize the workflow, pull flow, make process policies explicit, improve collaboration

© 2012 RMC Publications, Inc • 952.846.4484 • info@rmcproject.com • www.rmcproject.com

Answers

1. Answer: C
   Explanation: The three correct XP core values from the options presented are: simplicity, communication, and feedback. "Solutions" and "control" are not core values.

2. Answer: D
   Explanation: The three pillars are Transparency, Inspection, and Adaptation. Evolution and communication are both admirable goals, but they are not Scrum pillars.

3. Answer: A
   Explanation: The three questions asked in the daily Scrum meeting are: "What has been achieved since the last meeting?" "What will be done before the next meeting?" and "What obstacles are in the way?" Work started but not completed, or work that might be done before the next meeting, is not discussed to keep the meeting results-oriented.

4. Answer: B
   Explanation: The backlogs maintained in Scrum are the product backlog and the sprint backlog. Scrum calls iterations "sprints," so Scrum teams have a sprint backlog rather than an iteration backlog. Likewise, there is a product backlog but not a project backlog. Regardless of the term used, it is the practice that is really important. To be able to work effectively with people across methodologies, however, we do need to understand the differences in terminology.

5. Answer: D
   Explanation: The whole team, including the development team, product owner, and ScrumMaster, is responsible for creating a shared definition of "done." Since "process owner" is a made-up term, this is the correct choice for someone who would NOT be involved in defining done.

6. Answer: A
   Explanation: The correct set of XP core practices include: whole team, planning games, and small releases. The choices of "one team," "process game," and "quick releases" are not XP core practices.

7. Answer: C
   Explanation: The valid lean principles from this list are: eliminate waste, empower the team, build quality in, defer decisions, and amplify learning. "Exterminate waste," "Optimize learning," and "Deter decisions" are not lean principles. Make sure you read each answer choice carefully on questions like these—"defer" looks very much like "deter," especially when you are under pressure.

8. Answer: C
   Explanation: Scrum's planned opportunities for Inspection and Adaptation are the sprint retrospective, the daily scrum meeting, and the sprint review meeting. Velocity review meetings, sprint risk meetings, and retrospective planning meetings are not recognized Scrum events.

9. Answer: B
   Explanation: WIP stands for "Work in progress" or "Work in Process," not "waste" or "progressing."

10. Answer: B
    Explanation: The Agile Manifesto contains the value: "Working software over comprehensive documentation." The other choices express similar ideas, but they are not correctly stated.

11. **Answer:**   B
    Explanation: The Agile Manifesto value is "Individuals and interactions over processes and tools." Therefore, "individuals and interactions" is the correct choice.

12. **Answer:**   C
    Explanation: The value of "Working software over comprehensive documentation" is most closely related to WIP. This value speaks to the need to be focused on results and completed deliverables, rather than partially completed or in-progress work. If things like comprehensive documentation are holding up the ability to complete a deliverable—in other words, if a need for comprehensive documentation is keeping a lot of work in progress—it should be reduced as much as possible to support the ultimate goal of creating a useful, functional product.

13. **Answer:**   B
    Explanation: If work is timeboxed, it means it has a maximum duration assigned to it. This ensures the team spends an appropriate amount of time on the work without allowing waste.

14. **Answer:**   B
    Explanation: "Individuals and interactions over processes and tools" speaks to the concept that the benefits of empowerment outweigh the benefits of processes and tools on a project. The "customer collaboration over contract negotiation" choice is close, but that value is less about empowerment than about the need to respond to new information and changes instead of strictly adhering to old contracts and plans.

15. **Answer:**   B
    Explanation: The five core principles of Kanban development include: visualize the workflow, manage flow, make process policies explicit, and improve collaboratively. "Pull flow," "minimize the workflow," and "improve collaboration" all sound close to the real phrases, but they are not Kanban principles.

VALUE-DRIVEN DELIVERY

Chapter Three

Quicktest

- » Return on investment (ROI)
- » Net present value (NPV)
- » Internal rate of return (IRR)
- » Chartering
- » Value stream mapping
  - – Process cycle efficiency
  - – Waste
- » Customer-valued prioritization
  - – Prioritization schemes (MoSCoW, Kano analysis, Requirements Prioritization Model)
- » Relative prioritization/ranking
- » Product roadmap
  - – Story map
- » Risk-adjusted backlog
- » Agile contracting
- » Task/Kanban boards
- » WIP limits
  - – Work in progress (WIP)
  - – Cycle time
- » Incremental delivery
  - – Cost of change over time
- » Prototypes, simulations, demonstrations
- » Agile earned value
- » Cumulative flow diagram (CFD)
- » Risk burn down graph
  - – Risk probability and impact
  - – Expected monetary value
  - – Risk severity

Delivering value, specifically business value, is a core component of agile methods. This concept is woven into the agile DNA with its inclusion in the Agile Manifesto's values ("Working software over comprehensive documentation"[1]) and principles ("Deliver working software frequently" and "Working software is the primary measure of progress"[2]). The focus on delivering value drives many of the activities and decisions on an agile project, and it manifests itself in many of the tools and techniques and knowledge and skills used. This focus is such an essential component of agile methods that the value-driven delivery domain has the most T&Ts and K&Ss of any of the six domains. This means we are starting with the biggest section early in this book.

What Is Value-Driven Delivery?

Let's start by defining value-driven delivery. The reason projects are undertaken is to generate business value, be it to produce a benefit or to improve a service. Even safety and regulatory compliance projects can be expressed in terms of business value by considering the business risk and the impact of not undertaking them. So if value is the reason for doing projects, value-driven delivery must be the focus of the project throughout the planning, execution, and control efforts.

Aiming to maximize value delivery is an overarching theme, or mantra, for agile teams. When faced with a decision between two or more options, we often ask the question, "Which choice would add the most value for the business or customer?" to help determine the way forward. We also have an obligation to consider technical dependencies and risks. A choice that could lead to future problems or rework does not support the long-term goal of value-driven development, even if it gives the illusion of early progress. Therefore, we need to consider nonfunctional requirements and risks and advise the customer about how those elements will impact the project.

Risks as Anti-Value

The concept of risk is closely related to value, so much so that we can think of negative project risks (threats) as anti-value, or factors that have the potential to erode, remove, or reduce value if they occur. If value is the "heads" side of a coin, then risk is the "tails" side. To maximize value, we must also minimize risks, since risks can reduce value. This is why the value-driven delivery domain emphasizes risk-reduction concepts and techniques.

Here's another simple way to grasp the relationship of value and risks. Think of value-driven delivery as creating credits or deposits that are paid into your bank account. Risks—or at least threats that occur and become issues on your project—are then like withdrawals or charges that are taken out of your account. To create the most value, we need to maximize the inflow and minimize the outflow of value from the account.

Eat Your Dessert First—Early Value Delivery

Agile methods promote early value delivery. This means the team aims to deliver the highest value portions of the project as soon as possible. There are some key reasons for this approach. First, life is short, weird stuff happens, and the longer a project runs, the longer the horizon becomes for risks such as failure, reduced benefits, erosion of opportunities, and so on. To maximize success, we should aim to deliver as many high-value components as soon as we can, before things change or go sideways.

The second major reason is that stakeholder satisfaction plays a huge role in project success. Engaged, committed sponsors and business representatives who support a project are vital to removing project obstacles and defining success. All project teams are on a trial period when they start, since the sponsors may not be convinced that the team can deliver. By delivering high-value elements early, the team demonstrates an understanding of the stakeholders' needs, shows a recognition of the most important aspects of the project, and proves they can deliver. Tangible results raise stakeholders' confidence, build rapport with them, and get them on board early, creating virtuous circles of support.

In short, value-driven delivery is about making decisions that prioritize the value-adding activities and risk-reducing actions for the project, and then executing based on these priorities.

In This Chapter

Now that we've covered some of the basic concepts related to value-driven delivery, the rest of this chapter will focus on the practices of assessing, planning, delivering, confirming, tracking, and reporting value, including the tools and techniques and knowledge and skills involved in these practices, as shown in the chart on the following page. Although these practices are not official terms that will appear on the exam, they provide the context of why and how you use the T&Ts and K&Ss that you will be tested on.

Practice	Tool/Technique	Knowledge/Skill (Level)
Assessing value	» Return on investment (ROI) » Net present value (NPV) » Internal rate of return (IRR)	
Planning value	» Chartering » Value stream mapping » Customer-valued prioritization » Relative prioritization/ranking » Product roadmap » Risk-adjusted backlog	» Prioritization (Level 1) » Agile contracting methods (Level 3)
Delivering value	» Task/Kanban boards » WIP limits	» Incremental delivery (Level 1)
Confirming value	» Customer-valued prioritization	» Feedback through prototypes, simulations, and demonstrations (Level 1)
Tracking and reporting value	» Earned value management for agile projects » Cumulative flow diagrams (CFDs) » Risk burn down graphs » Task/Kanban boards	

Assessing Value

Business value is usually assessed in financial terms. Some projects are undertaken for safety or regulatory compliance purposes and do not have an easily determined monetary value. In these cases, the organization might want to look at the financial ramifications of not undertaking the project, such as the risk of the business being shut down, fines, or lawsuits. Or it can simply label the project as mandatory and not spend any additional time trying to quantify its value.

For business projects, value is commonly estimated using methods such as return on investment (ROI), internal rate of return (IRR), and net present value (NPV). ROI, IRR, and NPV are among the tools and techniques the exam will test your comprehension of. You will see examples of these calculations later in this section, but first let's look at the benefits these techniques provide.

 The PMI-ACP exam focuses on the *when* and the *why* of ROI, NPV, and IRR over the *how* and the *what*. In other words, you will be asked questions about *when* these techniques might be used and *why* these techniques are used, but you will not be asked to perform the calculations. I've included information in this chapter about how to calculate these metrics to help you more completely understand the concept, but you don't need to fret about memorizing the formulas for the exam.

Using economic models to assess value removes individual bias and emotion from the process of selecting and justifying projects. Instead, with economic models, you can focus on comparing a common variable (financial return) across projects. The results are "in the numbers," and are (in theory) more objective than other project selection models. (In practice, however, the inputs into the calculations can be manipulated to sway the outcome.)

T&T | Return on Investment (ROI)

Let's look at an example of return on investment. We have a project that will run from January until June and then deliver a solution that generates some financial return. From January until June, we will spend money on the project, paying hourly rates for the resources (shown in figure 3.1 by the green line with triangle markers indicating negative cumulative cash flow). In June, we will deploy our solution and start to get a positive income (shown by the dark line with circle markers).

Figure 3.1: Project Spending and Income

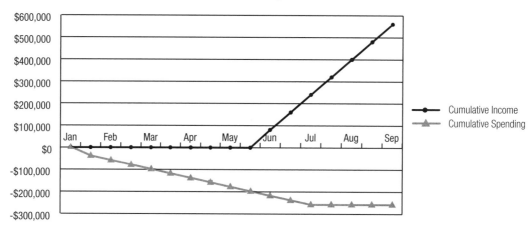

When we add the new income to the outflow figures, we can see the net cash flow (indicated in figure 3.2 by the gray line with square markers). Based on figure 3.2, when do you think we will have met our return on investment?

Figure 3.2: Net Cash Flow

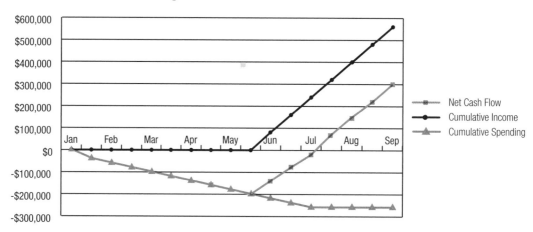

It is tempting to assume that when this net cash flow reaches zero (July in our example), we will have met our return on investment and that January to July is our payback period. In a way, this is true; we will have received back as much money as we spent. We need to consider the effect of inflation, however. Money that is received in the future is less valuable than money we hold, or spend, right now. This is especially true if, to fund the project, we have to borrow money that we will need to pay back with interest. So when determining ROI, we need a way to take into account the effect of inflation and the cost of borrowing money.

T&T Net Present Value (NPV)

This is where the concept of present value comes in. Present value is a way of calculating the value in today's terms of a future amount, given an assumed interest rate or inflation rate. Let's take a look at how present value is calculated.

Present Value

Present Value = The value in today's terms of a future amount

$$PV = \frac{FV}{(1+r)^n}$$

FV = Future value
r = Interest rate
n = Number of time periods

What is the present value of $200,000 received 4 years from now if the interest rate is 7%?

$$\frac{200{,}000}{(1+0.07)^4} = \$152{,}579$$

REMINDER: You don't need to know this formula for the exam.

Now let's apply the concept of present value to our sample project. In figure 3.3, the gray line with the "x" markers indicates the present value of the money we will receive in the future, based on a projected interest rate of 2 percent (to represent inflation).

Figure 3.3: Present Value

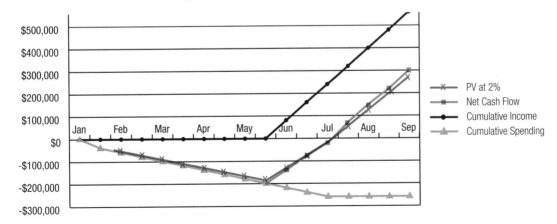

Now let's take the concept of present value further, to net present value (NPV). NPV is the total benefits (the income minus costs) for a revenue stream adjusted to today's value. Organizations have found present value calculations and the resulting ability to compare money going out and money coming in so valuable that NPV is widely used to evaluate project returns.

Net Present Value

Net Present Value = The total benefits (income minus the costs) for a revenue stream

$$NPV = I_o + \frac{I_1}{(1+r)^1} + \frac{I_2}{(1+r)^2} \cdots + \frac{I_n}{(1+r)^n}$$

I = Income for each year
r = Discount rate
n = Number of time periods

What is the net present value of a project that costs $300,000 in the first year and returns $80,000 for the next 4 years, assuming a discount rate of 5%?

$$-300,000 + \frac{80,000}{(1+0.05)} + \frac{80,000}{(1+0.05)^2} + \frac{80,000}{(1+0.05)^3} + \frac{80,000}{(1+0.05)^4} = -\$16,324$$

REMINDER: You don't need to know this formula for the exam.

By using NPV to assess our project cost and income streams, we can find, after adjustment for inflation, the true ROI point and payback period. In large multiyear projects, the payback period can be substantially longer, especially if money to invest in projects is borrowed at high interest rates.

T&T Internal Rate of Return (IRR)

Now let's look at the concept of internal rate of return. The IRR calculation helps simplify the evaluation of projects by turning the return on investment period around. Rather than using an interest rate to calculate a value of an investment in today's terms, it uses duration and payback information to calculate an effective interest rate for the project.

The definition of IRR is the discount rate "at which the project inflows (revenues) and project outflows (costs) are equal."[3] In other words, "What discount rate would I have to use to move the true payback period to the end of my project?" From an economic perspective, the higher the rate, the better the project.

Internal Rate of Return

From an economic perspective, the higher the discount rate, the better the project is.

If Project A has an IRR of 25% and Project B has an IRR of 18%, choose Project A to maximize the rate of return.

EXERCISE: UNDERSTANDING ROI, NPV AND IRR

Test yourself! See how well you understand ROI, NPV, and IRR by answering the following questions:

1. Which of the following definitions best describes return on investment (ROI)?

    A. The point in time when the revenue received equals the costs expended for the project
    B. How much revenue the project will bring in once it is completed and operational
    C. How much money, net of costs expended, will be returned when the project is over
    D. How much money the project will cost once all project expenditures are collected

2. A sponsor is trying to determine which project has the greatest business value. One project returns $5 million in 3 years, and another project returns $6 million in 4 years. The cost of borrowing capital to fund the project is 4 percent. Which of the following is the best approach to determine the project with the greatest value?

    A. Select the project that returns $6 million in 4 years, since it returns the highest amount.
    B. Select the project that returns $5 million in 3 years, since it has the shorter payback period.
    C. Calculate the NPV of the projects, and choose the project with the lowest cost.
    D. Calculate the NPV of the projects, and choose the project with the highest value.

3. A sponsor is considering the business value of two projects. Which of the following definitions best describes the approach for assessing and applying the concept of internal rate of return (IRR)?

    A. Calculate the internal rate of return, and choose the project with the highest rate.
    B. Calculate the internal rate of return, and choose the project with lowest cost.
    C. Calculate the internal rate of return, and choose the project with highest revenue.
    D. Calculate the internal rate of return, and choose the project with lowest revenue.

ANSWER

1. **Answer:** C. The question calls for us to identify the BEST definition, which is the amount of money that will be returned when the project is over, minus expenditures. ROI is actually a fairly loose term, since it does not specify at what point in time the measurement will be made, which is why concepts like NPV are used instead. In looking at the other choices, option A is more concerned with the point in time and is a closer match to a payback point or breakeven point for the project. Choice B focuses on revenue only, omitting any consideration of costs, and choice D is a better description for project costs than ROI. Therefore, choice C is our best option.

2. **Answer:** D. To evaluate the value of two projects that complete at different times, we can use net present value (NPV) to level the amounts into today's values. So calculating the NPV and choosing the project with the highest NPV value is the way to go. Choice A points us to the project with the highest return, but the question is asking for the best approach. Likewise, options B and C do not address the best approach to take.

3. **Answer:** A. Internal rate of return (IRR) shows the earning potential for a project. Like comparing investment interest rates, the higher the rate, the better the investment proposition. So to use IRR to evaluate projects, we calculate the IRR for each and then select the project with the highest IRR value. Costs and revenue are rolled into the calculation of IRR and are not part of the final IRR evaluation.

Planning Value

Now that we've discussed ways of assessing value when selecting projects, let's look at how value-driven delivery plays out in planning a project after it has been selected. The focus on value-driven delivery permeates the agile planning process. We prioritize the work to be done on a project according to business value, putting high-value deliverables at the top of the list, or backlog. When we start working on the project, we start with the items at the top of the backlog. Change requests and defect fixes—in fact any work that wasn't initially planned and is added later—are prioritized in the backlog based on their business value and whether they are deemed more important than the existing items on the list.

The concept of planning value comes up a lot in the PMI-ACP exam content outline, particularly in the T&Ts of chartering, value stream mapping, relative prioritization/ranking, and the product roadmap.[4] Since risks can reduce value, we also need to address them in planning through the use of tools like a risk-adjusted backlog. In addition, we'll touch on the concepts of value-based analysis and agile contracts. Let's review each of these T&Ts and K&Ss in turn.

T&T | Chartering

The technique of chartering in agile projects has the same general goal as the Develop Project Charter process defined in the *PMBOK® Guide*, but the level of detail and the set of assumptions are different.[5] Like a non-agile charter, the goal of an agile charter is to describe the project at a high level, gain agreement about the project's W5H (What, Why, Who, When, Where, and How) attributes, and obtain the authority to proceed. However, since agile methods are often used on projects where the requirements or technology are uncertain or high levels of changes are expected, the scope is typically less clearly defined.

As a result, agile charters generally have less detail than non-agile charters, are shorter documents, and focus more on *how* the project will be run than on exactly *what* will be built. When we are aiming at a static target (with unchanging requirements or technology), it is appropriate to plan, plan some more, and then execute. But on a dynamic project with a moving target, a high degree of planning may be inappropriate because key elements of the project are likely to change—and to do so quickly. For such projects, we need to allow for mid-flight adjustments and make sure we have the processes (such as prioritization, demos, retrospectives, etc.) in place to allow us to make such adjustments effectively and efficiently.

Any elements of the agile methodology that may be different from an organization's normal processes, such as how changes are approved and then prioritized into the backlog after approval, should be clearly outlined in the charter. This is especially important if the agile methods are new to the organization and if any part of the approach is a departure from how aspects of a project, such as change control and inclusion, were handled in the past.

We will discuss agile charters in more detail in chapter 6, Adaptive Planning. For purposes of the value-driven delivery domain, understand that chartering in an agile environment results in a flexible document that allows the team to respond to changing needs and technology and ultimately deliver high-value components that the organization can begin using quickly.

T&T | Value Stream Mapping

Value stream mapping is a lean manufacturing technique that has been adopted by agile methods. This technique illustrates the flow of information (or materials) required to complete a process. It can help determine the elements of waste that could be removed to improve the efficiency of a process. Value stream mapping usually involves creating visual maps of the process (known as value stream maps), following these steps:

1. Identify the product or service that you are analyzing.
2. Create a value stream map of the current process, identifying steps, queues, delays, and information flows.
3. Review the map to find delays, waste, and constraints.
4. Create a new value stream map of the desired future state of the process, optimized to remove or reduce delays, waste, and constraints.
5. Develop a roadmap for creating the optimized state.
6. Plan to revisit the process in the future to continually tune and optimize it.

To illustrate this technique, let's create a value stream map for buying a cake to celebrate passing your PMI-ACP exam with a friend. For purposes of the illustration, we'll say this process involves choosing a cake, waiting at the bakery counter to get the cake, paying for the cake at the checkout register, and walking home with the cake. We then unpack and slice the cake before enjoying the benefit of the process (eating the cake).

First, identify the starting point of the process (who initiates it) and the end point (who gets the end result).

Figure 3.4: Value Stream Map—Process Starting and End Points

Then identify the high-level steps, inventories, and queues through the process, focusing on the primary flow.

Figure 3.5: Value Stream Map—Primary Flow

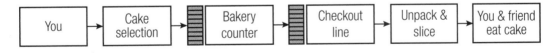

Identify any supporting groups (such as bakers and sales clerks) and alternative flows (such as selecting another cake if the bakery counter does not have the one you want).

Figure 3.6: Value Stream Map—Supporting Groups and Alternative Flows

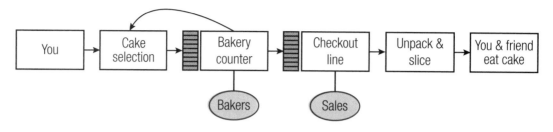

Measure the value-adding and nonvalue-adding activities; calculate efficiencies; and identify waste, bottlenecks, and improvement actions.

Figure 3.7: Value Stream Map—Measurements, Calculations, and Areas for Improvement

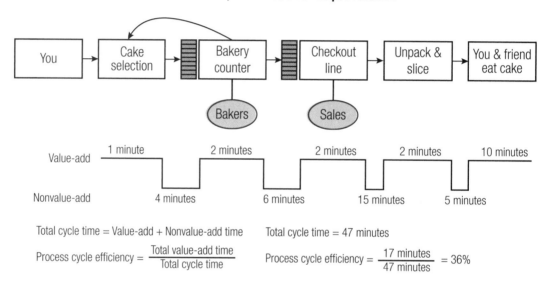

Total cycle time = Value-add + Nonvalue-add time

$$\text{Process cycle efficiency} = \frac{\text{Total value-add time}}{\text{Total cycle time}}$$

Total cycle time = 47 minutes

$$\text{Process cycle efficiency} = \frac{17 \text{ minutes}}{47 \text{ minutes}} = 36\%$$

This takes us through step 3 of the value stream mapping process, where we review the map to identify waste or process inefficiencies. The next steps are to remove waste and create a new value stream map of the future optimized state, along with a roadmap of how to get to that state. To complete the technique, we plan in the points where we will revisit the process in order to keep refining it.

In this example, we can see that there are waiting delays at the bakery counter and the checkout counter. We can also see that there are motion inefficiencies, with lots of time spent between paying for the cake and being able to eat it, as we travel from the store back home.

To design a more efficient process, we could consider phoning a specialty cake catering service and having the cake express-delivered to our house.

In this new, more efficient process, let's say that our time waiting to place the order is reduced from 4 minutes to 2 minutes. Our 6-minute wait to pay for the cake is reduced to 1 minute, and the 15-minute walk home is replaced by a 10-minute delivery period.

Figure 3.8: Value Stream Map—Improved Process Efficiency

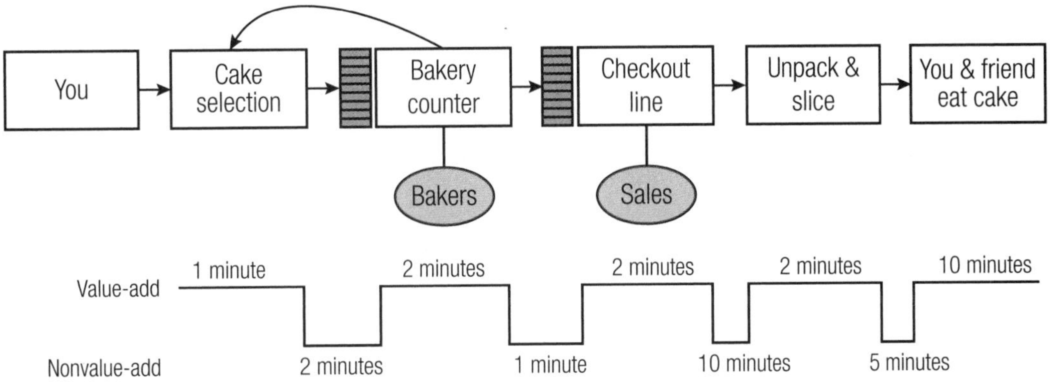

Total cycle time = Value-add + Nonvalue-add time

$$\text{Process cycle efficiency} = \frac{\text{Total value-add time}}{\text{Total cycle time}}$$

Total cycle time = 35 minutes

$$\text{Process cycle efficiency} = \frac{17 \text{ minutes}}{35 \text{ minutes}} = 49\%$$

With these changes, the value-added time remains at 17 minutes, but the nonvalue-added time is reduced from 47 minutes to 35 minutes, which means that the process efficiency goes up from 36 percent to 49 percent. Of course, process efficiency is not the whole story—if the express delivery of the cake triples the cost, we might think twice about using it. However, this design does maximize the efficiency of the transaction.

EXERCISE: PROCESS CYCLE EFFICIENCY—CAR WASH

Calculate the process cycle efficiency of waiting in line for 10 minutes to use a car wash for 5 minutes.

ANSWER

To do this calculation, we first need to know what the total cycle time is: 10 minutes in line + 5 minutes washing the car = 15 minutes total cycle time.

Now, let's calculate the process cycle efficiency, using the following formula:

Process cycle efficiency = Total value-add time / Total cycle time

So process cycle efficiency = 5 / 15 = 33.3%.

Our perception of what aspects of a process add value affects our calculations. Test yourself with this next exercise to see how well you understand the concept of process cycle efficiency.

EXERCISE: PROCESS CYCLE EFFICIENCY—CUPCAKES

On Saturday morning, Tom and his young son Tim make cupcakes together. Although Tom does not like cupcakes, he values the 30 minutes with his son that it takes to make them. Tim thinks that making the cupcakes is a chore, but he really values the 5 minutes that he spends eating them. What are the process cycle efficiencies for Tom and Tim?

ANSWER

This question involves two separate calculations of process cycle efficiency—one for Tom, who considers the baking process to be the value-added time, and one for Tim, who considers the eating process to be the value-added time. To work out the process cycle efficiency, we need to know both the total cycle time and the value-added time. The total cycle time is the same for both Tom and Tim: 30 + 5 = 35 minutes. The formula for calculating the process cycle efficiency is:

$$\text{Process cycle efficiency} = \text{Value-added time} / \text{Total cycle time}$$

For Tom, who values the baking time with his son, the process cycle efficiency is 30 / 35, or 86%.

For Tim, who values actually eating the cupcakes, the process cycle efficiency is 5 / 35, or 14%.

Before we move on to the discussion of the next topic, customer-valued prioritization, let's look further into the concept of waste on software projects. Mary and Tom Poppendieck have written extensively on the use of Lean principles for software projects. They have converted the seven traditional wastes of a manufacturing process into seven equivalent software-related wastes, as indicated in the following table:[6]

Waste	Description	Example
Partially done work	Work started, but not complete; partially done work can entropy	» Code waiting for testing » Specs waiting for development
Extra processes	Extra work that does not add value	» Unused documentation » Unnecessary approvals
Extra features	Features that are not required, or are thought of as "nice-to-haves"	» Gold-plating » Technology features
Task switching	Multitasking between several different projects when there are context-switching penalties	» People on multiple projects
Waiting	Delays waiting for reviews and approvals	» Waiting for prototype reviews » Waiting for document approvals

Waste	Description	Example
Motion	The effort required to communicate or move information or deliverables from one group to another; if teams are not co-located, this effort may need to be greater	» Distributed teams » Handoffs
Defects	Defective documents or software that need correction	» Requirements defects » Software bugs

EXERCISE: CATEGORIZE WASTES

Using the Poppendiecks' table of wastes as a reference, categorize the following day-to-day office wastes shown in the table below. The first one is done for you as an example.

Activity	Type of Waste
Queuing for elevator	Waiting
Rebooting a computer after a program crash	
Saving documents in old formats for compatibility	
Creating notices in French and Spanish to comply with company standards, even though nobody at your location speaks these languages	
Submitting stationery and letterhead orders for approval	

ANSWER

Activity	Type of Waste
Queuing for elevator	Waiting
Rebooting a computer after a program crash	Defects, waiting
Saving documents in old formats for compatibility	Extra processes, motion
Creating notices in French and Spanish to comply with company standards, even though nobody at your location speaks these languages	Extra processes, extra features
Submitting stationery and letterhead orders for approval	Extra processes, motion, partially done work

Of course, these types of activities aren't always waste. The waste comes in when there aren't really any benefits gained from the activity. So while safety notices should be in the languages of anyone likely to need it, the creation of such notices for people who do not need them can be considered waste. Likewise, approvals for stationery and letterhead orders might be useful to prevent abuse or petty theft, but for people who just need some basic supplies, the process adds no value and can be considered a waste.

K&S Level 1   **T&T**   ## Customer-Valued Prioritization

Customer-valued prioritization is concerned with working on the items that yield the highest value to the customer as soon as possible. This technique aims to engage the customer in the prioritization process, in which the team identifies high-value features and moves them up the backlog of items to work on. Prioritization is essential for the team to be able to adjust the scope to meet budget or timeline objectives while still retaining the useful set of functionality that makes up the minimally marketable feature (for an explanation of the minimally marketable feature, see chapter 6, Adapative Planning).

The use of customer-valued prioritization schemes is a common thread through the different agile methods. While the terminology often varies—Scrum, for instance, has a "product backlog," FDD has a "feature list," and DSDM has a "prioritized requirements list"—the idea is the same. The project works through a prioritized list of items that have discernible customer value.

Prioritization Schemes

The team should choose which prioritization scheme to use based on the needs of the project and what works best for the organization. Let's look at some common prioritization schemes.

Simple Schemes   One of the simplest schemes is to label items as "Priority 1," "Priority 2," "Priority 3," etc. While this approach is straightforward, it can be problematic in that people have a tendency to designate everything a "Priority 1." If too many items are labeled "Priority 1," the scheme becomes ineffective. Business representatives rarely ask for a new feature and say it should be a Priority 2 or 3, since they know that low-priority items risk getting cut out of the project. For the same reasons, "high," "medium," and "low" prioritizations can also be problematic. Without a shared, defendable reason for what defines "high" priority, we end up with too many items in this category and a lack of true priority.

MoSCoW Prioritization Scheme   The MoSCoW prioritization scheme, popularized by DSDM, is another example. This scheme derives its name from the first letters of the following labels:

» "**M**ust have"
» "**S**hould have"
» "**C**ould have"
» "**W**ould like to have, but not this time"

The categories used in MoSCoW are easier to identify and defend than the "Priority 1" or "High Priority" labels of the simpler schemes. "Must-have" requirements or features are those that are fundamental to the system; without them, the system will not work or will have no value. "Should have" features are important—by definition, we should have them for the system to work correctly; if they are not there, then the workaround will likely be costly or cumbersome. "Could have" features are useful net additions that add tangible value, and "Would like" requirements are the "nice-to-have" requests that are duly noted—but unlikely to make the cut.

Monopoly Money   Another approach I have seen work well is to give sponsors Monopoly money equal to the amount of the project budget and to ask them to distribute it amongst the system features. This approach is useful for identifying the general priority of system components, but it can be taken too far if the people distributing the money start to question activities, such as documentation, that they perceive as adding little value to the project. The Monopoly money technique is most effective when it's limited to prioritizing business features.

100-Point Method The 100-Point Method, originally developed by Dean Leffingwell and Don Widrig for use cases, is another way to prioritize features. In this method, each stakeholder is given 100 points that he or she can use to vote for the most important requirements. The stakeholders can distribute the 100 points in any way: 30 points here, 15 points there, or even all 100 points on a single requirement, if that is the stakeholder's only priority.

Kano Analysis Kano analysis, developed in the 1980s by Noriaki Kano, can also serve as a prioritization scheme. This technique can be used to classify customer preferences into four categories, which we will refer to in this book as Delighters/Exciters, Satisfiers, Dissatisfiers, and Indifferent. These categories can help the team better understand how needs relate to customer satisfaction. Kano analysis can set the context for questions about features and help build release plans that promote improved customer satisfaction.

Note: You do not need to know historical information for the exam.

Figure 3.9: Kano Analysis

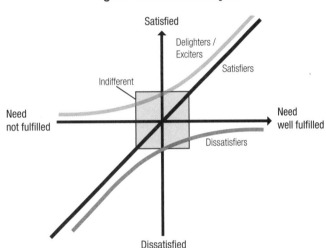

Let's look at each category in more detail:

» **Exciters**: These features deliver unexpected, novel, or new high-value benefits to the customer. For example, an exciter feature could be the visual mapping of data that was previously only available in tabular form. Exciters yield high levels of customer support.
» **Satisfiers**: For features that are categorized as Satisfiers, the more the better. These features bring value to the customer. For example, a useful reporting function could be a Satisfier.
» **Dissatisfiers**: These are things that will cause a user to dislike the product if they are not there, but will not necessarily raise satisfaction if they are present. For example, the ability to change a password within the system could be a Dissatisfier.
» **Indifferent**: These features have no impact on customers one way or another. Since customers are indifferent to them, we should try to eliminate, minimize, or defer them.

Requirements Prioritization Model The Requirements Prioritization Model created by Karl Wiegers is a more mathematically rigorous method of calculating priority than the other schemes we've discussed. With this approach, the benefit, penalty, cost, and risk of every proposed feature is rated on a relative scale of 1 (lowest) to 9 (highest). Customers rate both the benefit score for having the feature and the penalty score for not having it. Developers rate the cost of producing the feature and the risk associated with producing it. All the numbers for each feature are then entered into a weighted formula that is used to calculate their relative priority.

EXERCISE: MUST HAVE, SHOULD HAVE, COULD HAVE

Categorize the following features for a child's bicycle into "must-have," "should-have," and "could-have" features. The first one is done for you as an example.

Feature	Category
Two wheels and a frame	Must have
Ability to adjust the saddle to accommodate growth	
Brakes for safe stopping	
Bell or horn to alert others in proximity	
Safety cover for the chain	
Attractive color scheme	
Stabilizers or the ability to fit them	
Front suspension	
Valves for inflating tires	
Pedals	

ANSWER

Feature	Category
Two wheels and a frame	Must have
Ability to adjust the saddle to accommodate growth	Should have
Brakes for safe stopping	Should have
Bell or horn to alert others in proximity	Could have
Safety cover for the chain	Should have / Could have
Attractive color scheme	Could have
Stabilizers or the ability to fit them	Should have / Could have
Front suspension	Could have
Valves for inflating tires	Could have
Pedals	Should have / Could have

My answers may seem extreme—surely bikes need pedals, valves to put air in the tires, and brakes! However, a bicycle is a two-wheel transportation device. By definition, it must have two wheels and a frame to link the wheels together, but beyond that, everything else is up for discussion and negotiation. My son learned to ride a bike on a "balance bike," which had solid tires and no pedals or brakes; instead, he just scooted it along with his feet.

Often there is a disconnect between expectations and requirements, and this disconnect is highlighted in this exercise. As sophisticated consumers of products today, we often have a high level of expectations, but high expectations are quite different from true must-have requirements. The qualifying question for a must-have requirement is closer to "Can it work without it?" than "Would I buy one that did not have it?"

T&T Relative Prioritization / Ranking

Regardless of the prioritization scheme that is used, the focus should be on the end goal—understanding the priority of features. Sometimes the effort involved in refereeing the schemes can detract from meaningful discussions about prioritization. For this reason, I am personally a fan of simply asking the business to list features in priority order—no category 1, 2, or 3; no high, medium, or low; no must-haves, etc. A simple list (whether it is created in a spreadsheet or in an agile requirements management tool) removes the categories that people tend to fixate on from the debate and allows the focus of the discussion to be on priorities.

Let's look at an example of a simple priority list:

Figure 3.10: Simple Priority List

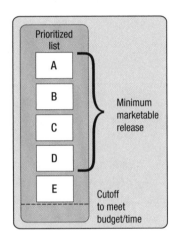

In figure 3.10, the features are listed in order of priority. The items at the top of the list—features A through D—are part of the defined minimum marketable release. If scope needs to be cut to meet the budget and schedule objectives, it's clear by looking at this simple list that adjustments should be made to item E.

Relative prioritization also provides a framework for deciding if and when to incorporate changes. When a change is requested, the team can ask the business representatives, "What items are more important than this change?" The new change can then be inserted into the prioritized work list at the appropriate point, as shown in figure 3.11.

Figure 3.11: Incorporating Changes into a Simple Priority List

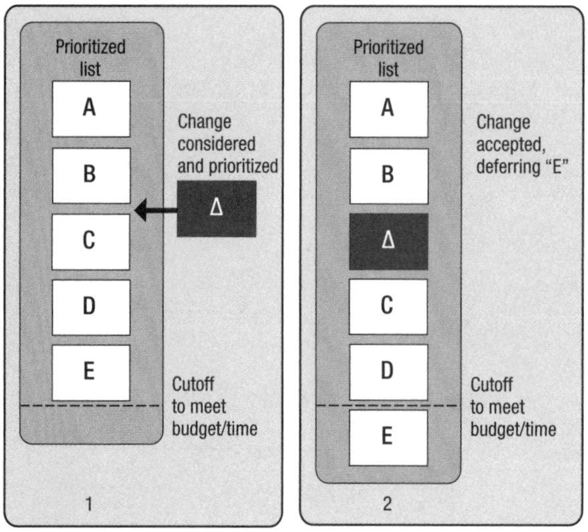

While agile methods provide tremendous flexibility in accepting late-breaking changes, they cannot bend the laws of time and space. So if our project time or budget was estimated to be fully consumed with the current scope, then adding a new change will inevitably force a lower priority feature below the "cutoff point" of what we expect to deliver. So, yes, we can accept late-breaking changes on projects—but only at the expense of lower-priority work items.

A single prioritized work list is useful for simplifying the view of all the remaining work; rather than having separate "buckets" of work that represent change requests, defect fixes, and new features, a single prioritized list combining these items gives everyone a clear, complete view of everything that remains to be done on the project. When first adopting an agile approach, many teams miss this point and instead retain separate buckets for bug fixes and changes. This separation muddies velocity, however. A single prioritized list of work-to-be-done, regardless of its origin, offers better transparency and control over trade-offs, because the relative priority of the work is clearly shown by where each item is placed on the list.

TRICKS OF THE TRADE® Although I endorse the use of a simple list, there is no single best method to always use in prioritizing features on every project. Whatever technique you use, try to diagnose any issues that arise in the prioritization process, be it "lack of involvement" or "too many priority 1s." You can then add in different approaches, such as using Monopoly money, applying the MoSCoW prioritization scheme, or simply listing the features in order of priority, to see if you can resolve the issues by framing the discussion in a new way. The goal of such efforts is to understand where features lie in relation to each other, rather than to simply assign a category label. You will then end up with a flexible list of prioritized requirements that you can revisit and reprioritize as needed. This allows you to maintain the agility to deliver the highest value set of features within the available time and budget.

T&T Product Roadmap

A product roadmap is a visual overview of a product's releases and its main components. It is a communication tool that provides project stakeholders with a quick view of the primary release points and intended functionality. There is no one set way of depicting a product roadmap, but story maps, popularized by Jeff Patton, are a commonly used approach.

Story Maps

Story maps help select and group features for a release. These diagrams show the sequence of the features and indicate their importance to the project by classifying them as "backbone," "walking skeleton," or additional features. All products and systems have some essential functionality that they need to perform. This essential functionality makes up the backbone of the system. There is little point in overly prioritizing such functions; they just need to be in the system. Hanging off of the backbone is the walking skeleton functionality. The walking skeleton describes the smallest system that could possibly work. Finally, any remaining features hang below the walking skeleton and are prioritized by their importance to the system. Figure 3.12 is an example of a story map.

Figure 3.12: Story Map

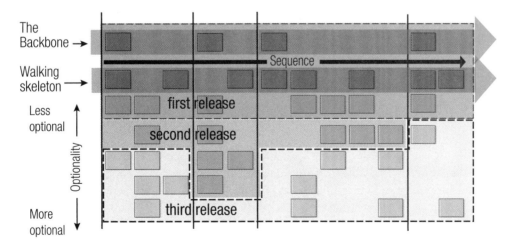

Once the features are placed on the map according to their importance and sequence, the customer's priorities are balanced with the team's capacity to deliver, and the releases that will make up the product roadmap are identified. Figure 3.13 provides an example of a product roadmap that shows the first, second, and third release.

Figure 3.13: Product Roadmap

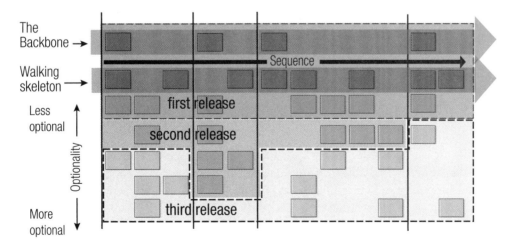

Using this approach, the final product roadmap consists of collections of story maps and shows what will go into each release. It depicts what is absolutely essential for the system (the backbone) and necessary for the solution (the walking skeleton), along with the other features that will comprise later releases.

T&T Risk-Adjusted Backlog

As we discussed at the start of this chapter, negative risks (project threats) are like anti-value; if a risk occurs, it takes time and resources away from efforts that deliver value and threatens the project benefits. Therefore, we should not only plan to deliver high-value features early, we should plan to execute risk avoidance and risk mitigation activities early, too.

Risk management may seem like a traditional, process-driven project management effort that would not work well in an agile environment. However, agile methods are great risk reduction vehicles and are actually very well suited for rapidly identifying and reducing risks. Let's explore risk management in more detail, starting with the definition of a risk.

A risk is an event or circumstance that could transpire and impact the project. Most risk literature focuses on events that have the potential to negatively impact or threaten the project, but the *PMBOK® Guide* also talks about good risks, or opportunities, for the project.[7]

Figure 3.14 represents the risk management process that is outlined in the *PMBOK® Guide*:

Figure 3.14: Risk Management Process

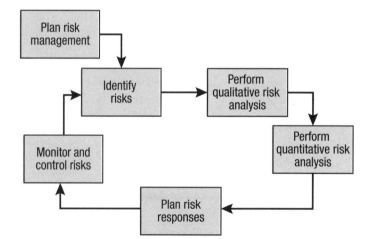

One step that appears to be absent from this process is a "risk response doing" step in which the actions identified in the risk response plan are completed. This step is not actually missing; instead, these activities are scheduled with the project's regular work activities. The apparent lack of a "doing" step does mirror a problem seen on many projects, however—namely, that risk management is undertaken as a separate (sometimes one-time only) passive activity that does not drive enough action on the project to prevent the risks from happening. As a result, we see risks occurring and can point to where they were identified on the risk list, yet not enough was done to prevent them.

The iterative nature of agile projects helps overcome this issue. Through iterations, we can tackle high-risk areas of the project sooner rather than later. This approach gets problems out in the open while there is still room in the schedule and budget to work on them. It also reduces the amount of effort invested in work that may end up being scrapped.

Figure 3.15: Agile Projects Are Both Business-Value and Risk-Driven

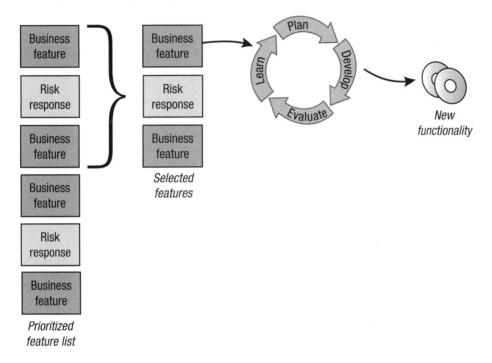

Agile projects are said to be both business-value- and risk-driven. This means we choose practical bundles of work based on the assigned business priority and what high-risk items remain in the prioritized feature list (or user story backlog). So if we have stories with residual risk, we would want to move the risky items up the queue and undertake them as appropriate.

Most teams are comfortable with ranking requirements (stories, features, use cases) by business value and levels of risk. This process is often subjective, based on a customer's or proxy user's gut feeling or preference. If we want to get more scientific about it, however, we can focus on the return on investment per feature. This calculation starts with understanding the ROI for the project as a whole. For example, before approving a $2 million project, a company (presumably) does a cost-benefit analysis to determine whether the revenue or savings to be gained from the project justify the cost of undertaking it, and calculates the return on investment for the project (e.g., $4 million in three years). For regulatory compliance or maintenance projects, we can still come up with a dollar figure; the dollar amount will be related to the economic penalties for noncompliance (fines, lost business, etc.). (For more on how ROI is used to select projects, see the Assessing Value discussion earlier in this chapter.)

Once we have an ROI figure for a project, the business representatives (not the development team) should distribute or prorate this amount across the identified features. Business representatives often push back at this idea with comments like, "I can't put a dollar value on a sales report; that would be too subjective or misleading." It can be helpful to remind them that someone came up with a projected payback for this project. If that figure cannot be divided across the product's features, then where did it come from in the first place?

After the business representatives have (perhaps somewhat arbitrarily) attributed a dollar value to the product features, we will have a prioritized feature list with ROI values, as shown in figure 3.16.

Figure 3.16: Prioritized Feature List with ROI Values

Prioritized
requirements
list

Must	$5,000
Must	$4,000
Must	$3,000
Should	$2,000
Should	$1,000
Should	$500
Could	$100

Now we need some way to monetize all the risk avoidance and risk mitigation requirements. To get this figure, we can calculate the expected monetary value of the risk. For purposes of a sample calculation, let's assume that using an in-house reporting tool has no cost to the project, but buying a high-performance reporting engine will cost $10,000. There is a 50 percent chance that we will end up needing the high-performance tool. With this data, we can use the following formula to calculate expected monetary value:

Expected Monetary Value (EMV) = Risk Impact (in dollars) × Risk Probability (as a percentage)

So in our example, EMV = $10,000 × 50% = $5,000. This figure allows us to say to the project sponsors that we believe the economic value to the organization of mitigating this risk is $5,000; therefore, the development priority of its response action should be on par with functional features that are valued at $5,000.

The EMV calculation can be done for most risks. Technical risks usually have an associated purchase cost (e.g., $10,000 for a high-performance reporting engine) or time penalty (e.g., it will take two developers an additional three weeks) that can be translated into a dollar amount. Human resource and business risks can likewise be estimated in monetary terms. We tend to think that we cannot assign a monetary value to certain things, but remember that insurance companies are able to determine a value for a lost finger or emotional distress for their clients. The same concept applies to assigning value to project risks. It is important to keep in mind that we are looking for relative scorings rather than precise numbers. In many cases, the initial ROI figure that the business established to justify the project is suspect anyway, so we should not get hung up on the level of accuracy of the risk values or try to create a perfect balance sheet of risk. Instead, we should focus on coming up with general, justifiable numbers that have consensus from the project stakeholders to use as a basis for prioritization.

Using this approach, we can rank the project risks to produce a prioritized risk list, ordered by risk severity, as shown in figure 3.17.

Figure 3.17: Prioritized Risk List, Ordered by Severity

Prioritized risk list

Risk 1 ($9,000 × 50% = $4,500)
Risk 2 ($8,000 × 50% = $4,000)
Risk 3 ($3,000 × 50% = $1,500)
Risk 4 ($6,000 × 25% = $1,500)
Risk 5 ($2,500 × 25% = $625)
Risk 6 ($500 × 25% = $125)
Risk 7 ($500 × 20%= $100)

Of course not all risks have avoidance or mitigation steps that we can schedule into the project. Some risks may have to be accepted (e.g., "We are waiting for service pack 2") or transferred (e.g., "We have taken out insurance"). For the risks that can be proactively tackled, however, the response actions can be prioritized alongside functional features. When combined, we will have a risk-adjusted backlog, as indicated in figure 3.18.

Figure 3.18: Risk-Adjusted Backlog
(with Requirements and Risk Response Actions)

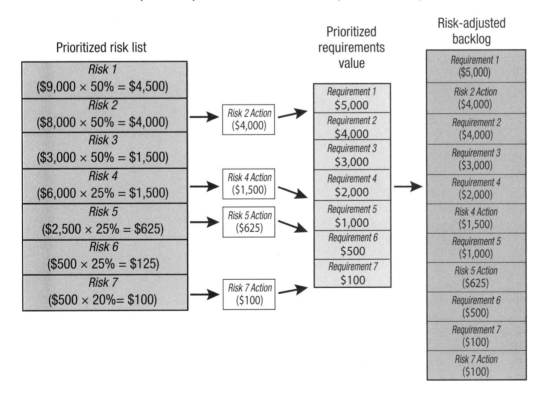

Attributing a dollar figure to both functional and nonfunctional requirements allows the team to have a more meaningful discussion with the sponsors and users. For example, in figure 3.18, we can see that Risk 2 has an expected monetary value of $4,000; as a result, when it is time to select requirements or features for an upcoming iteration, the risk response action associated with Risk 2 now has a similar ranking to Requirement 2. In other words, a risk response action that did not seem to have a compelling business value now makes sense because we can show that it is of equal value to the organization.

Again our focus here is not really on the precision of the numbers. A guess multiplied by a guess is unlikely to be highly accurate. Instead, the purpose of this exercise is to facilitate better discussions with business representatives about how to best sequence the work items. If people start rigging the numbers to serve their personal agendas, the purpose and true power of the process will be lost, and technical dependencies and sponsor mandates will take precedence over sequences derived from this approach. So think of the risk-adjusted backlog as a tool that uses numbers only to get at what is truly important—the priority of the work items that need to be done. The true benefits of this tool are that it helps the business representatives and the development team bridge a communication gap and have meaningful discussions about schedule and scope trade-offs. So although we assign numerical values to help level the playing field, creating a risk-adjusted backlog is really more of a qualitative practice than a quantitative practice.

K&S Level 3 — Agile Contracting

Portions of the Agile Contracting section were originally published by gantthead.com in "Agile Contracts (Part 1)" by Mike Griffiths on February 8, 2011, and "Agile Contracts (Part 2)" by Mike Griffiths on March 15, 2011, copyright © 2011 gantthead.com. Reproduced by permission of gantthead.com.

Now that we've discussed the tools and techniques used in planning value on agile projects, how does this agility work when a project is done on a contract basis? While agile methods provide great flexibility and allow us to manage changing requirements and priorities, this adaptability and scope flexibility can create problems when defining acceptance criteria for contracts and when outsourcing work.

These challenges have existed since the creation of agile methods. Fortunately as a result, a lot of effort has been put into resolving the issues. In 1994, the first edition of the DSDM Manual presented the inverted triangle model, shown in figure 3.19.

Figure 3.19: Inverted Triangle Model

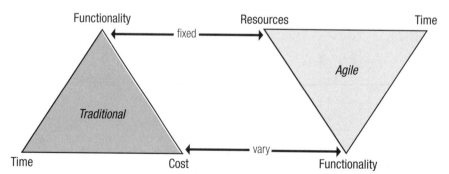

Agile projects attempt to fix resources and time (which are key components of cost) and vary functionality to achieve the highest-priority, best-quality product possible within those constraints. In contrast, when functionality is fixed, there is a risk that the project will run out of money or time—or even worse, produce a poor-quality outcome.

This idea of potentially not delivering all the functionality does not sit well with many people. They want an upfront estimate for delivering the whole product, not some subset of the easy parts; they also want a written contract to hold the vendor or project manager accountable to. However, in order for any knowledge worker project to achieve this (i.e., complete functionality within the contracted cost and schedule), lots of time-consuming and costly analysis must be done, carefully crafted specifications must be produced, and substantial contingencies have to be incorporated into the contract to accommodate reasonable and unforeseen changes, technical issues, and setbacks. Customers can have fixed scope and firm estimates, but it will cost them—estimates will be inflated as a buffer for uncertainty, and the customer will pay for activities that do not add much value to the business after going live.

The goal of agile methods and agile contracts is closer cooperation between the project team and the business or customer. This cooperation helps redirect the team's efforts toward delivering value-adding features. This goal is represented in the third Agile Manifesto value that ranks "Customer collaboration over contract negotiation." An agile approach requires more trust between parties than the traditional approach, but it focuses resources on what they are trying to build, rather than bogging them down in debates about how changes will be negotiated or what the completion criteria really is.

An agile approach also requires the business to be more involved in providing feedback on iterations, reprioritizing the backlog, and evaluating the value of change requests against the remaining work items. For trusting, invested clients, agile contracts are great tools for extracting more value, and they give the clients a competitive advantage. For untrusting or hands-off clients, agile contracts will be a tough sell and may not be suitable.

There are different ways agile contracts can be structured. Let's briefly look at some of them, starting with the DSDM contract.

DSDM Contract

The DSDM contract was commissioned by the DSDM Consortium and continues to evolve. This contract focuses on work being "fit for business purpose" and passing tests, rather than matching a specification. The DSDM contract is used primarily in the United Kingdom and other areas of Europe.

Money for Nothing and Change for Free

Jeff Sutherland also promotes a structure for an agile contract in his popular presentation, "Money for Nothing and Your Change for Free."[8] Sutherland suggests including early termination options and proposes a model that allows for flexibility in making changes. Sutherland's structure starts with a standard fixed price contract that includes time and materials for additional work, but he then inserts a "change for free" option clause.

The customer can only use this "change for free" clause if they work with the team on every iteration. Failure to be engaged in such a way voids the clause, and the contract reverts back to time and materials. Assuming the customer stays engaged, the product owner can reprioritize the backlog at the end of an iteration, and changes are then free if the total contract work is not changed. This allows new features to be added for free if lower-priority items that require equal or greater amounts of time and effort are removed.

Figure 3.20: Change for Free

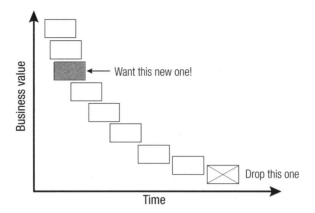

Like the "change for free" clause, the "money for nothing" concept is also only valid if the customer plays their part in the agile project. "Money for nothing" allows the customer to terminate the project early when they feel there is no longer sufficient ROI in the backlog to warrant further iterations. For example, the seller might allow termination of the contract at any time for 20 percent of the remaining contract value.

Figure 3.21: Money for Nothing

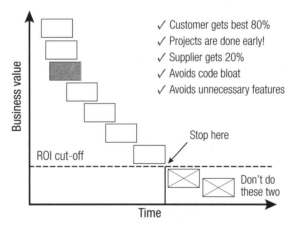

The 20 percent of the remaining contract value is the "money for nothing" part and helps offset the risk of having a team idle while the seller pays their salaries. Using the "money for nothing" approach, the customer gets their top-priority business value, projects always finish early, and good relations are maintained with the seller. In addition, the system stays efficient without leading to code bloat (for software projects) and unnecessary features. The arrangement remains open to additional releases if required at the contracted rates for time and materials.

Graduated Fixed Price Contract

Graduated fixed price contracts are promoted by Thorup and Jensen as another type of agile contract.[9] With this kind of contract, both parties share some of the risk and reward associated with schedule variance. Thorup and Jensen suggest using different hourly rates based on early, on-time, or late delivery. For example:

Project Completion	Graduated Rate	Total Fee
Finish early	$110 / hour	$92,000
Finish on time	$100 / hour	$100,000
Finish late	$90 / hour	$112,000

Under this arrangement, if the seller delivers on time, they get paid for the hours worked at their standard rate. If they deliver early, they get paid for fewer hours—but at a higher rate. The customer is happy because the work is done early and they pay less overall. The seller is happy because they make a higher margin. However, if the seller delivers late, they will get paid for more hours, but at a lower rate. When this occurs, both parties are somewhat unhappy since they are both making less money, but at a gradual, sustainable rate that hopefully will not lead to the contract being abandoned.

Fixed Price Work Packages

Another approach to setting up an agile contract is to establish fixed price work packages. Fixed price work packages mitigate the risks of underestimating or overestimating a chunk of work by reducing the scope and costs involved in the work being estimated. For example, Marriott International successfully broke down their statements of work (SOW) into individual work packages, each with its own fixed price.[10] Then as the work progressed, the seller was allowed to re-estimate the remaining work packages in the SOW based on new information and new risks.

> Reminder: You won't need to know historical examples (such as the Marriott International case) for the exam.

This approach allows the customer to reprioritize the remaining work based on evolving costs, and it gives the contractor the ability to update their costs as new details emerge, removing the need for the contractor to build excess contingency funds into the project cost. The changes are then localized to small components (i.e., the work packages), and if extra funding is required, it is easy to identify the need and justify it. Figure 3.22 illustrates the difference between a traditional SOW and fixed price work packages.

Figure 3.22: Money for Nothing

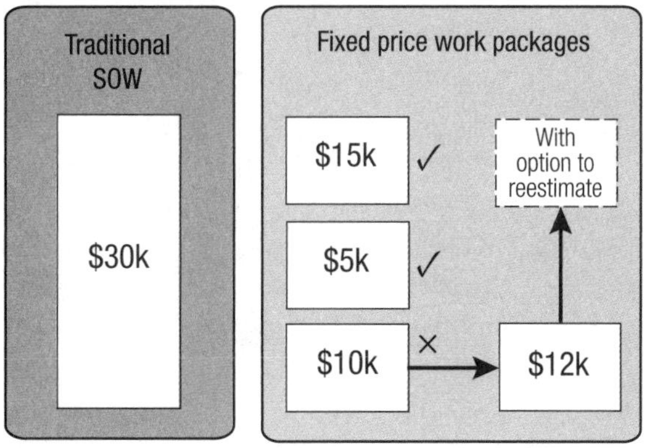

Customized Contracts

These different agile approaches to contracts can be pieced together to create a customized contract that benefits both the customer and the seller. With such contracts, the customer retains flexibility to reprioritize work and the seller is not penalized for sharing information about increased costs. They also remove the incentive for the seller to add large amounts of contingency costs to the project price. By combining elements of a graduated fixed price contract and fixed price work packages and incorporating the concepts of early termination (money for nothing) and reprioritization (change for free), we can create a contract that protects both parties and encourages positive behavior.

Although agile contracts can be highly beneficial to both parties, we must remember that creating a contract between one party that wants to minimize the cost for a product or service and another party that is in business to maximize its revenue will always be a balancing act. On agile projects, procurement has always been particularly challenging, since the scope is often not fully defined early in the project. In addition, the intangible nature of products like software can make it difficult to evaluate and get acceptance for the work. Any type of procurement—whether it's for agile or traditional contracts—works best when both parties want successful results that lead to future work. A project's success is ultimately determined by the level of ongoing collaboration between the customer and the seller. Agile contracts cannot generate or enforce that collaboration, but with some work and creativity, they can at least be better structured to support it.

Delivering Value

Now that we've discussed what's involved in assessing and planning value for agile projects, let's look at what it means to deliver value. The goal of delivering value is emphasized throughout the execution of agile projects. To accomplish this goal, the team should apply the lean concepts of maximizing value-delivering activities and minimizing "waste" or compliance (nonvalue-adding) activities. For example, activities that may be necessary for an organization but are not directly focused on delivering value, such as time tracking and reporting, may be reduced or transferred while a project is being executed. When aiming to maximize value, it is useful to revisit the Poppendiecks' seven software-related wastes, which we discussed in the Value Stream Mapping section of this chapter.[11]

Waste	Description	Example
Partially done work	Work started, but not complete; partially done work can entropy	» Code waiting for testing » Specs waiting for development
Extra processes	Extra work that does not add value	» Unused documentation » Unnecessary approvals
Extra features	Features that are not required, or are thought of as "nice-to-haves"	» Gold-plating » Technology features
Task switching	Multitasking between several different projects when there are context-switching penalties	» People on multiple projects
Waiting	Delays waiting for reviews and approvals	» Waiting for prototype reviews » Waiting for document approvals

Waste	Description	Example
Motion	The effort required to communicate or move information or deliverables from one group to another; if teams are not co-located, this effort may need to be greater	» Distributed teams » Handoffs
Defects	Defective documents or software that need correction	» Requirements defects » Software bugs

Where we see activities on our projects that are wasteful, we can aim to eliminate them. Let's look at some tools and techniques that can clarify the project work and help identify and eliminate waste activities.

 Task and Kanban Boards

Task and Kanban boards can help deliver value on agile projects in a number of ways. While it may seem like a step backward to go from sophisticated software scheduling tools to cards on a wall, this transition offers many benefits.

Figure 3.23: Moving from Scheduling Software to Task/Kanban Boards

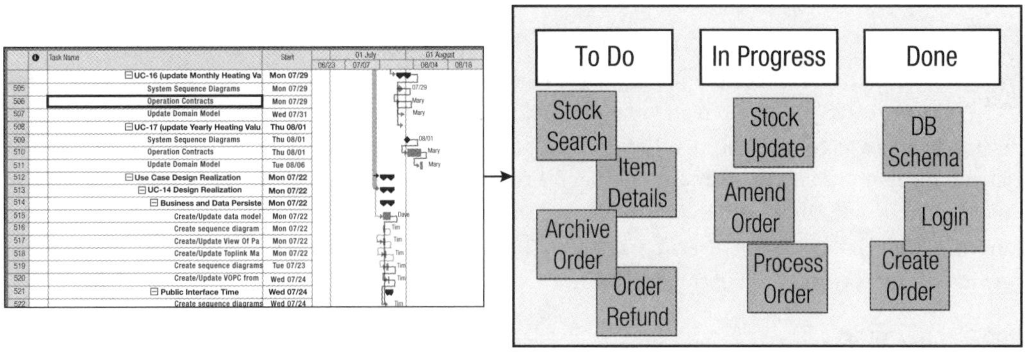

The technical features that Gantt charts provide can actually present some disadvantages on agile projects. Scheduling software can illustrate very deep hierarchies of tasks, support task dependency integrity checks, and calculate interesting metrics, such as slack, subassembly costs, and resource utilization. Yet the technical sophistication of these tools is the principal reason they are not ideal for agile methods. The math, statistics, and quantitative reports that can be produced with these tools disguise the volatile nature of what is being analyzed—project tasks and estimates. In addition, sophisticated scheduling tools can alienate the team and discourage whole-team collaboration.

When we use tools that perform scheduling calculations and forecasting, two problems arise: data accuracy perception increases, and barriers for stakeholder interaction are created. Let's look at these problems in more detail.

1. **Data accuracy perception increases**: Just because we can enter a developer's estimate into an expensive scheduling tool does not alter the fact that it may be a lousy estimate or, more likely, today's best estimate that will change as the project progresses and more information surfaces. Scheduling tools can create sophisticated models of the future that imply more credibility than their base data supports.

2. **Barriers for stakeholder interaction are created**: Once tasks and estimates are codified into a Gantt chart, the number of project stakeholders who can readily enhance, improve, and update the plan is drastically reduced. With a sophisticated schedule, it is usually just the project manager who is responsible for updating the plan. The project manager regularly asks the team how work is progressing and updates the task durations based on what has already occurred on the project and the estimate to complete (ETC) figures, but how often do team members get to reschedule the tasks and insert new task groups?

These observations are reflected in Donald Reinertsen's book, *Managing the Design Factory*, in which he warns of sophisticated models:

> *There is a solid practical reason for not using a more sophisticated analysis: not everyone will understand it. The more complex we make a model, chasing after a bit more accuracy here and there, the more we create a formidable maze of calculations that will not be trusted by the team. It is far better to choose a simple modeling technique and have 100 percent of the team understand the model than it is to risk confusing half the team with an elaborate model that is 5 percent more accurate.*[12]

> You won't need to know quotes or other such observations for the exam. They are provided for context and understanding only.

In contrast, agile planning and tracking tools employ a low-tech, high-touch approach. As implied by the name, these tools are simple, such as cards and charts, and are easy for all team stakeholders to manipulate by doing things like moving the cards, reordering lists, etc. By adopting these deliberately primitive techniques, we avoid a tool-related data accuracy perception and allow more people to update the plans as appropriate for the reality of the project.

TRICKS OF THE TRADE® So What Should the Smart Project Manager Do?

If you are not already doing so, try these low-tech, high-touch approaches. Encourage the team to use a visual system to plan iterations and track overall project status. For example, you could dedicate a wall in a team room or high-traffic corridor for big visible charts (as the name implies, these are large information charts that are easy for people to see and understand). Get the customer in front of the planning wall and show them the work that is done and the work that is planned for the upcoming iterations. When changes are requested, work with the team and the customer to visually prioritize the new work against the backdrop of the existing features.

TRICKS OF THE TRADE® If this all sounds too loosey-goosey and lacking in professional best practices, back it up with a traditional planning approach. When I first started managing agile projects in the early 1990s, I was working at IBM in the United Kingdom, and the company had standardized project planning and reporting formats. My PMO was not flexible in its processes and demanded standard plans, so I maintained a set of plans for reporting purposes and let the team maintain the work plan. After several projects, I had the proof I needed. The team plans tracked what was really happening on the project and reacted to project changes and challenges faster than I could rebaseline and level a resource profile. I could make my plans and statistics indicate whatever I wanted, but the low-tech, high-touch team plans were a faithful reflection of project status (good and bad).

If you operate in a highly regulated environment, you may also need to keep parallel traditional plans—but let your traditional plans be driven by the progress reported in the team's low-tech, high-touch plans. If you are concerned about losing the data in the low-tech plans, take digital photographs of the story cards and planning boards on a regular basis as a low-interference safeguard.

T&T WIP Limits

Work in progress (WIP), also sometimes known as "work in process" or even "work in play," is the term given to work that has been started but has not yet been completed. Having excessive levels of WIP is associated with a number of problems, including:

» WIP consumes investment capital and delivers no return on the investment until it is converted into an accepted product. It represents money spent with no return, which is something we want to limit.
» WIP hides bottlenecks in processes that slow overall workflow (or throughput) and masks efficiency issues.
» WIP represents risk in the form of potential rework, since there may still be changes to items until those items have been accepted. If there is a large inventory of WIP, there in turn may be a lot of scrap or expensive rework if a change is required.

Because of these problems, agile approaches generally aim to limit WIP. A common way to apply WIP limits on agile projects is to use Kanban boards that restrict the amount of work in the system and help ensure that WIP limits are not exceeded. The boards can indicate WIP limits by displaying a preset number for how many tasks should be worked on at any given time. Another option is to restrict the amount of space designated for where the task cards can be placed on the board so only a select number of cards will fit into the space. Agile teams use tools such as Kanban boards with WIP limits to help identify and remove bottlenecks so they can keep the process running efficiently with optimal levels of WIP. As a result, these tools help reduce the risks of tied-up capital, rework, and waste on the project.

Without limits on WIP, a project team may be tempted to undertake too many different pieces of work all at once. This might be done with the best intentions, such as to fully utilize everyone's availability and to keep people busy working on the project. But the problem is, if we have a bottleneck in processing database requests or designing user interfaces, for example, then tasks may end up sitting for a while, and work accumulates in the system. When this occurs, it is difficult to identify where the bottleneck is, because everyone appears to be busy.

Figure 3.24 illustrates a Kanban board with no WIP limit. We can see that there is a lot of WIP, which means the team is busy. But we cannot see which tasks are idle and where the bottlenecks are that are contributing to a slow workflow.

Figure 3.24: Task/Kanban Board with No WIP Limit

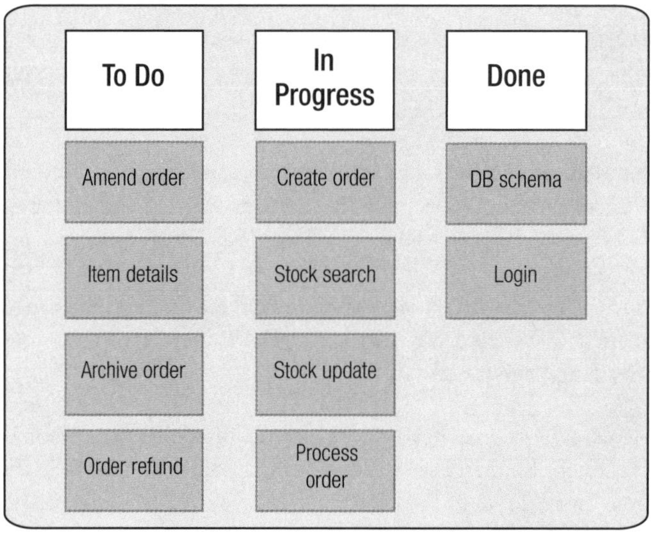

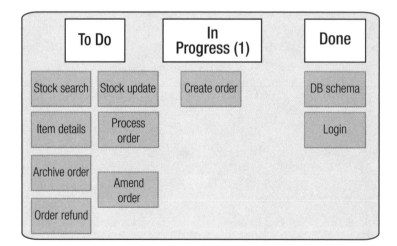

Limiting WIP is like draining the water out of a river; it shows us where all the boulders and obstacles are. We don't want to run the system with next-to-no WIP for too long—this would slow throughput because everyone but the bottleneck would be waiting for work. However, having a very low WIP limit for a short period of time is an effective method for identifying bottlenecks (or "constraints," if we use Theory of Constraints terminology, which is the origin of this concept).

Figure 3.25 shows a Kanban board with a WIP limit that is set too low. There is only one item in progress, which means some people are idle and there is a slow workflow. This low limit makes it very easy to identify which item is holding up the workflow, however.

Figure 3.25: Task/Kanban Board with the WIP Limit Too Low

Once the bottleneck item is identified, we can elevate the constraint and remove the bottleneck by making it more efficient. For example, we may have other team members do some preprocessing for that activity, ask downstream consumers if they are willing to take a less-polished output, or increase resources for the constrained activity.

With the first constraint removed, we can run the process again and see if there is another item that is causing a slow workflow. We repeat the process until people are sometimes idle but tasks are being worked on most of the time and the throughput is fast.

Figure 3.26 shows a Kanban board with an appropriate WIP limit for the project. We can see that there is sufficient work occurring. People are sometimes idle, or have some slack, but the bottlenecks are cleared and there is a fast workflow.

Figure 3.26: Task/Kanban Board with the WIP Limit Just Right

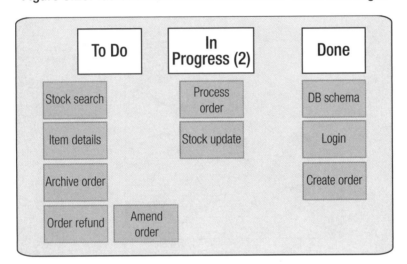

The aim of WIP limits is to optimize throughput of work, not to optimize resource utilization. This is often counterintuitive to people at first. We tend to think team members should be busy working at all times and anything else is laziness or inefficiency. Consider a highway, however. When does it flow best—when it is fully utilized at rush hour (busy), or during off-peak hours when it has some slack (less busy)?

Figure 3.27: A Fully Utilized Highway

Figure 3.28: A Highway with Some Slack

Limiting WIP helps identify bottlenecks and maximize throughput on a project, just like limiting the number of cars on a road helps traffic flow faster. On software projects, WIP limits equate to the number of features that are being worked on but are not yet accepted by the business.

Little's Law, which is shown in figure 3.29, is related to WIP. This law states that the cycle time—how long we are going to have to wait for benefits—is proportional to the size of our queue—how much WIP we have. In other words, we can predict completion times based on the size of the WIP queue. We will discuss this concept in more detail later in this chapter.

Figure 3.29: Little's Law

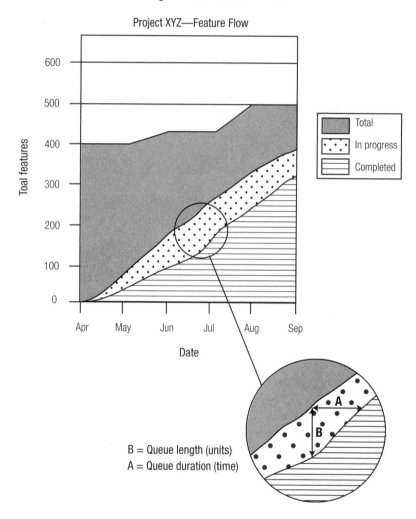

B = Queue length (units)
A = Queue duration (time)

K&S Level 1 — Incremental Delivery

Incremental delivery is another way to optimize the delivery of value on a project. With incremental delivery, the team regularly deploys working increments of the product over the course of the project. In the case of software development projects, the working software is usually deployed to a test environment for evaluation, but if it makes sense for the business, the team could deliver functionality to production in increments. If we can deliver the "plain-vanilla" version of a product or service while working on the more complex elements, we have an opportunity to start realizing the benefits of the product and get an early return on investment.

Even if we are incrementally delivering software into test environments, rather than into production, this approach can still help with the overall delivery of value. Issues that are found in software deployed in a test environment for evaluation (point 1 in figure 3.30) are much cheaper to fix than issues found during production (point 2). Incremental delivery reduces the amount of rework by finding issues earlier and, therefore, contributes to the delivery of value on the project.

Figure 3.30: Cost of Change

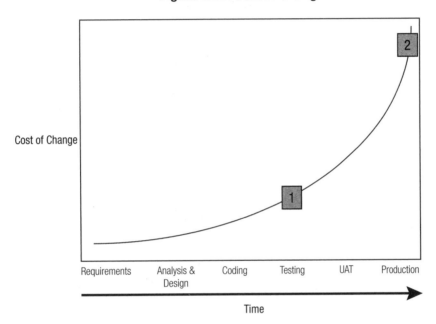

Image copyright © Scott Ambler, www.agilemodeling.com

Confirming Value

It is one thing to think we are building great products and services and another thing entirely to have our sponsors and business users confirm this. Agile methods are often used on projects that are intangible (e.g., designs, software, etc.). The intangible nature of these projects means it is all that much more important to validate that what we are building is, in fact, on the right track and seen as highly valuable by the business. This challenge is illustrated in figure 3.31.

Figure 3.31: Project Cartoon

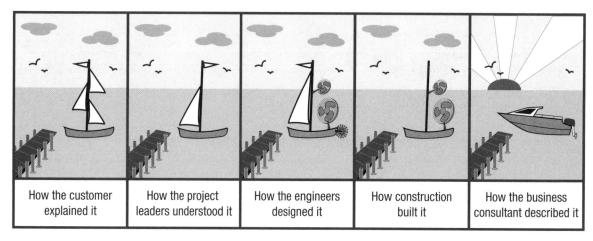

| How the customer explained it | How the project leaders understood it | How the engineers designed it | How construction built it | How the business consultant described it |

| How the project was documented | What was operational | How the customer was billed | How it was supported | What the customer really needed |

Cartoons such as this have been around for many years to highlight the communication failures that can occur when we try to describe something intangible. What one person describes is often very different from how the listener interprets it. This semantic gap is called the "gulf of evaluation."

Because having a gap between requested and delivered features may lead to rework, it is important to discover these differences early. Therefore, confirming value—meaning verifying the team is building the right thing and that it works as desired rather than as first described, which could be different—is a key practice when using agile methods.

T&T Customer-Valued Prioritization

We discussed customer-valued prioritization as part of the practice of planning value earlier in this chapter. This tool and technique can also be used to confirm value. Working with the customer to prioritize the remaining items to be done helps ensure the work is progressing toward the target of the project, which may itself be moving. Together the team and the customer answer the questions of, "Have things changed?" and "Do we still want to move on to item X next?" These reprioritization sessions, which are typically done at the end of each iteration, serve as important checkpoints for agile projects. New and evolving priorities are then captured in the user story backlog, which is revisited again at the next session.

I am often surprised by what the customer ranks highly when we first begin to prioritize the features and stories to work on. As we discuss these seemingly unlikely first choices, the conversation usually brings political concerns and residual risks to the surface. For example, "We are doing Premium Rates first because it is an objective for our Quarter 1 milestones," or "We need to deliver the CIO dashboard to secure project funding for next year." While we might be tempted to argue these are not really true system business benefits, we are often wise to listen to these motivators since the business representatives or customers are our allies in the project and the people who declare what success looks like.

By asking the business representatives or customer what their top-priority features are, we learn about their motivations, risks, and acceptance criteria. Projects that do not engage in customer-valued prioritization are likely to miss out on identifying critical success factors.

K&S Level 1   Prototypes, Simulations, Demonstrations

Demonstrations of functionality are critical to confirming success on software projects. Software is intangible and difficult to reference. In addition, companies rarely build the same system twice, which means projects are developing products that, for the most part, are new to the users. Therefore, users will need the opportunity to look at something and try it out to be able to confirm whether the functionality is suitable. The term IKIWISI (I'll Know It When I See It) is often used in software development, because the true requirements may only emerge once the product is demonstrated and used.

In addition to helping clarify requirements, demonstrations can uncover the need for new features. Often, it is not until the business representatives actually see the functionality that they realize additional elements are required. For example, "The order entry screen looks great, but after trying it, we realize we need a duplicate order function."

When teams demonstrate functionality, two things occur. First, we learn about the differences between what was asked for and what was interpreted and built (the gulf of evaluation). Second, we learn about new or adjusted functionality (IKIWISI).

So requirements evolve with prototypes, simulations, and demonstrations. Giving people a chance to evaluate and use something helps uncover the true business requirements. Our solution then converges toward the emerging requirements, and the gulf of evaluation grows smaller. This concept is illustrated in figure 3.32, where X_1, X_2, and X_3 are the emerging requirements and O_1, O_2, and O_3 represent what was interpreted and implemented. As we can see here, the solution takes form as the requirements and what is being built move closer together over three iterations.

Figure 3.32: Requirements Evolve with Iterations

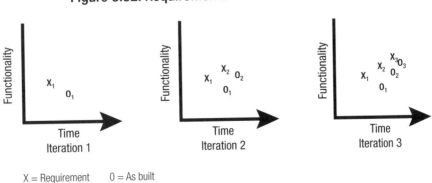

X = Requirement   O = As built

Tracking and Reporting Value

We've talked about the practices of assessing, planning, delivering, and confirming value. Now let's look at tracking and reporting value. In an agile environment, it is important to monitor the rate at which features and value are being delivered to make sure we are on track to complete the project as agreed upon. Once we determine the project's status, we need to communicate that status to stakeholders. There are several tools and techniques that we can use to track and report value, including earned value, cumulative flow diagrams, risk burn down graphs, and task and Kanban boards.

T&T   Agile Earned Value

When it comes to tracking and reporting progress on our projects, S-curves are great tools to track project spending. They are simple to interpret, and they quickly convey whether the project is over- or under-budget, as shown in figure 3.33.

Figure 3.33: S-Curve Graph

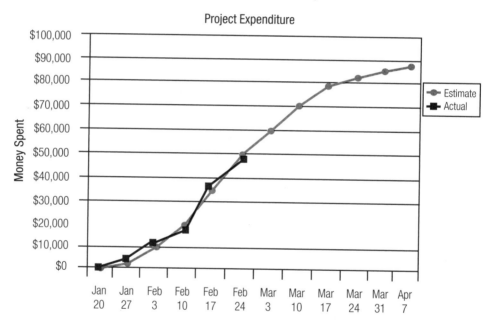

This S-curve doesn't reveal any information about the schedule, however. We could be doing fine spending-wise, but be behind from a schedule perspective. To report schedule status, people often use tracking Gantt charts, as shown in figure 3.34.

Figure 3.34: Gantt Chart

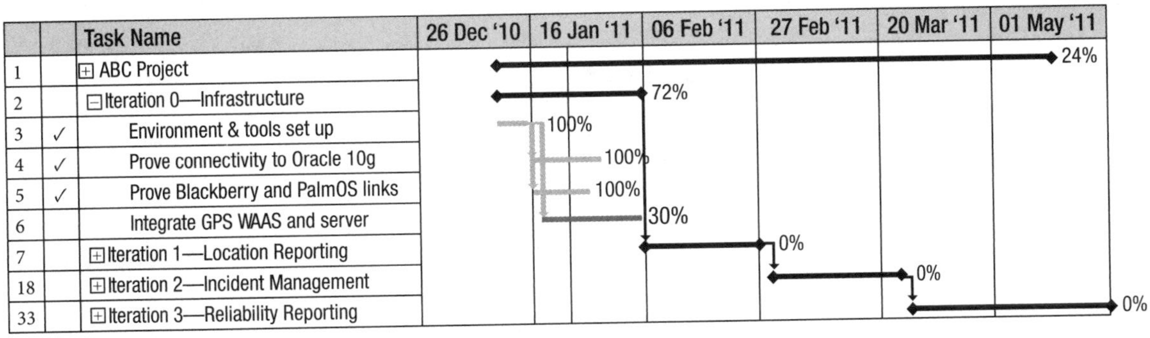

		Task Name	26 Dec '10	16 Jan '11	06 Feb '11	27 Feb '11	20 Mar '11	01 May '11
1		⊞ ABC Project						24%
2		⊟ Iteration 0—Infrastructure			72%			
3	✓	Environment & tools set up	100%					
4	✓	Prove connectivity to Oracle 10g		100%				
5	✓	Prove Blackberry and PalmOS links		100%				
6		Integrate GPS WAAS and server			30%			
7		⊞ Iteration 1—Location Reporting				0%		
18		⊞ Iteration 2—Incident Management					0%	
33		⊞ Iteration 3—Reliability Reporting						0%

But we have a similar limitation with Gantt charts. They lack the spending component, just like S-curves lack the schedule component. Pretty soon most projects get ahead of or behind budget and schedule, so trying to gauge the overall project health can become difficult. In addition, the iterative nature of agile projects means Gantt charts can become deeply nested and confusing.

These are the reasons why earned value analysis (EVA) and earned value management (EVM) were created. Earned value combines spending and schedule data to produce a comprehensive set of project measures and metrics.

People ask me if you can use earned value on agile projects. The answer is yes. But while the math still works in the same way as on non-agile projects, we do need to be careful about what we are measuring against. Earned value compares actual project performance to planned performance at a particular point in time. That means if our initial plan is wrong, we could be trying to do the equivalent of tracking our progress on a road trip from Calgary to Salt Lake City on a map of France! The quality of the baseline plan is a critical success factor in using earned value. On agile projects, we acknowledge that initial plans will likely need to change, so the basis for effective EVM is quickly eroded with evolving plans.

Another note of caution regarding earned value is that it does not truly indicate whether the project is successful. We could be on time and on budget, but building a horrible, low-quality product that the business does not like or need. Remember that cost and schedule are not the whole picture, which means our project might still be going badly even if it looks good from an earned value standpoint.

What's Good about Earned Value?

We've just discussed some aspects of earned value to be wary about on agile projects. So why use it at all? One of the key benefits of earned value is that it is a leading indicator. Perfect rearview vision is not much use to us. EVM looks forward, trying to predict completion dates and final costs. After all, imperfect leading metrics are generally more valuable than perfect trailing metrics, since the leading metrics give us the opportunity to replan and change our approach.

Another benefit of earned value is that it is visual. People often forget the EVM diagrams and just focus on the numbers, but at the heart of this technique are some useful graphs. Visual representations of information engage the right side of our brains and help us absorb the data while we work to understand, interpret, and plan appropriate responses. Visual depictions are also better when discussing information and working collaboratively, since people can point, annotate, and extrapolate more easily with pictures than with words or numbers.

Agile Earned Value Constructed

So how can we maintain the forecasting and visual components of EVM and reduce some of the downsides? Well, double S-curves are a good start.

Figure 3.35: Double S-Curve Graph

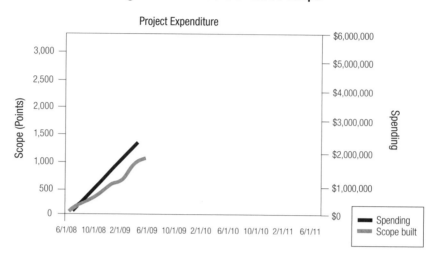

In figure 3.35, we have a familiar spending line, shown in black, which is tracked against the dollar scale on the right-hand axis. We also have a feature-based line (the scope built to date on the project) shown in green, which is tracked against the points scale on the left.

The gradient of the green line indicates project velocity. Where it rises steeply, we developed a lot of points in a short period of time. Where it is flat, progress was slow.

Adding a background to the graph can be a useful way to show functional areas of the project. In figure 3.36, we can see that the "Configuration" and "Stock" components of the system have been built, and we are currently in the "Sales" piece of the scope, with just over 1,000 points' worth of functionality completed. Also, in October of 2008, the step in the background lines shows where the scope of the "Sales" portion of the system was increased, shifting the remaining functional areas up to accommodate the new work.

Figure 3.36: Double S-Curve Graph with Functional Areas

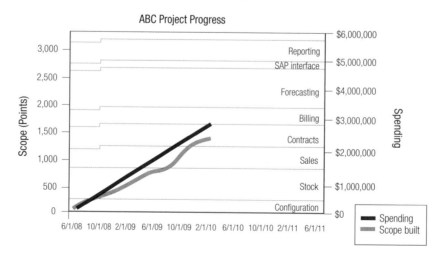

So we have a graph that shows scope, schedule, and cost performance to date, but we are still missing the projections that give us a sense of whether we are ahead or behind from the budget and schedule perspectives. This is where predicted values come in, as shown in figure 3.37.

Figure 3.37: Scope, Schedule, and Cost Performance and Predicted Value

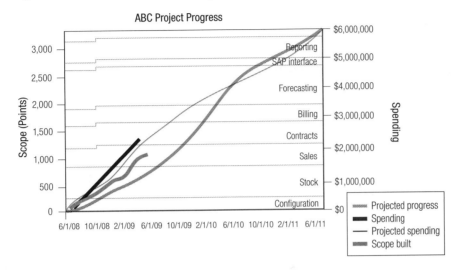

Now we can see how the project's actual progress compares to our projections. Figure 3.37 shows that, at this point on the project, we have overspent and are a little ahead in building the scope.

These graphs can serve as a replacement for earned value management, providing the same metrics and indices but in a visual way, as shown in figure 3.38.

Figure 3.38: A Visual Way to Represent Earned Value Management

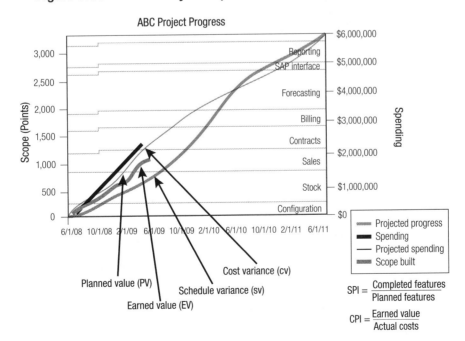

Note that you should not have to perform earned value calculations for the exam, but you do need to be aware of how such measurements can be used on agile projects.

Traditional EVM metrics like Schedule Performance Index (SPI) and Cost Performance Index (CPI) can be easily translated into agile terms. For example, we planned to complete 30 story points in this iteration, but only completed 25. To get SPI, we can divide 25 by 30 for an SPI of 0.83 (meaning we are working at only 83 percent of the rate planned). Likewise, CPI is the earned value (EV, or the value of completed features to date) divided by the actual costs (AC) to date. So in the example in the previous chart, CPI = $2,200,000 / $2,800,000 = 0.79. This means we are only getting 79 cents on the dollar compared to what we had predicted.

T&T   Cumulative Flow Diagrams (CFDs)

Cumulative flow diagrams are valuable tools for tracking and forecasting agile projects. CFDs can help us gain insight into project issues, cycle times, and likely completion dates. Figure 3.39 is an example of a CFD.

Figure 3.39: Sample Cumulative Flow Diagram

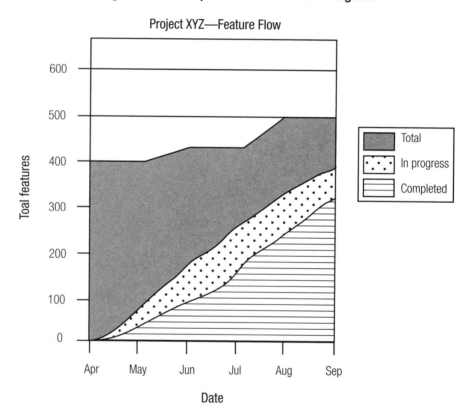

Figure 3.39 shows the features completed versus the features remaining for a fictional project that is still in progress. The green area represents all the planned features to be built. This number rose from 400 to 450 in June and then to 500 in August as additional features were added to the project. The dotted section plots the work in progress, and the striped section shows the total number of features completed on the project.

Little's Law

Little's Law is a concept introduced by Donald Reinertsen that can be used to analyze queues from CFDs. This concept is illustrated in figure 3.40.[13]

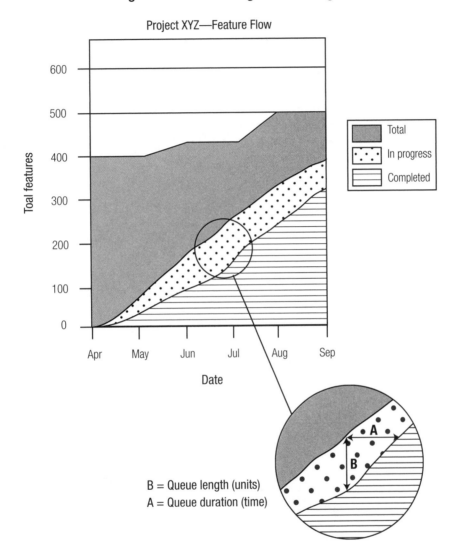

Figure 3.40: Examining Work in Progress

The dotted section representing work in progress (WIP) is our queue; it is the work we have started but not yet completed. We can see how many items are in the queue by looking at the vertical (B) distance, and we can determine the cycle time, or how long it will likely take to complete the items in the queue, by examining the horizontal (A) distance.

Cycle times are important metrics for lean production systems. This data helps us predict when all the work currently in progress will be done. We should aim to keep WIP and cycle times as low as possible, since they represent sunk investment costs that have not yet resulted in business benefits. The more WIP and the longer cycle times we have on the project, the higher the amount of potential scrap we have in the system if we encounter a problem.

Looking for Bottlenecks and the Theory of Constraints

We talked about bottlenecks, the Theory of Constraints, and WIP in the Delivering Value section of this chapter, but let's look at these concepts again from the perspective of tracking and reporting value on agile projects.

Eli Goldratt introduced the Theory of Constrains (TOC) as a tool for optimizing a production system. He observed that "Changes to most of the variables in an organization usually have only small impacts on global performance. There are few variables (perhaps only one) for which a significant change in local performance will effect a significant change in global performance."[14] So to achieve the greatest benefits, we should find these constraints (or bottlenecks in the system) and focus on improving these issues.

Question 3 from the daily stand-up meeting, which asks for any impediments (or blockers) to making progress, is an adoption of TOC thinking. With this question, we are looking for roadblocks on the project and removing them. (Daily stand-up meetings are discussed in chapter 5, Boosting Team Performance Practices.)

Constraints can also manifest themselves as restrictions on throughput capacity. For example, the database group might not be able to keep up with the changes coming from the development team, or perhaps the customer proxy cannot keep up with questions about validation rules for a new screen the team is designing. In both cases, the database group and the customer proxy are constraints, but as a project manager, these bottlenecks are not always easy to spot. We usually have a feeling where the bottlenecks are, but short of standing over people with a stopwatch and counting how many features they can process in a day, how can activity throughput and bottlenecks be objectively measured? This is where CFDs come into play.

We can use a CFD to find the bottlenecks if, instead of lumping all the work in progress as a single measure, we break it out by activity and plot the flow of this work. Figure 3.41 shows an example of a detailed CFD.

Figure 3.41: Detailed CFD

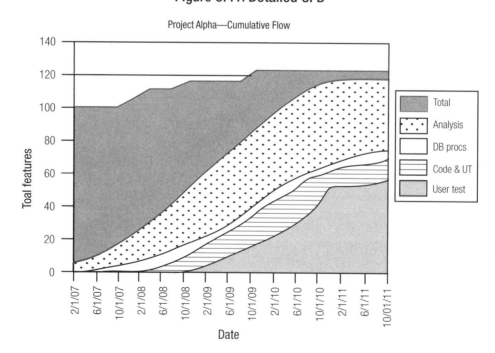

In Figure 3.41, the work in progress has been broken out by activity, and the activities are stacked sequentially. Analysis, database procedures, coding and unit testing, and user testing work are being done on the project by different groups. When examining CFDs for bottlenecks, we look for areas that widen before the final activity is done. In this example, user testing is the final activity. The widening of an area indicates the growing completion of work. To explain this idea using mathematical concepts, a widening area is created when one line is followed by another line of shallower gradient. Since the line gradient indicates the rate of progress for an activity (features over time), a widening area is created above an activity that is progressing at a slower rate. In figure 3.42, you can see that Analysis is a widening area activity, while Database Procedures is a bottleneck activity.

Figure 3.42: Detailed CFD with Bottleneck Identified

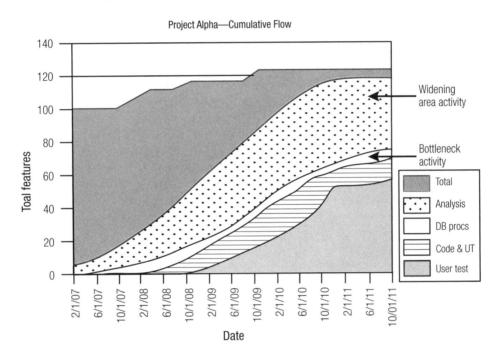

Regardless of whether the mathematical explanation makes sense to you, all you need to remember for the exam is that the bottleneck is the activity that lies below the widening band. The widening band is the feeding activity, not the problem activity. So in the example shown in figure 3.42, Analysis is going okay. However, the activity that lies below the widening band—creating the database stored procedures (DB Procs)—shows a slower rate of progress. The CFD gives us a warning that creating the database stored procedures is currently a bottleneck in the system.

So we do not need to micromanage team throughput to determine where the bottlenecks are. Instead, by using CFDs to track progress, we can identify bottlenecks unobtrusively. Then once we know where the problem is, we can start addressing the issue by applying the Five Focusing Steps of Goldratt's Theory of Constraints, starting with step 2:[15]

1. Identify the constraint.
2. Exploit the constraint.
3. Subordinate all other processes to exploit the constraint.
4. If after steps 2 and 3 are done, more capacity is needed to meet demand, elevate the constraint.
5. If the constraint has not moved, go back to step 1, but don't let inertia (complacency) become the system's constraint.

The use of agile methods inherently reduces the likelihood of activity-based bottlenecks because these methods promote multidisciplined or cross-trained teams. By avoiding role specialization, people are able to move between roles more effectively and share the workload. However, while the goal is to have fully multidisciplined teams, in practice some role specialization and workflow management is the norm on projects.

T&T Risk Burn Down Graphs

As we've discussed at earlier points in this chapter, risk and value are closely related. Therefore, risk management is an important activity on agile projects. Risk management should serve as a driver for work scheduling, moving high-risk activities into earlier iterations of the project and incorporating risk mitigation actions into the backlog. As the project progresses, we need to continue to manage risks and track the effectiveness of our efforts.

We need to actively attack threats before they become problems on the project. Unfortunately, all too often we simply conduct risk analysis and risk management steps alongside the regular project tasks, rather than having risk management be a driver for work scheduling. Many projects create risk management plans and risk lists, but then do not allow these findings to influence task selection and scheduling. As a result, the risk response steps do not make it into the project plan.

With an agile approach, there are many opportunities to actively attack the risks on a project before they can become tomorrow's problems. Iterative development allows high-risk work to be tackled early in the life cycle. Features or stories that carry high levels of risk can be undertaken in early iterations to prove the technological approach and remove doubts. We need to carefully balance the goals of delivering business value and reducing risk when we select features or stories.

Risks are generally assessed via two measures—risk probability (a measure of how likely a risk is to occur) and risk impact (a measure of the consequence to the project should the risk actually occur). When the probability is indicated as a percentage and the impact is defined in monetary terms, these measures can be used to calculate the risk's expected monetary value (EMV), as we discussed earlier in this chapter. For example, if a risk is estimated to have a 25 percent probability of occurring and its impact is estimated at $8,000, the EMV = 0.25 × $8,000 = $2,000.

When we rank probability and impact on a numerical scale, we can use these measures to calculate risk severity, as indicated in the following formula:

$$\textbf{Risk Severity} = \textbf{Risk Probability} \times \textbf{Risk Impact}$$

Calculating the risk severity allows us to rank risks and determine risk response priorities. For example, if we give scores of low (1), medium (2), and high (3) to both risk probability and risk impact, we will see that high-probability and high-impact risks get a risk severity score of 3 × 3 = 9. A high-probability but low-impact risk would be given a risk severity score of only 3 × 1 = 3.

It is possible to take the analysis of risks much further using techniques such as expected monetary value, but for the purposes of illustrating risk profiles and trends, the abstract values of risk severity scores of 1 through 9 are all we require.

For any project, we should engage the development team, sponsors, customers, and other relevant stakeholders in the process of risk identification. Their ideas, along with reviews of previous projects' lessons learned notes, risk logs, and industry risk profiles, should be used to identify the known and likely risks for the project. Once we have the list of risks, we can undertake risk analysis and assign probability and impact scores to each risk. We can then use these scores to calculate the risk severities. Similar to estimation, we engage the team members in risk analysis because they are closer to the technical details and because including them generates increased buy-in to the risk management plan and response actions. If we have no involvement, we have no commitment.

Figure 3.43 presents some identified risks for a fictitious project and their associated probability, impact, and severity scores.

Figure 3.43: Identified Risks with Impact, Probability, and Severity Scores

ID	Short Risk Name	Impact	Prob.	Sev.
1	JDBC driver performance	3	2	6
2	Calling Oracle stored procs. via web service	2	2	4
3	Remote app. distribution to PDAs	3	2	6
4	Oracle warehouse builder stability	2	2	4
5	Legacy system stability	2	1	2
6	Access to user community	2	1	2
7	Availability of architect	2	2	4
8	Server upgrade necessary	1	2	2
9	Oracle handheld warehouse browser launch	3	1	3
10	PST changes for British Columbia	0	0	0
				33

As the project progresses, we expand the table to record how our attempts to manage the project risks are working. Figure 3.44 shows the progress of the risks through the first four months of the project.

Figure 3.44: Progress of Risks

ID	Short Risk Name	January			February			March			April		
		Imp.	Prob.	Sev.	Imp.	Prob.	Sev.	Imp.	Prob.	Sev.	Imp.	Prob.	Sev.
1	JDBC driver performance	3	2	6	3	0	0	3	0	0	3	0	0
2	Calling Oracle stored procs. via web service	2	2	4	2	0	0	2	0	0	2	0	0
3	Remote app. distribution to PDAs	3	2	6	3	1	3	3	0	0	3	0	0
4	Oracle warehouse builder stability	2	2	4	2	3	6	2	2	4	2	0	0
5	Legacy system stability	2	1	2	2	1	2	2	0	0	2	0	0
6	Access to user community	2	1	2	2	2	4	2	1	2	2	1	2
7	Availability of architect	2	2	4	2	3	6	2	2	4	2	0	0
8	Server upgrade necessary	1	2	2	1	1	1	1	0	0	1	0	0
9	Oracle handheld warehouse browser launch	3	1	3	3	1	3	3	3	9	3	1	3
10	PST changes for British Columbia	0	0	0	0	0	0	2	2	4	2	1	2
				33			25			23			7

Image originally published in "The Game of Risk" by Mike Griffiths on gantthead.com on September 20, 2011, copyright © 2011 gantthead.com. Reproduced by permission of gantthead.com.

During these four months, many of the project risks were mitigated or avoided completely. For example, the first risk, "JDBC driver performance," ended up not being a problem because database features and performance testing were deliberately included in the first (one-month) iteration. As a result, the probability of this risk occurring was reduced from 2 (Medium) to 0, and so the risk severity went from 6 to 0.

These types of details can be difficult to determine from just looking at tables. To make them clearer, we can convert this information into risk burn down graphs, which are excellent tools for showing status and trends. Figure 3.45 is a sample risk burn down graph:

Figure 3.45: Risk Burn Down Graph

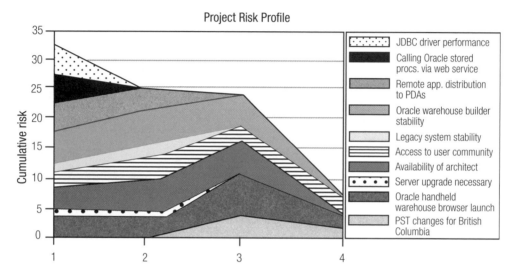

Image originally published in "The Game of Risk" by Mike Griffiths on gantthead.com on September 20, 2011, copyright © 2011 gantthead.com. Reproduced by permission of gantthead.com.

Risk burn down graphs are essentially stacked area graphs of cumulative project risk severity. The severity scores for each risk are plotted one on top of another to show the project's cumulative severity profile. When risks and their history of severity are displayed in this format, it is much easier to interpret the overall risk status and trends of the project.

For instance, we can tell from the general downward trend of figure 3.45 that the project risks are being reduced. This kind of visual graph is an excellent way to demonstrate the value of "Iteration 0" activities—activities that may not directly deliver much (or any) business value, but are extremely useful in proving whether a particular approach will work and reducing project risks.

Escalating risks and new risks are also easy to spot on risk burn down graphs. In our example, Risk 9, "Oracle handheld warehouse browser launch," escalated from a severity 3 risk to severity 9 risk in month 3 (March). Risk 10, "PST changes for British Columbia," is a new risk that was assessed as a severity 4 risk in month 3 (March) and went down to a severity 2 risk in month 4 (April).

Risk burn down graphs quickly inform stakeholders if the risks are moving in the right direction (downward), or if they are escalating. These graphs provide an easy-to-interpret way to check the health of your project and can be quickly produced in tools like Microsoft Excel. Although project risk is not a core metric, like features delivered, it is useful to track. We need to actively try to control risks, since how effective we are in these efforts ultimately impacts whether we achieve our goal of delivering a successful project.

T&T   Task/Kanban Boards

The final tools we will discuss in this section are task boards, or Kanban boards. While these boards are primarily thought of as planning and monitoring tools (as discussed in the Delivering Value section of this chapter), they can also be a great way to track and report value.

Figure 3.46 shows a task board used on one of my projects:

Figure 3.46: Sample Task Board

Image copyright © 2012 Leading Answers, Inc. Reproduced with permission from Leading Answers, Inc. www.leadinganswers.com

In this example, we were tracking all the activities that needed to happen for a release to production. One of the benefits of meeting at the board and updating it daily was that the team saw a gradual left-to-right migration of cards across the board as work items moved from "To Do," to "In Progress," to "Done." It was rewarding to the team—and reassuring to the sponsor—to see a growing collection of completed work as the deadline approached. It also focused everyone's attention on the few remaining issues, which really began to stand out since they were the last ones to move.

Tools like task boards help with tracking and reporting value, and their results are often shown on information radiators, which are large charts that are displayed in prominent places. We will explore information radiators further in the next chapter, Stakeholder Engagement.

Professional Responsibility and Ethics

Before we move on to the next chapter, let's look at how PMI's Code of Ethics and Professional Conduct (available on PMI's website: www.pmi.org) applies to value-driven delivery concepts.[16] There are four main areas of this code—Responsibility, Respect, Fairness, and Honesty—and we'll cover each in turn, looking at examples of how they relate to the topics discussed in this chapter. As you read this section, think about your real-world projects and how they are impacted by these different aspects of professional responsibility and ethics.

Responsibility

» **Make decisions based on the best interests of the company**: This duty fits in very well with the concepts of value-driven prioritization and delivery. We set the order of the project work according to business value. In other words, our projects are driven by the reason the company is doing the work, rather than by the preferences of the project manager or team.

This aspect of professional responsibility also speaks to the development team's duty to identify and help prioritize technical risks that might otherwise go unnoticed. We are not making decisions based on the best interests of the company if we let technical problems disrupt our ability to deliver business value.

» **Protect proprietary information**: Although to many people this is common sense, we should think about the implications of entering requirements into web-hosted prioritization tools. Is the information secure and protected? If we use the tools, who owns the information we enter into them? Who has rights to see the data? We need to be careful when adopting new tools to not compromise proprietary information.

» **Report unethical behavior and violations**: Hopefully we will not see any severe behavior or violations on our projects, but we do need to watch out for things like a pushy product owner bullying or cajoling the development team to build requirements not approved for the iteration.

Respect

» **Maintain an attitude of mutual cooperation**: This professional duty also relates to balancing business requests with the need to reduce technical risks. The business representatives and development team should work collaboratively to select items for an iteration, balancing the delivery of new business features with risk response actions.

» **Negotiate in good faith**: When we create estimates and negotiate priorities, the budget, and the schedule, we need to act in good faith and with transparency for the process to work. Padding estimates and creating comfortable buffers in iteration and release plans undermines the close partnership model that the business representatives and development team strive to create. Such actions also make it difficult to track estimates accurately and measure the true rate of progress.

Another aspect of this professional duty affects our interactions with external vendors. When we solicit bids for work and negotiate agile contracts with external vendors, we need to make sure we share information fairly between all sellers.

» **Do not use your position to influence others**: On agile projects, the project manager does not get veto power over what goes into an iteration, nor does the project manager get to decide the priority of an item or how much work the team can do within an iteration.

Fairness

» **Look for and disclose conflicts of interest**: This point is particularly important when negotiating contracts for agile projects. We have a responsibility to disclose relationships with sellers and any potential conflicts of interest.

Honesty

» **Understand the truth**: In terms of value-driven delivery, this means we need to check that the business or customer is getting what they want.

» **Be truthful in all communications**: We should not engage in or condone behavior that is designed to deceive others, such as making misleading or false statements, stating half-truths, providing information out of context, or withholding information. This can be especially relevant when working with business representatives on priorities and estimates and also when working with sellers on contracts and negotiations. Another point to consider here is that when negotiating with vendors, we must not engage in dishonest behavior with the intention of personal gain or at the expense of others.

1. Which of the following is NOT an advantage of limiting work in progress (WIP)?

    A. It reduces the potential need to rework a large collection of flawed, partially completed items.
    B. It helps optimize throughput to make processes work more efficiently.
    C. It brings bottlenecks in the production process to the surface so they can be identified and resolved.
    D. It maximizes resource utilization to make processes work more efficiently.

2. Project X has a IRR of 12%, and project Y has a IRR of 10%. Which project represents the better rate of return?

    A. It depends on the payback period
    B. Project Y
    C. Project X
    D. Project X or Y, depending on NPV

3. Which of the following is NOT a recognized prioritization scheme?

    A. Prioritization based on business value
    B. Prioritization based on reducing risk
    C. Prioritization based on iteration velocity
    D. Prioritization based on business value and risk

4. What is a product roadmap?

    A. A list of reports and screens
    B. A view of release candidates
    C. Instructions for deployment
    D. A backlog prioritization scheme

5. Which of the following is true about agile contracts?

    A. They only work when the specs are fully defined.
    B. They only work for time and materials agreements.
    C. They can accommodate changes.
    D. They cannot easily accommodate changes.

6. We put risks in the backlog to:

    A. Avoid having to keep separate risk lists
    B. Keep the team focused on risks
    C. Ensure that they get worked on in the early iterations
    D. Prevent the team from forgetting about the risks

7. Which of the following combinations is a valid mix for story prioritization?

    A. Customer importance and business urgency
    B. Risk reduction and technical dependency
    C. Customer value and risk reduction
    D. Team preference and customer value

8. To cut costs, company X has decided to cancel one of its money-losing projects. Project A has a IRR of –4%, project B has a IRR of –5%, and project C has a IRR of –6%. Which project should be cut?

   A. The more negative the results are, the better, so cut project A.
   B. Less-negative results are bad, so cut project B.
   C. To reduce losses, choose project C.
   D. Cancel projects A, B, and C, as they are all losing money.

9. A sponsor is trying to determine which project has the greatest business value—one that returns $4 million in 3 years or one that returns $5 million in 4 years. The interest rate is 5 percent for borrowing capital to develop the projects. The best approach to determine the highest value project is:

   A. Select the "$5 million in 4 years" project, since it returns the highest amount.
   B. Select the "$4 million in 3 years" project, since it has the shorter payback period.
   C. Calculate the NPV of the projects, and choose the project with the highest value.
   D. Calculate the NPV of the projects, and choose the project with the lowest cost.

10. Which of the following statements best describes the role of the project charter?

    A. Forms the basis of the prioritized backlog and identifies the work to be completed by the project
    B. Describes the issues and risks the project may encounter and describes mitigation strategies for avoidance
    C. Defines the what, why, when, who, and how details of the project and provides authority to proceed
    D. Outlines the roles and responsibilities for the project stakeholders and identifies any third-party companies

11. Your new team spends 10 minutes waiting for people to turn up for the daily stand-up meeting, which then lasts 15 minutes. The stand-up meeting is then followed by another 5 minutes of the team discussing the hockey game last night, and yet another 5 minutes brainstorming issues to solve. Calculate the total cycle time of this process (assuming that the hockey discussion is not categorized as a value-adding activity).

    A. 15 minutes
    B. 20 minutes
    C. 30 minutes
    D. 35 minutes

12. Your sponsor has asked for clarification on when releases of your product will ship and what those releases will contain. Which agile deliverable would best answer their needs?

    A. Product demo
    B. Product roadmap
    C. Product backlog
    D. Product owner

13. You have been asked to outline the basics of agile contracting for your steering committee. Which of the following statements best matches the recommended approach taken to contracting on agile projects?

   A. The contract is worded to allow for early completion of scope, and acceptance is based on items matching the original specification.
   B. The contract is worded to allow for reprioritization of scope, and acceptance is based on items matching the original specification.
   C. The contract is worded to allow for early completion of scope, and acceptance is based on items being fit for business purpose.
   D. The contract is worded to allow for reprioritization of scope, and acceptance is based on items being fit for business purpose.

14. In agile methods the terms MoSCoW and "Priority 1, Priority 2, Priority 3" are forms of:

   A. Estimation
   B. Risk identification
   C. Prioritization
   D. Reporting

15. Customers or business representatives are involved in the prioritization of work for which primary benefit?

   A. To proactively engage the business between acceptance testing cycles
   B. To answer business-related questions about the requirements
   C. To aid communications about when features will be delivered
   D. To better reflect the business needs and wants for the project

16. Which of the definitions shown below best describes the agile concept of incremental delivery?

   A. The product is built and evaluated in chunks that are selected and developed by the development team.
   B. The product is built and evaluated in chunks that, by the end of the project, comprise the complete product, including agreed-upon change requests that arose during the process.
   C. The product is built and evaluated in chunks that, by the end of the project, comprise the complete product, excluding agreed-upon change requests that arose during the process.
   D. The product is built and evaluated in agreed-upon increments that, by the end of the project, comprise the complete product, factoring in the support demand that will be required after delivery.

17. Your team on average has to wait 3 business days (24 business hours) to get approval to make changes to their user acceptance environment. Making the changes usually takes about an hour. Which of the answers below represents the correct process efficiency time, rounded to one decimal place?

   A. 4.0%
   B. 4.1%
   C. 4.2%
   D. 4.3%

18. You have been asked to explain what the project team has been doing during iteration 0, an early portion of the project. Which of the following graphs would be a good choice?

    A. Budget burn up chart
    B. Risk burn down graph
    C. Work breakdown structure
    D. Project organization chart

Answers

1. **Answer: D**
   Explanation: Since this question is looking for the answer that is NOT an advantage of limiting WIP, if an option is true, that means it is not the answer we are looking for. Limiting WIP does reduce the potential need for rework. It also improves process efficiency and helps us find production bottlenecks. The only option listed here that is NOT an advantage of limiting WIP is the one that refers to maximizing resource utilization. Limiting WIP focuses on optimizing throughput, not resources, and we may actually decrease resource optimization to get more throughput.

2. **Answer: C**
   Explanation: The answer is project X, simply because it has the larger internal rate of return (IRR). We don't need to consider the payback period or the NPV because the question asks which project has the better rate of return, which is its IRR.

3. **Answer: C**
   Explanation: To get the correct answer, we need to examine each option to find the one that is NOT a prioritization scheme (or that sounds least likely to be one). Prioritization based on business value is the most common prioritization method, so it is certainly a valid prioritization scheme. Prioritization based on risk is also a valid prioritization scheme. Likewise, prioritization based on both business value and risk is valid. The only option presented here that is NOT a valid prioritization scheme is iteration velocity. This term measures the work done and the team's capacity; it is not a prioritization scheme. So prioritization based on iteration velocity is the correct answer.

4. **Answer: B**
   Explanation: Creating a product roadmap is a release planning technique. A roadmap is not a list of screens and reports, because we can build a roadmap for a product even if the project has no screens and reports. The other options of deployment instructions and a backlog prioritization scheme are also incorrect.

5. **Answer: C**
   Explanation: Since agile contracts have to take into account the difficulty of defining the required product characteristics in advance, they need to work even when the specs are not fully defined. Agile contracts can be used with time and materials agreements but they also work well for fixed price projects where a cost limit cannot be exceeded and functionality is trimmed to meet the budget. A major reason agile contracts were developed was to accommodate changes, so that is the correct answer.

6. **Answer: C**
   Explanation: Here we have a few reasonable choices to consider, but only one option is the main reason. Putting risks in the backlog does prevent us from having to maintain a separate list, but that is not the reason we do it. It also helps keep the team focused on the risk, but again, that is not the main reason we do it. Preventing the team from forgetting about the risk is a lot like the previous idea, and is also not the real reason we put risks into the backlog. Instead, the main reason is to ensure that those items get worked on in early iterations, since delivering value early also means removing opportunities for value reduction.

© 2012 RMC Publications, Inc • 952.846.4484 • info@rmcproject.com • www.rmcproject.com

7. Answer: C

   Explanation: Here we need to eliminate the incorrect options to find the remaining valid combination. At first glance, "customer importance and business urgency" sounds like it might be a plausible option—but since both components are based on the customer's preference, they are similar enough that this isn't really a valid mix. "Risk reduction and technical dependency" can be eliminated because this combination doesn't take into account the customer's priorities—a mix is not balanced (and therefore not valid) if it doesn't consider value to the customer. "Team preference and customer value" is not a valid mix because team preference is not a valid selection criteria on its own. Although the team might prioritize a story for good reasons (for example, because it reduces risk), we don't know that from the question. The correct option is "customer value and risk reduction." These are the classic elements that we seek to balance in prioritizing work, so this option is the most valid story prioritization mix of the choices given here.

8. Answer: C

   Explanation: Without more information, such as ROI (though we are actually looking at loss instead of return in this case), the logical option is to cut the project that has the highest rate of loss. This means that we would cut project C, since it has the largest negative internal rate of return. Canceling all the projects is not the answer, since the question says that company X has decided to cancel ONE of its projects. On the exam, look out for questions like this that appear to present multiple "correct" answers but include information within the question that rules out certain choices.

9. Answer: C

   Explanation: To evaluate the value of two projects that are completed at different times, we can use net present value (NPV) to translate the amounts into today's values. Therefore, the approach of calculating the NPV and choosing the project with the highest value is the way to go. The other answers may make valid arguments, but the question is asking for the BEST approach, which is to calculate NPV.

10. Answer: C

    Explanation: The project charter defines the what, why, when, who, and how details of the project and provides authority to proceed. It may also list the scope that ends up in the backlog and the risks that should go into a risk register or risk list, but these are all just portions of the charter that do not "Best describe the role."

11. Answer: D

    Explanation: Since the total cycle time is the value-add time + the nonvalue-add time, we do not actually need to determine what falls under the value-add category. Instead, we just need to add up all the times involved: 10 + 15 + 5 + 5 = 35 minutes.

12. Answer: B

    Explanation: The product roadmap shows release dates and the high-level contents of releases, so it would be the best deliverable for answering these questions. A product demo might be good for showing the sponsor what has already been built, but demos are not targeted at communicating the release schedule for upcoming features, and neither is the backlog. The product owner will likely know the answers to these questions, but the question asked "Which agile deliverable," and the product owner is not a deliverable.

13. **Answer:** D

    Explanation: Two components common to agile contracts are an ability to reprioritize work and the goal of satisfying the business, rather than conforming to a spec. The closest match to these characteristic is the option "The contract is worded to allow for reprioritization of scope, and acceptance is based on items being fit for business purpose."

14. **Answer:** C

    Explanation: MoSCoW and "Priority 1, Priority 2, Priority 3" are forms of prioritization. They are ways the business representatives or customer can classify requirements or user stories to rank the work that needs to be done by the project.

15. **Answer:** D

    Explanation: While involving the customer does help with communications and business question clarifications, the primary reason we engage them is to better reflect the business needs and wants for the project. Keeping the customer busy is not a concern.

16. **Answer:** B

    Explanation: The best explanation here is "The product is built and evaluated in chunks that, by the end of the project, comprise the complete product, including agreed-upon change requests that arose during the process." The other choices contain concepts that are contrary to the incremental delivery approach or are completely unrelated. We don't just let the team, rather than the business or customer, select work, and we wouldn't exclude agreed-upon changes. As promoted by the Agile Manifesto, agile methods can harness change requests to deliver competitive advantage. And support demand has nothing to do with incremental delivery.

17. **Answer:** A

    Explanation: Process cycle efficiency = Total value-add time/Total cycle time. So, in this example, the value-add time is 1 hour, and the total cycle time = 24 + 1 = 25 hours. This gives us 1/25, which is 0.04, or 4 percent. If you used 24 for the total cycle time, you would have calculated 1/24 for an answer of 4.2%, which is incorrect.

18. **Answer:** B

    Explanation: Since iteration 0 is concerned with establishing tools and environments and proving approaches, a risk burn down graph is a good chart to show what the team has been working on. While there may not be business functionality to speak of, hopefully the team has reduced some technical risks and proven some key approaches that will be used.

STAKEHOLDER ENGAGEMENT

Chapter Four

Quicktest

Stakeholders, as defined in the *PMBOK® Guide*, are any people or groups who will be impacted by or have an impact on the project.[1] This is a pretty broad term that includes people in the role of the customer, sponsor, and/or business representative, as well as the project manager, the development team, any vendors involved in the project, and other people in the organization affected by the work of the project or its results, including the product's end users.

Getting stakeholders involved—in other words, engaging them in the project—is absolutely essential for an agile project's success. This chapter brings together a wide variety of topics related to stakeholder engagement, from soft skills related to leadership theory and active listening to technical skills used to gather information and communicate value. If this diversity seems hard to reconcile at times, keep in mind that the uniting theme of this chapter is working successfully with project stakeholders.

Why the Big Focus on Stakeholders?

Projects are undertaken by people, for people. Knowledge worker projects often have no tangible product; therefore, effective communication and stakeholder engagement are critical to ensure that team members know what they are building and what the customer is asking for. For example, if a team is developing a large business system that will operate in a frequently changing environment, it is vital for the team to engage customers throughout the project to ensure the team understands the correct details for each component and that they are able to incorporate late-breaking changes. Only through such ongoing stakeholder engagement can the team be confident they will deliver an optimum product or service.

Let's look again at the cartoon we saw in chapter 3:

Figure 4.1: Project Cartoon

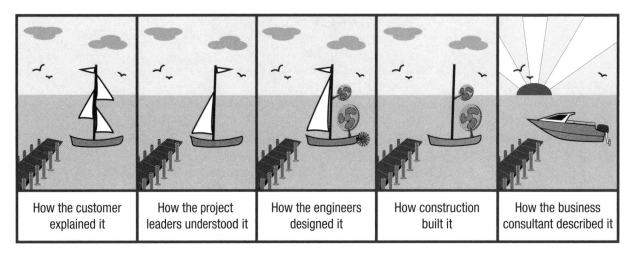

Variations of this image have been around for more than 20 years. Such cartoons are popular and still relevant because they highlight the frequent expectation mismatches that occur between stakeholder groups. In computer science, we call this mismatch the "gulf of evaluation." It is the difference between what one person envisioned and tried to describe and what another person heard and interpreted. If these mismatches are left unchecked for too long, then costly rework or project failure can (and often do) result.

On physical engineering projects, the work is visible, tangible, and familiar; therefore, the gulf is small and quickly crossed. In contrast, on knowledge worker projects, the work is often invisible, intangible, and new; this leads to a greater gulf of evaluation, and misunderstandings are more common. Agile methods aim to frequently bridge this gulf with demos, joint design sessions, multiple feedback loops, and repeated discussions about what "done" will look like.

 The PMI-ACP exam will test your competence in and understanding of the following aspects of stakeholder engagement. Keep this summary in mind as you read through the chapter, and think about how each concept we discuss relates back to these items.

» **Get the right stakeholders**: Projects won't be successful without the right stakeholders, so we should push hard to get the people we need. Of course, we want to have the right people on the development team, but we also need to have access to people in the organization who can most effectively help us understand the requirements of the project and make the necessary decisions to move things forward. Often the best people are the busiest people. Therefore, it may be beneficial for the project to pay to backfill these resources (bring additional people in) to help them complete their other duties so they have more time to contribute to the project.

» **Cement stakeholder involvement**: It is essential for stakeholders to stay engaged with the project, so we need to do all we can to make stakeholder involvement "stick." For example, we could document in the project charter how important the various stakeholders' involvement is on the project. We could also report on the benefits or issues resulting from the stakeholders' involvement (or the lack thereof) in the project's status reports and other reports to steering committees. Whatever specific methods we choose, we need to make sure stakeholders' involvement is visible and monitored on the project.

» **Actively manage stakeholder interest**: To keep stakeholders engaged, we should add some carrots to the mix. This means we take actions to recognize and reward stakeholder involvement, such as celebrating project milestones with the stakeholders, talking to their managers about how to recognize their contributions, and making sure project-related feedback becomes part of their performance reviews.

» **Frequently discuss what "done" looks like**: Since knowledge worker projects often create intangible products and services, there is a lot of potential for a gap between what the customer wants and describes and what the development team hears and interprets. It is critical to bridge that gap early and often, with each new idea presented on the project. Frequent discussions of what "done" looks like are essential if the team hopes to avoid nasty surprises, gaps in expectations, or poorly accepted products.

» **Show progress and capabilities**: Projects take a long time, and people generally want things as soon as possible after they've described them. For these reasons, it is important to frequently show stakeholders what has been built on the project. Such demos or presentations not only allow us to check that we are building the right thing before we get too far into the project, but they also show progress to our customer and sponsor. In turn, stakeholders stay engaged and informed about when things will be completed.

» **Candidly discuss estimates and projections**: One advantage of engaging the customer and showing them pieces of the project as those pieces are built is that the true rate of project progress is highly visible. On the negative side, the true rate of progress is often not what the sponsor or customer wants to hear. If it's delivered early enough, however, bad news can be valuable. By tracking and discussing the features delivered versus the features remaining, the team and the customer can make important trade-off decisions based upon solid data.

In this chapter, we'll examine the practices necessary to work successfully with project stakeholders. These include aligning the stakeholders' understanding of the project, communicating with stakeholders, using critical soft skills, and leading effectively. The following chart shows the tools and techniques and knowledge and skills associated with each of these practices. Although the names of these practices are not official terms and will not appear on the exam, organizing the concepts in this way provides the context of why and how you use the T&Ts and K&Ss that you will be tested on.

Practice	Tool/Technique	Knowledge/Skill (Level)
Aligning stakeholders' understanding	» Wireframes » Personas » User stories/backlogs » Story maps	» Incorporating stakeholder values (Level 1) » Stakeholder management (Level 1) » Vendor management (Level 3)
Communicating with stakeholders	» Information radiators » Burn down/up charts » Velocity » Agile modeling	» Communications management (Level 1)
Using critical soft skills	» Negotiation » Conflict resolution	» Active listening (Level 1) » Facilitation methods (Level 2) » Distributed teams (Level 2) » Participatory decision models (Level 2) » Globalization, culture, and team diversity (Level 3)
Leading effectively	» Servant leadership	» Leadership tools and techniques (Level 1)

Aligning Stakeholders' Understanding

Agile methods recognize the importance and challenge of overcoming the "semantic gap" between what customers ask for and how the development team interprets what they ask for. A variety of techniques have been created to help facilitate discussions, quickly bring mismatches to the surface, and work toward consensus and agreement. On agile projects, failing is okay as long as the failure is fast and cheap and it's still possible to recover the project. We ideally want to uncover disconnects in understanding at the lowest possible cost. By doing so, we save the organization money that it can then invest in other projects.

 Wireframes

Wireframe models are a popular way of creating a quick mock-up of the product. For example, in software development, a wireframe depicts individual screens and the flows between the screens. This diagram helps confirm that everyone has the same understanding of the product. If there are discrepancies in understanding, the wireframe serves as a useful visual for stakeholders to refer to and adjust until they

© 2012 RMC Publications, Inc • 952.846.4484 • info@rmcproject.com • www.rmcproject.com

achieve consensus. Wireframes are a form of "low-fidelity prototyping." In other words, they are quick and cheap ways to get feedback on something.

Figure 4.2: Sample Wireframe

MoviesOnline Basic Ordering Workflow

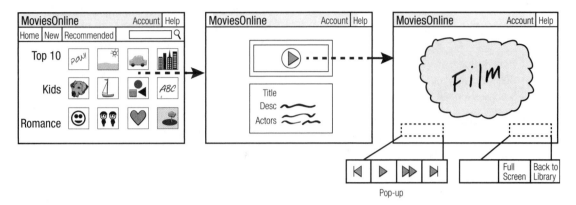

Agile teams may use wireframe models created in tools like Visio®, Balsamiq® Mockups, or PowerPoint®,[2] or they may draw the models freehand on whiteboards or sheets of paper stuck to a wall that allow for easy repositioning to change workflows. The purpose of these tools is to help clarify what "done" looks like and validate the approach the team plans to take before they commit large amounts of time to building (potentially wrong) increments of the product.

T&T Personas

Personas are quick guides or reminders of the key stakeholders on the project and their interests. Software projects, for example, commonly create personas for the different types of people who will use the system being built. Personas may be based on profiles of real people or composites of multiple users. When they are used as a project tool, personas should:

» Provide an archetypal description of users
» Be grounded in reality
» Be goal-oriented, specific, and relevant
» Be tangible and actionable
» Generate focus

Personas are not a replacement for requirements, but instead augment them. Personas help the team prioritize their work, stay focused on the users, and gain insight into who the users will be. These tools help team members empathize with users of the product or solution.

Figure 4.3 is a sample persona:

Figure 4.3: Sample Persona

Name: Bob the Movie Buff	
 **Description:** Bob loves movies. On average, he rents 5 movies a week from his local rental store. His two children also like to watch children's TV shows. They often like to watch the same shows more than once, which means that Bob sometimes has to pay late fees. Bob's wife has different movie tastes than Bob and often spends a lot of time choosing a movie.	**Values:** Bob would like to be able to order movies from the comfort of his home. He would like to be able to search for movies by title, actor, genre, and director. He would also be interested in knowing how other viewers rated the movie. He is looking forward to unlimited movies so his children can watch shows multiple times without having to pay additional fees. He would also appreciate a "recommended" feature to help him and his wife choose movies.

Personas can help keep a team focused on delivering the features that users will find valuable, and this leads to better decision-making on the project. These tools can also shorten project discussions. For example, team members may reference a persona that is familiar to the rest of the team. A question like "Does Samantha need it?" or a declaration like "Samantha doesn't need that!" can serve as a shortcut to help the team make decisions more quickly and keep them connected to the project vision.

EXERCISE

Referring to figure 4.3 for guidance, create the beginnings of a persona for the typical reader of this book—someone who is preparing for the PMI-ACP exam. Think about their goals, motivation, and definitions of success when completing the personal and professional goals section of the table.

Personal Profile	
Project Experience	
Personal Goals	
Professional Goals	

T&T User Stories/Backlogs

User stories are bite-sized, understandable chunks of business functionality. Agile project teams commonly rely on user stories and a backlog of these stories to help align team priorities with the needs of the business. User stories are often written in the following format:

"As a *<Role>*, I want *<Functionality>*, so that *<Business Benefit>*."

Example: "As a MoviesOnline customer, I want to search movies by actor, so that I can more easily find movies I would like to rent."

The advantages of this role, function, and business benefit template is that it forces the project to identify the user (Who is asking for this?) and the business benefit (Why are we doing this?) for every required piece of functionality. All too often, projects are bloated with requirements that have no clear owner or universally understood benefit.

EXERCISE

Rewrite the following requests so they are in the user story format: "As a *<Role>*, I want *<Functionality>*, so that *<Business Benefit>*." You will need to make some assumptions to complete this exercise. For example, I have not identified who is requesting the requirement in each item below, so you will need to assign a logical role.

1. Code the system to support banner advertisements from external advertisers to drive website revenue.

2. System needs to allow reports to be run on membership trends, including age and location demographics.

3. All financial transactions should be handled via the SecureServe system.

ANSWER

The following are examples of user stories for each item. Depending on the assumptions you made, your answers may be different.

1. As a business manager, I want the system to support banner advertisements so that we can generate additional website revenue.
2. As a marketing manager, I want membership reports including age, location, and trends so that we can run better-targeted incentive programs to drive up membership, referrals, and revenue.
3. As CFO, I want all financial transactions to be handled via SecureServe so that credit card information is protected and fraud is reduced.

Another format, often used for nonfunctional or system-based requirements, is "Given, When, Then." For example:

> **Given** the account is valid and the account has a MovieCredit balance of greater than $0,
> **When** the user redeems credit for a movie,
> **Then** issue the movie and reduce the user's MovieCredit balance.

The way user stories are phrased is important, but there are also other aspects of user stories that contribute to their value on a project. The INVEST mnemonic, shown in figure 4.4, is often used as a reminder of the characteristics of effective user stories.[3]

Figure 4.4: Characteristics of Effective User Stories

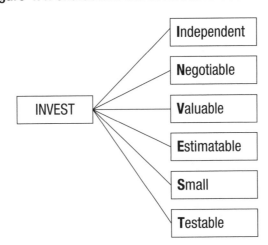

Let's look at this mnemonic in more detail:

» **I – Independent**: Ideally, we want to be able to reprioritize and develop user stories in any order. This is hard to achieve, but it is a goal. We try to create independent user stories that can be selected on merit, rather than dragged into the release because other user stories are dependent on them.
» **N – Negotiable**: The team should be able to discuss user stories with business representatives and make tradeoffs based on cost and function. For example, does "Printing" mean "hit the PrintScreen button and paste the image into a word processing program," or does the business need a fully formatted Crystal Reports document with headers and footers? Negotiating user stories leads to an improved understanding of the true requirements, costs, and acceptable compromises.
» **V – Valuable**: If we cannot determine the value of a requirement, then we should question why it is part of the project. Even if a user story is phrased in some way other than the role, function, and business benefit format, a portion of the user story should explain the value, or benefit, of the requirement. User stories without clearly understood business benefits will be difficult to prioritize, since backlogs are usually ranked on business value.
» **E – Estimatable**: Although "estimatable" is not really a word, it conveys the idea that we have to be able to estimate the effort of a user story. If it's not possible to say whether the request will take a day or will require two weeks' worth of work, we will not be able to prioritize the user story based on its cost/benefit trade-off.
» **S – Small**: Small user stories are easier to estimate and test than large user stories. As work units get larger, people's ability to estimate them reliably decreases. Also, by the time a large user story is reported as late, it may take an equally long time to correct or redo the work. Therefore, user stories should be

kept small. A common range is between a half day and 10 days. Another advantage of smaller user stories is that they can usually be completed within one iteration. But this doesn't mean, "the smaller, the better." Extremely small user stories, such as those that will take 2 hours or less to complete, should also be avoided, since there is an overhead cost involved in creating and tracking them.

» **T – Testable**: If we cannot test something, how will we know when it is done? Having testable user stories is important for tracking progress because we measure progress based upon how many user stories have been successfully accepted.

To summarize, we are looking for small, independent, valuable chunks of work—functions of which can be negotiated with the business to find the right level of cost versus performance—and we must be able to readily estimate and test these pieces of work. When developing software systems, stories should typically be vertical slices of functionality that cut through all the relevant architectural layers of the system, as indicated in figure 4.5.

Figure 4.5: User Stories That Impact All Architectural Layers

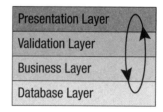

For example, a user story that involves saving and retrieving a customer balance is preferable to one that is focused on mocking up the customer account screen. The first example uses all the components of the system that the final solution will use (the presentation, validation, business, and database layers), whereas the second example just refers to the user interface (presentation) layer. Because it only focuses on one layer, creating a mock-up of the customer account screen will not reveal any issues in the other layers. In addition, the user story will not act as a reliable indicator of true development speed, since other work still remains to be done to achieve the desired functionality.

User Story Backlog

After the user stories are created, they are organized into a backlog. This backlog of user stories is a visible list of the work to be done, as shown in figure 4.6.

© 2012 RMC Publications, Inc • 952.846.4484 • info@rmcproject.com • www.rmcproject.com

Figure 4.6: User Story Backlog

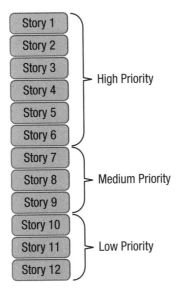

The user story backlog helps guide discussions of the team's priorities. It also serves as a planning tool for managing releases and iterations, and it helps direct the team's focus during scope discussions and when managing changes. This tool helps coordinate the project and keeps the team working toward the agreed-upon mission, while still allowing for revisions and updates as new and better information arises.

Requirements Hierarchy

A large project in its entirety is a complex, overwhelming amount of work that cannot be accurately planned or estimated as a whole. So we need to break the project down into smaller chunks, with increasingly refined requirements, until we reach a level that is small enough to actually estimate and build the items. This is done through iterative planning on agile projects (discussed in more detail in chapter 6, Adaptive Planning). Although user stories are the most commonly discussed planning tool, they are not the only one that agile projects use. In the hierarchy of requirements on a project, user stories are generally in the middle. Figure 4.7 provides an example of a common way to structure the requirements hierarchy:

Figure 4.7: Basic Standard Format for Requirements Hierarchy

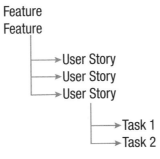

Some methodologies extend this basic model with the addition of epics (large user stories that span one or more iterations). Unfortunately there is no single universally approved version of the extended requirements hierarchy. Some project teams will have "epics" above the user story level. An epic may also be above, below, or simply replace the feature node. Figures 4.8 through 4.10 illustrate different ways epics can be positioned in requirements hierarchies.

Figure 4.8: Requirements Hierarchy with Epics Instead of Features

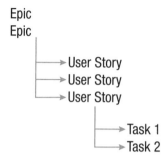

Figure 4.9: Requirements Hierarchy with Epics Above Features

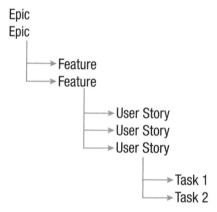

Figure 4.10: Requirements Hierarchy with Epics Below Features

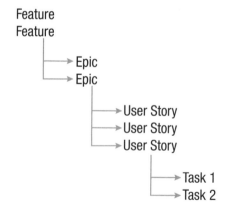

TRICKS OF THE TRADE® If the different hierarchy terms sound too confusing, don't worry. Because of the inconsistencies, the exam does not ask questions about where epics fall in the hierarchy. It is still useful to understand how they may be used on projects, however. If you are faced with both epics and features in use on a project, just ask the team what structure, or precedence, they are using.

T&T Story Maps

As discussed in chapter 3, Value-Driven Delivery, story maps are useful tools for indicating customer-valued prioritization, but this tool can also serve as a product roadmap to show when features will be delivered. Story maps are great tools for explaining what will go into the first release, second release, and subsequent releases. As such, they are often used in stakeholder communications and can be posted on a wall as an information radiator of the project plan. They have the added benefit of engaging people in a different way than if the same information was depicted on a Gantt chart, since the story map format is more visual and inviting.

Figure 4.11: Story Map Showing the Project Plan and Product Road Map

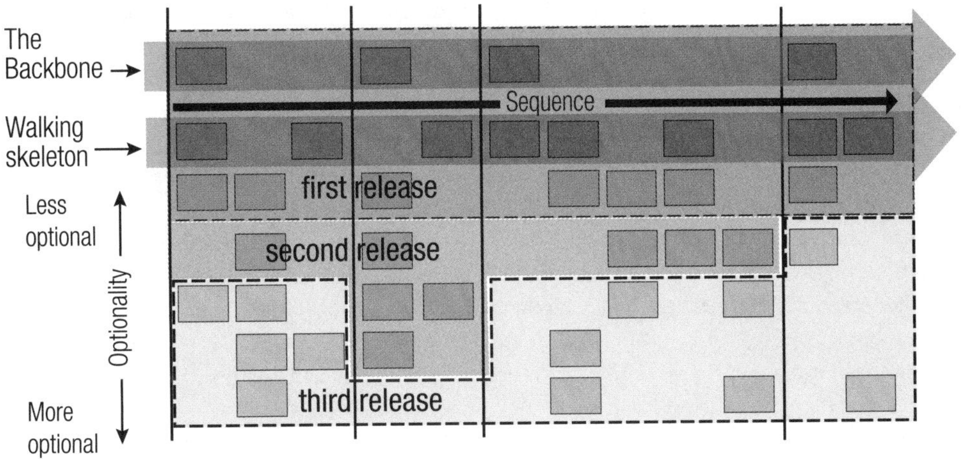
The Backbone
Walking skeleton
Less optional
Optionality
More optional
Sequence
first release
second release
third release

K&S Level 1 Incorporating Stakeholder Values

This K&S is about incorporating the sponsor's and users' priorities into the project's priorities and execution. In other words, it's about bringing project priorities into alignment with stakeholder priorities. Incorporating stakeholder values means we make sure we do not plan and initiate work that the stakeholders do not support or value at this time.

One way to incorporate stakeholder values on a project is to engage business representatives in the prioritization of the backlog. By executing the work in the order that the business representatives specify (taking into account the necessary dependencies and risk mitigation work, of course), the project delivers the highest-priority items early to the business.

Another way to incorporate stakeholders' values and interests into the project activities is to invite our stakeholders to retrospectives and planning meetings. At the end of the day, our customers and sponsors are the ones who determine if the project is a success or a failure, so it is smart to base the project team's work and actions on what those stakeholders value.

K&S Level 1 — Stakeholder Management

Stakeholder management is about comprehensively looking after stakeholders, including in the initial efforts to identify who the stakeholders are. Some roles are obvious; for example, we typically know who the sponsor, users, and department managers will be. However, some of the other roles may be trickier to identify, such as auditors, the upstream providers of inputs to the project, or the downstream consumers of its outputs. It is important to identify all the stakeholders and effectively manage their involvement in the project, because excluding or alienating any of them will put the successful execution of the project at risk.

If project stakeholders are new to agile methods, they may need some basic education about how agile projects operate to help them understand the approach, address any myths about agile projects, and manage their expectations. This education should include the goals, values, practices, and benefits of the agile approach so they understand why the project will be executed in this manner.

It is normal for any change to be met with some degree of skepticism and caution. This isn't necessarily a bad thing. After all, the world would be pretty chaotic if we adopted every new idea, operating system, or suggestion to change something as systemic as which side of the road we drive on. Some resistance to change is healthy because it helps ensure that only worthwhile changes prevail. So when we are initially engaging stakeholders in an agile project, we need to recognize some of the concerns the various stakeholder groups may have. The following are examples of common concerns:

» **Executives and project sponsors**: Executives and sponsors are often concerned about the risk of failure due to the use of unprecedented practices and counterintuitive planning approaches, even though an agile approach actually provides better feedback loops for preventing failure.
» **Managers**: Managers may fear a loss of control or erosion of their role when projects assume an agile approach.
» **The project team**: The project team may resist having a new method forced upon them by "management."
» **The user community**: The user community is often worried they will not get all features they want or require, or that the early iterations will result in poor quality deliverables.
» **Supporting groups**: Other groups may be concerned about an apparent lack of control, continual requests for their involvement, or the lack of a clear end point.

In addition to the initial efforts to identify stakeholders, educate them, and address their concerns, stakeholder management involves continuing to engage them in the project as it progresses. One benefit of two- to four-week iterations is that they are short enough to prevent stakeholders from losing interest in the process. During an iteration, we meet with stakeholders, agree on what should be done, do some work, and then two to four weeks later, we show them what we have developed. Since brief iterations are good for maintaining stakeholder engagement, they are preferable to long development phases where visibility is low and stakeholder interest tends to wane as a result.

One key reason to keep stakeholders engaged is to ensure we will hear about change requests as soon as possible. An ongoing dialogue with our stakeholders will also help us identify potential risks, defects, and issues. Agile methods provide multiple touch points with stakeholders and deliberate communication events designed to facilitate early and continuous feedback.

For example, in Scrum, sprint planning and sprint review meetings act like the bookends to an iteration, during which the team initiates and reviews stakeholder involvement. Other agile methods also have similar events. One point to keep in mind when engaging people in such events is that not all stakeholders can be handled the same way. Some people may cause problems and actually be impediments to project progress. In such cases, the ScrumMaster, project manager, or other designated person needs to use emotional intelligence skills to try to understand these stakeholders' concerns and find a positive way to engage them with the project. If this is not possible, it may be necessary to try and shield the team from their disruptive or corrosive influence.

Another aspect of stakeholder management is establishing a process for escalating issues that need a high level of authority to resolve. Agreement on such a process is essential to keep the project operating smoothly. Then if the team encounters a problem or issue that they do not have the authority or influence to resolve, they will be able to follow the established procedure to quickly escalate it to the appropriate stakeholders for resolution.

Vendor Management

Vendor management focuses on stakeholders who are external to the organization but are involved in the project because they are providing some product or service. As with internal stakeholders, we should be careful in selecting vendors and we may need to educate them about the unique aspects of working in an agile environment.

If a vendor needs to use an agile approach to participate in the project, then this requirement should be outlined in the request for proposal (RFP). Depending on their role in the project, however, some vendors may not need to use or understand agile practices. Before setting a requirement that the vendors be familiar with agile, or developing an educational event for vendors, we should ask if it's worth it. If the vendor plays a minor role, perhaps it is not. For those who will play a major or critical role, it probably is worthwhile. Like all decisions, we need to consider the cost/benefit trade-off.

Since agile projects acknowledge that requirements may change and scope is negotiable, traditional vendor engagement contracts based on formal specifications are problematic. Instead, agile projects typically use the contracting models described in chapter 3, Value-Driven Delivery, including fixed price work packages (pay as you go) and graduated fixed price contracts.

Frequently Discuss What "Done" Looks Like

Before we move on to the next practice, Communicating with Stakeholders, let's talk about another essential concept related to Aligning Stakeholders' Understanding—the definition of "done." Creating a shared definition of done is crucial for managing our stakeholders' expectations. This initiative will affect the project from the user story level (e.g., "Done will mean developed, documented, and user acceptance tested"), to the release level (e.g., "The first release will be deemed done when system Alpha is replaced and there are no priority 1 defects or change requests"), all the way up to the final project deliverable level (e.g., "Done for the project means all high- and medium-priority features are implemented, there are two months of trouble-free operation, and the project receives satisfaction scores of greater than 70 percent from the user community").

For software projects, James Shore provides the following list of elements that should be discussed and checked before we declare that anything is "done"[4]:

> These elements are software-specific and are not tested on the exam.

- » **Tested**: Are all unit, integration, and customer tests finished?
- » **Coded**: Has all code been written?
- » **Designed**: Has the code been refactored to the team's satisfaction?

» **Integrated**: Does the user story work from end to end (typically user interface to database) and fit into the rest of the software?
» **Builds**: Does the build script include any new modules?
» **Installs**: Does the build script include the user story in the automated installer?
» **Migrates**: Does the build script update the database schema if necessary? Does the installer migrate data when appropriate?
» **Reviewed**: Have customers reviewed the user story and confirmed that it meets their expectations?
» **Fixed**: Have all known bugs been fixed or scheduled as their own user stories?
» **Accepted**: Do customers agree that the user story is finished?

Agile works best when you make a little progress on every aspect of your work every day, rather than reserving the last few days of your iteration for getting user stories "Done Done." As we develop the user stories and features, we need to make sure we are involving the onsite customer and that the various aspects of the product work together.

Communicating with Stakeholders

Since work is often invisible on knowledge worker projects, we cannot easily tell the state of things by looking around the office. Therefore, it is critical for the project team to communicate frequently with the stakeholders to ensure everyone is on the same page and kept up to date. In addition, project failures can often be traced back to communication failures. On many projects, somewhere along the way, an issue or overrun occurred that was not communicated in a timely manner. Instead of the issue being corrected, things on the project went from bad to worse. To help combat these potential issues, agile methods provide a host of communication tools and events. Let's explore these now, starting with the K&S of communications management.

 ### Communications Management

The preferred way to communicate on agile projects is through face-to-face (F2F) communications. F2F communications have the highest bandwidth of all forms of communication; this means that F2F communications can transfer the most information in a given time period. F2F communications also allow for immediate questions and answers, whereas static methods, like paper documentation, do not. Alistair Cockburn's communication effectiveness diagram compares some of the most common communication methods, including paper documentation, multimedia methods, e-mail exchanges, telephone conversations, and F2F communication.[5] Figure 4.12 (an adaptation of Alistair Cockburn's original diagram) indicates where different methods lie in terms of communication effectiveness and richness, or "temperature."

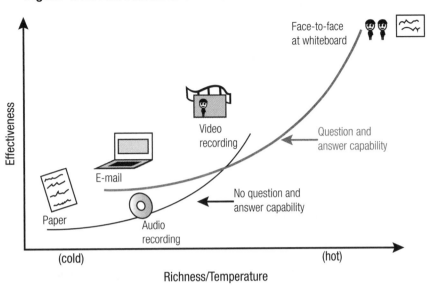

Figure 4.12: Effectiveness of Different Communication Channels

Looking at this diagram, we can see that paper-based communications are rated lowest in terms of communication effectiveness (the Y axis). This form of communication takes a long time to create and, because it has no option for interactivity, the documents have to be written in such a way that all recipients can understand the information, regardless of their level of knowledge or expertise. Paper documents are also low on the richness, or "temperature," scale (the X axis), which means that they typically do not convey a lot of emotion.

Now compare paper communication with F2F communication, such as two people working together at a whiteboard. In F2F communication, the two participants can quickly shortcut information when both people understand the concept, and they can ask each other questions and get immediate feedback. Such conversations also convey a lot of emotional bandwidth through nonverbal communication such as gestures, facial expressions, and tone of voice. In F2F communication, we can quickly tell if people are puzzled, angry, or passionate about a topic. However, while we prefer F2F communications for their efficiency and high bandwidth, we cannot always rely on them; there are times when information does need to be recorded on paper.

T&T Information Radiators

"Information radiator" is an umbrella term for a number of highly visible ways to display information, including large charts, graphs, and summaries of project data. These tools, also sometimes referred to as "visual controls," quickly inform stakeholders about the project's status, and they are usually displayed in high-traffic areas to maximize exposure. The term "information radiator" was developed by Alistair Cockburn in contrast to the practice of locking project information away in an "information refrigerator," where nobody knows what is going on. Instead, information radiators use highly visible charts or graphs to convey, or radiate, information about the project quickly to anyone who is interested.

The sort of data that might be displayed on an information radiator includes:

» The features delivered to date versus the features remaining to be delivered
» Who is working on what
» The features selected for the current iteration
» Velocity and defect metrics
» Retrospective findings
» Risk registers

Figure 4.13 is an example of an information radiator that shows defects work in progress. For the project featured on this chart, we were interested in keeping on top of the defects—in other words, keeping the volume of open defects low—to minimize the cost of changes and the amount of code that might be written on top of faulty code.

Figure 4.13: Sample Information Radiator Tracking Defects Work in Progress

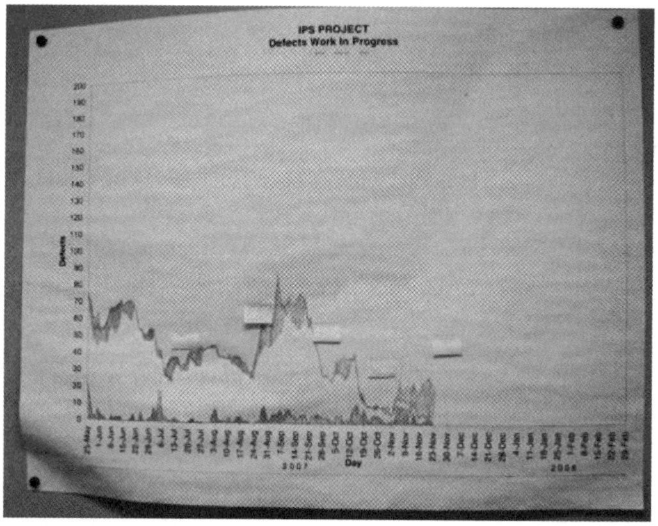

Image copyright © 2012 Leading Answers, Inc. Reproduced with permission from Leading Answers, Inc., www.leadinganswers.com

We also tracked defect cycle time, which was the total time taken between defect injection (when the defect was introduced) and defect correction (when it was fixed). Our goal was to fix each defect within one business day. Figure 4.14, another example of an information radiator, shows the defect cycle time for the project.

Figure 4.14: Sample Information Radiator Tracking Defect Cycle Time

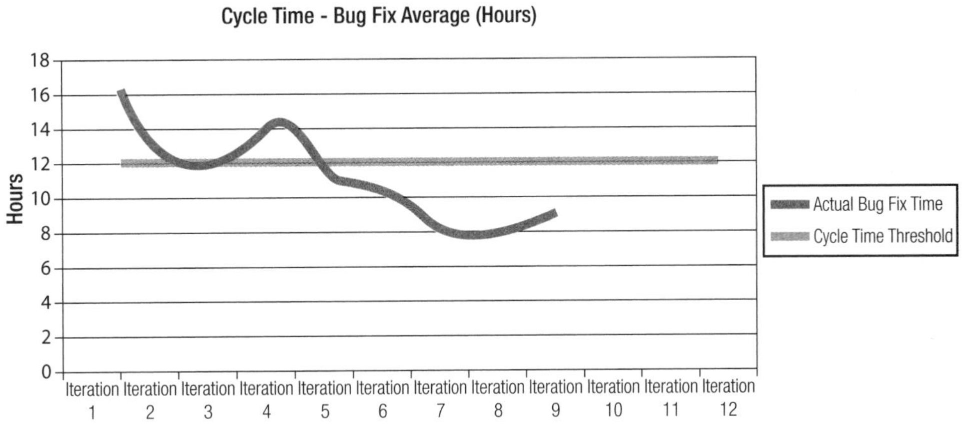

Cycle Time - Bug Fix Average (Hours)

Story maps, discussed earlier in this chapter, and burn down and burn up charts, which we will discuss next, are other common examples of information radiators.

T&T Burn Down and Burn Up Charts

Burn down and burn up charts are used to show progress and to help determine when the project (or a release within the project) should be complete. Burn down charts show the estimated effort remaining on the project, and burn up charts show what has been delivered. This means as more work is completed, a burn down chart will show a progress indicator moving downward to indicate the reduced amount of work that still needs to be done. In contrast, the progress indicator on a burn up chart will move upward, to show the increasing amount of work completed. Figure 4.15 is an example of a burn down chart.

Figure 4.15: Sample Burn Down Chart Using Time to Measure Progress

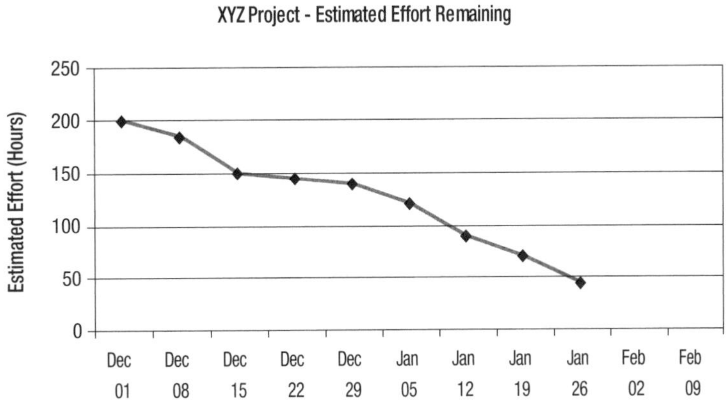

XYZ Project - Estimated Effort Remaining

Burn down charts typically show the estimated time remaining or, if the project team is tracking progress in points, the estimated points remaining. Burn down charts can be created in Microsoft Excel®.[6] In looking at the chart in figure 4.15, we can estimate that this project will be completed (in other words, reach "0" hours of estimated effort remaining) in early February.

Figure 4.16 is another example of a burn down chart. This example is based on points. In addition to the project progress, this chart shows the future points effort (in green—an unlikely increase) that would be required to meet the target release date.

Figure 4.16: Sample Burn Down Chart Using Points to Measure Progress

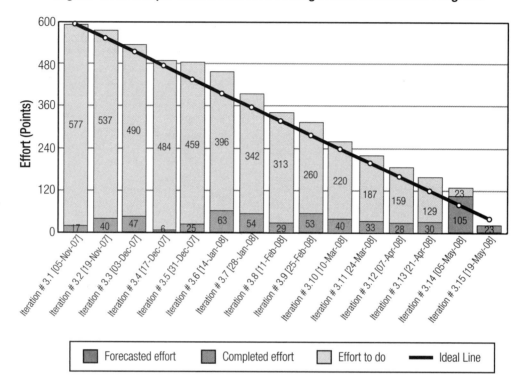

One drawback of burn down charts is that they can mix scope creep and progress variables together. If we look again at the first example (figure 4.15), we can see that progress was slow (the line was flatter) between December 15 and December 29. This slowdown could have been caused by people taking vacation around the holidays, or it could have resulted from the team being given or discovering more scope on the project. We cannot discern the reason for the slow progress by looking at the burn down chart. In contrast, burn up charts usually separate out progress from scope, making these factors easier to distinguish.

Figure 4.17 is an example of a burn up chart, in which we can see that the scope increased first from 300 points to 330 points, and then eventually to 350 points.

4.17: Sample Burn Up Chart Using Points to Measure Progress

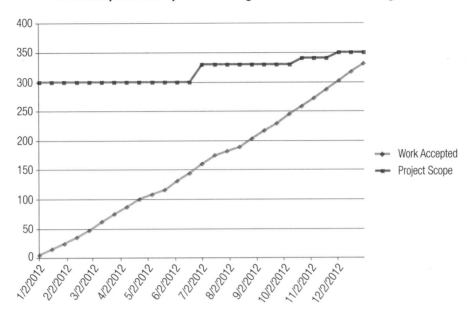

If the data in this burn up chart was plugged into a burn down chart, we would see areas when the rate of effort line would flatten, but we wouldn't be able to tell from the burn down chart whether we should attribute that flattening to an increase in scope or slower progress. By separating progress and scope, burn up charts offer additional insight into scope variances.

The burn up chart in figure 4.17 showed work accepted, or completed. But what about work in progress? If we add work in progress to our burn up chart, to track both work started *and* work completed, we create a cumulative flow diagram (CFD; also discussed in chapter 3, Value-Driven Delivery). Figure 4.18 is an example of a CFD.

Figure 4.18: Sample Cumulative Flow Diagram

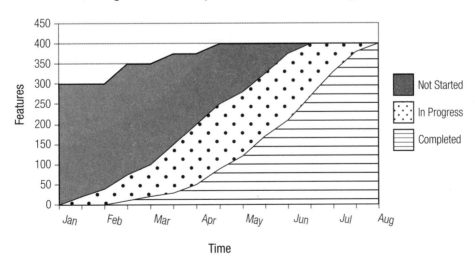

In figure 4.18, we can see how the overall scope (the green section) increased from 300 features to 400 during the project. The CFD also shows work in progress (the dotted section) and the completed work (the striped section). The true rate of progress is the gradient of the line at the top of the "Completed" section, because it indicates the rate of feature completion.

T&T   Velocity

Velocity is the measure of a team's capacity for work per iteration. This metric helps us gauge how much work the team is able to do, based on the number of user stories completed in past iterations. This metric provides a way to communicate what we have accomplished, what we will likely be able to accomplish, and when we expect the project (or release) to be done. Velocity is measured in whatever units the team uses for its work, so those units could be hours, days, points, or even jelly beans (yes, jelly beans are actually used on many projects).

Figure 4.19: Sample Velocity Tracking Chart

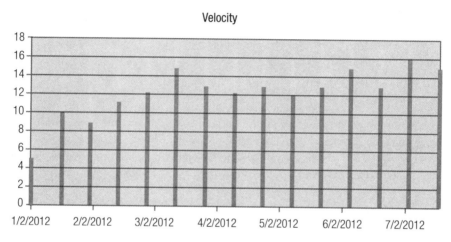

When velocity is tracked over multiple iterations, this metric can be used to determine when a project will likely be completed. For example, if a project's velocity averages 50 points per iteration, and the backlog contains 500 points' worth of undeveloped work, then we would divide 500 by 50 to get 10 (500 / 50 = 10). The data indicates that the project will likely be completed in 10 more iterations.

Velocity usually varies most in the first few iterations and then begins to stabilize. This is because the team has to get used to working together, familiarize themselves with the project tools, and get comfortable interacting with the project stakeholders.

Figure 4.20: Velocity Stabilizes as a Project Progresses

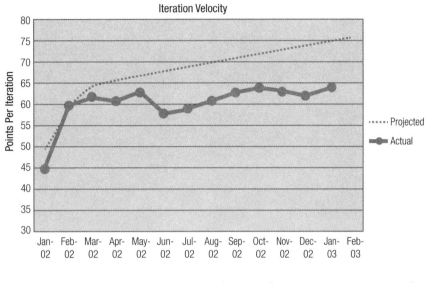

While it may seem logical to predict ever-increasing velocity as the team gains experience, velocity does typically plateau. One reason for this is that, as the product being built gets bigger, there is more to maintain, refactor, and possibly support if early versions of the product have been deployed.

EXERCISE

Your team's velocity has been 40, 48, 52, 59, and 51 points per iteration since starting the project. Your backlog of remaining work has 600 points of functionality in it. Your sponsor wants to know when you expect to be done. How many more iterations of work will be required to complete the backlog?

ANSWER

You first need to calculate the average number of points per iteration:

$$(40 + 48 + 52 + 59 + 51) / 5 = 50$$

You then divide the remaining work by the average points per iteration:

$$600 / 50 = 12$$

Therefore, the backlog will likely require 12 more iterations of work to complete.

T&T | Agile Modeling

The term "agile modeling" refers to the various modeling techniques that are commonly used on agile projects. While models are important in agile methods, their main value often lies in the discussion and creation of the model, rather than the final output. As a reflection of this, agile models are often sketched on whiteboards and then photographed as a means of recording them. The value is in the creation, not the beautification and preservation of the model in a specialized modeling tool.

So agile models are typically lightweight, or "barely sufficient," capturing the design without a need for further polish. We can create a model for predictive purposes to help clarify a design and identify the issues, risks, and elements that we need to test. We can also use modeling for reflective purposes to investigate problems and help find solutions.

Scott Ambler, an agile modeling expert, asserts that the value of modeling peaks earlier than traditional theory has led us to believe. This earlier peak is indicated in figure 4.21.

Figure 4.21: The Value of Modeling

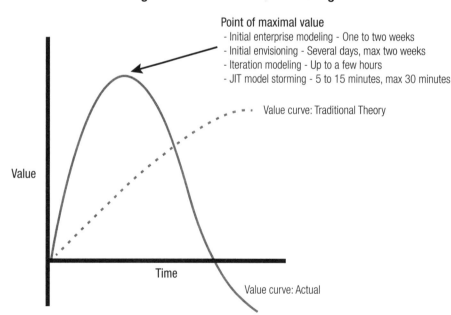

Image copyright © Scott Ambler, www.agilemodeling.com

Ambler recommends limiting modeling to the point of the model being "barely good enough," and then moving on to the next task. The types of agile models that can be created during agile modeling include:

» Use case diagrams (see figure 4.22)
» Data models (see figure 4.23)
» Screen designs (see figure 4.24)

Figure 4.22: Sample Use Case Diagram

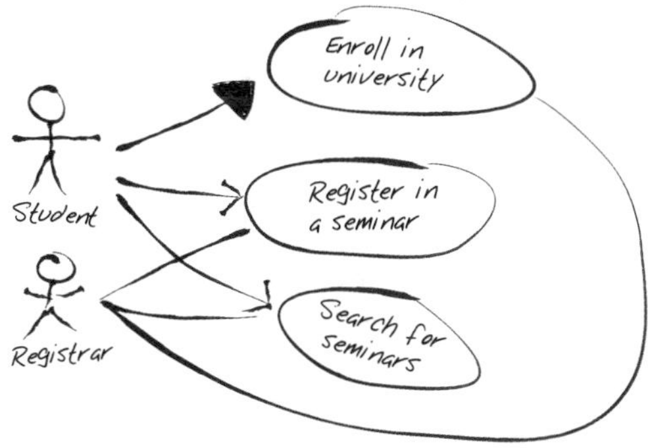

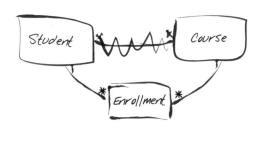

Image copyright © Scott Ambler, www.agilemodeling.com

Figure 4.23: Sample Data Model

Image copyright © Scott Ambler, www.agilemodeling.com

Figure 4.24: Sample Screen Design

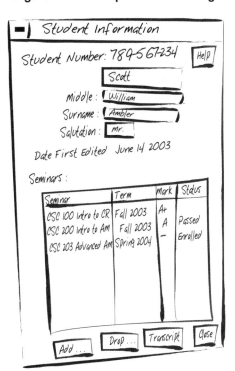

Image copyright © Scott Ambler, www.agilemodeling.com

Regardless of the type of model you create, remember that the goal is still to deliver valuable but not extraneous documentation. So keep it light, move on quickly, and be adaptable to changes.

Using Critical Soft Skills

The adage "The soft stuff is the hard stuff, and the hard stuff is the easy stuff" speaks to the fact that soft skills are often more difficult to master than technical skills. The good news is that while our Intelligence Quotient (IQ) peaks when we are in our 20s, our Emotional Quotient (EQ) continues to develop through our 40s and 50s. Critical soft skills are included in the PMI-ACP exam because they are just that—critical. Poor soft skills can quickly demoralize and disenchant a technically strong team, while someone who effectively uses soft skills can extract amazing results from average teams.

We use the term "critical soft *skills*" instead of "critical soft *talents*" because unlike talents, which we are largely born with, skills can be acquired and improved through education and practice. The following are the critical soft skills that will be tested on the PMI-ACP exam:

- » Negotiation
- » Active listening
- » Facilitation methods
- » Globalization, culture, and team diversity
- » Conflict resolution
- » Distributed teams
- » Participatory decision models

T&T Negotiation

Negotiation happens throughout an agile project, especially when discussing the requirements or priorities of features and what "done" would best look like. For example, let's say that a customer asks for the ability to print out product codes. In negotiating this requirement, the team presents options to the customer. The low-cost option might be to use the Print Screen function on the product code screen, paste the screen shot into Microsoft Word®, and then print that document to get the product codes.[7] A more costly solution might be a fully formatted report with headers, footers, and page numbers. And then there would be additional options that fall between these low-cost and high-cost solutions. The team and the customer can negotiate the tradeoffs between functionality and cost to come up with a balanced solution.

Negotiating on agile projects does not have to be—and typically should not be—a zero-sum game (i.e., with a winner and a loser). Instead, healthy negotiations allow each party to investigate the trade-offs and present alternative perspectives. There should be an opportunity for each viewpoint or business case to be fully described, noting the pros and cons of the different options. Negotiations are most effective when the interactions between participants are positive and there is some room for give and take on each side.

K&S Level 1 Active Listening

Active listening is hearing what someone is really trying to convey, rather than just the meanings of the words they are speaking. The expression, "Do what I mean, not what I say," speaks to this concept. On agile projects, we need to listen for the message, not just the string of words being spoken.

Active listening is a skill that can be improved with practice. According to the book *Co-Active Coaching: Changing Business, Transforming Lives*, our listening skills progress through three levels, as shown in figure 4.25.[8]

Note: You don't need to know the titles of resources or the names of authors for the exam.

Figure 4.25: Three Levels of Listening

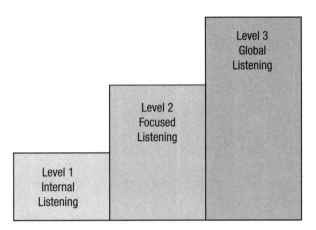

Level 1: Internal Listening

We hear the words being spoken, and although we may be very attentive, we interpret them through our own lens. When listening, we are thinking "How is this going to affect me?" and miss the speaker's real message. For example, if someone on our team starts talking about challenges with a new team member, we might be thinking about our goal of quickly getting the new team member integrated and up to speed and miss what the speaker is trying to say about the team member.

Level 2: Focused Listening

When listening at this level, we let go of our own thoughts and put ourselves in the mind of the speaker. We empathize with their thoughts, experiences, and emotions as they tell us about the situation. In our example of the person who is encountering challenges with a new team member, we are able to empathize with the speaker's feelings and recognize that the training of this new person has added to her workload at a stressful time. We look for emotional indicators in the speaker's words and pauses, their voice and tone, and their facial expressions for more information about how the person feels about what they are describing.

Level 3: Global Listening

When listening at this level, we build on the approach taken in level 2, adding a higher level of awareness, like an antennae function, to pick up on subtle physical and environmental indicators. These indicators can include the speaker's movements or posture, their energy level, and the atmosphere or vibe in the room. We notice factors like whether the speaker is voicing the information openly in front of others or privately, the mannerisms of others who are within earshot (e.g., do they seem to agree, or are they averting their eyes or otherwise distancing themselves from the conversation?), and many other subtle clues help us understand a fuller context of the information being shared. In our example, as the speaker is telling us about the new team member, we recognize the importance and sensitive nature of the conversation because she came to us privately to discuss the matter. We also notice that she is physically tense, clenching her hands into a fist, and then standing up and pacing as she is speaking. Taking these clues into account, we can help her recognize and explore her feelings to better understand her reaction to working with the new team member.

Coaching agile teams requires that we listen intently to people. And we cannot listen when we are talking ourselves, so talk less and listen more. Wait for others to speak. Try counting slowly to 10 to give other people enough time to get comfortable and speak up. In general, we are not learning while our mouths are flapping.

 ## Facilitation Methods

The questions about facilitation methods on the PMI-ACP exam are essentially testing whether you understand how to run effective meetings and workshops. When facilitating a meeting or session (or when you encounter such questions on the exam), keep the following in mind:

» **Goals**: People often feel that meetings are a waste of their time, especially if the meeting discusses a wide range of topics and the participants don't understand why they need to be there or what their contribution should be. Establishing a clear goal for each meeting or workshop session can help people get engaged in the discussion from the start. Plus, having a clear goal and keeping everyone focused on that goal, rather than allowing the session to be sidetracked, can shorten the session time, making the discussion feel more valuable to all involved.

» **Rules**: Establishing some basic ground rules is another important technique for holding effective sessions. For example, there might be rules regarding the use of cell phones, starting and ending the sessions on time, and respecting the views of all participants. It is not enough to simply set the rules, however. The rules must also be enforced during each session.

» **Timing**: Timing is always important when we are trying to get a group of people together, and it can be easy to lose track of the time once the session is going. Therefore, the duration of the session should be established ahead of time, and someone should be designated as the timekeeper. It is also useful to determine in advance when the session breaks will take place.

» **Assisting**: The session facilitator needs to make sure the meeting is productive and that everyone has a chance to contribute. In addition to keeping the group focused on the session goal and enforcing the ground rules, this may include making sure junior or quieter members have the opportunity to express their thoughts, coping with dominant or aggressive participants, and otherwise keeping the session flowing smoothly.

 ## Globalization, Culture, and Team Diversity

As our communication options expand and become less expensive, and as our partner and customer bases widen, factors like globalization, culture, and team diversity are becoming increasingly important. It is not uncommon to have team members from three or four continents working on the same project. Since knowledge work is invisible, we rely primarily on communication to share project information. Different cultures bring communication challenges, but they can also bring efficiency to a project because you have a broader pool of resources to choose from.

Even when people from different regions of the world speak the same language, there are still differences to take into account. As an example, when I first made the relatively easy transition from the United Kingdom to Canada, I discovered surprising differences in culture, expressions, and terminology, despite the supposedly common language. For instance, I remember someone saying to me, "We'll need biweekly status reports." Thinking that "biweekly" meant twice a week, I replied, "Okay, can we make that every Wednesday and Friday?"

"Oh no, every two weeks."

"Wait, you mean every fortnight?"

"What's a "fortnight?" And things continued to decline from there.

TRICKS OF THE TRADE® One great way to help the members of a global team learn about each other's communication preferences and styles is to hold a face-to-face kickoff meeting. It is so much easier to e-mail, call, or instant message someone whom you have already met in person. And if possible, extend the model of face-to-face kickoff events so that team members work together for the first one or two iterations before they return to their respective countries, as shown in figure 4.26.

Figure 4.26: Bringing Geographically Dispersed Teams Together Early Improves Communications Later

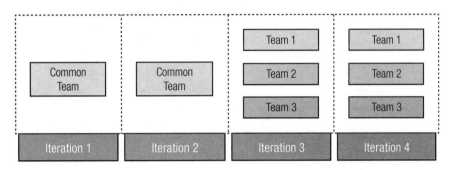

This model can be further extended by arranging for face-to-face release and planning meetings as the project progresses. Other models that work well include a rotating secondment, or temporary assignment, of team members between locations to give the team members in each region an opportunity to work in person with people from the other teams and experience their cultures.

Of course, diversity may be a factor on our local teams, too. The XP practice of pairing can help overcome local issues related to diversity. Pairing gives team members a great opportunity to learn about how others communicate progress, raise problems, and brainstorm. When conducting retrospectives (see chapter 8, Continuous Improvement), we should keep in mind cultural differences. For example, people from some cultures may not feel comfortable raising problems with the current process when they are in the presence of their managers. In such instances, it can be helpful to rephrase "What did not go well?" types of questions to "What areas could use improvement?" It can also be helpful to leave retrospective questions open at the end of the meeting so people can respond to them in meeting rooms outside of the retrospective group and via e-mail or anonymous forms.

T&T   Conflict Resolution

Conflict is an inevitable part of project work. Whenever people come together to solve problems, there will be differences of opinion and competing interests. Some degree of conflict is healthy, to ensure that ideas are sufficiently tested before they are adopted. However, we need to make sure the conflict does not escalate beyond healthy skepticism and friendly teasing, or we will end up with a negative and repressive team environment.

Creating an environment in which people can use conflict constructively is a key part of successfully engaging stakeholders on a project. We must watch for instances when conflict moves beyond normal, healthy debate and becomes destructive and harmful to the relationships and the team. Speed B. Leas offers a framework that helps us judge the seriousness of a conflict and better understand the escalation path from Level 1 (Problem to Solve) to Level 5 (World War).[9]

Level	Name	Characteristic	Language Type	Atmosphere/Environment
Level 1	Problem to Solve	Information sharing and collaboration	Open and fact-based	» People have different opinions or misunderstandings » Conflicting goals or values » Not comfortable, but not emotionally charged either
Level 2	Disagreement	Personal protection trumps resolving the conflict	Guarded and open to interpretation	» Self-protection becomes important » Team members distance themselves from the debate » Discussions happen off-line (outside of the team environment) » Good-natured joking moves to half-joking barbs
Level 3	Contest	Winning trumps resolving the conflict	Includes personal attacks	» The aim is to win » People take sides » Blaming flourishes
Level 4	Crusade	Protecting one's own group becomes the focus	Ideological	» Resolving the situation is not good enough » Team members believe that people "on the other side" will not change and need to be removed
Level 5	World War	Destroy the other!	Little or nonexistent	» "Destroy!" is the battle cry » The combatants must be separated » No constructive outcome can be had

Understanding Leas's framework on the stages of conflict can help us look at a situation more objectively, moving past our own judgments to see what is really happening. Identifying the conflict stage can also help us determine what actions we should take or what tools or techniques may work in the given situation.

Therefore, when a team is in a state of conflict, we should first take some time to observe the conflict and make sure we are seeing both sides of the dispute, not just jumping in with a knee-jerk reaction. We need to allow time for proper observation, conversation, and intuition about the issues before taking action. This means that at first we simply listen to the complaints, without immediately trying to solve them. We feel the energy of the group, and assess the conflict levels. We look for glances, eye rolling, and words that halt conversations to ascertain if the conflict is out in the open, or if it is playing out in subsurface snippets.

One way to assess the level of conflict is to focus on the language the team uses and then compare the conversation against the 1 to 5 conflict scale. Let's look at the language used at each level in more detail:

» **Level 1 (Problem to Solve)**: The language is generally open-hearted and constructive, and people frequently use factual statements to justify their viewpoints. For example, team members may make statements such as, "Oh, I see what you are saying now. I still prefer the other approach, however, because in the past we've seen fewer bugs and less rework using that technique."
» **Level 2 (Disagreement)**: The language starts to include self-protection. For example, team members may make statements like "I know you think my idea won't work as well, but we tried your approach last time, and there were a lot of problems."

» **Level 3 (Contest):** The team members start using distorted language, such as overgeneralizations, presumptions, and magnified positions. They may make statements like, "He always takes over the demo" and "If only she wasn't on the team…"
» **Level 4 (Crusade):** The conflict becomes more ideological and polarized. The team members begin to make statements like "They're just plain wrong," and "It's not worth even talking to them."
» **Level 5 (World War):** The language is fully combative. The opposing team members rarely speak directly to each other, instead speaking mostly to those "on their side," expressing sentiments like "It's us or them," and "We have to beat them!"

Once we have observed and diagnosed the level of conflict, we can decide what to do about it. If the conflict is at level 1 through 3, do not take any immediate action to resolve the conflict. Instead, first give the team a chance to fix it themselves. If the team can overcome the conflict on their own, they will have built and exercised an important skill. It is okay for them to have some discomfort during the conflict because that experience will better equip them to self-manage similar conflicts in the future. However, if the situation does not improve and instead seems to be escalating, the following guidelines can be useful in resolving the conflict:

» **Level 1 (Problem to Solve):** For a level 1 conflict, try constructing a collaborative scenario to illustrate the competing issues and use that scenario to help build consensus around a decision that everyone can support.
» **Level 2 (Disagreement):** At level 2, conflict resolution typically involves empowering the relevant team members to solve the problem. This approach builds the team members' support for the decision and restores a sense of safety to the group.
» **Level 3 (Contest):** At this level, the conflict has become accusatory. To help fix the issue, we need to accommodate people's differing views. Although this may involve compromising on the work to be done, we should not compromise the team's values.
» **Level 4 (Crusade):** Resolving a level 4 conflict requires diplomacy. Since the communications between opposing sides have largely broken down, the team may need a facilitator to convey messages between the different parties. Our focus should be on de-escalating the conflict in an effort to take it down a level or two.
» **Level 5 (World War):** If a conflict gets to level 5, it may actually be unresolvable. Instead of trying to fix it, we may need to figure out how we can give people ways to live with it. Only at level 5 do we separate the opposing individuals to prevent further harm to each other.

In summary, conflict is normal and inevitable when people work closely together. Coaches, ScrumMasters, and managers often feel obliged to help resolve conflict, but before rushing in, it is best to observe the situation to get a better view of the issues. Leas's model can help us objectively assess the severity of a conflict. We should pay attention to the language being used and give the team an opportunity to resolve the conflict themselves. If we do need to intervene, we should focus on de-escalating the problem by separating facts from emotions and looking for ways to help people move forward, despite their differences.

EXERCISE

Review the following snippets of conversation, and determine the conflict level illustrated in each.

Snippet	Conflict Level
"They have no idea, yet again. We would be better off without them!"	
"Okay, I get that you will have extra work if we choose this option. But so will I if we go with your method. And I'll have to redo this piece each time we set up a new page."	
"That's it! I warned you before. You and me—outside, right now!"	
"I know you have told me before, but I must be losing it. How do I request a ticket again?"	
"You're just pushing for this option because it makes your job easier. You never care about how it impacts anyone else! I'm tired of it. I think we should try something else for once."	

ANSWER

Snippet	Conflict Level
"They have no idea, yet again. We would be better off without them!"	Level 4
"Okay, I get that you will have extra work if we choose this option. But so will I if we go with your method. And I'll have to redo this piece each time we set up a new page."	Level 2
"That's it! I warned you before. You and me—outside, right now!"	Level 5
"I know you have told me before, but I must be losing it. How do I request a ticket again?"	Level 1
"You're just pushing for this option because it makes your job easier. You never care about how it impacts anyone else! I'm tired of it. I think we should try something else for once."	Level 3

 ### Distributed Teams

Distributed stakeholders present a challenge to both face-to-face communication and tools such as information radiators that rely on co-location to work best. However, this is a challenge that most projects have to deal with; surveys have found that more than 50 percent of agile teams have at least one team member in a different physical location than the rest of the team.[10]

To help address this challenge, distributed teams can use communication technologies like video conferencing, live chat, Skype, and other tools to simulate a shared team environment and allow distributed stakeholders to chat and interact as if their colleagues were within earshot. In addition, there are online agile tools that offer features like electronic task boards and story boards that can be used by people in multiple remote locations.

Participatory Decision Models

Participatory decision models present different ways to engage the team in the decision-making process. The speed at which we make decisions and our team's level of agreement with these decisions will impact both project performance and team cohesion. Also, since knowledge worker projects have no tangible, emerging product moving down a production line, communication and decision-making processes become more critical to keep everyone informed and engaged.

Although agile methods use many tools to promote effective communication among stakeholders (e.g., co-location, daily stand-up meetings, planning workshops, retrospectives, etc.), less is written about decision-making tools. This does not mean that stakeholder participation in decisions isn't important, however. If we do not ask team members for their opinions when making decisions, we run the risk of alienating some members of the team. This in turn leads to reduced levels of stakeholder commitment and participation, and could result in missing an important perspective that would help avoid pitfalls later in the project.

Agile methods favor more team empowerment and less command-and-control direction on projects. Although the higher level of team empowerment increases stakeholders' satisfaction and productivity, it also raises the need for effective decision-making processes. So without a project dictator, how do teams make decisions and move forward?

The first thing to realize is that it is not realistic to expect the team to achieve total agreement on all issues and decisions. Sooner or later, we will need some mechanisms in place for making tough decisions while still keeping everyone engaged in the project. These mechanisms are called participatory decision models. Let's look at some examples of these models, along with the advantages and disadvantages of each.

Simple Voting

One simple approach would be to ask the team to vote "for" or "against" an idea by a show of hands. Although this is an easy technique, it limits our opportunities to refine the resulting decision. In striving for a quick result, this method can prevent the team from discussing better alternatives. What if someone has a suggestion for tweaking the options that are being voted on? A simple "for" or "against" vote omits refinement as an integral step. To help address this limitation, teams might discuss their thoughts before voting—but for most straightforward decisions, this discussion would be a poor use of the team's time. Personally, I would vote "No" on this approach.

Figure 4.27: Simple Voting

Thumbs Up/Down/Sideways

Asking for a show of thumbs up, down, or sideways around the room is a more efficient way of achieving a simple vote while still allowing some time to discuss other options. With this technique, we ask those who are holding their thumb sideways why they cannot make up their mind. Sometimes these people are just neutral on the idea, but other times they have a conflict, concern, or question that needs further investigation. This approach is quicker than polling everyone in the group for input, since most people will have no concerns and will just want to move forward.

Figure 4.28: Thumbs Up, Down, or Sideways

Jim Highsmith's Decision Spectrum

Jim Highsmith outlines a great decision-making tool in his book *Agile Project Management: Creating Innovative Products*. Using Highsmith's model, team members indicate how they feel about a decision by placing a check mark on a spectrum ranging from "fully in favor" to "mixed feelings" to "absolutely no, or veto." Highsmith's model is effective because it allows people to both indicate their support for a decision and express their reservations at the same time. It's important to give people an opportunity to voice their concerns if we hope to reach an agreement to go forward while still respecting dissenting views and keeping everyone engaged. This method invites those who are not entirely in favor of an option to share their concerns. Often, just being given the opportunity to register their reservations is enough to allow them to commit to a new direction.

The following is a sample decision spectrum. It can be created on a whiteboard with tape and permanent markers and then easily reused for multiple decision-making sessions.

Figure 4.29: Jim Highsmith's Decision Spectrum

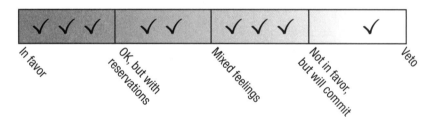

Fist-of-Five Voting

The "fist of five" approach has the advantage of speed (similar to the simple voting method), while still allowing people to indicate their degree of agreement (similar to the decision spectrum method). Using the fist-of-five approach, people vote by showing the number of fingers that indicates their degree of support.

Figure 4.30: Fist-of-Five Voting

© 2012 RMC Publications, Inc • 952.846.4484 • info@rmcproject.com • www.rmcproject.com

A small problem with this approach is that two standards have emerged. To counter this issue, we need to make it clear upfront whether five fingers means "full agreement" or "no, stop." One version of this method, which has been popularized by the American Youth Foundation, registers the level of support by number of fingers raised; a fist (no fingers) means no support, while raising five fingers indicates full support and a desire to lead the charge.

The other popular version of this method uses finger votes to register the amount of resistance or objection to an idea. With this method, the number of fingers raised indicates the following:

» **One finger**: "I totally support this option."
» **Two fingers**: "I support this option with some minor reservations that we probably don't need to discuss."
» **Three fingers**: "I have concerns that we need to discuss."
» **Four fingers**: "I object and want to discuss the issue."
» **Five fingers** (an extended palm like a stop sign): "Stop; I am against this decision."

With participatory decision models, a key point to remember is, "not involved means not committed." We need to find ways to get our stakeholders involved in important project decisions, including iteration and release planning, estimation sessions, and retrospectives. If people are not involved, they will not be committed to the decision and, ultimately, will not be committed to the project.

Leading Effectively

Agile is more humanistic than mechanistic, as evidenced by the agile value of "Individuals and interactions over processes and tools." The concept of valuing people over processes goes beyond how we manage the work to be done on the project; it also impacts how we organize and motivate our team members, and how we assume our role as leaders. Leadership is about tapping into people's intrinsic motivations. To be effective leaders, we need to discover why our people want to do things, understand what motivates them, and then align their project tasks and goals accordingly. It is when we align project objectives with personal objectives that we get higher levels of productivity.

Management versus Leadership

Management has a more mechanical focus than leadership; it is concerned with tasks, control, and speed. In contrast, leadership assumes a humanistic focus on people and purpose; it is more concerned with empowerment, effectiveness, and doing the right things. The following table illustrates the differences between a management focus and leadership focus:

Management Focus	Leadership Focus
Tasks/things	People
Control	Empowerment
Efficiency	Effectiveness
Doing things right	Doing the right things
Speed	Direction
Practices	Principles
Command	Communication

So does this mean that leadership is better than management? Can we have just leadership without management? No; we definitely need the mechanics of management in place. But to be truly effective, we then need to layer leadership on top of those mechanics. We can best amplify team productivity through a combination of management and leadership.

EXERCISE

Review the activities in the table below, and determine whether they are mainly leadership- or management-based.

Activity	Mainly Leadership or Management?
Human resource management	
Career planning	
Team time tracking	
Team member recognition	
Task assignment	
Team brainstorming	
Planning workshops	
Creating Gantt charts	

ANSWER

Activity	Mainly Leadership or Management?
Human Resource management	Management
Career planning	Leadership
Team time tracking	Management
Team member recognition	Leadership
Task assignment	Management
Team brainstorming	Leadership
Planning workshops	Leadership
Creating Gantt charts	Management

T&T | Servant Leadership

Agile promotes a servant leadership model that recognizes that it is the team members, not the leader, coach, ScrumMaster, or project manager, who get the technical work done and achieve the business value. The servant leadership approach redefines the leader's role in relation to the team. It focuses the leader on providing what the team members need, removing impediments to progress, and performing supporting tasks to maximize the team's productivity.

There are four primary duties a leader performs in this role of serving the team:

1. **Shield the team from interruptions**: Servant leaders need to isolate and protect the team members from diversions, interruptions, and requests for work that aren't part of the project.

   When business representatives are closely involved in a project, it can be tempting for them to make side requests for changes or enhancements directly to the developers that would sidetrack the planned development effort. While agile projects positively encourage these business insights and requests, they need to go through the proper channels. Business representatives should make such requests during the iteration planning meeting or submit them to the product owner, who manages the backlog. Part of being a servant leader involves reminding people about the designated channels so the team can maintain their focus on the iteration and establish a reliable velocity. Such progress metrics can then be used to help plan future work.

   Although it is important to shield the team from internal diversions, the project manager must be especially vigilant in protecting the team from external diversions. Time fragmentation— breaking people away from focusing on the project work and moving them back and forth between initiatives—saps productivity. In contrast, shielding the team from noncritical external demands enhances productivity. Physically co-locating team members is an effective way to prevent external interference. If people are still located in their old departments or workspaces, it is too easy for them to be drawn back into nonproject work.

2. **Remove impediments to progress**: Servant leaders need to clear obstacles from the team's path that would cause delay or nonvalue-adding work. These obstacles may include wasted work or compliance activities that divert the team from completing the objectives of the current iteration. In the lean vocabulary, compliance work refers to efforts that do not directly contribute toward delivering business value. For example, this could include duplicated time recording tasks, nonproject meetings, and other administrative activities.

   At the daily stand-up meeting where the team reports on its progress, planned work, and issues, the leader needs to note the issues and work to resolve them, that same day if possible. Removing or easing such impediments will allow the development team to work faster and ultimately deliver more value to the business.

   Some agile project management tools now support impediment backlogs. These backlogs are a kind of prioritized obstacle removal list. Servant leaders can use such tools to track their impediment removal work.

3. **(Re)Communicate project vision**: This may seem like an odd duty to place in the category of servant leadership, but communicating and re-communicating the project vision is critical to successfully leading a team. Only if stakeholders have a clear image of the goals for the completed product and project can they align their decisions with, and work toward, the common project objective. In their best-selling book *The Leadership Challenge*, James Kouzes and Barry Posner say that leaders need to reveal a "beckoning summit" toward which others can "chart their course."[11] Simply stated, a common vision helps to keep people all pulling in the same direction. Divergent views commonly develop between well-intentioned team members. In software projects, for example, a developer's desire for simplicity or a new technology can cause his or her work to diverge from the user's requirements. An analyst's or quality assurance specialist's desire for completeness and conformance may diverge from the

project manager's and sponsor's requirements for progress and completion. Communicating and re-communicating the project vision helps stakeholders recognize these divergences and bring them back in line with the project's objectives.

The most effective leaders (level 5 leaders) dedicate a much higher percentage of their work time to communicating and re-communicating project and corporate vision than do people in the lower leadership levels. Kouzes and Posner believe it is almost impossible for leaders to overcommunicate project vision and state that it is a critical step for effective leadership.

So agile projects should not just have a vision exercise at the project kickoff or when developing the iteration goals. Such a limited focus is not enough. Instead, servant leaders need to continually look for opportunities to communicate the project vision and find new ways to illustrate and reinforce that vision.

4. **Carry food and water.** This duty isn't literally about food and water, it is about providing the essential resources a team needs to keep them nourished and productive. Such resources could include tools, compensation, and encouragement. People who are fueled by professionalism and duty alone can't continue to contribute to the best of their ability, iteration after iteration. Leaders need to learn what motivates their team members as individuals and find ways to reward them for good work. As a simple measure, a great place to start is a sincere "thank you" to someone for their hard work.

Leaders also need to celebrate victories—the large ones, of course, but also the small ones— as the project progresses. It is often tempting to save the project celebrations for the end, but if the team members aren't receiving some regular recognition, the project may never reach a successful conclusion. Celebrations and recognition help build momentum, and leaders need to nourish their teams with such rewards frequently to keep the project moving forward productively.

Training and other professional development activities are also examples of resources the team may need to be productive. The project manager should take an interest in and arrange appropriate training for the individuals on the team. By building the team members' skills, the project will not only gain the benefits of their new knowledge, but such actions also show that we want the team members to grow as individuals, not just extract work and information from them.

Twelve Principles for Leading Agile Projects

In addition to the four core duties we've just discussed, there are other activities that servant leaders should keep in mind. Jeffrey Pinto, in *Project Leadership: from Theory to Practice*, offers the following great list of principles for leaders to follow:[12]

1. Learn the team members' needs.
2. Learn the project's requirements.
3. Act for the simultaneous welfare of the team and the project.
4. Create an environment of *functional accountability*.
5. Have a vision of the completed project.
6. Use the project vision to drive your own behavior.
7. Serve as the central figure in successful project team development.
8. Recognize team conflict as a positive step.
9. Manage with an eye toward ethics.

10. Remember that ethics is not an afterthought, but an integral part of our thinking.
11. Take time to reflect on the project.
12. Develop the trick of *thinking backwards*.

In point 12, thinking backwards means we visualize the end goal and then work backwards to determine what needed to happen to get there and what problems and risks may have occurred. We've already discussed some of these principles in other parts of this chapter, but this list provides a nice summary to keep in mind as we strive to be effective servant leaders.

Leadership Tools and Techniques

The leadership tools and techniques employed on agile projects involve taking a soft-skills approach, rather than a directing, command-and-control project structure. There is a famous quote from Warren Bennis that speaks to the difference between these two approaches: "Management is getting people to do what needs to be done. Leadership is getting people to want to do what needs to be done."[13] Instead of telling people what to do, we need to create an environment where people want to do what needs to be done. The difference between the two environments is like trying to pull a rope (when people want to do what needs to be done) rather than pushing the rope (when people are simply told what to do).

As leaders, we can help create a productive project environment by using practices like modeling the behavior we want the team to follow, using different communication tools to express the project vision, enabling stakeholders to act, and being willing to challenge the status quo.[14] Let's look at these leadership practices in more detail.

Modeling Desired Behavior

In *The Leadership Challenge*, Kouzes and Posner describe a 10-year study that asked more than 75,000 people, "What values, personal traits, or characteristics do you look for or admire in your leader?"[15] The following were the highest-ranked values:

» **Honesty**: People will not follow leaders they know are deceptive, since doing so undermines their own feelings of self-worth. Therefore, leaders should pay special attention to transparency and make sure they follow through on what they say they will do. So we shouldn't hide our mistakes—we should admit them openly. This is not only a healthy approach for us as leaders, but it also sets an example for how we want our team to operate. And we shouldn't do things like ask our team members for estimates and then say we will double the estimates before we give them to management. Such statements hurt our credibility with our team and give them reason to doubt our integrity. A better approach would be to explain the concept of adding a contingency to estimates and discuss how to base that contingency on realistic expectations of the risks involved in the project.
» **Forward-looking**: People expect those who lead them to understand where they are going. Leaders should be able to paint the picture for the team so everyone understands what they are ultimately aiming for.
» **Competent**: Leaders do not need to have the strongest technical skills on the team, since team members are typically happy to provide specialist knowledge when required. But leaders should be competent and not be an embarrassment or liability to the group.
» **Inspiring**: People want to be inspired in their work, rather than be met each day with a sense of doom and gloom. Therefore, leaders need to find ways to explain the project's vision and journey with genuine enthusiasm and spirit.

When we embody these traits as leaders, not only do we encourage people to follow us, we also model the behaviors that we want our team members to emulate. We are, in effect, leading by example.

Communicating the Project Vision

In our earlier discussion of the duties of a servant leader, we talked about the importance of communicating and re-communicating the project vision to keep stakeholders aligned with the project objectives. A leader can use a variety of practices to achieve this, based on what is most effective for the particular team. For example, XP teams use metaphors, some teams develop mantras, and other teams create elevator pitches or project tweets, in which they explain the project purpose in 140 characters or less. Whatever the method used, it is important to frequently communicate the project's goals and objectives to ensure that all stakeholders are aware of and aligned with the vision.

Enabling Others to Act

In order to enable our team members to feel confident in making decisions and taking actions that move the project forward in a productive way, we need to foster a collaborative environment. This involves building trust among team members and strengthening others by sharing power. We also need to create a safe work environment where people are not afraid to ask what they may think are dumb questions. People learn much more quickly when they can raise questions without fear of reprisal or ridicule.

Strengthening others by sharing power means the project manager, ScrumMaster, or leader does not keep the project plan or estimates to him- or herself. Instead, the leader makes sure that information and knowledge are spread throughout the team. For example, this might involve switching from planning tools like Gantt charts that only one or two people update and maintain to using a task board that the whole team engages with. In doing so, the planning and status information is more accessible to the team, and the project benefits because more people vet, update, and optimize the plan.

Figure 4.31: Switching from Exclusive Tools Like
Gantt Charts to Inclusive Tools Like Task Boards

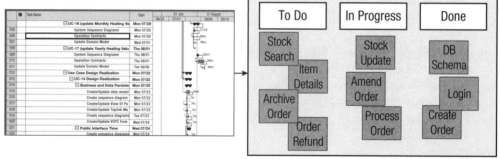

Being Willing to Challenge the Status Quo

Challenging the status quo means we search for innovative ways to change, grow, and improve and then experiment and take risks by constantly generating small wins and learning from our mistakes. Iterations are perfect microcosms for experimentation. We can try new ideas for one or two iterations before committing to them. If the ideas work, we can institutionalize them. If they do not work, it's no big loss; at least we tried, and we learned something from the experience.

Allowing stakeholders to suggest new ideas for improvement and then giving them a chance to try out those ideas is one way to cement the concept that everyone's ideas have value. There is nothing more disheartening than having a good idea fall on deaf ears. If this happens, people will soon stop trying to make suggestions and will no longer care about the project. So to keep our stakeholders engaged, we should take advantage of the opportunities agile projects present us for small-scale, localized experiments in a supportive, low-risk environment.

As leaders, we need to encourage our team to challenge the status quo of how we operate, not only because the team members are in a great position to suggest process improvements, but also because doing so helps to motivate them. To be successful in this effort, we need to have analytical-thinking skills to help our team brainstorm ideas and solutions and active-listening skills to make sure we accurately understand their suggestions.

Professional Responsibility and Ethics

Before we move on to the next chapter, let's look at how PMI's Code of Ethics and Professional Conduct (available on PMI's website: www.pmi.org) applies to stakeholder engagement.[16] We'll cover each of the four main areas of the code—Responsibility, Respect, Fairness, and Honesty—in turn and look at examples of how they relate to the T&Ts and K&Ss discussed in this chapter. As you read this section, think about your real-world projects and how they are impacted by these different aspects of professional responsibility and ethics.

Responsibility

» **Make decisions based on the best interests of the company**. This aspect of professional responsibility affects vendor management and negotiations. When we are selecting vendors and negotiating contracts, we must be sure to put the company's interests first. This rule also impacts conflict resolution and facilitation. When we are faced with a difficult situation, we need to ask ourselves, "Am I making this decision because it is the easiest option for me or the project team, or because it is the best decision for the company?"

» **Protect proprietary information**. This is another aspect of professional responsibility that affects vendor management and negotiations. When we are working with external vendors, how much information can we share? We need to be sure to keep the company's proprietary information confidential during such discussions.

» **Report unethical behavior and violations**. This aspect of professional responsibility may come into play during conflicts, especially if the conflict has escalated to level 4 or 5. When people are no longer behaving appropriately to each other, we have the duty to report unacceptable behavior to our human resources department. If we know that damaging behaviors are occurring but do not act on them, we are ignoring our ethical duty.

Respect

» **Maintain an attitude of mutual cooperation**. The team might want to do things the easy way, while the customer may want things that are technically difficult to develop. Maintaining an attitude of mutual cooperation means we accept and respect such differences and find ways to amicably resolve disputes.

» **Respect cultural differences**. Respecting cultural differences has a strong connection with the K&S of globalization, culture, and team diversity. We need to respect stakeholder differences and find work practices that are mutually agreeable and productive.

» **Negotiate in good faith**. When dealing with vendors, we should not ask for a quote or enter into a negotiation if we have no intention of ever using that vendor. And we should not bring vendors into a bidding situation just to "make up the numbers" or to satisfy political motivations.

> » **Deal with conflict directly**. We have an ethical duty to deal with conflict directly. This means that when we see a conflict increasing in intensity, we should try to de-escalate it by working directly with those who initiated it. This doesn't mean we always intervene rather than allowing stakeholders to try to resolve the conflict themselves, but we do have to know when a situation is getting out of control, and step in when appropriate. Some team conflict is normal and healthy, especially when a team is forming, but when relationships between stakeholders begin to deteriorate, we need to act quickly to intervene.
> » **Do not use your position to influence others**. The person in charge, whether called the ScrumMaster, leader, or project manager, has some level of positional power and authority on the project, even if their role is to serve the team. When facilitating meetings and participatory decision-making sessions, leaders have to be careful to not unduly influence the other team members; it is best for the project if each team member voices his or her own perspective and opinion, rather than simply supporting the leader's view of an issue.

Fairness

> » **Act impartially without bribery**. This one seems pretty obvious, right? But where do we draw the line? What about accepting a holiday gift basket from a vendor? Is a lunch meeting at a fancy restaurant okay? Depending on the value of the items received, these types of things are probably acceptable. Now what about off-site customer appreciation events that might be offered by a vendor, such as a fully funded trip to a vacation destination? Such extravagant gifts are probably a problem. When accepting any kind of vendor offer, we need to be very careful about complying both with our company's gift acquisition rules and PMI's Code of Ethics and Professional Conduct.[17]
> » **Look for and disclose conflicts of interest**. When negotiating, we need to make sure we disclose any potential conflicts of interest, such as board memberships or having some level of ownership of competing companies or products. As an example, imagine you are asked to help a company select an agile planning tool, and you happen to have a relationship with a company that offers such a tool. (Such a relationship could be anything from having an ownership stake in the company to simply receiving referral bonuses from them.) In this case, you have an ethical duty to disclose the connection, and you may even want to (or be obliged to) suggest that you should not be involved in the selection or negotiation process.
> » **Do not discriminate**. This point has become increasingly relevant as the diversity and globalization of project teams has increased. We need to make sure that any personal prejudices do not influence our facilitation duties or our role as a servant leader.
> » **Do not use your position for personal or business gain**. This aspect of professional responsibility includes not asking vendors or more junior team members for favors on pet projects or outside contracts. And while it is acceptable to network and build mutual connections, it would not be ethical to use your position as a hiring manager at a company to get a job for a friend or family member.

Honesty

> » **Understand the truth**. This point applies to all discussions, meetings, and investigations of issues with our stakeholders. We have an obligation to discover and understand the truth, even if it is not what we want to hear—such as when a customer does not like our design or we find that our own lack of communication was the source of a problem. In order to effectively resolve issues and make decisions, we need to have a clear and common understanding of the facts before we begin brainstorming solutions.
> » **Be truthful in all communications**. When reporting project progress, we want to emphasize all the good work the team has done, but if we are behind plan, then we need to honestly report that we are behind. Agile progress reporting is very transparent and encourages truthful communications; if the customer has only accepted 50 percent of the required features, then we are only 50 percent done.

Practice Exam

1. User stories feature which of the following components?

    A. Role, Function, Benefit
    B. Reason, Functionality, Benefit
    C. Risk, Function, Benefit
    D. Risk, Feature, Business Reason

2. Wireframes, personas, and user stories can all play a part in understanding stakeholder objectives. Which of the circumstances outlined below would be a good fit for the use of personas?

    A. When the conversation is centered on the high-level flow of a process
    B. When we are trying to better understand stakeholder demographics and general needs
    C. When we need to capture the high-level objective of a specific requirement
    D. When we want to communicate what features will be included in the next release

3. When comparing communication styles, which of the following is true?

    A. Paper-based communication has the lowest efficiency and the highest richness.
    B. Face-to-face communication has the highest efficiency and the lowest richness.
    C. Paper-based communication has the highest efficiency and the lowest richness.
    D. Face-to-face communication has the highest efficiency and the highest richness.

4. Your project team has some conflict, and you are trying to diagnose what level of conflict they are at. You notice that statements such as "Team B has no clue again!" are becoming commonplace. What level of conflict would you say the team is experiencing?

    A. Level 1
    B. Level 2
    C. Level 3
    D. Level 4

5. High-visibility project displays are sometimes called:

    A. Project radiators
    B. Information refrigerators
    C. Information radiators
    D. Project distributors

6. The INVEST mnemonic for user stories looks for attributes that include:

    A. Independent, Negotiable, Smart
    B. Valuable, Easy-to-use, Timely
    C. Negotiable, Estimatable, Small
    D. Independent, Valuable, Timely

7. Burn down charts display the following attributes on their axes:

    A. X axis = points remaining; Y axis = calendar time
    B. X axis = estimated time remaining; Y axis = calendar time
    C. X axis = calendar time; Y axis = estimated effort remaining
    D. X axis = calendar time; Y axis = calendar time

8. Wireframe models help agile teams to:

    A. Test designs
    B. Confirm designs
    C. Configure reports
    D. Track velocity

9. What is velocity not used for?

    A. Gauging the work capacity of the team
    B. Checking our release plan validity
    C. Getting a sense of work done per iteration
    D. Defining feature requirements

10. The definition of done is frequently discussed with stakeholders so that:

    A. Functionality can be negotiated until the last responsible moment.
    B. Everyone has a clear understanding of what completion means.
    C. Team members get to improve their negotiation skills.
    D. Active listening reveals previously undiscussed requirements.

11. Wireframes, personas, and user stories can all play a part in understanding stakeholder objectives. Which of the circumstances outlined below would be a good fit for the use of user stories?

    A. When the conversation is centered on the high-level flow of a process
    B. When we are trying to better understand stakeholder demographics and general needs
    C. When we need to capture the high-level objective of a specific requirement
    D. When we want to communicate what features will be included in the next release

12. Agile modelling aims to:

    A. Capture the intent of the design in a barely sufficient way
    B. Capture the intent of the design in detail-oriented way
    C. Deliver extraneous documentation for the project
    D. Recognize that the value of modeling increases with time spent

13. Which of the following is a valid requirements hierarchy progression from large to small?

    A. Task, User Story, Epic
    B. Feature, User Story, Task
    C. Epic, User Story, Feature
    D. Epic, Task, Feature

14. Your team seems to unproductively debate even trivial decisions. To help them along, you could try:

    A. Fist-of-five voting
    B. Bare fist fighting
    C. Wideband Delphi
    D. Retrospectives

15. Which of the following statements is true for measuring team velocity?

    A. Velocity is not accurate when there are meetings that cut into development time.
    B. Velocity measurements are disrupted when some project resources are part-time.
    C. Velocity tracking does not allow for scope changes during the project.
    D. Velocity measurements account for work done and disruptions on the project.

16. You have been assigned to lead a geographically distributed agile team. To assist with communication, the best option would be to:

    A. Ask team members to send photos of themselves so you know what they look like.
    B. Choose a common language for project communications.
    C. Set up some initial face-to-face meetings for everyone to meet.
    D. Define common working hours so everyone can better communicate.

17. The relationship between leadership and management in agile methods is:

    A. Leadership replaces all aspects of management.
    B. Leadership is subservient to management.
    C. Management and leadership are used together.
    D. Management and leadership are not compatible.

18. Wireframes, personas, and user stories can all play a part in understanding stakeholder objectives. Which of the circumstances outlined below would be a good fit for the use of wireframes?

    A. When the conversation is centered on the high-level flow of a process
    B. When we are trying to better understand stakeholder demographics and general needs
    C. When we need to capture the high-level objective of a specific requirement
    D. When we want to communicate what features will be included in the next release

Answers

1. Answer: A
   Explanation: The format of a user story is "As a <Role>, I want <Functionality>, so that <Business Benefit>." Risks and reasons are not common attributes of user story templates.

2. Answer: B
   Explanation: Personas would be a good fit when we are trying to better understand stakeholder demographics and general needs.

3. Answer: D
   Explanation: Recall that in the communication effectiveness graph, paper-based communication is in the lower left corner (low effectiveness, low richness) and face-to-face communications (two people at a whiteboard) are in the upper right corner (high effectiveness, high richness).

4. Answer: C
   Explanation: "Team B has no clue again" falls into the category of overgeneralizations, presumptions, and magnified positions, which indicates a level 3 type conflict. At level 2, they wouldn't have said the "no clue again" overgeneralization, and at level 4, the language likely would have been more ideological and hostile.

5. Answer: C
   Explanation: The term Alistair Cockburn coined for these high-visibility displays of project data is "information radiators." Cockburn compares this to the practice of locking information away in plans that few people get to see (information refrigerators).

6. Answer: C
   Explanation: INVEST is the mnemonic for Independent, Negotiable, Valuable, Estimatable, Small, and Testable. So option C is the only choice with a valid combination of the attributes. Smart and Timely are not part of the acronym.

7. Answer: C
   Explanation: Burn down charts always show calendar time on the X axis. They may show either points remaining or estimated time remaining on the Y axis. Option D, which plots calendar time against calendar time, would just produce a straight line that does not tell us much.

8. Answer: B
   Explanation: Wireframes are used to confirm designs; they are not detailed enough to test designs or configure reports.

9. Answer: D
   Explanation: Velocity is a versatile metric that does indeed provide insight into team capacity (how much work the team can likely deliver in an iteration), release plan validity (if we are averaging 50 points per iteration and have 500 points of work remaining, then it looks like we are on track to complete the project within the 11 iterations remaining), and finally work done per iteration (the team is averaging 50 points per iteration). It is not used in defining the requirements of a feature, but velocity does impact which features can be built within a given period of time.

10. Answer: B
    Explanation: The reason to have frequent discussions on the definition of done is to help mitigate the differences in opinion that can result when new functionality is described from a variety of

viewpoints. The definition of done is not intended to be used to negotiate functionality, improve negotiation skills, or surface new requirements (although that may occur). Instead, we have these discussions to make sure everyone has a common understanding of what completion or success will look like.

11. **Answer: C**
    Explanation: User stories are used when we need to capture the high-level objective of a specific requirement.

12. **Answer: A**
    Explanation: Agile models are lightweight, barely sufficient (just enough detail) models to capture the high-value benefits of modeling without too much of the lower-value development time taken to create very detailed or polished models. We want to focus on the product being developed, rather than on generating extraneous documentation.

13. **Answer: B**
    Explanation: The question asks for the progression from large to small. Since Task is the smallest planning unit, options that end in Epic or Feature are not a valid progression. (Note: Although you will not be tested on the alternate requirements hierarchies that include epics, you may still see the term "epics" as a distractor in answer choices.)

14. **Answer: A**
    Explanation: When struggling to make simple decisions effectively, we should introduce participatory decision models such as fist-of-five voting. Wideband Delphi is a group estimation approach that would only really help if the question said they were having difficulty agreeing on estimates. Retrospectives are group-based reflection and learning sessions that would probably not help with decision making, and bare fist fighting is, sadly, now in conflict with PMI's Code of Ethics and Professional Conduct.[18]

15. **Answer: D**
    Explanation: Velocity is a measure of work done (and team capacity) net of all the interruptions and other things that occur on projects. So it does account for meetings, part-time resources, and scope changes that are all common on today's projects.

16. **Answer: C**
    Explanation: If possible, setting up some initial face-to-face meetings for everyone to meet is an effective way of improving remote communications later in the project. Once people have met face-to-face, it is generally much easier to follow up with e-mail, phone calls, etc. Defining common working hours or a common language might appear to help, but it can also be viewed as not being respectful. Sending photos is also unlikely to assist much, and it is certainly not the best option.

17. **Answer: C**
    Explanation: Agile methods employ a combination of management and leadership. Leadership neither totally replaces nor is subservient to management, and since the two approaches can be used together, they are not incompatible.

18. **Answer: A**
    Explanation: Wireframes would be a good fit when the conversation is centered on the high-level flow of a process.

BOOSTING TEAM PERFORMANCE PRACTICES

Chapter Five

Quicktest

» People over process
» Adaptive leadership
  – Stages of team formation
» Emotional intelligence
» Empowered teams
  – Self-organizing and self-directing
  – Servant leadership

» Building high-performance teams
  – Guidelines for managers
  – Characteristics of high-performing teams
  – Team dysfunctions
» Personal and team motivation
» Daily stand-up meetings
» Coaching and mentoring
» Brainstorming
  – Quiet writing, round robin, free-for-all
  – Dot voting, multi-voting

» Team space
» Co-located and distributed teams
  – Osmotic communication
  – Tacit knowledge
  – Communication tools
» Agile tooling
  – Low-tech, high-touch tools
  – Digital tools

This chapter is all about teams. For the exam—and to be successful on real-world agile projects—you need to understand when and how teams work best, and how to create self-organizing, empowered teams. We touched on related ideas in chapter 4, Stakeholder Engagement, so in this chapter you will see some overlap in concepts like shielding team members from outside interruptions and building team consensus. However, we will also discuss new topics, including attributes of high-performance teams and agile coaching.

In This Chapter

This chapter is broken into two sections, or practice areas, related to team performance. In the first section, Understanding Team Performance, we'll discuss the leadership, emotional intelligence, and team performance concepts that are tested on the exam. In the second section, Team Practices, we'll cover the techniques and activities that high-performing teams use on agile projects.

The following chart shows the tools and techniques and knowledge and skills associated with each practice. Although the names of these practices are not official terms that will appear on the exam, organizing the concepts in this way provides the context of why and how you use the T&Ts and K&Ss that you will be tested on.

Practice	Tool/Technique	Knowledge/Skill (Level)
Understanding team performance	» Adaptive leadership » Emotional intelligence	» Building empowered teams (Level 1) » Building high-performance teams (Level 2) » Team motivation (Level 1)
Team practices	» Daily stand-ups » Co-located teams » Team space » Agile tooling	» Coaching and mentoring (Level 1) » Brainstorming techniques (Level 1) » Distributed teams (Level 2)

 Remember, knowledge and skill subject areas are tested by recall-type questions that assess whether you remember the *How* and *Why* of the topics being tested. Tool and technique subjects are typically examined through *Do, Calculate,* or *Describe what happens next* types of questions. Be ready for both of these *Tell Me* and *Show Me* types of questions on the exam.

Understanding Team Performance

Agile methods talk a lot about process with their focus on concepts like iterations, backlogs, and reviews. This focus is ironic when the first value in the Agile Manifesto is "Individuals and interactions over processes and tools." So why does this occur? A major reason is that processes and tools are simply easier to describe, classify, and provide guidance for than trickier topics related to individuals and interactions. Individuals and interactions cannot readily be referred to in general terms because people vary so much—in skill sets, attitudes, experiences, perspectives, culture, etc. Individuals and interactions are less definite than processes and tools; in other words, the right thing to do with one team might be the wrong approach to take with another.

While we hear expressions like "The soft stuff is the hard stuff," we need to recognize it's not just the hard stuff—it's also the most important stuff. Trying to quantify the significance between good process versus good people is in itself problematic, but it can help emphasize the need to focus on the people side of projects, even if that focus may not be your area of expertise or where you are most comfortable. Let's look at an example of such a quantification, as it relates to coming up with realistic project estimates.

Estimating software projects is notoriously difficult because of all the inherent risk involved in developing solutions for new business problems that have high rates of change. Despite this difficulty, software companies still need a way to bid on projects and estimate their likely budgets. As a result, many smart people have studied the subject extensively to come up with solutions.

The content you need to understand for the exam will be covered in this book, but if the soft skills topics discussed in this chapter, including agile coaching, conflict resolution, and negotiation, are new to you or if you want to learn more about them for personal development purposes, I recommend Lyssa Adkins' book, *Coaching Agile Teams* (Addison Wesley, 2010).

One of the most popular solutions is the software estimation model called COCOMO (from the term "Constructive Cost Model"). This model was created by reverse engineering the inputs from thousands of completed software projects that had a known exact cost. The idea behind the model was to assess a large number of projects to see if there was some correlation between project input variables and the final cost and to then use this data as a basis for estimating future projects. The method has proven successful; the COCOMO II model is at the heart of many commercial estimation systems used today. Figure 5.1 shows the COCOMO II weighting factors for seven of the input variables, one of which is "people factors."

Figure 5.1: Weighting Factors for COCOMO Input Variables

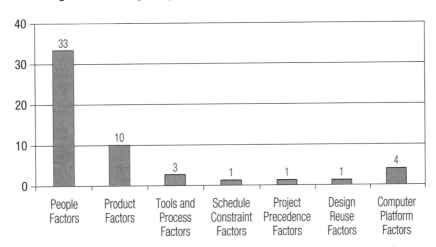

In looking at figure 5.1, we can see that "People Factors" has a score of 33 and "Tools and Process Factors" has a score of 3. This means when calculating the final cost of a software project, the impact of people factors (such as poor, average, or best-in-class ability and skills) is over 10 times more significant than the tools and processes those people follow.

As evidenced by this data, the Agile Manifesto's idea of valuing individuals over processes is indeed the path to project success. Good people who have few or no processes in place can succeed even on difficult projects, yet poorly skilled or poorly aligned teams often fail, even with the best processes. As leaders of teams, we should be focusing our efforts on people factors to get the maximum return on performance. This is why boosting team performance practices is so important.

T&T Adaptive Leadership

Adaptive leadership refers to the concept of adapting how we lead a team based on the specific circumstances and how mature the team is in its formation. Team formation typically follows the stages of *Forming, Storming, Norming,* and *Performing*. These stages are just what they seem—in Forming, people come together as a team. Then there is some turmoil, or Storming, as people learn to work together. The team normalizes (Norming), becoming comfortable in the roles and relationships, before becoming a highly functional, or Performing, team that works effectively together. These stages, originally identified by Bruce Tuckman, are followed by a disengagement phase called *Adjourning* or *Mourning*, since people often miss being on a high-performing team after it's disbanded.[1]

Figure 5.2 illustrates the different phases of the model, showing that the team may cycle through Storming, Norming, and Performing multiple times. This is particularly true when changes happen to the project team, such as people leaving or joining the group. Team members then have to reset and sort out the roles, relationships, and responsibilities within the new team structure.

Figure 5.2: Five Stages of Team Formation and Development

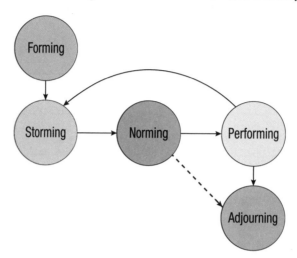

As a results-oriented team driver, I personally prefer another way to illustrate this model—from a performance perspective. As indicated in figure 5.3, we need to get to the Performing phase to get the most out of the team.

Figure 5.3: Stages of Team Formation and Development

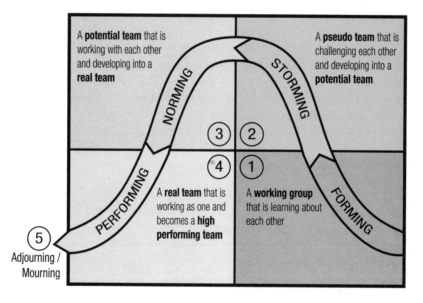

Here we see that teams start in the lower right Forming quadrant as they learn about each other. Then they move through Storming (challenging each other) and Norming (learning how to work with each other), before finally arriving at the Performing phase (working as one). Figure 5.3 also points out that we typically start with a collection of people on our project, rather than a "real team." During Storming, we have a "pseudo team," which transforms into a "potential team" during Norming, and becomes a real team once they are Performing.

Now let's look at how this concept applies to situational leadership. As leaders, we can help the team through the stages by adjusting our focus according to figure 5.4, which was developed by Ken Blanchard and Paul Hersey:[2]

Figure 5.4: Situational Leadership Model

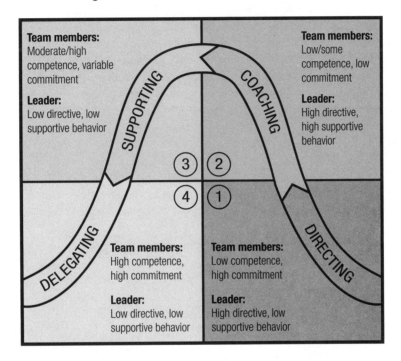

This model shows that Tuckman's Forming stage maps to Blanchard and Hersey's Directing style of leadership. Early in a team's formation, the role of an agile team leader is to directly help with project activities and present a clear, tactical picture of what needs to be done. The leader may also make a lot of requests like "Help me see it" or ask questions like "Where is the problem?" to assist team members in identifying and articulating the issues.

As teams pass into the Storming phase, there is generally plenty of disagreement, open conflict, and harsh dialogue. During this stage, the leader needs to assume the Coaching role to help team members resolve conflicts without damaging relationships. Keep in mind that some conflict is good, so we shouldn't mollycoddle our team too much. Let the disputes occur, but act as a referee or safety value to ensure the conflict does not go too far.

When a team is in the Norming phase, it means the team has essentially created rules to help govern itself. This stage does not mean the team leader can simply go into cruise control mode, however. Instead, the leader needs to play a Supporting role. The team will still need help with conflict resolution, as well as reminders to enforce the rules (norms) they have just created. This is a good time for the leader to challenge the team with high-level goals such as "The team is responsible for tracking velocity on the project," or "Everyone owns testing." This stage is also a good time to tackle issues raised at retrospectives.

The final Performing stage is not a given—many (if not most) project teams never reach this phase because organizations make too many changes to the teams, which instead sends the teams through the Storming and Norming phases again. Perfoming teams are autonomous, empowered, self-managing, and self-policing. They require little more than to be pointed in the right direction and to be given regular recognition and appreciation for their high performance. Blanchard and Hersey's Delegating leadership style in this phase means the leader brings work and challenges to the team for them to solve.

It seems so neat and clean to define the stages of team formation like this. Does that mean all teams go through these phases in a predictable way? No, each team is different. The people who make up the team and factors like whether any of the team members have worked together in the past affect the way in which the team moves through the stages. This brings us to another question: Do teams progress as a whole unit through the stages? Not really. People and teams are complex and messy. The best we can do is be aware of these models, look for signs that the team is in a particular phase, and then act accordingly as leaders. Such general pointers are useful, but we should never expect teams to proceed in an orderly fashion and follow the stereotypical stages.

EXERCISE

In the columns below, match the Tuckman stage of team formation with the corresponding Blanchard and Hersey situational leadership style by drawing lines between the two columns.

Stages of Team Formation	Situational Leadership Styles
Forming	Supporting
Storming	Delegating
Norming	Directing
Performing	Coaching

ANSWER

The team formation stages and the adaptive leadership styles match up as follows:

Stages of Team Formation	Situational Leadership Styles
Forming	Supporting
Storming	Delegating
Norming	Directing
Performing	Coaching

T&T Emotional Intelligence

One of the best ways to stay flexible in leading or managing unpredictable teams is to continuously try to improve our emotional intelligence. Emotional intelligence is our ability to identify, assess, and influence the emotions of ourselves, other individuals, and groups. Figure 5.5 presents different aspects of emotional intelligence, broken into quadrants.

Figure 5.5: Aspects of Emotional Intelligence

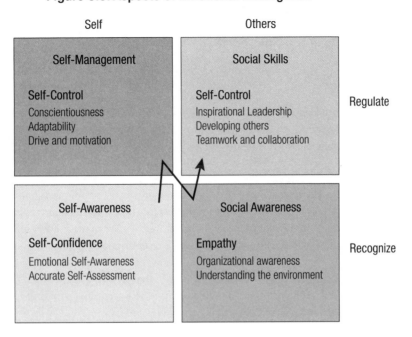

This diagram places "Self" on the left side and "Others" on the right side, and the model vertically splits into the skills of "Recognize" and "Regulate." While everyone has some level of skill in all quadrants, it is usually easiest to start improving our emotional intelligence with ourselves at "Self-Awareness" (bottom left). Next we can learn how to regulate ourselves through "Self-Management" (top left), then build "Social Awareness" (bottom right), and finally hone our "Social Skills" (top right).

In other words, we first need to recognize our own feelings. Once we understand our emotions, we can begin to control them. So as a start, we recognize what makes us angry, frustrated, happy, or thankful. We then need to realize we have the power to choose how we feel and respond. We could simply follow the normal pattern of stimulus leading to a response, but as humans, we have the unique ability to insert a decision between stimulus and response. We have the ability to choose if we will allow something to continue to upset us or if we will respond to it differently. Recognizing that we have a choice is a key part of becoming self-aware and moving on to mastering self-management.

We should also keep in mind that how well we manage ourselves and our attitude has an impact on those around us, particularly if we are in a position of leadership. As emotional intelligence expert Daniel Goleman explains, "The leader's mood and behaviors drive the moods and behaviors of everyone else. A cranky and ruthless boss creates a toxic organization filled with negative underachievers who ignore opportunities."[3]

Once we've sorted ourselves out in the areas of self-awareness and self-management, we should work on developing social awareness and empathy for others. As an agile coach or manager, we need to be able to identify when team members are stuck, frustrated, or upset in order to help them. Then once we're able to recognize when others need help, we use social skills, such as the ability to influence, inspire, lead, and develop others, to help our team members do their work and collaborate with each other.

Building Empowered Teams

Empowered teams are both self-organizing and self-directing. Let's discuss each of these characteristics in turn.

Self-Organizing Teams

Being told what to do is never a recipe for runaway success. The receivers of tasks end up second-guessing the direction or sequence of upcoming activities, and the providers of instructions get frustrated with unforeseen obstacles and technical issues. Pushing out instructions is like pushing rope—it's not very effective and it never really brings out the best in people.

In contrast, members of empowered teams are freed from command-and-control management and can use their own knowledge to determine how best to do their job. Empowering teams also enables organizations to tap into people's natural ability to manage complexity. We manage complexity every day, by juggling our work life, home life, e-mails, phone calls, and appointments. Organizations often fail to capitalize on this ability when it comes to executing project tasks, however. Instead of presenting team members with a number of items that have to be accomplished, they present a set of ordered tasks that, in reality, might best be done in a different way. Allowing teams to self-organize enables us to use the individual complexity management skills that we all have.

In addition, managers and schedulers do not have the same technical insight into task execution as do the people performing the work on a daily basis. So managers and leaders of agile teams are better served by allowing team members to self-organize their own work. Instead of providing detailed task lists, leaders of agile teams should describe the iteration goals at a high level and let the team determine how to best accomplish the work, within the ground rules of what is acceptable within the organization.

This recognition that the team is in the best position to organize the project work is liberating and motivating for the team members. People work harder and take more pride in their work when they are recognized as experts of their domain. When self-organizing teams select work items from the queue of waiting work, they have the expertise to choose those items that are not blocked for any reason, that they are capable of doing, and that will bring them toward the iteration goal. This practice alleviates many of the technical blockages seen in push systems where the task list and sequence is imposed on the team.

So we need to delegate responsibility for success to the team and allow them to do what is necessary to achieve the goals. This is the "downward serving" or servant leadership model used by agile methods. Instead of a "directing" style, which is a command-and-control approach where instructions are passed from the project manager to team leads down to team members, agile projects take a servant leadership approach, where the project manager or leader shields the team from interruptions, removes impediments, communicates the project vision, and provides support and encouragement.

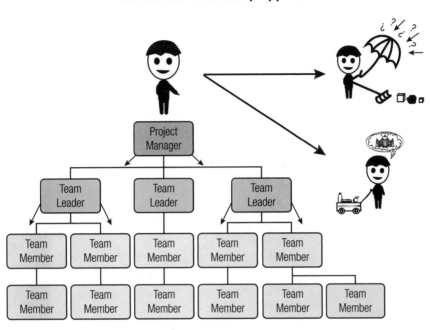

Figure 5.6: Moving from a Command-and-Control Approach to a Servant Leadership Approach

Self-Directing Teams

Self-directing teams are teams that work collectively to create team norms and make their own local decisions. This means they not only figure out the best way to accomplish the work they committed to for an iteration, but they also resolve many of the day-to-day issues that crop up along the way. Project managers or leaders can support and reinforce this behavior by respecting the team's estimates and decisions and by allowing them to make mistakes and correct them.

This does not mean the project manager abdicates responsibility to the team. Instead it means the team is given freedom within the confines of an iteration. If the team's estimates are way off or if they make poor technical decisions, these items will be detected and discussed at the iteration retrospective. The issues should then improve during the next iteration, and within a more few iterations, the team's estimates and technical decisions will likely be better than what the project manager could have produced.

Keep in mind that the self-organizing and self-directing attributes of agile teams are goals; we do not start there. Teams initially need support and guidance as they come to grips with the project scope, tools, and Forming and Storming aspects of the project. Then when they are in the Norming phase, the project manager can introduce the goals of self-organization and self-direction as long-term objectives for the group.

EXERCISE

For each behavior listed below, place a check mark in the appropriate column to indicate whether it is a command-and-control approach to managing projects or a servant leadership approach.

Behavior	Command and Control	Servant Leadership
Handing out detailed task lists		
Doing administrative work for team members		
Creating the entire project's WBS one weekend so as not to disturb the team		
Posting the project Gantt chart on the office wall		
Posting a "suggestions" box on the office wall		

ANSWER

A command-and-control management approach does not accept that team members have the majority of the answers and excludes them from planning and scheduling activities.

Behavior	Command and Control	Servant Leadership
Handing out detailed tasks lists	✓ (This behavior means the project manager does not recognize that team members are best placed to determine task-based work.)	
Doing administrative work for team members		✓ (By doing administrative work for the team, the project manager is allowing the team to spend more time on value-added work.)
Creating the entire project's WBS one weekend so as not to disturb the team	✓ (By creating the project's WBS without the team, the project manager is not incorporating the team's local knowledge.)	

Behavior	Command and Control	Servant Leadership
Posting the project Gantt chart on the office wall	✓ (Gantt charts are typically controlled by one person and are not easy for team members to adjust. By relying on such a tool, the project manager is not recognizing that the team may want to change things as the project progresses.)	
Posting a "suggestions" box on the office wall		✓ (This behavior means the project manager is looking for input from the team members.)

K&S Level 2 — Building High-Performance Teams

In their book *The Wisdom of Teams*, Jon Katzenbach and Douglas Smith define a team as "a small number of people with complementary skills who are committed to a common purpose, performance goals and approach for which they hold themselves mutually accountable."[4] There are some valuable aspects of this definition that are worth discussing further. First, note that teams are described here as generally "small." We often see teams of 10 or 20 people. As team sizes grow, larger groups usually need to be broken into multiple subteams and include people from several different departments or divisions. Keeping a team small (12 or fewer members, for example) allows team members to develop better relationships and communicate more directly.

Second, team members have "complementary skills." While individual team members may not possess all the skills required to complete a project on their own, the team collectively has the necessary skills. This could mean the team consists of specialists who all own their role in the project, but agile methods also promote the use of generalizing specialists (multiskilled individuals who can readily move between roles). For example, an agile project in a software environment might have business analysts who can also perform quality assurance work or developers with good analysis skills. Generalizing specialists with cross-functional skills can perform many different tasks on projects and can help smooth resourcing peaks and troughs.

Third, teams are defined as being "committed to a common purpose." This means team members are aligned behind a project goal that supersedes their personal agendas. Teams also share common "performance goals" and a common "approach." In other words, team members are in alignment (if not always in agreement) as to how the goals will be measured and how the team should go about the work. Finally, there's the idea that team members "hold themselves mutually accountable." In other words, the team has shared ownership for the outcome of the project.

Many people have researched how we build such high-performance teams, including Carl Larson and Frank LaFasto, authors of the book *Teamwork*. The following guidelines for managers are influenced by their research:[4]

» **Create a shared vision for the team**: Doing so enables the team to make faster decisions and builds trust.
» **Set realistic goals**: We should set people up to succeed, not fail, so goals need to be achievable.
» **Limit team size to 12 or fewer members**: Small teams communicate better and can support tacit (unwritten) knowledge.
» **Build a sense of team identity**: Having a team identity helps increase each team member's loyalty to the team and their support for other team members.
» **Provide strong leadership**: Leaders should be there to point out the way, and then let the team own the mission.

Lyssa Adkins has also explored the concept of high-performance teams and identifies the following characteristics of such teams:[5]

» They are **self-organizing**, rather than role- or title-based.
» They are **empowered** to make decisions.
» They truly believe that **as a team they can solve any problem**.
» They are committed to **team success** vs. success at any cost.
» The team **owns its decisions and commitments**.
» **Trust**, vs. fear or anger, motivates them.
» They are **consensus-driven**, with full divergence and then convergence.
» And they live in a world of constant **constructive disagreement**.

Most of these items are self-explanatory or have been discussed already in this book. Let's look at the last two items in more detail, however. Item 7 ("They are consensus-driven, with full divergence and then convergence") speaks to establishing a safe environment in which team members debating or arguing over issues is seen as healthy and is encouraged because this practice ultimately leads to better decisions and stronger buy-in to those decisions once they are made. Divergence (the argument and debate) and convergence (the agreement about the best solution) increase the team's commitment.

Item 8 ("High-performance teams live in a world of constant constructive disagreement") is related to item 7. Constructive disagreement is vital for really understanding and working out issues. Patrick Lencioni, author of *The Five Dysfunctions of a Team*, lists the following dysfunctions that damage and limit team performance:[6]

1. **Absence of trust**: Team members are unwilling to be vulnerable within the group.
2. **Fear of conflict**: The team seeks artificial harmony over constructive, passionate debate.
3. **Lack of commitment**: Team members don't commit to group decisions or simply feign agreement with them.
4. **Avoidance of accountability**: Team members duck the responsibility of calling peers on counterproductive behavior or low standards.
5. **Inattention to results**: Team members prioritize their individual needs, such as personal success, status, or ego, before team success.

These dysfunctions all stem from avoiding conflict (or constructive disagreement) and not having a safe environment where it is okay to ask questions. Establishing a safe environment for disagreement is key to success; such an environment allows team members to build a strong commitment to decisions. If they have such a commitment when they encounter the inevitable obstacles on a project, rather than returning to management with a list of reasons why something cannot be done, they instead push past the obstacles or find a way around them.

K&S
Level 1

Team Motivation

What motivates people goes far beyond paying them a salary. Salaries simply encourage people to show up to work every day. Once they are at work, employees' productivity levels vary from someone who undermines or is a net drain on the project to a critical contributor who brings passionate innovation to the organization.

Figure 5.7: Net Contribution

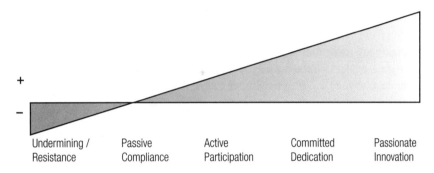

Team motivation is the art of encouraging people toward the right-hand side of the continuum illustrated in figure 5.7. Alistair Cockburn has described team motivation as an overall propulsion vector of team members in a raft. In other words, if the team members' individual motivations are personal and have no alignment toward the project goal, then the overall team vector (direction and speed) is likely to be small and not well directed toward the project goal.

Figure 5.8: Effect of Not Aligning Team Members' Motivations Toward the Project Goal

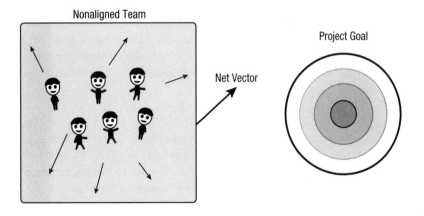

If, however, we can find a way to align team members' personal goals with the project goal, we greatly magnify the project's net vector toward successful project completion, as illustrated in figure 5.9.

Figure 5.9: Effect of Aligning Team Members' Motivations Toward the Project Goal

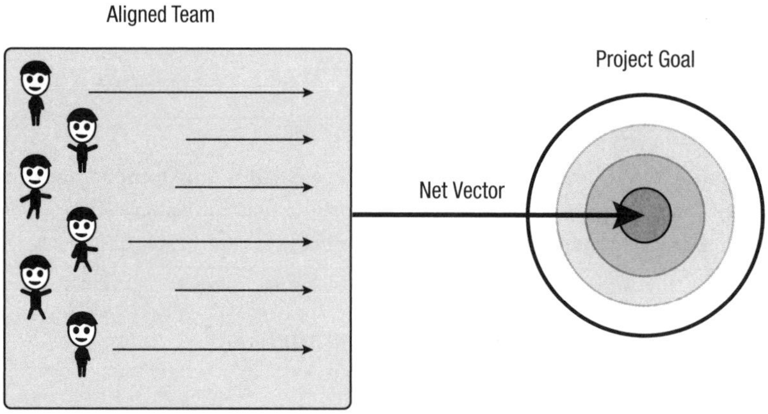

To achieve this alignment, we need to research and fully understand the personal motivators of individuals on the team and the motivators for the team as a group, using techniques like one-on-one interviews. Imagine, for example, that you have a team member named Bob who is six months away from retirement and just wants his last months of work to be as easy as possible. You have another team member, Tim, who is mad because he wanted to use a particular technology for the website but the architecture group chose a different tool. And yet another team member, Jane, is looking for a new job because she was not given the team lead role she wanted.

Once we've done the research and fully understand what motivates (and demotivates) people, we can begin to determine if some elements of what they want can be worked into the project plan. For example, this may mean saying, "Bob, I know you are retiring in six months, but wouldn't winning 'Project of the Year' be a great way to be remembered? We have a good chance if we can pull this off." For Tim, the motivator may be, "I know we did not select your preferred technology for the new site, but could we use it to build our help system and knowledge base? Can we put you in charge of that part of the project?" And for Jane, you may offer a motivator like, "Jane, how about we make you team lead for the next two iterations with a review at the retrospectives? I know it is not the full-time role you wanted, but it will be good experience and you can honestly put it on your resume."

These are artificially easy examples in the interest of keeping the descriptions short, but they help illustrate that most projects have opportunities for incorporating team members' personal goals into the project goals—even if it is only temporarily, for a couple of iterations. By finding a way to align personal goals with project goals, people see what's in it for them and their motivation and productivity levels increase substantially.

Candid conversations explaining why the project is important to the company can also help motivate the team. Try getting an executive or sponsor to outline for the team what success on the initiative means. Having a senior member of the organization communicate an inspiring vision of what the organization hopes the project will achieve is well worth the phone calls and e-mails to make it happen. Plus, having the team members know that someone who is significant to them cares if the project is a success is also a powerful motivator.

The final point I'd like to make regarding team motivation is that, while it is good to understand and incorporate individual motivators, we want to make sure we cement company and team objectives over individual objectives. It is important to do things like celebrating victories as a team and coming up with whole-team rewards, rather than individual rewards for discrete pieces of project work. We need to promote the "mutually accountable" aspect of teamwork.

Team Practices

Now let's move on to the Team Practices section of this chapter. Team Practices refers to the activities teams do to be more effective. In this section, we will discuss daily stand-up meetings, brainstorming techniques, and other tools and techniques used for both co-located and distributed teams.

T&T   Daily Stand-Ups

Daily stand-up meetings are a core practice of agile teams. They are short, focused meetings that negate the need for most other team status meetings. Daily stand-ups are timeboxed to 15 minutes or less and are kept on schedule by having attendees only answer three questions. Stand-ups are "for-the-team" and "performed by-the-team" communications that help keep everyone focused on the agreed-to scope and iteration goal.

The following are the three questions each team member answers during the stand-up meeting to report his or her status:

1. What have you worked on since the last meeting?
2. What do you plan to finish today?
3. Are there any roadblocks or impediments to your work?

When people are reporting issues, conversations about how to fix the issues should be taken off-line (i.e., outside of the meeting environment) to keep the meeting on track and within the 15-minute timeframe.

EXERCISE

Consider the following conversation snippets and indicate whether they are valid topics to discuss at a stand-up meeting by placing a check mark in the appropriate column.

Conversation Snippet	Valid Topic	Invalid Topic
"My PC still needs more RAM."		
"I finished testing the launcher."		
"I think we should add a turbo booster."		
"I just finished adding the supercharger."		
"Bill from accounting did not approve my trip to see the users."		
"Wendy from marketing won't go on a date with me."		
"I am still stuck trying to attach the nose cone."		
"If you thread it backwards, the nose cone should go on easily."		

ANSWER

During daily stand-up meetings, we need to be strict about keeping people focused on reporting progress, work planned, or impediments. Anything else is supplemental and should be taken off-line.

Conversation Snippet	Valid Topic	Invalid Topic
"My PC still needs more RAM."	✓ (This is an impediment and is therefore a valid topic.)	
"I finished testing the launcher."	✓ (This snippet is about project progress and is therefore a valid topic.)	
"I think we should add a turbo booster."		✓ (This conversation is about suggested new scope, so the discussion should be taken off-line.)
"I just finished adding the supercharger."	✓ (This comment is a report on project progress, which makes it a valid topic.)	
"Bill from accounting did not approve my trip to see the users."	✓ (This is an impediment, so it is an appropriate topic for a stand-up meeting.)	
"Wendy from marketing won't go on a date with me."		✓ (This comment is completely off-topic and doesn't belong in the daily stand-up meeting.)
"I am still stuck trying to attach the nose cone."	✓ (This is an appropriate topic, because it's an impediment.)	
"If you thread it backwards, the nose cone should go on easily."		✓ (This is related to solving the issue, rather than simply reporting it. The discussion should be taken offline.)

TRICKS OF THE TRADE® Daily stand-ups are a pretty basic topic, so questions on the exam related to this T&T should be fairly straightforward. Remember that the daily stand-up meeting is for the team, so team members answer the three questions to the team at large, not just to the ScrumMaster or project manager.

K&S Level 1 | Coaching and Mentoring

Coaching and mentoring agile teams help them stay on track, overcome issues, and continually improve their skills. Coaching is done simultaneously at two levels, the individual level and the whole-team level. Figure 5.10 shows how the emphasis switches from the whole team at the iteration boundaries to the individuals during the iteration:[7]

Figure 5.10: Coaching at the Whole-Team and Individual Levels

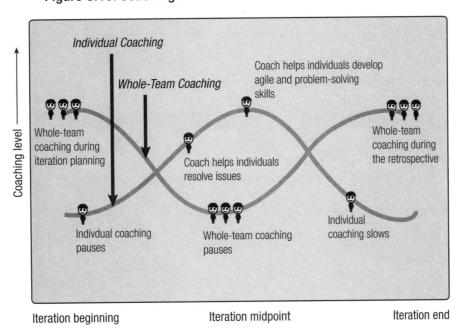

Whole-team coaching happens more at the iteration boundaries because that's when we have the team assembled for events like iteration planning, iteration reviews, and retrospectives. These are great times to get agile practices working well and to really help the team embody their agile role. Process changes are made between iterations rather than in the middle of the iteration, because the iteration is the team's dedicated period for completing the work within an unchanging environment.

During the iteration, we provide individual coaching and mentoring to team members. This may mean meeting with a team member one-on-one in a safe, confidential environment if the individual has any problems or complaints to report. During such conversations, it is important to keep the discussion frank, but be positive and respectful. To solve issues, we may need to partner with other managers, set up frequent check-ins, and follow up to make sure the issues have been resolved or at least reduced.

Adkins outlines the following actions that help set the groundwork for one-on-one coaching and mentoring:[8]

» **Meet them a half-step ahead**: Don't try to push people directly to the end point. Instead, coach them so that they move toward the end goal and take the next step from where they are now. As an example, if our aim is to have team members select their own work tasks but they are not there yet, instead of just telling them that agile teams self-select their work, try to get them halfway there by asking them questions like "Who can do this one?"

> » **Guarantee safety**: Declare to the team members that all coaching conversations will be kept confidential, and then make sure they are. People are more willing to contribute and share without fear of things being repeated out of context.
> » **Partner with managers**: Often team members' functional managers are not on the project team. Furthermore, these functional managers may not be using or even aware of agile methods, so how the team members are measured in their functional roles may not match agile values. We need to partner with functional managers to align everyone's goals and ensure the team members' project contributions get reported appropriately to their functional managers.
> » **Create positive regard**: We may not personally like every individual we coach, but we do have to help them. If we dislike someone, this sentiment can show through, often in subtle ways. Therefore, it is important to develop a true compassion for others and a desire to help people improve in their roles.

 ## Brainstorming Techniques

Agile teams use brainstorming techniques to help identify options, solve issues, and find ways to improve processes. For example, the team may brainstorm:

> » Product roles that will be featured in personas
> » The items that should go into a minimally marketable feature list for a release
> » Potential risks that could impact the project
> » Solutions to a problem raised at a retrospective

Brainstorming can be done in different ways, including through quiet writing, a round-robin approach, or a free-for-all format.

Quiet Writing

With the quiet writing method, team members are given time to generate a list of ideas individually. This approach limits peer influence because the ideas are first generated in isolation before the team members share them.

Round-Robin

A round-robin format can also be used. With this approach, everyone takes a turn suggesting their idea. This format has the advantage of allowing ideas to build on each other, but the group has to be comfortable sharing their ideas in front of each other for it to work.

Free-for-All

Another brainstorming approach is the free-for-all format. With this method, people just shout out their ideas. It's spontaneous and can be collaborative as team members vet and improve on suggestions through discussion, but it can only work in a supportive environment. Even in a supportive environment, however, quieter members may not be heard or may not feel like they had an equal opportunity to participate.

When choosing which brainstorming method to use, it is important to understand the team's openness to collaborating as a group. Lyssa Adkins recommends the "Green Zone, Red Zone" model as a way to understand and diagnose how much support there is for collaboration.[9]

A Person in the Green Zone...	A Person in the Red Zone...
Takes responsibility for the circumstances of his or her life	Blames others for the circumstances of his or her life
Seeks to respond nondefensively	Feels threatened or wronged
Is not easily threatened psychologically	Responds defensively
Attempts to build mutual success	Triggers defensiveness in others
Seeks solutions rather than blame	Is rigid, reactive, and righteous
Uses persuasion rather than force	Uses shame, blame, and accusations
Can be firm, but not rigid, about his or her interests	Is unaware of the climate of antagonism he or she creates
Thinks both short term and long term	Has low awareness of blind spots
Is interested in other points of view	Does not seek or value feedback
Welcomes feedback	Sees others as the problem or enemy
Sees conflict as a natural part of the human condition	Sees conflict as a battle and seeks to win at any cost
Talks calmly and directly about difficult issues	Does not let go or forgive
Accepts responsibility for consequences of his or her actions	Communicates high levels of disapproval and contempt
Continuously seeks deeper levels of understanding	Focuses on short-term advantage and gain
Communicates a caring attitude	Feels victimized by different points of view
Seeks excellence rather than victory	Is black/white, right/wrong in thinking
Listens well	Does not listen effectively

Effective coaches and facilitators live in the Green Zone and demonstrate Green Zone behavior at every interaction. They also encourage and solicit Green Zone thinking and behavior from team members. It is only when people spend most of their time in a Green Zone state of mind that they can be truly effective and helpful during brainstorming sessions. It is acceptable—and human—to have a few Red Zone thoughts some of the time, but we need to keep such thoughts in check and move back to the Green Zone as soon as possible.

Once the ideas have been captured through brainstorming sessions, the next steps are to sort the ideas, prioritize them, and then act on them. Sorting the ideas is often done by putting them on a board, consolidating similar ideas, and removing duplicates until a list of distinct suggestions are visible.

Agile teams can then use the following prioritization techniques:

» **MoSCoW**: This technique is used for hierarchical prioritization. Designations like "1, 2, 3," or "High, Medium, Low," can also be used.
» **Dot Voting or Multi-Voting**: With this technique, public or private prioritization of votes is spread across the total constellation of items.

Let's discuss these two techniques in more detail.

MoSCoW

As we discussed in chapter 3, Value-Driven Delivery, the "MoSCoW" term comes from the DSDM agile method and is derived from the first letters of the phrases "**M**ust have," "**S**hould have," "**C**ould have," and "**W**ould like to have, but not this time." When using MoSCoW to prioritize brainstorming ideas, the team categorizes the suggestions under the headings of "Must have," "Should have," etc., until they reach consensus on a hierarchy.

Dot Voting or Multi-Voting

With this technique, team wisdom emerges through individual priorities. Everyone gets a predetermined number of dots (or check marks, sticky stars, etc.) to distribute among the options presented.

To illustrate how this works, let's look at an example. Imagine we have completed a brainstorming session to come up with potential risks for the project. The session has resulted in a list of 40 unique risks that now need to be prioritized. Each person is given eight votes in the form of check marks that they can use to indicate which items they feel are most important. Each team member is limited to a total of eight check marks, but how the team member distributes his or her check marks is up to each person. It could be one check mark on eight different items, four check marks on one item and two check marks on a couple of other items, or any other combination that reflects the team member's assessment of priorities.

The leader of the brainstorming session then sums the votes for each item and creates a ranked list based on how many votes the items received. The voting can be public, or it can be private with someone tallying the totals off-line to prevent power struggles and strategic voting.

When deciding how many votes to give each person, a good rule of thumb is 20 percent of the total number of items. So if there are 40 risks to be voted on, we would calculate $40 \times 0.2 = 8$, and everyone would get 8 votes to distribute.

 ## Team Space

The team space is the designated environment where team members conduct their everyday work. Since agile methods recommend face-to-face interactions as the preferred means of communication, it is no surprise that they also recommend co-located teams with a common work area for collaboration and information sharing.

Agile teams often commandeer an open space like a conference room to serve as their team space. Such a space can also be known as a war room. Whatever you call it, there should be plenty of wall space for whiteboards to be used during collaborative discussions and room to post information radiators of project metrics.

 ## Co-located Teams

Although agile methods promote using co-located teams and creating a collaborative team space, this approach also comes with challenges. Let's look at some important aspects of co-located teams you should understand for the exam, including some of the challenges and ways to address them.

Caves and Common

Open work environments are great for overhearing useful project information that may help you in your work, but they are also great for overhearing private telephone conversations with spouses and financial managers. To help resolve this issue, most companies provide access to private offices where people can go to make private calls. These offices can also be used by team members who want to work in quiet isolation for short periods if they are having problems concentrating in a noisy environment.

This model is called "caves and common." "Caves" refer to the space where team members can retreat to when they need some quiet time or privacy for phone calls, and "common" is the area where the team members can work as a group.

Osmotic Communication

Osmotic communication refers to the useful information that flows from team members as part of everyday conversations and questions when they work in close proximity to each other. For example, imagine Bob asks Jim, a co-located team member, how to restart the build server. Mary, another team member, is just about to use that machine and overhears the conversation. She can now intervene on the restart and save a potential conflict. This ability to pick up on things that would otherwise be missed is a major benefit of co-location.

The more separation we have between team members, the more difficult this osmotic information flow becomes. So when we are faced with the challenge of working with a physically separated team, agile methods recommend that we remove as many barriers to face-to-face and osmotic communications as possible.

Alistair Cockburn likens osmotic communication to energy fields that radiate from people. If you are too far away, you receive very little, but if you are working in close proximity, you get the full benefit, as indicated in figure 5.11. In other words, if we can get people sitting and working closely together with fewer barriers between them, osmotic communication improves.[10]

Figure 5.11: Effect of Proximity on Osmotic Communication Flows

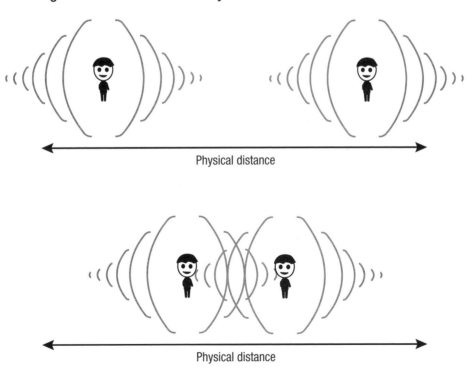

Physical distance

Physical distance

Tacit Knowledge

Tacit knowledge, which refers to information that is not written down but is instead supported through collective group knowledge, is also more effective when teams are co-located. For example, how to restart the printer may not be written down anywhere, but since everyone is in earshot and has seen and heard people do it before, the information is shared and supported by the team.

As teams grow in size, it becomes physically more difficult to maintain face-to-face communications with everyone, and tacit knowledge begins to break down. As a result, teams needs to start committing more things to writing to keep everyone informed. Written documentation is much slower to create, so some of the time savings that come from small team collaboration are lost.

To better facilitate face-to-face communications and to maintain tacit knowledge, agile methods recommend limiting the team size to 12 or fewer people. As projects grow in size and require more resources, the preferred approach is to split large teams into smaller subteams. Representatives of the subteams then need to come together everyday to coordinate and synchronize work across the project.

K&S Level 2 Distributed Teams

You will not have to know these types of statistics for the exam.

Distributed teams are those that have at least one team member working off-site. The 2010 and 2011 VersionOne State of Agile Surveys, which received feedback from several thousand projects, reported that over 50 percent of agile projects have at least one person working remotely. This means that, rather than being the exception, distributed teams are the norm. One reason distributed teams are used so frequently is that the Internet has opened up new communication options and reduced communication costs, which makes forming geographically distributed teams not only possible but also cost effective.

A big challenge for distributed teams is finding ways to replicate the benefits of face-to-face collaboration, osmotic communication, tacit knowledge, and improved relations that come from people working in close proximity to each other. Luckily the same factors that have made distributed teams more common also allow for tools that can help us restore some level of the benefits we get from face-to-face collaboration. The following are examples of such tools:

» **Videoconferencing** can be especially useful for stand-up meetings and retrospectives to provide a visual presence for distributed team members.
» **Web-based meeting facilitators** help keep track of participants and provide a central hub for connection information.
» **Survey applications** can be an effective way of polling team members in real time or off-line to get answers to questions and opinions.
» **Instant messaging (IM)** and **VoIP (Voice over Internet Protocol) headsets** can make it seem like people halfway around the world are much closer. With Skype headsets, for instance, team members can chat away with each other as if they were in the same (dark) room.
» **Presence-based applications** build on and extend IM capabilities by managing the "currently online" status of participants to create a virtual office environment for sharing information. These applications usually offer document and file management services, as well as a rudimentary project plan integration capability, to help team members collaborate.
» **Interactive whiteboards** can share content with multiple locations and allow participants to collaborate in a visual whiteboard-type environment that is much richer than a telephone conversation.

Beyond the tools technology can offer us, we can also take the step of bringing team members together at least once at the beginning of the project. As we discussed in chapter 4, Stakeholder Engagement, communications are much easier once people have met face to face. Personally, I would be happy to spend up to 80 percent of my travel budget early in the project getting people to meet face to face, because it makes such a difference in subsequent communications.

Another aspect of distributed teams to keep in mind is that the team formation phases of Storming and Norming are more difficult when team members are not co-located. Some people are more likely to just disengage from an e-mail or VoIP debate, rather than stand up for their viewpoint the way they would if they were in the same room as the other person. If people are out of sight, it is easier to dismiss them and their crazy ideas. However, other people seem more comfortable debating via e-mail, perhaps because they feel protected by distance and a sense of being somewhat anonymous. In contrast, when you meet in person, such individuals may suddenly be very agreeable and meek.

Storming and Norming are critical to help teams build commitment to decisions and results. Therefore, leaders of distributed agile teams need to ensure there is enough debate and collective decision making early on in the project for the team to fully work through these stages. This may mean introducing certain pieces of work earlier in the project just to get the team talking and working through issues.

Jean Tabaka, author of *Collaboration Explained*, offers the following tips for managing distributed teams:[11]

» **Maintain a metaphor**: Metaphors can help the team stay focused on the project mission or vision. For example, a metaphor for a project to build a security system may be "We are building the Great Wall of China."
» **Apply frequent communications**: When team members aren't in close proximity to each other, adding in more scheduled communications may help. For example, a distributed team may have two stand-up meetings a day plus scheduled one-on-one calls to compensate for the lack of spontaneous communications.
» **Intensify facilitation**: This may mean asking more questions, repeating responses more frequently when on conference calls, and working to keep everyone engaged.
» **Collaboration practices for conference calls**: It also important to keep conference calls effective and productive so people are willing to attend and contribute. Here are some basic guidelines to follow when facilitating conference calls:

   – *Keep on track*: There should be no fuzzy agendas.
   – *Keep on time*: As a general rule, keep calls to a one-hour limit.
   – *Keep track of who is on the call*: This can be done by maintaining a seating chart.
   – *Keep the decisions flowing*: Sending out agendas in advance can help achieve this goal.
   – *Keep the answers coming*: To do so, we need to engage participants with questions.
   – *Keep it fair*: This means we need to maintain fair telephone control.
   – *Keep it facilitated*: In other words, don't take control of decisions.
   – *Keep it documented*: Not only should we document the conference call, but we should also send feedback promptly.

Jim Highsmith points out that there is an important difference between distributed and outsourced projects. As he explains, "Distributed projects basically have multiple development sites that can span buildings, cities, or countries. Outsourced projects involve multiple legal entities, therefore contracting, contract administration, and dealing with different development infrastructures are added to the team's workload."[12]

As projects get bigger and require more resources, it is inevitable that teams become distributed. It is simply not possible to accommodate large numbers of people in one space. But even with distributed teams, Highsmith asserts that agile methods result in greater success for teams and projects than non-agile approaches because of the following factors:

» The short iterations in agile development force continuous close collaboration and coordination.
» Control of distributed agile projects is better because a releasable product is built each iteration.[13]

In other words, if you have to manage a distributed team, it is best to employ agile practices, because the frequent feedback is more helpful than just adding documentation for keeping the team on track.

 Agile Tooling

In addition to the tools we just discussed that help with distributed communications, there are other tools agile teams can take advantage of. Just as the Agile Manifesto values "Individuals and interactions over processes and tools," agile teams tend to prefer low-tech, high-touch tools over sophisticated computerized models.

Low-Tech, High-Touch Tools

One key reason agile methods value these types of tools is that low-tech, tangible objects promote communication and collaboration, which is where learning and knowledge transfer really occur on a project. In contrast, sophisticated tools can produce impressive-looking reports and graphs but often lose participants due to their complexity and the learning curve required to master them.

This preference for low-tech, high-touch tools is not unique to agile. The coordination of military battles is often still performed by manipulating physical tokens for boats and troops, despite huge budgets for computer models, because moving tokens around better engages the participants and leads to less confusion.

In keeping with the low-tech, high-touch approach, we see the widespread use of manual tools like task boards (shown in figure 5.12), user stories written on 3-inch x 5-inch cards, and playing cards with numbers on them used for planning poker estimation (discussed in chapter 6, Adaptive Planning).

Figure 5.12: Task Board

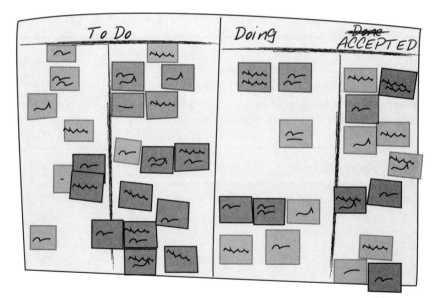

Digital Tools

There are also a host of electronic tools and gizmos that can be used with distributed teams, including:

» **Agile project management software**: These tools can help with backlog creation and prioritization. They also produce velocity tracking statistics and help the team own the process of tracking velocity.

» **Virtual card walls**: These virtual walls can mimic physical card walls, but they are accessible anywhere to team members with an Internet connection.

» **Smart boards**: These tools are great for capturing the output of design sessions without having to spend extra time creating formal documents.

» **Digital cameras**: Taking a digital picture is another way to quickly capture whiteboard sessions without the need to spend time polishing designs.

» **Wiki sites, document management tools, and collaboration websites**: Such tools allow stakeholders to create, view, amend, and discuss project elements.

» **Automated testing tools, automated build tools, and traffic-light-type signals**: These tools are typically used on software projects to show the status of the build. For example, if the build is stable and all tests are running, the tools give a green light. If some code has been checked in that breaks the build, they give a red light.

» **CASE tools**: These tools were popular in the 1990s to generate code from designs. They are now being used to reverse engineer documentation from source code and data models. So rather than spending valuable time keeping systems documentation up to date, teams can now use CASE tools every week to perform tasks like reverse engineering new database models, depth-of-inheritance metrics, and code coverage statistics from the evolving system. The capabilities of such tools free up developer time to focus on adding new features, rather than maintaining documentation.

Professional Responsibility and Ethics

Before we move on to the next chapter, let's look at how PMI's Code of Ethics and Professional Conduct (available on PMI's website: www.pmi.org) applies to boosting team performance practices.[14] We'll cover each of the four main areas of the code—Responsibility, Respect, Fairness, and Honesty—in turn and look at examples of how they relate to the T&Ts and K&Ss discussed in this chapter. As you read this section, think about your real-world projects and how they are impacted by these different aspects of professional responsibility and ethics.

Responsibility

» **Make decisions based on the best interests of the company**: Empowered teams are very effective, but we still need to check team decisions against shareholder values. For example, the team may recommend buying a new server to provide faster response time, but if the server is very expensive, purchasing it for the project may not be in the company's interest.

» **Protect proprietary information**: Distributed teams make extensive use of Web-based collaboration tools, but we do need to make sure that hosting company information on these off-site services doesn't break company data protection policies. Before using such tools, we need to understand their security models, as well as their terms and conditions related to information usage and resale.

Respect

» **Maintain an attitude of mutual cooperation**: When we have distributed team members, we have to be extra vigilant in making sure that "out of sight" does not equal "out of mind." Before making decisions, we should ask ourselves if we have properly engaged the off-site members in the dialogue.

» **Respect cultural differences**: Not everyone will be comfortable with free-for-all brainstorming sessions in the presence of peers and mangers. We need to figure out how to engage team members in ways that respect their cultural norms.

» **Negotiate in good faith**: At all times during the project, but especially in the early stages of team formation, we need to make sure everyone gets their fair say in negotiating things like what approach to take after a brainstorming session or which features to include in an iteration.

» **Deal with conflict directly**: Conflict can be good and should be allowed to occur, but boosting team performance becomes almost impossible if the conflicts aren't dealt with in a direct and productive way and are instead left to resurface throughout the project.

» **Do not use your position to influence others**: Leaders should facilitate, rather than dictate. This means we let team members debate issues and empower them to make local decisions.

Fairness

» **Look for and disclose conflicts of interest**: We should always be alert for conflicts of interest between internal project parties, but this concept also applies when choosing which tools to use for our projects, particularly remotely hosted systems. Are such tools safe? Will they protect corporate data and not sell it to other parties?

» **Do not discriminate**: With distributed teams, discrimination can mean treating remote team members differently than local team members. For example, if we organize a team lunch for the local team to celebrate an event, we should find a way to recognize our remote team members as well.

Honesty

» **Understand the truth**: Part of emotional intelligence is understanding our own strengths and weaknesses. When coaching and collaborating, we should look for "Red Zone" behavior in ourselves and others and work to adjust it.

» **Be truthful in all communications**: Teams perform best when team members openly and honestly report progress and issues during daily stand-ups and other meetings. In addition, when mentoring we should not sidestep difficult issues for fear of hurting someone's feelings; instead we need to find an appropriate way to discuss the topic.

Practice Exam

1. Which are the recommended pairings of adaptive leadership and team phases?

   A. Supporting and Norming, Delegating and Performing, Directing and Forming, Coaching and Storming
   B. Directing and Forming, Coaching and Storming, Delegating and Norming, Supporting and Performing
   C. Directing and Forming, Supporting and Storming, Delegating and Norming, Coaching and Performing
   D. Directing and Forming, Supporting and Norming, Coaching and Performing, Delegating and Storming

2. _____ is the agile name given to undocumented information supported through team communications.

   A. Unwritten knowledge
   B. Tribal knowledge
   C. Tacit knowledge
   D. Common knowledge

3. Self-organizing teams are most readily characterized by their ability to:

   A. Do their own filing
   B. Sit where they like
   C. Make local decisions
   D. Make project-based decisions

4. Which of the following is not a recommendation for one-on-one coaching?

   A. Meet them a half-step ahead
   B. Create positive regard
   C. Partner with managers
   D. Let the team resolve conflicts

5. High-performing teams feature which of the following sets of characteristics?

   A. Consensus-driven, empowered, low trust
   B. Self-organizing, plan-driven, empowered
   C. Consensus-driven, empowered, plan-driven
   D. Constructive disagreement, empowered, self-organizing

6. Which of the following sets of tools is least likely to be utilized by an agile team?

   A. Digital camera, task board
   B. Wiki, planning poker cards
   C. WBS, PERT charts
   D. Smart board, card wall

7. Which of the following is a valid list of the quadrants of emotional intelligence?

   A. Self, Others, Recognize, Optimize
   B. Self, Others, Regulate, Recognize
   C. Self, Team, Regulate, Recognize
   D. Self, Team, Recognize, Optimize

8. The three questions answered in daily stand-up meetings aim to:

   A. Identify problems, discuss accomplishments
   B. Identify opportunities, discuss accomplishments
   C. Fix problems, discuss accomplishments
   D. Fix problems, discuss work planned

9. Who typically has the best insight into task execution?

   A. Project managers
   B. Team members
   C. ScrumMasters
   D. Agile coaches

10. Which of the following are recommended brainstorming techniques?

    A. Quiet writing
    B. Decision spectrum
    C. Fist-of-five voting
    D. Participatory decisions

11. Servant leadership roles include:

    A. Shielding team members from interruptions
    B. Leading conflict resolution
    C. Determining which features to include in an iteration
    D. Assigning tasks to save time

12. Which of the following statements is false for distributed teams?

    A. Should consider instant messaging tools
    B. Should have an easier Storming phase
    C. Need to spend more effort communicating
    D. Have a higher need for videoconferencing

13. Another project manager of an agile project in your organization comes to you for advice. She is having trouble getting her team to take ownership of the project and get comfortable selecting the work to be done. She keeps finding herself making the decisions and directing their work. What advice can you offer her?

    A. Play round-robin at stand-up meetings, assigning a different person each day as the decision maker to get them comfortable in the role.
    B. Implement an incentive plan and officially report any lack of participation to team members' functional managers.
    C. Meet them halfway and work with their functional managers to align each team member's goals with the project goals.
    D. Explain to them that agile teams self-select their work and tell them to get on with it.

14. Tuckman's stages of team formation and development progress in what sequence?

    A.   Norming, Storming, Performing, Forming
    B.   Norming, Storming, Forming, Performing
    C.   Forming, Storming, Performing, Norming
    D.   Forming, Storming, Norming, Performing

15. Blanchard and Hersey's adaptive leadership phases, in sequence, are:

    A.   Supporting, Directing, Coaching, Delegating
    B.   Supporting, Coaching, Directing, Delegating
    C.   Delegating, Coaching Supporting, Directing
    D.   Directing, Coaching, Supporting, Delegating

16. Which of the following emotional intelligence pairings is an appropriate combination?

    A.   Self-management deals with influence
    B.   Self-awareness deals with self-control
    C.   Social skills deals with self-confidence
    D.   Social awareness deals with empathy

17. The primary reason constructive disagreement is valued on high-performing agile teams is to:

    A.   Weed out the weak
    B.   Test requirements for robustness
    C.   Generate buy-in for decisions
    D.   Build negotiation skills

18. At what team formation and development phase is conflict likely to be highest?

    A.   Forming
    B.   Fuming
    C.   Storming
    D.   Debating

Answers

1. Answer: A

   Explanation: The pairings align the Tuckman model with the Blanchard and Hersey model. The correct pairings are Directing and Forming, Coaching and Storming, Supporting and Norming, and finally Delegating and Performing. Option A is correct, even though it has them out of sequence; the question just asked for the pairings, not the correct sequence.

2. Answer: C

   Explanation: While the terms "tribal knowledge," "common knowledge," and "unwritten knowledge" may still convey the idea, the correct term is "tacit knowledge."

3. Answer: C

   Explanation: This question can be confusing because teams may have the opportunity to make some project-based decisions, but remember to always look for the BEST choice in the options presented. Self-organizing teams primarily have control over local decisions related to the project execution. For example, they may decide what to do next and how to solve a technical problem. Sponsors typically make external decisions, such as increasing the budget or extending the schedule. Doing their own filing or sitting where they like may or may not occur, but these choices are not readily associated with characteristics of a self-organizing team. Therefore, choice C is the best option.

4. Answer: D

   Explanation: The recommendations for one-on-one coaching are to meet team members a half-step ahead, create positive regard, partner with managers, and guarantee safety. While we should let the team work through conflict, this is not a recommendation for one-on-one coaching.

5. Answer: D

   Explanation: Through a process of elimination, we can determine that the correct answer is choice D. High-performing teams work in high-trust, rather than low-trust, environments, and they are consensus-driven, not plan-driven.

6. Answer: C

   Explanation: While tools like work breakdown structures and PERT charts can still work on agile projects, these tools are used less than the other choices presented in the question. This is a result of the frequent reprioritization of work and the high rates of changes. Agile teams tend to use tools that take a minimal amount of time to update and keep current.

7. Answer: B

   Explanation: Vertically the emotional intelligence model has two columns—Self and Others. Horizontally it has two rows representing Recognize and Regulate. "Optimize" and "Team" are not model category names.

8. Answer: A

   Explanation: The three questions asked at stand-up meetings are: 1) "What have you worked on since the last meeting?" 2) "What do you plan on finishing today?" and 3) "Are there any roadblocks or impediments to your work?" These questions aim to discuss accomplishments, discuss work planned, and identify problems. Fixing problems or identifying opportunities, while worthy goals, are not objectives of the stand-up meeting.

9. Answer: B

   Explanation: Servant leadership recognizes that the "doers" of the work, the team members, are closest to the work and therefore have the best insight into its execution. Project managers, ScrumMasters, and agile coaches should defer to the team's decision regarding how best to execute the work.

10. Answer: A

    Explanation: Recommended brainstorming techniques include quiet writing, round-robin, and free-for-all. Decision spectrum, fist-of-five voting, and participatory decision models are team decision-making tools.

11. Answer: A

    Explanation: Servant leaders recognize that it is the team that adds value, so their role is to shield the team from interruptions. They should not immediately take the lead in resolving conflicts but first let the team try to resolve issues on their own. And the team determines the iteration features; they are not dictated by the project leader. Task assignment is not a servant leadership role; agile teams are encouraged to select their own work, based on the backlog and their skills.

12. Answer: B

    Explanation: Distributed teams have a tougher time, rather than an easier time, getting through the Storming phase since it is difficult to resolve conflicts when people are geographically distributed. The other statements are true for distributed teams.

13. Answer: C

    Explanation: The project manager in this situation should assume a coaching role with her team to help the team members get to the point where they are comfortable selecting their own work. The recommendations for one-on-one coaching include meeting team members a half step ahead, guaranteeing safety, partnering with managers, and creating positive regard. Assigning someone as a decision maker at stand-up meetings isn't an effective approach, since teams should be consensus-driven. Incentive plans can be useful and a project manager should work with a functional manager to help resolve issues, but what the team really needs is guidance, not strictly rewards and punishments. Simply explaining that agile teams self-select their work isn't enough to get team members to the point where they are comfortable assuming more ownership of the project.

14. Answer: D

    Explanation: The correct sequence is forming, storming, norming, performing.

15. Answer: D

    Explanation: The correct sequence is directing, coaching, supporting, delegating.

16. Answer: D

    Explanation: The only correct choice is the combination of social awareness and empathy. Self-management is paired with self-control, not influencing; self-awareness is paried with self-confidence; and social skills is paired with self-control.

17. Answer: C

    Explanation: Constructive disagreement is a form of healthy conflict, where team members work through issues to find a solution that is right for the team and the project. As a result, constructive disagreement generates team buy-in for decisions. Agile methods do not seek to "weed out the weak," and while constructive disagreement could help clarify requirements and build negotiation skills, those are not the primary reasons it is valued on a project.

18. Answer: C

    Explanation: The stage where conflict is highest is the storming phase. When the team is in the forming stage, they are still getting to know each other and move from that phase into storming. Fuming and debating are not team formation and development phases.

© 2012 RMC Publications, Inc • 952.846.4484 • info@rmcproject.com • www.rmcproject.com

ADAPTIVE PLANNING

Chapter Six

This chapter is about planning, but not just any kind of planning; agile projects call for *adaptive planning*. An adaptive approach acknowledges that planning is an ongoing process and has multiple mechanisms in place to proactively update the plan. Adaptive planning differs from more static planning approaches that create most of the plan upfront. The more static approaches are reactive, rather than proactive; after the initial plan is created, planning is typically done only in response to exceptions to the plan and change requests.

As we've discussed throughout this book, agile methods are value-driven. This means they aim to maximize the delivery of business value to the customer. So the backlog is prioritized with high-business-value items at the top, and releases are targeted to maximize the value of the functionality being delivered. Given this focus on value in planning, there are strong connections between this chapter and chapter 3, Value-Driven Delivery.

Adaptive Planning

As part of the focus on value delivery, agile methods also look to minimize any nonvalue-adding work. Since planning activities do not directly add business functionality, they could be considered waste. So if we want to minimize waste, we should take the most efficient approach to planning, right? From an efficiency standpoint, doing the necessary planning for the project only once and then not returning to the planning effort would seem like the best thing to do. Unfortunately, this is not an effective approach for knowledge worker projects due to their high rates of change, nor is it safe or responsible to plan once. The only way we can be successful on such projects is to plan to replan.

Adaptive planning is the conscious acceptance that early plans are both necessary and likely to be flawed; therefore, replanning and adaptation activities should be scheduled into the project. Uncertainty drives the need to replan. To help illustrate this concept, think about a project as a journey. If we are going to a well-known destination and traveling over well-known terrain, we can use maps and GPS units to create detailed, reliable upfront plans for the entire trip. Our rate of progress may vary from the original schedule, but that's why we have status reviews—to compare where we are to where we thought we would be by now, always referring back to the baseline plan. Taking the variances from the plan into account, we can recalculate our consumption and estimated time of arrival projections. Perhaps we'll encounter a roadblock or diversion, or maybe we'll have to go back to the steering committee to ask for permission to go a different way, but such events are exceptions; they are infrequent deviations from the plan.

In contrast, the uncertainty of undertaking a novel knowledge worker project is more like a journey across a deserted island that few people have ever visited, using a rough treasure map as a guide. It is quite likely that no one on our team has ever been to the island before. There are no GPS capabilities or drive-time averages to help us plan our trip. Instead, as a team we discuss the goal, agree on a general plan, and set off in the direction we think is most likely correct. If we come to an obstacle such as a cliff or a lake that is not on our map, we do not blindly attempt to follow the plan. Instead, we accept that our plan was flawed and needs updating, and we adapt our journey based on the new information we have learned.

And so it is with many agile projects; the unprecedented nature of the work means that we frequently discover issues and experience high rates of change. Therefore, we should go into the project with the expectation that we will be adapting the plan. To quote Alfred Korzybski, "The map is not the territory."[1] This expression speaks to the need to adapt our approach as we encounter unplanned obstacles.

In This Chapter

This chapter is broken into three sections or areas of practice: planning-related concepts, estimation, and agile plans. The following chart shows the tools and techniques and knowledge and skills associated with each section. Although the names of these practices are not official terms that will appear on the exam, organizing the concepts in this way provides the context of why and how you use the T&Ts and K&Ss that you will be tested on.

Practice	Tool/Technique	Knowledge/Skill (Level)
Planning concepts	» Timeboxing » Progressive elaboration » Process tailoring » Minimally marketable feature (MMF)	» Value-based analysis (Level 2) » Value-based decomposition and prioritization (Level 1) » Agile games (Level 3)
Estimation	» Wideband Delphi and planning poker » Ideal time » Relative sizing/story points » Affinity estimating	» Time, budget, and cost estimation (Level 1) » Agile project accounting principles (Level 3)
Agile plans	» Iteration and release planning	» Agile charters (Level 2) » Business case development (Level 2)

Planning Concepts

The planning concepts embodied by agile methods promote an acceptance that details will emerge as the project progresses, that it is necessary to adapt the project based on feedback, and that frequent reprioritization is the norm. This acceptance that things will change and the resulting realization that it is better to embrace uncertainty than to resist the change are what drive the agile practices covered in this chapter.

 The PMI-ACP exam will test your knowledge and ability to apply the following planning concepts:

1. Plan at multiple levels.
2. Engage the team and the customer in planning.
3. Manage expectations by frequently demonstrating progress and extrapolating velocity.
4. Tailor processes to the project's characteristics.
5. Update the plan based on the project's priorities.
6. Ensure encompassing estimates that account for risks, distractions, and team availability.
7. Use appropriate estimate ranges to reflect the level of uncertainty in the estimate.
8. Base projections on completion rates.
9. Factor in diversions and outside work.

Make sure you read through these points carefully. When you review the tools and techniques and knowledge and skills discussed in the rest of the chapter, think about how the different topics relate back to these concepts. Then keep this list in mind when answering questions on the exam. For example, if the answer choices for a question suggest that either a) "Planning is done by the project manager in isolation" or b) "Planning is done by the project manager, with the team and the customer," you should choose option B, which addresses concept 2 in this list.

 Timeboxing

Timeboxes are short, fixed-duration periods of time in which activities or work are undertaken. If the work planned for the timebox is not complete when the time runs out, then we stop what we're doing and move the uncompleted work into another timebox. Examples of timeboxes include:

» Daily stand-up meetings that are timeboxed to 15 minutes
» Iterations that are timeboxed to (typically) two weeks

Let's explore the concept of timeboxed iterations a little further. Imagine that we plan to complete 10 user stories within a timeboxed iteration, but we only have 8 of the user stories done when the timebox ends. Even though we didn't complete all the planned user stories, we do not extend the timebox. Instead, we report that 8 items were completed and return the remaining 2 user stories to the backlog for consideration in the next timeboxed iteration.

Agile projects often have a lot of uncertainty when the domain of the project is novel to the organization or when new technologies are being used on the project. Timeboxes help bring some level of order and consistency to an otherwise highly variable work environment. They offer an opportunity to assess results, gather feedback, and control the costs and risks associated with an endeavor.

Timeboxes have been referred to as "the control in the chaos." They provide frequent checkpoints to gauge progress and replan the ongoing approach. Another way to think about timeboxed iterations is to imagine a physical box that represents the team's capacity to accomplish work, as illustrated in figure 6.1.

Figure 6.1: Assigning Work to a Timeboxed Iteration

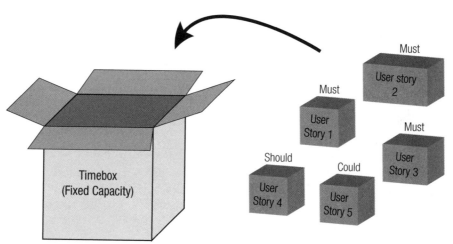

Work is loaded into the timebox in priority order. If something doesn't fit in the box—in other words, if the team doesn't have the capacity to complete a piece of work within the iteration—it will have to wait for subsequent iterations.

Figure 6.2: Work that Does Not Fit Into the Timebox Waits for Subsequent Iterations

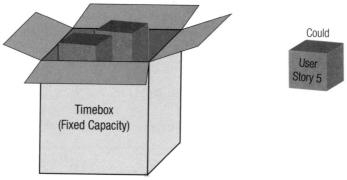

An architectural spike (also discussed in chapter 2, Agile Framework) is a period of time dedicated to a proof of concept. An architectural spike is another activity that is often timeboxed on agile projects. In an example of a software project, this may mean "We will spend one week testing performance of the native database drivers before making a decision on connectivity."

Timeboxes are also powerful motivation tools for completing focused work. For example, when working individually, some people use Pomodoro timers (25-minute timers, often shaped like a tomato) to help keep themselves focused and on task for short periods of time. The 25-minute setting allows for two sessions per hour, with a few minutes outside of the focused session to check e-mails, get a drink, stretch your legs, etc. The reason the Pomodoro technique is effective is that most people get distracted and multitask inefficiently. For some activities, instead of answering every e-mail or message as it comes in, it is better to work hard without any distractions or interruptions for 25 minutes and then take a short break.

The timeboxing technique can be used in preparing for the PMI-ACP exam as well. Get a one-hour sand timer, and commit to setting aside one solid hour each evening for study, with no distractions. Don't check your e-mail or let yourself get sidetracked; dedicate that time to studying alone. The power of using the sand timer is that the volumes in the two halves give an immediate visual of time remaining, and the falling sand generates a sense of rapidly depleting time that is lost with the digital counters we are so familiar with. A sand timer portrays a visual "time is passing by, so you had better get on with it" message.

 Progressive Elaboration

Progressive elaboration is the name given to the process of adding more detail as information emerges. We use progressive elaboration to evolve and create increasingly accurate:

» Plans
» Estimates
» Risk assessments
» Requirements definitions
» Architectural designs
» Acceptance criteria
» Test scenarios

Progressive Elaboration in Plans and Estimates

At the beginning of a project, we need to plan and estimate the work involved to determine how big the endeavor is likely to be and to create a reasonable strategy and execution approach. However, we also need to understand that the beginning of a project is when we know the least about the endeavor. At this early point, there has not yet been any "learning by doing" on the project. We would be foolish to limit our planning and estimation activities to the start of the project. Instead, we must continually refine our plans and estimates as the project progresses and new details emerge. This process of continual updates is the essence of progressive elaboration.

The concept of progressive elaboration is illustrated in figures 6.3 and 6.4. In figure 6.3, the "Now" arrow indicates we are at the start of the project and are creating the upfront plans. The lines in the early iterations show how detailed the plans for those iterations are. As you can see, the first iteration has a lot of detail, but there is less and less detail for the subsequent iterations.

Figure 6.3: The Level of Planning Early in a Project When Using Progressive Elaboration

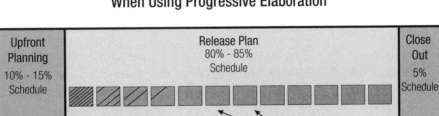

Figure 6.4 shows that, as the project goes on and new information arises, the plans are progressively elaborated and details are added. In this diagram, the "Now" arrow indicates that we are in the third iteration. The fourth iteration is planned in detail, while the fifth, sixth, and seventh iterations have decreasing levels of detail. This process of refining the plans as we get closer to working on the iterations continues throughout the project.

Figure 6.4: The Level of Planning as the Project Is Being Completed

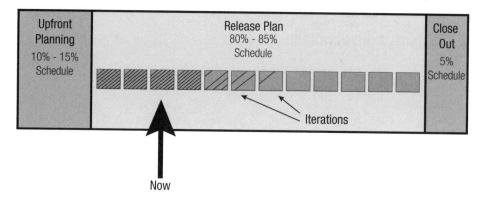

Process Tailoring

Just as our plans evolve as we learn more about a project, its environment, and its stakeholders, so too does our approach. Retrospective reviews are the main trigger for driving process changes. At the end of each iteration, we meet with the extended team (our development team and other business stakeholders) to ask the following questions:

» What is going well?
» What areas could use improvement?
» What should we be doing differently?

As problems are identified, we engage the team in brainstorming solutions. We then commit to trying the selected solutions for one or two iterations before meeting again to discuss whether the situation has improved. If the actions helped—great! We adopt them as part of our processes on the project. If they did not help, we consider the effort a learning opportunity and decide whether to try something else or revert to the earlier process.

Through this cycle of regular inspection, reflection, and adaptation, we tailor our project processes to the unique situation of the project and organization.

T&T Minimally Marketable Feature (MMF)

When planning a release of features to customers, the release has to make sense, be useful, and be valuable. This applies to all types of agile projects, whether it's a release of software, a new electrical product, or an engineering increment. The term "minimally marketable feature" (MMF) refers to this package of functionality that is complete enough to be useful to the users or market, yet small enough that it does not represent the entire project.[2]

For a cell phone, for example, a minimally marketable feature could be a phone that can be used to make and receive calls, store contact names and numbers, and access voice mail, but the phone would not need to have a camera, Internet connectivity, or a music player in its first release. Instead, these sets of functionality could be added in subsequent releases and evaluated independently. Keep in mind, however, that the functionality of the phone that is released in the MMF needs to be complete. So all the attributes related to making phone calls should be present as part of the MMF to allow the customer or business to comprehensively review this functionality.

In software development, it may be possible to transfer increments of the final product to the user community early so that the business can start getting some benefits from the application before the entire project is completed. For example, if the order entry and billing system is complete but the management reporting and marketing links have not been built yet, the company might still gain benefits from deploying this early version of the system. This incremental release can allow for some return on investment while the team develops the remaining functionality. It also provides an opportunity to field-test the functionality of the order entry and billing system. These field tests may then result in change requests that can be rolled into the final product while the development team is still in place.

EXERCISE

Create a list of the functionality that should be included in the minimally marketable feature for each product listed here, and then also list other potential functionality that could be developed for subsequent releases.

Pencil

MMF	Additional Releases

Car

MMF	Additional Releases

Automated teller machine (ATM)

MMF	Additional Releases

ANSWER

There could be a wide range of correct answers for this exercise. The following are some possible options.

Pencil

MMF	Additional Releases
» Makes a mark on paper » Can be held in one hand	» Eraser » Visually attractive » Self-sharpening or continuous lead » Comfortable

Car

MMF	Additional Releases
» Transport occupants from point A to point B » Road legal » Safe	» Air conditioner and heater » Fuel efficient » Aesthetically pleasing » Sporty performance » Comfortable

Automated teller machine (ATM)

MMF	Additional Releases
» Dispenses money » Displays balance » Protects against attack » Keeps user information secure	» Accepts cash deposits » Accepts check deposits » Remembers user's favorite withdrawal amounts

 Value-Based Analysis
K&S Level 2

Value-based analysis is the process of considering the business value of work items and then acting accordingly. It affects the full life cycle of agile projects and is holistic in the sense that the business value impacts how we scope, plan, schedule, develop, test, and release work. At every stage of the project, we are asking, "What is the business value of this item or practice?" and "What items in this set have the highest business value?" We then prioritize the work to deliver the highest-value items first.

Figure 6.5: Analyzing the Business Value of Work Items

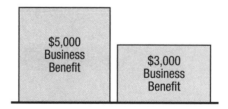

To fully understand an item's value, we also need to understand the development and delivery cost. For example, a feature that is worth $5,000 to the business but costs $4,000 to develop (or even $6,000 to develop) is not as valuable as something that delivers $3,000 in value to the business and only costs $1,000 to develop.

Figure 6.6: Considering Both Development Cost and Business Value

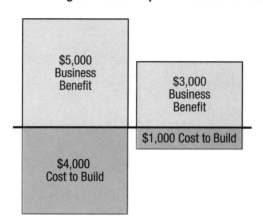

So we need to factor in likely development costs when performing value-based analysis. This is one reason why we estimate the backlog items at a high level early in the project. Doing so allows us to make benefit-versus-cost value comparisons. This information is then used in prioritizing items for development. For example, to maximize the value delivered in a release, a product manager may choose several medium-value features that the team can quickly develop rather than a higher-value item that would consume all the remaining development time.

The other component we need to consider is payback frequency. Does the feature generate business value every week or month (such as a time savings for staff) or just once (such as a compliance check). Therefore, when we evaluate the return over a one- to five-year period, the extended view of the return should be used to assess the true business value.

Keeping these components in mind, we analyze the real business value of features so that we can then prioritize the features appropriately. However, we need to remember that some high-business-value items may be dependent on some lower-business-value items, and so these lower-business-value items will need to be undertaken first, to allow the team to deliver the high-business-value items as soon as possible.

Value-Based Decomposition and Prioritization

Value-based decomposition and prioritization is the process of eliciting requirements from stakeholders, ranking those requirements, and then pulling the prioritized requirements into the development process. This process is illustrated in figure 6.7.

Figure 6.7: Value-Based Decomposition and Prioritzation

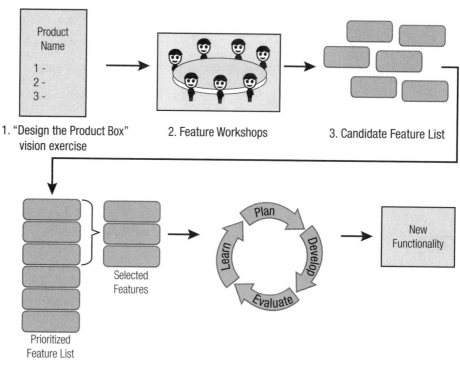

1. "Design the Product Box" vision exercise

2. Feature Workshops

3. Candidate Feature List

Prioritized Feature List

Selected Features

4. Iterative Development Cycle

The way the project is kicked off may vary from project to project, but regardless of the approach taken, there should be an initial effort to define the vision. In figure 6.7, we see a "Design the Product Box" activity at the start of the project. This activity captures the high-level vision for the project and helps align the stakeholders behind a common mission, goals, and success criteria. In step 2, we have a series of feature workshops in which the project vision is broken down into potential features of the system. These workshops result in a candidate feature list (step 3), which is then prioritized based on business value and risk and forms the prioritized feature list for the iterative development cycle (step 4).

At this macro level, we can see examples of value-based decomposition and prioritization. The top three things the project must deliver are captured on the vision box. (The limit of three is intentional, to keep the team focused on prioritizing the features and making trade-offs.) The major functional elements of the vision are drawn out in the feature workshops. The features are then prioritized and consumed by the development cycle. As we get into development and try to implement the features, we are likely to discover the need for supporting features and other elements that previously had not been considered. The process of identifying additional requirements, grouping or breaking them down into functional elements, and prioritizing those elements repeats over and over at an increasingly refined and more detailed level, similar to a fractal leaf pattern (see figure 6.8).

Figure 6.8: Fractal Leaf Pattern

This is another example of how agile methods tackle what the *PMBOK® Guide* calls "progressive elaboration" (discussed earlier in this chapter).[3] In value-based decomposition and prioritization, we pull forward elements of the project—in whatever size and level of detail is appropriate for the project phase we are in and how much we currently know about the project—into a format that we can work with for the next process. We then continue to refine and elaborate those elements, adding increasing levels of detail and transforming them into a format that can be further refined in subsequent processes. The end product of the progressive elaboration is a highly detailed deliverable that is still true to the original design objectives.

With agile methods, we do not attempt to specify fully detailed requirements upfront. Instead, we initially keep the requirements "coarse grained," and then progressively refine them as the process progresses. This approach has a number of advantages:

» It helps keep the overall design balanced so the product does not become lopsided by over-development in any particular area.
» It delays decisions on implementation details until the "last responsible moment." This means we are not rushing to develop things that may later need to be changed as a result of new information or late-breaking change requests.

As a side note, this is one of the many paradoxes or balancing decisions involved in agile projects. We aim to make decisions late to incorporate changes, while we build increments of the system early to gain feedback, which can then result in system changes. It may sound silly, but this approach is really a way to mitigate risks and find out about problems and changes within the friendlier project environment, where changes cost less, than in the more hostile production environment where changes are much more expensive to make.

TRICKS OF THE TRADE® If this all sounds well and good, but you are still not sure how you would answer a question about value-based decomposition and prioritization in the exam, just remember this: on agile projects, we refine the requirements from the backlog into the iteration goal. We then further refine the iteration goal requirements into the iteration plan and then into user stories. And we continue to refine the user stories' requirements during discussions and even mention them in the daily stand-up meetings. These are all practical examples of how project elements get decomposed and prioritized at the last responsible moment.

Agile Games (Collaborative/Innovation Games)

Innovation games, also known as collaborative games, are facilitated workshop techniques that agile teams use to help stakeholders better understand complex or ambiguous issues and reach consensus on an agreed-upon solution.

The following are examples of collaborative games used on agile projects:

» **Remember the Future**: This is a vision-setting and requirements-elicitation exercise.
» **Prune the Product Tree**: This exercise helps gather and shape requirements.
» **Speedboat**: The purpose of this exercise is to identify threats and opportunities (risks) for the project.
» **Buy a Feature**: This is a prioritization exercise.
» **Bang-for-the-Buck**: This exercise looks at value versus cost rankings.

Let's discuss the most commonly used of these games in more detail, starting with the Remember the Future exercise.

Remember the Future

This facilitated exercise engages project stakeholders in imagining that the release or iteration is now complete. They then describe what they imagine has occurred for the iteration or release to be successful.

How It Works For purposes of this discussion, let's use the example of planning a release six months out. We get the project stakeholders, including the team, users, and sponsors, together and ask them to imagine that it is now six months plus two weeks from the current date. The reason we tell them to imagine two weeks after the end of the release is because that's often how long it takes for the acceptance and implementation "dust" to settle.

The exercise starts with each stakeholder working independently. For the next 20 minutes, each person's job is to list what was completed for the release to be successful. One way to explain this part of the exercise is to ask people to imagine they are writing a report for their boss or department about how the release went, in which they list all the things that were completed and delivered. The stakeholders should record the completed and delivered items on sticky notes, with one item on each note.

Once the 20 minutes are up, everyone transfers their sticky notes to a wall. Then, as a team, the stakeholders work together to group the sticky notes into associated clusters and remove any duplicates. This process can take another 20 minutes as people clarify the meaning of their sticky notes and create headings to correctly identify each group of items.

Figure 6.9: Remember the Future

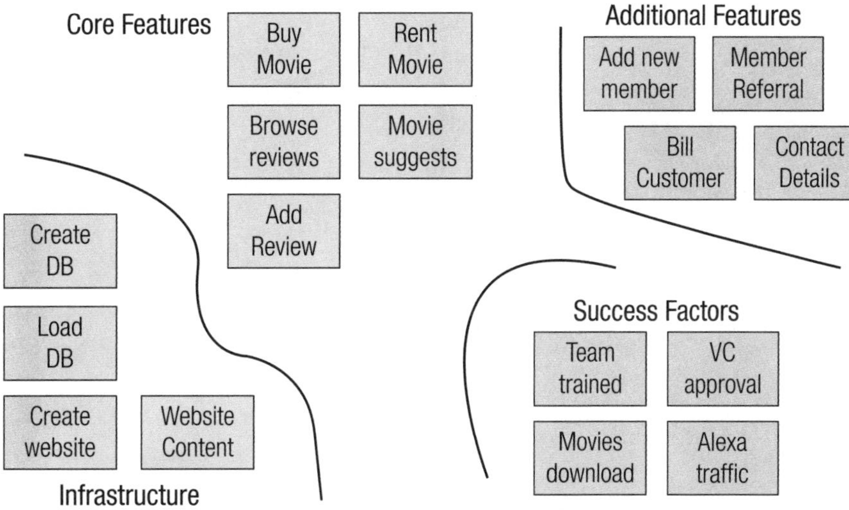

Core Features

| Buy Movie | Rent Movie |

| Browse reviews | Movie suggests |

| Add Review |

Create DB

Load DB

Create website | Website Content

Infrastructure

Additional Features

| Add new member | Member Referral |

| Bill Customer | Contact Details |

Success Factors

| Team trained | VC approval |

| Movies download | Alexa traffic |

Image originally published in "The Melin Exercise" by Mike Griffiths on gantthead.com on April 20, 2009, copyright © 2009 gantthead.com. Reproduced by permission of gantthead.com.

Theory Behind the Game   The game is designed in this way because of findings from numerous studies in cognitive psychology. When asked the open question of "What should a system or product do?" people struggle to generate a complete list of features and interim steps. However, if we vary the question just slightly and ask people to imagine that it is now some point after the delivery date and ask them to "remember" all the things the system or project has done to be successful, we get significantly different results. Because the event is now "in the past," the participants must mentally generate a sequence of events that led to this result. This exercise leads to improved definitions and more detailed descriptions of the interim steps.

Of course, the purpose of the Remember the Future game is not really to predict the future. Instead, we are trying to better understand the stakeholders' definition of success and how we can achieve that successful outcome.

Prune the Product Tree

This exercise engages the participants in brainstorming a product's functionality and features.

How It Works   For this game, we start by drawing a big tree with a trunk and branches on a whiteboard or flip chart. Artistic ability does not matter here—we are just creating a placeholder for features. We then invite the participants to add the features as leaves to the product tree. A good way to explain this part of the exercise is to say that the tree is the product, in that the trunk represents what we already know or have built so far, and the outer branches represent new functionality that has yet to be designed. Encourage the stakeholders to group related features close to each other on the tree. Supporting features should be closer to the trunk, and features that are dependent upon those supporting features should be further out or higher up on the tree.

Figure 6.10: Prune the Product Tree

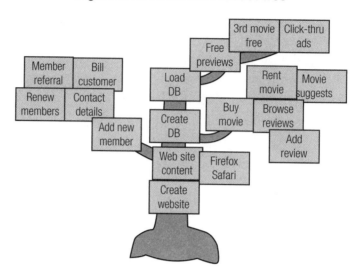

Theory Behind the Game   By thinking about how the features relate to each other and to existing functionality, stakeholders can better understand the process of setting priorities and defining development sequences. This exercise assists participants in the process of progressive elaboration. We encourage stakeholders to add new sticky notes to the tree to identify additional features. We then expand into more details of the product as the features are split out into user stories and other supporting requirements emerge. If you use yellow sticky notes, the features end up looking like autumn leaves, and you can expect to see a lumpy tree with patchy leaves emerge as the participants continue to identify and add more feature "leaves."

Speedboat or Sailboat

Once the features and user stories are identified on our product tree, we may be tempted to jump right into prioritizing and scheduling these tasks, but there is one very important step that should occur first. We need to identify and plan to either mitigate (reduce) or avoid potential project threats and take advantage of potential opportunities. This step has to happen before we prioritize our user stories because many of the risk response steps will need to be factored into the prioritization process. If we leave risk mitigation until after we've finished prioritizing our user stories, we will find ourselves trying to shoehorn important tasks into already-full iterations, and this approach simply will not work.

The Speedboat game, which is also sometimes called Sailboat, uses the features and user stories identified in the Prune the Product Tree game. It focuses on gathering project risks—both bad risks, which are threats to the project, and good risks, which are potential opportunities. This exercise is very quick to set up and facilitate, and it typically results in a good list of project risks.

How It Works   To start, we place a whiteboard or flip chart to the left of the Product Tree diagram from the previous exercise. We then draw a waterline and a picture of a boat, with the boat facing in the direction of the Product Tree. We explain to participants that the boat represents the project. For example, we may say "Here is the project heading toward the goal we just developed. What are the anchors (or threats) that could slow us down or even sink us? And what other factors (or opportunities) could be wind in our sails and help propel us toward our goal?"

The stakeholders then work as a group to create "anchor" sticky notes for the threats and impediments to the project. Anchor notes are posted below the waterline. The stakeholders also create "wind" sticky notes for opportunities, which they post above the waterline. To further distinguish the project threats from the opportunities, teams often use yellow or red sticky notes for the threats and blue or white sticky notes for the opportunities.

Figure 6.11: Speedboat or Sailboat

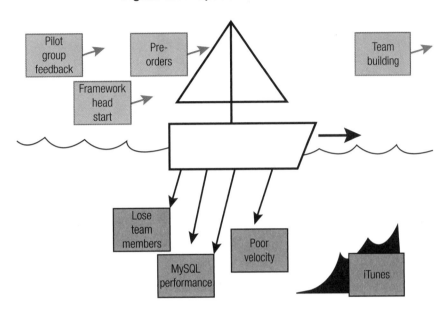

Theory Behind the Game   This game provides a benefit beyond identifying threats and opportunities for the project. Some people need a way to articulate their concerns before they are comfortable committing to work. Once their worries are recorded and recognized, they are less encumbered by these concerns and are happier to contribute. They have said their piece and done their duty in identifying the risk, so they can now move on more effectively than if they were still carrying unvoiced concerns.

This is not to say that simply recording the risks will make the threats go away or the opportunities happen. The record of risks is really just where the hard work of threat reduction and avoidance or opportunity enhancement begins. We still have to go through the effort of determining how to respond to risks, assessing those actions, and building the responses into the project. However, this game helps people remove mental obstacles so they can move on more happily, knowing that their concerns are on the project's "radar" of things to watch for and manage.

Estimation

Estimation is a large topic. For the exam, you will be tested on your knowledge of agile estimation theory and your ability to perform simple agile estimating techniques. Estimating knowledge worker projects is especially difficult, because these projects are complex and are often new to the organization. This means the organization may not have undertaken similar projects before, the approach or technology being used might be new, and there are likely to be some unknowns. This combination of complexity and uncertainty makes it more problematic to estimate knowledge worker projects than other types of projects.

The following are some general points and good practices for agile estimation to keep in mind, both for the exam and for your real-world projects:

» **Why do we estimate?** Estimates are necessary for sizing and approving projects, calculating ROI and IRR, and determining which pieces of work can be done within a release or iteration.

» **How are estimates created?** Estimates are created by progressing through the stages of determining the project's size, effort, schedule, and finally cost. To create a holistic estimate, the project's development, rollout, and sustainment costs also need to be factored in.

» **How should estimates be stated?** We use the term "estimates" and not "predictions" because there is some degree of uncertainty in an estimate. Therefore, estimates should be stated as ranges (e.g., "$4,000 to $4,500," or "16 to 18 months") to manage expectations about the project's uncertainty.

» **When do we estimate?** We should not reserve estimating for when we know the least about the project—at the beginning. Upfront estimates are certainly necessary, but they are also the least accurate. This means we need to estimate continuously throughout the project, factoring in the actual costs or durations to date to create better estimates for the project going forward.

» **Who estimates?** Just as with *when* we estimate, we shouldn't reserve estimating for *the person* who knows the least about the project's execution or acceptance—the project manager. Instead, we need to get the team members who will be doing the work involved with the estimation process. After all, they know the most about the technology, and their involvement will increase their buy-in to the estimates.

Now let's break down the how-to aspect of agile estimation by looking at the T&Ts and K&Ss used to create the estimates.

T&T Wideband Delphi and Planning Poker

Wideband Delphi is a group-based estimation approach. This technique asks a panel of experts to submit estimates anonymously so no one knows which estimates belong to whom. The anonymous approach produces improved estimates because it minimizes both the "bandwagon effect" (where people tend to agree with a prominent viewpoint) and the "halo effect" (where people gravitate to the ideas of experts or superiors, rather than judging the ideas on their own merit).

A wideband Delphi estimation session starts with a planning effort to define the problem. Instead of estimating the whole project in one meeting, the group breaks down the project or large problem into more manageable chunks. The team creates a problem specification, identifies the assumptions and constraints, and outlines the process for subsequent rounds of estimation. For example, details such as whether people should omit documentation time from the estimates, the estimation units (e.g., person weeks, hours, dollars, etc.), and the exit criteria (e.g., we want to get to +/- 20 percent tolerance on the estimate range) are included in the plan, and a kickoff meeting for the team of estimators is scheduled.

Before they begin creating estimates, participants read the problem specification and have an opportunity to raise and discuss qualification questions. They also receive sheets of paper with spaces where they can enter their estimates for different tasks. The facilitator then gathers the estimates and plots them on a chart, without identifying which estimate is from which estimator.

Figure 6.12: Wideband Delphi Technique—Round 1 Estimates

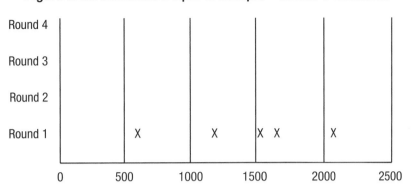

In figure 6.12, we can see that after the first round of the estimation process, the estimates range from approximately 600 person hours to 2,100 person hours. It doesn't matter if the 600-hour estimate came from the project manager or if the 2,100-hour estimate came from the most experienced developer. All of this information is kept anonymous.

The participants then discuss the different tasks and any assumptions or other significant factors that influenced their estimates before repeating the estimating process. For example, Bill might report "I added two weeks for regression testing of downstream applications, because we are amending the accounting table; the last time we did that, it broke the billing system, so we need to allow some time for additional testing and possible remediation." Once all the tasks, assumptions, and significant factors have been discussed, the group repeats the anonymous estimation process. After several rounds of this process, we usually start to see more consensus around the estimates, as shown in figure 6.13.

Figure 6.13: Wideband Delphi Technique—Getting Closer to Consensus

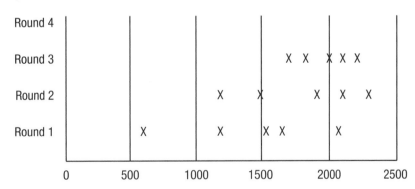

In this chart, we see that with each estimating round, there has been a "northeast" drift toward a tighter set of estimates. This drift demonstrates the emerging consensus that the particular problem or part of the project being estimated will require a higher range of person hours. Once the estimates have come together enough for the group to reach their exit criteria (in this example, the highest and lowest estimates must be within a range of +/- 20 percent of the median estimate), the process stops. A single master task list is then created from everyone's task lists. If any tasks were excluded from estimation (such as documentation in this case), then those tasks are added to the master list. The team reviews the results to make sure everyone agrees on the final task list and estimate range.

Wideband Delphi estimation is a good technique for agile teams to use, because it is:

» **Iterative**: The process is repeated several times.
» **Adaptive**: Based on feedback from other participants, team members have a chance to update and improve their next round of estimates.
» **Collaborative**: It is a team-based collaborative process that improves participants' buy-in to the results.

Planning Poker

The wideband Delphi technique is often implemented as "planning poker." This variation of the technique combines all of the essential elements of wideband Delphi in a fast, collaborative process. Planning poker uses playing cards with numbers on them. The numbers, which are often based on the Fibonacci sequence (described later in this chapter), represent sizing units, such as developer days or story points. A set of cards, as shown in figure 6.14, is given to each planning participant.

Figure 6.14: Planning Poker Cards

Once the cards have been distributed, a moderator (often the product owner or customer) reads a user story, which the group then discusses briefly before each estimator selects a card to represent his or her estimate for the user story. The participants all turn over their cards simultaneously so that everyone can see the numbers. For example, imagine the moderator reads, "Create password change functionality." Once the team discusses the user story, someone counts to three and everyone reveals the card that they believe best represents the effort required to develop that user story.

If there is a group of four people, and three of them turn over cards with the number 5 and one person turns over a card with the number 3, the task is recorded as a "5." Since the range was small and there is little debate about the estimate, the process moves onto the next story to keep the game moving quickly. If, however, there were three cards with the number 5 and one card with the number 13, then the outlier (the "13") would be discussed. For example, the conversation might go something like this:

Facilitator: Okay, Bob, can you tell us why you think this is a 13?
Bob: Well, we are using LDAP authentication to keep the passwords synchronized with other applications. Password changes will need to be pushed back to the LDAP server, and we don't have security permissions to do that. So we need to get the security group engaged and that takes time.
Facilitator: Hmm, I didn't know that. Okay, let's estimate this again.

The process is then repeated—everyone picks up their card and estimates again, taking the new information into account. In doing so, we might see a new consensus emerge around the number 13.

Like fist-of-five voting (discussed in chapter 4, Stakeholder Engagement), planning poker is an example of a participatory decision model. As stakeholders' involvement in the process increases, so too does their commitment to the outcome, as illustrated in figure 6.15.

Figure 6.15: Commitment Increases as Involvement Increases

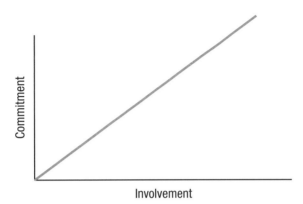

Planning poker is faithful to the wideband Delphi approach in that it combines the following elements:

» It has multiple iterations of estimation, where needed.
» It requires participants to submit estimates at the same time to help counter the bandwagon effect and the halo effect.
» It allows group convergence on supported estimates.

In addition, studies at Motorola and Microsoft show that many project teams find planning poker to not only be as accurate as their previous approach to estimation, but also quicker and more enjoyable.[4] That said, the goal of the exercise is not to create precise estimates. Instead, this technique helps the team quickly and cheaply achieve consensus around reasonable estimates to move the project forward.

T&T   Ideal Time

When asking a team to estimate work, the topic of how best to factor in interruptions, diversions, and nonproject work usually crops up. Such nonproject activities may include attending staff meetings, checking e-mails, and going to the occasional doctor's visit. For example, for salaried team members who have 40-hour workweeks, should we estimate 35 hours a week for them to work on the project and allow 5 hours for them to do these other activities? And what about contract staff? They have fewer staff meetings and seem to come in when sick anyway, so should we count on 38 hours for them?

Putting stereotypes or our own expectations aside, we can simplify the discussion by talking about ideal time. This means we ask team members to estimate as if there were no interruptions. In an eight-hour day, we tell team members to assume all eight hours would be available for work. This is obviously not a very realistic approach, but the purpose of talking about ideal time is to simplify the estimation process and take the variable of availability out of the equation. In doing so, we can get a more accurate sense of the effort involved in the work.

So ideal time is how long something would take, if all the other peripheral work and distractions were removed. It assumes that the user story being estimated is the only thing being worked on, that there will be no interruptions, and that we have everything we need, meaning we are not waiting for someone to deliver work or provide information.

EXERCISE

For this exercise, assume that after you have slept and performed essential activities like washing, preparing food, and eating, you have 12 available hours left to you in your day. Now let's say that studying for the PMI-ACP exam will take you 60 hours. (Note: This is a made-up number; the amount of time you will need to prepare for the exam will vary based on your experience.) Using this information, calculate the ideal time estimate and the likely time estimate for studying for the exam.

Ideal Time:	
Likely Time:	

ANSWER

Ideal Time:	If preparing for the exam theoretically takes 60 hours and we have 12 hours a day available, then we do the following calculation: $$60 / 12 = 5$$ So in ideal time, it should only take us 5 days to complete all studying required to pass the PMI-ACP exam.
Likely Time:	To come up with a likely time estimate, we take other factors, like work and family, into account and the fact that there are nights when we arrive home and are too tired to think about anything. Perhaps it is more realistic to assume that, on average, we will likely get 4 hours per week to spend on preparing for the PMI-ACP exam. Using this information, we can do the following calculation: $$60 / 4 = 15$$ So at this rate, it will take 15 weeks to prepare for the exam.

This exercise brings forward another point to consider—the effectiveness of the timeline. Even if we did have 12 hours a day for 5 straight days to study for the exam, we would not be able to retain or absorb all the information in that time. So studying over a more extended period of time may not only be more realistic, but in this example, it is also probably more effective. In the same way, we need to be careful the timeline isn't too long, to avoid the risk of "knowledge leak," or the slow decline of knowledge that we don't use every day. While too short of a timeline can be a problem, so can too slow of a process.

© 2012 RMC Publications, Inc • 952.846.4484 • info@rmcproject.com • www.rmcproject.com

T&T Relative Sizing / Story Points

Relative sizing and story points help solve two common problems with estimation:

1. People are not very good at predicting the absolute size of work.
2. The estimation process is difficult and unpopular.

Oftentimes on projects, what should be trivial work takes much longer to complete than anticipated, and sometimes new and unforeseen tasks appear. The whole process takes longer than we expected. We could try to factor these issues into all estimates, but then we would be criticized for padding the estimates. This apparent no-win situation is why estimating has become so unpopular with team members.

So how do we counter this frustration? It turns out that while people are not very accurate at making absolute estimates, they are better at (and at least more comfortable with) making comparative estimates. The difference between absolute and comparative estimates can be illustrated with the example of giving directions. We could explain that you get to the grocery store by traveling 1.3 miles southeast (an absolute approach to giving directions), but it is easier both to estimate and to understand if we say you should go straight out the door for about 8 or 9 blocks until you reach the park, and then the grocery store is another 5 blocks past the park. This second explanation is relative to common and recognizable surroundings (blocks) and not stated in absolute measurements.

Like estimating distance via blocks rather than mile measurements, if we have known chunks of work already done, we can estimate new pieces of work more quickly and accurately by referencing the known entities. Using the creation of a software system as an example, imagine we have developed a simple input screen and have given that task a relative score of 2 story points. We can then estimate other tasks in reference to the input screen score. So we might assign 1 story point to a simple fix or change to a screen because we think it's only about half as much work as developing the simple reference screen. We might also estimate the development of other simple screens as 2 story points, and bigger pieces of work could be 3-point or 5-point stories. In this example, "2 story points" has become the equivalent of a city block, in that it now serves as the reference that we use to estimate other things by.

Now, of course, taking a comparative approach to estimating does not stop weird things from happening or keep activities from taking longer than anticipated on our projects, but switching the estimation unit from hours to story points does make it easier to accept. Rather than saying we are bad at estimating, we recognize that a couple of stories took longer than we thought. The estimates weren't based on our own sense of time; they were based on how well we understood how the new activities compared to what was already completed on the project.

Another advantage of estimating in story points versus hours or days is that we remove the artificial ceiling of "hours per week." If a team member completed user stories that totaled 40 hours of estimated work by noon on Friday, what is the incentive to take the next story off the stack and carry on working in the afternoon? Hour and day estimates are too close to our workweeks and our sense of duty and accomplishment; the connection can actually cause productivity issues. So instead we say, "Last week the team delivered 42 story points, and this week they delivered 45." Can you see how this feels different than saying "Last week the team did 120 hours of work, and this week they did 130 hours"?

The term you use for the relative measures of work—whether it be "story points," just "points," or "gummy bears"—does not matter. The idea is to get away from estimating in hours, which not only creates artificial ceilings but can also create issues when some people have other demands on their time and never really stand a chance of delivering 40 hours' worth of work functionality in a week.

In his book, *User Stories Applied: For Agile Software Development*, Mike Cohn asserts that the best approach for estimating user stories is one that:[5]

» Allows us to change our mind whenever we have new information about a story
» Works for both epics and smaller user stories
» Doesn't take a lot of time
» Provides useful information about our progress and the work remaining
» Is tolerant of imprecision in the estimates
» Can be used to plan releases

In addition, we should keep the following points in mind when estimating user stories:

» **Teams should own the story point definition**: The story point sizing being used on the project should be created and owned by the team. For example, the team can decide 1 story point equals the effort involved in creating a simple screen, or that 1 story point is equal to the amount of work done in an ideal day (with no interruptions for meetings, e-mail, etc.). Whatever size unit the team chooses, that is what should be used. By accepting the team's decisions about the estimating unit, we reinforce their ownership of the estimates. And it doesn't matter if another team's story point unit represents an ideal developer *week*, rather than a *day*. The unit doesn't have to be consistent across the organization; it just needs to be used consistently within the project. We shouldn't try to compare velocities between teams, because the unique composition and definition of each team's story point makes such comparison meaningless.

» **Story point estimates should be all inclusive**: We should not need to add time to the project for unit testing or refactoring. Instead, the story point estimates should include all known activities. Otherwise, we end up trying to shoehorn in extra tasks or resort to multiplying the estimates by a preset factor (e.g., 1.5) to account for additional work. Inclusive story point estimates are preferred over a "magic multiplier" approach, because the inclusive estimates are more accurate and transparent. In contrast, multipliers can mistakenly be applied several times or forgotten about and are harder to defend.

» **When disaggregating, the totals do not need to match**: When breaking epics into user stories, it is okay if the sum of the estimates for the user stories exceeds the estimate for the epic. One reason the epic had to be broken down in the first place was that it was too big to estimate accurately. As we break down the epic and learn more about the work involved, we should expect the estimates for the user stories to reflect the new information. The same goes for breaking down user stories into tasks; the sum of the estimates for the tasks might not equal the estimate for the user story.

» **Sizes should be relative:** A 2-point user story should be equivalent to about twice as much effort or time as a 1-point story. A 3-point story should be equivalent to about three times as much effort or time as a 1-point story and about equal to the combination of a 1-point story and a 2-point story. Although this sounds obvious, it's still worth stating. On some scales, numbers can indicate placement on a range from low to medium to high or from small to medium to large to enormous. But with a relative scale, the base unit needs to be mathematically equivalent so that we can use the units to calculate velocity, compare iterations, and validate our release plan. So completing four 5-point user stories should be equivalent to completing twenty 1-point user stories.

» **Complexity, work effort, and risk should all count**: The total time required to complete work is a function of the work's complexity (does the work require analysis or is it likely to result in surprises?), the effort involved (do we have to add a single data field, or 30 fields?), and its risk (if we can't complete the work using plan A, we might have to rethink this piece of the project). We need to ensure all three attributes are assessed when the team is estimating user stories.

EXERCISE

Test your knowledge of agile estimating concepts by answering the true or false questions in the following table:

Question	True or False
Agile estimates are all encompassing; they should include time for documentation and testing.	
Agile estimates are timeboxed; once the estimates are set, they cannot be altered.	
Agile estimates are created by the product owner.	
Story points are preferable to ideal days, because story points better match estimate characteristics; they are called "stories," because not all stories are true.	
Agile teams create their own estimates.	
Risk should be not factored into user story estimates.	
Teams new to agile should rely on the experienced project manager to create the estimates for them.	

ANSWER

Question	True or False
Agile estimates are all encompassing; they should include time for documentation and testing.	True
Agile estimates are timeboxed; once the estimates are set, they cannot be altered.	False
Agile estimates are created by the product owner.	False
Story points are preferable to ideal days, because story points better match estimate characteristics; they are called "stories," because not all stories are true.	False
Agile teams create their own estimates.	True
Risk should be not factored into user story estimates.	False
Teams new to agile should rely on the experienced project manager to create the estimates for them.	False

The Fibonacci Sequence

Planning poker cards and story points are often estimated using the Fibonacci sequence, or variations of this sequence. The first numbers in the Fibonacci sequence are "0, 1, 1, 2, 3, 5, 8, 13, 21..." This sequence is derived by adding the previous two numbers together to get the next number in the sequence. So, $0 + 1 = 1$, $1 + 1 = 2$, $1 + 2 = 3$, $2 + 3 = 5$, and so on. Teams use the Fibonacci sequence to estimate size. It is a naturally occurring sequence that crops up frequently in connection with how things get bigger. Rabbit populations, shells, and tree branches follow the Fibonacci sequence, as do problem sizes and the effort to solve them. For the exam, you don't need to understand how to apply the Fibonacci sequence, but it is helpful to understand that this sequence can be used in estimating. With this sequence, there is enough variation in the number values to eliminate most of the squabbling over slight differences in estimates.

Figure 6.16: The Fibonacci Sequence

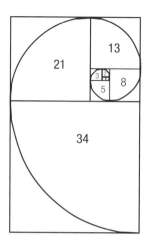

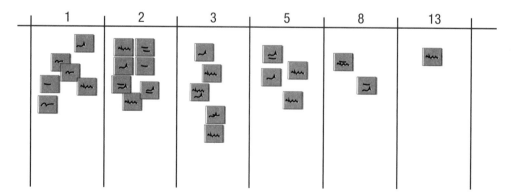

T&T Affinity Estimating

Affinity estimating is the process of grouping requirements into categories or collections. For agile projects, this technique is often used to group similarly sized user stories together. Affinity estimating is a form of triangulation; it provides a comparative view of the estimates and gives the team an opportunity to do a reality check. By placing the user stories into size categories, it is easier to see whether user stories that are assigned similar estimates are in fact comparable in size. This technique helps the team make sure they have not gradually altered the measurement value of a story point.

A good way to do this triangulation is to establish columns on a wall that represent different sizes of user stories, and then place each user story card into the appropriate column. As a new user story is estimated, it should also be placed in the appropriate column and compared to the cards that are already there. If the new user story looks like it fits in with the others already posted in the column, then great—the estimation scheme has not warped. If it is wildly different, however, we need to do a checkpoint with the team to discuss what exactly a story point means and then recalibrate the estimates.

Figure 6.17: Affinity Estimating

© 2012 RMC Publications, Inc • 952.846.4484 • info@rmcproject.com • www.rmcproject.com

Time, Budget, and Cost Estimation (via Size, Effort, and Cost Estimation)

We've talked about different tools and techniques used to create estimates. Now let's look at the steps involved in estimating:

1. **Determine the size** of the project in story points or ideal time.
2. **Calculate the effort** for the work in hours or person days (or person weeks or months) by determining the availability and capacity of the team.
3. **Convert the effort into a schedule** by factoring in the team size, required resources, and dependencies.
4. **Calculate the cost** by applying labor rates and adding in other project cost elements.

Let's discuss each of these steps in more detail:

Step 1: Determine the size of the project in story points or ideal days.

To complete this step, we use the techniques we discussed earlier in this section, including wideband Delphi estimation and planning poker.

Step 2: Calculate the effort for the work in hours or person days (or person weeks or months).

To complete this step, we need to determine the availability and capacity of the team. This means if we had chosen to estimate the work in ideal time for the sake of simplicity and speed, we now have to determine what the blended team availability is likely to be. We do this by calculating the average of the team members' expected availability and then dividing the ideal time estimate by this average.

For example, imagine a small team of three people—Bob, Bill, and Mary. Bob is typically available to work on the project 80 percent of the time, Bill is available 70 percent of the time, and Mary is available 75 percent of the time. Using this information, we calculate the team's average availability: (0.80 + 0.70 + 0.75) / 3 = 0.75, or 75%. So if our ideal time estimate for the project totalled 500 days, we can calculate the likely effort by dividing the ideal time by the average availability: 500 / 0.75 = 670 person days.

As the project progresses, we need to check the team's availability and capacity against this calculation to determine whether the original approximations were correct. If the same team of three people repeatedly completes a combined total of 100 hours' worth of work per 40-hour workweek, then their actual capacity is 100 / (40 x 3) = 83%. In other words, they actually work a little faster than they estimated.

As work progresses, we increasingly rely on the actual velocity of the team when we gauge the future progress of the project. Using the availability rate of 83 percent (which is the team's actual velocity), we can recalculate the effort of the 500-ideal-day project: 500 / 0.83 = 603 person days.

Step 3: Convert the effort into a schedule by factoring in the team size, required resources, and dependencies.

Now we have to translate the effort into a schedule duration and determine if our 603-day project will be completed by our team of three people in 201 days (603 / 3 = 201) or in some other duration.

When creating the schedule, we have to address questions such as:

» Can the work be done independently from other pieces of the project?
» Can it be worked on by any developer at any given time?
» Or are there scheduling dependencies or skill constraints that will require a longer duration?

As represented by the "I" in the INVEST mnemonic (see chapter 4, Stakeholder Engagement), "independent" is one of the characteristics of a good user story. This means good user stories should not be tightly coupled to other stories. Of course, reality has a way of messing up this goal, but the PMI-ACP exam will take the simpler approach. For the exam, assume user stories are truly independent, which makes the calculations as simple as dividing the effort by the number of resources.

Using our previous example, this means our project duration is indeed expected to be 201 days. If we want to translate this duration into months, we simply have to divide the total number of days by the number of working days in a month. If you assume a five-day workweek, there are about 21 working days in a typical month, so 201 / 21 = 9.6 months. Therefore, our project's schedule duration is 201 days, or 9.6 months.

For those who are interested in understanding the relationship between effort and schedule beyond what you need to know for the exam, visit **www.rmcproject.com/ agileprep** to access a free article about the Putnam Norden Rayleigh curve.

Step 4: Calculate the cost by applying labor rates and adding in other project cost elements.

Once we have a duration calculated for our project, it is fairly easy to calculate the costs in monetary terms. The formula for this calculation is:

$$\text{Total cost} = (\text{Time} \times \text{Resource rate}) + \text{Other project costs}$$

Let's look at an example, using our project time estimate of 9.6 months. To do this calculation, we need to know the team members' rates. Let's say Bob's rate is $50 per hour, Bill's rate is $80 per hour, and Mary's rate is $95 per hour. Then we need to convert our project time estimate into hours. With an 8-hour workday and approximately 21 work days per month, there are about 168 work hours per month (8 x 21 = 168). So 9.6 x 168 = about 1,613 project hours.

Using this information, we can calculate the labor cost:

$$(1,613 \times \$50) + (1,613 \times \$80) + (1,613 \times \$95) = \$80,650 + \$129,040 + \$153,235 = \$362,925$$

Now we need to add other project costs, such as part-time resources involved in the project, hardware, software, training, supplies, travel, backfilling business representatives to free them up to contribute to the project, a warranty period after the product goes live, plus whatever else the project needs to fund. Once we've calculated in these additional costs, we will have our total cost. At this point, we would add agreed-upon contingency funds to the total cost to get our project budget. The amount of these funds is based on the project's risk and uncertainty and the organization's policies regarding contingency. For example, some companies use a standard range of 10 to 20 percent of the project's total costs for the contingency amount.

© 2012 RMC Publications, Inc • 952.846.4484 • info@rmcproject.com • www.rmcproject.com

EXERCISE

Convert the cost elements outlined in the following scenario into a final project budget:

Team Alpha's labor costs are $20,000 per month. The team will need 10 two-week iterations to complete the project. Deployment costs are estimated at $5,000. Half the team will be retained for a one-month warranty period. What do we expect the costs to be from now until the end of the warranty period (omitting contingency)?

ANSWER

The labor cost of $20,000 is a per-month cost. Since each iteration is 2 weeks, 10 iterations will be about 5 months. So $20,000 × 5 = $100,000.

We already know deployment costs are estimated to be $5,000, so there's no calculation necessary there.

Now let's look at the warranty costs. If half the team is retained for the warranty period, we assume the burn rate for that period will be half of what it was during the project. So we calculate 0.5 × $20,000 = $10,000.

Using all of this data, we can calculate the total cost between now and the end of the warranty period:

$100,000 (labor) + $5,000 (deployment) + $10,000 (warranty) = $115,000

K&S Level 3 — Agile Project Accounting Principles

Understanding the value and benefits of a project is one side of the equation, while understanding the costs is the other. When we consider the costs of running a knowledge worker project, labor costs often comprise a large portion of the expenses. So while there will also be costs associated with equipment, travel, licenses, specialized services, etc., labor costs typically make up the largest segment.

There are different ways to account for labor expenses on the project. Many companies take a team member's annual salary and divide that number by 52 to determine a weekly salary cost. They then use that figure for project estimates and for budgeting purposes. Other companies consider the fully burdened labor cost, which is the team member's salary plus the cost of providing office space, computers, benefits, etc. This fully burdened labor cost can easily be 50 percent higher than the salary expense alone for employees.

As project managers trying to estimate projects, we need to know what the organization's policy is for using burdened versus unburdened costs. We also need to consider the team member's involvement on the project. Are they dedicated to the project full time, 50 percent of the time, or some other percentage? Once we understand these variables, we can calculate labor costs for the project, as shown in the following table:

Role	Annual Salary	Fully Burdened Labor Cost	Burdened Cost per Iteration	Time on Project	Adjusted Cost per Iteration
Product Owner	$120,000	$180,000	$6,925	100%	$6,925
Developer	$100,000	$150,000	$5,770	100%	$5,770
Developer	$80,000	$120,000	$4,615	50%	$2,310
Analyst	$100,000	$150,000	$5,770	100%	$5,770
Tester	$90,000	$135,000	$5,195	100%	$5,195
				Total	**$25,970**

This table tells us our likely real cost per iteration is about $26,000. So if our project has 10 iterations, the labor portion will be $260,000.

Using these figures and the team's velocity metrics, we can also calculate a cost per story point. For example, if the team averages 26 points of work per iteration and each iteration costs $26,000, then each story point is costing $26,000 / 26 = $1,000 to develop.

Knowing the cost per story point can be helpful in quickly validating new functionality. For example, if the product owner asks about the likely effort and cost to develop a new report and the team estimates it at 5 story points, we can report that it will cost about $5,000 to develop.

Estimate Ranges

Estimates should be presented in ranges to indicate our level of confidence in the estimate and to manage stakeholder expectations. When working with estimates, we need to be aware of the quality of our input variables—it is all too easy to apply math to a bunch of highly speculative estimates and then begin to believe there is more accuracy to our estimates than is realistic.

We also want to avoid single point estimates. For example, saying "The project will cost $784,375.32" gives the wrong impression of accuracy. Instead, we should present estimates as ranges, such as "We believe the project will cost between $775,000 and $820,000."

Estimate ranges should be narrower when we are more certain about the estimates and wider when we are less certain. The diagram in figure 6.18 represents Barry Boehm's Estimate Convergence Graph, which shows how estimates for software projects move from a very broad range early in the life cycle to more manageable ranges once scope and specifications are understood and agreed upon. The ranges continue to narrow as we learn more about the project. Beneath the graph, I have added green text in parenthesis to indicate how the stages of an agile project often map to the degree of confidence in the estimate ranges.

Figure 6.18: Estimate Convergence Graph

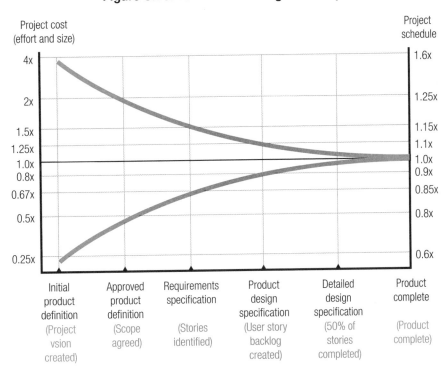

Estimating agile projects has some important similarities and differences from estimating traditional, noniterative projects. For example, near the start of an agile project when we know least about the project, our estimation techniques are quite similar to traditional estimation methods. We apply heuristic (expert-knowledge-based) approaches, such as looking at data from projects that created similar products or that were about the same size and complexity, to see how long those projects took. We can also perform parametric (calculation-based) estimates, such as bottom-up estimates that are based on the number and complexity of user stories.

As an agile project progresses, the iterations provide hard evidence of real progress. We can now start factoring in the velocity of completed iterations to better judge our true progress and estimate the remainder of the project.

Figure 6.19: Agile Versus Traditional Estimation Approaches

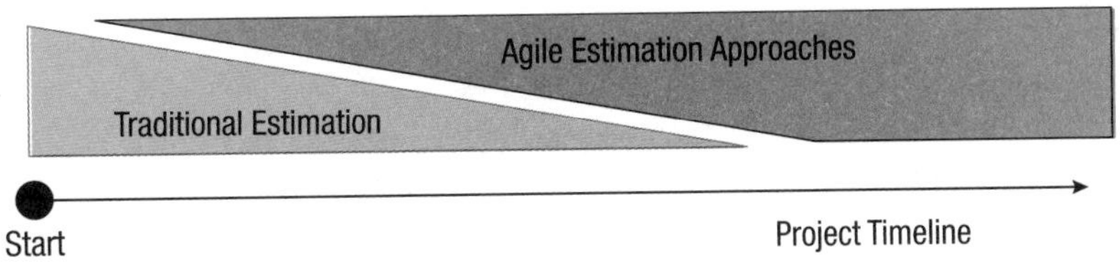

Image originally published in "Estimation for Agile Projects," by Mike Griffiths on gantthead.com on January 1, 2008, copyright © 2008 gantthead.com. Reproduced by permission of gantthead.com.

The reason why the velocity of completed iterations can be used to fairly accurately estimate project progress is because iterations involve all disciplines of development. As we discussed in chapter 4, Stakeholder Engagement, the user stories assigned to an iteration should involve all the components of the system that the final product will use. This means we get exposure to the different aspects of the development effort in each iteration, so soon into the project we are able to rely less and less on traditional upfront estimates and instead rely more heavily on the emerging velocity. We can also compare our velocity to the remaining backlog to estimate the timeline for project completion.

For example, if after the first three or four iterations, our velocity has stabilized and averages 50 points per two-week iteration, and the backlog of remaining work contains 500 points' worth of functionality, it is reasonable to assume that it will take 10 more iterations to complete the remaining work (500 / 50 = 10). Now let's calculate the burn rate per iteration, using Bob, Bill, and Mary again as our team members:

» For Bob, we would multiply 10 days by 8 hours by his rate of $50 per hour, for a total of $4,000.
» For Bill, we would multiply 10 days by 8 hours by his rate of $80 per hour, to get $6,400.
» For Mary, we would multiply 10 days by 8 hours by her rate of $95 per hour, to get $7,600.

Now if we add these numbers together ($4,000 + $6,400 + $7,600), we get an iteration burn rate of $18,000. Since we assume it will take 10 more iterations to complete the remaining work, we can calculate how much it will cost to complete the remaining backlog features: $18,000 x 10 iterations = $180,000.

This frequent feeding back of actual results into the estimates is a valuable reality check for the project. Underachievement is uncovered early, since agile projects measure progress by the number of accepted user stories, rather than an estimate of "percent complete" against analysis or design deliverables. It is very easy to be overly optimistic in interpreting "percent complete" on deliverables, whereas measuring progress based on acceptance is a much more solid indication of work accomplished. Uncovering underachievement is never pleasant, but it is best to uncover it early in the project, since we still have most of the project left to take corrective action.

Parkinson's Law and Student Syndrome

Agile practices also help mitigate the effects of Parkinson's Law and Student Syndrome. Parkinson's Law states that work tends to expand to fill the time available. In other words, if we have three months designated for gathering requirements, we will definitely spend all three months gathering requirements. Because agile projects focus on short time spans, such as iterations of one or two weeks, there is less "time to fill."

The idea behind Student Syndrome is that when people are given a deadline, they tend to wait until they have nearly reached the deadline before starting work. Again, the two-week iterations on agile projects mean the deadline is never far away, and this helps keep people focused.

Agile Plans

Before we get into talking about the actual planning documents and tools used on agile projects, let's take some time to compare the planning approaches of agile and traditional projects. Agile planning varies from traditional planning in three key ways. On agile projects:

1. Trial and demonstration uncover true requirements, which then require replanning.
2. Agile planning is less of an upfront effort, and instead is done more throughout the project.
3. Midcourse adjustments are the norm.

Let's explore each of these points in more detail.

1. **Trial and demonstration uncover true requirements, which then require replanning**. When undertaking uncertain endeavors like knowledge worker projects, getting stakeholder agreement is critical to the project's success. But how do we get stakeholders to agree on the requirements? It is often best to have an initial discussion about the vision for the product and iteratively progress from there with a tangible prototype. We can then allow stakeholders to adjust the project based on their experience with the prototype, rather than expecting them to fully describe in words what the product should look like and what it should do when there is still uncertainty about the scope and the proposed solution.

   So instead of creating very detailed specifications and plans, agile projects build a prototype to better understand the domain and use this prototype as the basis for further planning and elaboration.

2. **Agile planning is less of an upfront effort, and instead is done more throughout the project**. The *PMBOK® Guide* has a strong emphasis on upfront planning; it suggests focused planning efforts for a project's scope, schedule, budget, quality, human resources, communications, risk, procurements, change management, configuration management, and process improvement, all before beginning work on the project.[6] In contrast, agile methods recognize that the level of risk and uncertainty on knowledge worker projects can make heavy upfront planning problematic, so they spread the planning out more evenly throughout the project's life cycle. Spreading the effort out allows the project to better adjust to emerging information.

   As we've discussed repeatedly in this book, knowledge worker projects are often intangible and requirements are difficult to articulate. Rarely is the same system built twice, which makes it difficult to create analogies to existing functionality. These issues can lead to "evaluation difficulties," where mismatches develop between the team's interpretations of the original requirements and the customer's true goals.

   Executing a knowledge worker project is a complex, creative, and high-risk endeavor. Unlike many predictable manufacturing projects, the work is often an unprecedented, research-and-development-based process. Attempts to create detailed, task-oriented plans for knowledge worker teams are likely to lead to fragile, soon-abandoned plans. Or, if the plans are not abandoned, there will be a great deal of project management time spent updating these large plans, rather than managing the project.

   Unfortunately, many projects undertake the bulk of their planning too early in the life cycle, when little concrete data is known about the problem domain, the business environment, or the team dynamics. The planning emphasis with a traditional project management approach is illustrated in figure 6.20. As indicated by the green region, planning has predominantly been an early project life cycle activity.

Figure 6.20: Planning Focus with a Traditional Project Management Approach

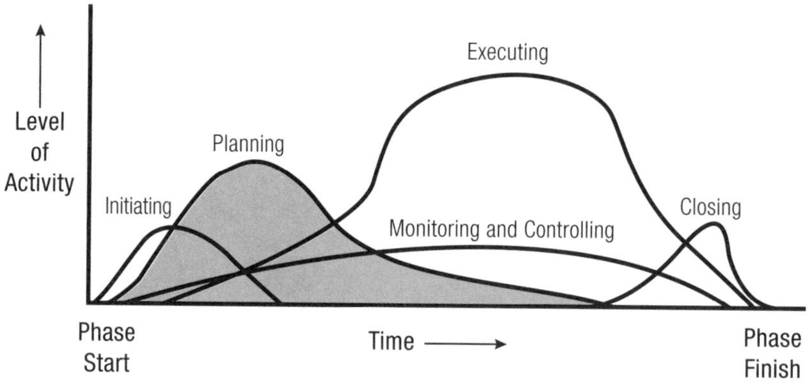

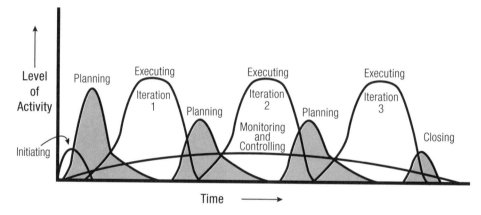

Image originally published in "Collaboration over Command and Control" by Mike Griffiths on gantthead.com on April 3, 2007, copyright © 2007 gantthead.com. Reproduced by permission of gantthead.com.

Agile methods accept the realities of knowledge worker projects and deliberately make planning a more highly visible and iterative component of the project life cycle. In figure 6.21, the repeated green sections indicate that planning happens throughout the life cycle.

Figure 6.21: Planning Focus with an Agile Project Management Approach

Image originally published in "Collaboration over Command and Control" by Mike Griffiths on gantthead.com on April 3, 2007, copyright © 2007 gantthead.com. Reproduced by permission of gantthead.com.

The total amount of planning on an agile project (combining all the green areas) often ends up being more than is done on a traditional project. So on agile projects, we end up doing more planning, not less, but the planning activities are distributed differently. No matter what the endeavor, there is always a responsible amount of upfront planning that should be done. Barry Boehm has illustrated the risks of not doing enough upfront planning, as represented in figure 6.22.

Figure 6.22: "Planning Risks" Graph

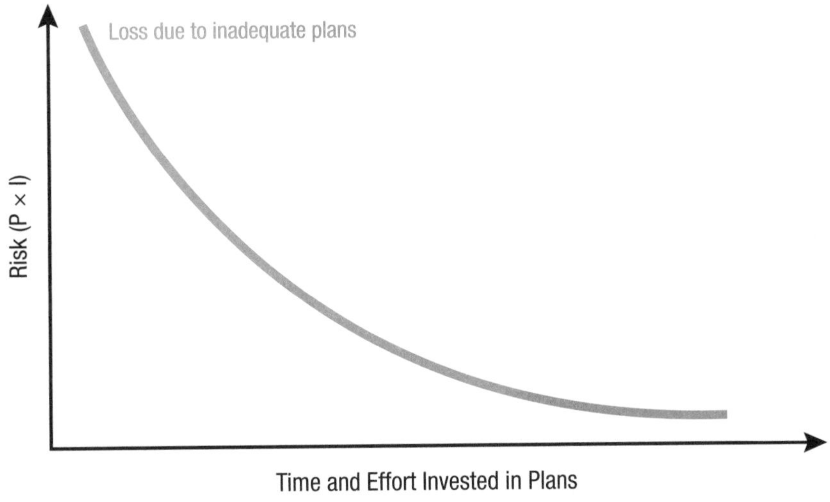

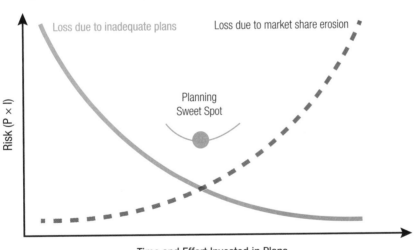

We can see on the left-hand side of figure 6.22 that when little time and effort is invested in planning, the risk of oversight and of delays due to rework is high. Then, as more time and effort is invested into planning, this risk drops away. But what some people miss is that there is a corollary risk of doing too much upfront planning. Barry Boehm's illustration of this risk is represented in figure 6.23.

Figure 6.23: Corollary Risk of Doing Too Much Upfront Planning

In figure 6.23, we can see that the dotted line represents the risks involved in doing too much upfront planning. The risk starts off low, but as more time and effort is invested in upfront planning, the risk of creating very detailed, brittle plans increases, as do the risks of delaying the project delivery and the return on investment because too much time was spent planning.

So we should aim for the sweet spot, where the sum of these two risks is lowest. We need to do enough upfront planning to reduce the bulk of the duplication and rework risk, while avoiding overplanning to minimize the risk of a late ROI and a brittle project plan. These curves are true for any kind of project, but due to the changeable nature of agile projects, the risk of the plan breaking escalates sooner than on more stable, predictable projects. Therefore, the amount of upfront planning required for agile projects is typically less than other projects.

3. **Midcourse adjustments are the norm**. When aiming at a static target, it is appropriate to aim very carefully and then fire toward the fixed target. When aiming at a moving target that is not following a predictable path, we need more of a guided-missile approach, making a lot of mid-flight adjustments to ensure we reach our target.

A guided missile is pointed in a general direction and then, once it is released, a sophisticated system of sensors, thrusters, and feedback systems takes over, guiding the missile to the moving target. This analogy is appropriate for agile projects, because they often have moving targets. The product the customer wants may be transformed by late-breaking change requests, which are triggered by changes in the business environment or offerings from competitors. To stay on target, agile methods use sophisticated sensing and adaptation systems to gather feedback and make adjustments to the backlog and plans as the project work is being done.

As a side note, I do realize that missiles have a lot of negative connotations—they are destructive, and they blow up and hurt people—none of which are good ways to describe a project environment! With the missile analogy, however, let's focus on the missile's ability to steer toward a moving target and, instead of exploding, imagine it delivers something pleasant, such as a bunch of flowers, once it reaches its target.

Figure 6.24: Agile Methods Take a Guided Missile Approach

Another way to explain this concept would be to quote my first project manager, who used to say, *"You cannot chase a dog with a train!"* It comes to roughly the same thing—a train that has to stay on prelaid tracks cannot adjust to the movements of a free-running dog.

The point to take away from all these analogies is that agile methods do not shy away from planning. Although to a casual observer, it may look like planning has been largely skipped while the team just goes ahead and develops things, there is instead an evolution of planning processes being done. This approach to planning better suits a high-change environment. Planning still exists, first with an overall release plan, and then at multiple points throughout the project to plan subsequent iterations and releases. Agile projects also factor a lot of feedback into their ongoing planning processes. For example:

» Backlog reprioritization affects iteration and release plans.
» Feedback from iteration demonstrations generates change requests and new requirements.
» Retrospectives generate changes to processes and techniques.

EXERCISE

Test your knowledge of the concepts we've just discussed by completing the following True or False quiz.

Statement	True or False
1. Agile projects typically do more upfront planning than traditional projects.	
2. Agile projects typically do more overall planning than traditional projects.	
3. By creating plans at the last responsible moment, the plans do not change.	
4. Midcourse adjustments on agile projects are not common.	
5. Knowledge worker projects tend to have high rates of change.	
6. If the project diverges from the original plan this could be a sign our initial plan was flawed.	

ANSWER

Statement	True or False
1. Agile projects typically do more upfront planning than traditional projects.	False
2. Agile projects typically do more overall planning than traditional projects.	True
3. By creating plans at the last responsible moment, the plans do not change.	False
4. Midcourse adjustments on agile projects are not common.	False
5. Knowledge worker projects tend to have high rates of change.	True
6. If the project diverges from the original plan, this could be a sign our initial plan was flawed.	True

Agile Charters

The project charter is one of the first documents produced for a project. It describes the project's goal, purpose, composition, and approach, and it provides authorization from the sponsor for the project to proceed. Agile charters can range from very lightweight worksheets and barely expanded vision statements to fairly detailed documents.

Agile charters acknowledge that scope may change and that initially some aspects of a project may be unknown. Therefore, rather than trying to fully specify the scope, agile charters characterize the goals envisioned for the project. They also describe the processes and approaches that the team should use to iterate toward the final product, as well as the acceptance criteria that will be used to verify the project outcomes.

Agile charters typically answer a subset of (or all of) the W5H questions:

» **What** is this project about? (A high-level description of the project's vision, mission, goals, and objectives)
» **Why** is it being undertaken? (The business rationale for the project)
» **When** will it start and end? (The project start and target end dates)

» **Who** will be engaged? (A list of the project participants and involved stakeholders)
» **Where** will it occur? (Details of work sites, deployment requirements, etc.)
» **How** will it be undertaken? (A description of the approach, which is particularly important for agile projects if agile methods are new to the organization; changes from the standard approach, such as the increased involvement of the customer, need to be explained.)

The process of chartering helps align stakeholders with the project. One way to help stakeholders explore and cement the basics of the project is to have them jointly develop a project elevator statement. Elevator statements are short descriptions of the project goals, benefits, and discriminators. These statements quickly describe the project or product. The following is a popular format for elevator statements:

For:	Target customers
Who:	Need (opportunity or problem)
The:	Product/service name
Is a:	Product category
That:	Key benefits/reason to buy
Unlike:	Primary competitive alternative(s)
We:	Primary differentiation

Let's use the scenario of describing a new course to prospective students for an example of an elevator statement:

For:	Project managers
Who:	Want to become agile project leaders
The:	"Learning to Lead Agile Teams Class"
Is a:	Three-day course
That:	Takes project managers through a comprehensive agile development life cycle, incorporating real case studies and hands-on exercises
Unlike:	Agile courses from generic training organizations
We:	Only use instructors with hands-on agile project experience to ensure they can answer all your questions, and our supplementary materials include valuable tools, case studies, and cheat sheets.

The final text format of this elevator statement would read:

> *For project managers who want to become agile project leaders, the "Learning to Lead Agile Teams Class" is a three-day course that takes project managers through a comprehensive agile development life cycle, incorporating real case studies and hands-on exercises. Unlike agile courses from generic training organizations, we only use instructors with hands-on agile project experience to ensure they can answer all your questions, and our supplementary materials include valuable tools, case studies, and cheat sheets.*

Another quick exercise that can help align stakeholders around the project is to create a project Tweet. This exercise requires stakeholders to describe the goal of the project in 140 characters or less. The intent of this activity is not to create an all-encompassing description, but to gauge stakeholders' high-level understanding of the project and their priorities.

Exercises like creating an elevator statement or a project Tweet ultimately help in developing the charter. Then, once the charter is complete and approved, it serves as a device to launch the project, giving authority for the team to proceed, following the approach described or referenced in the charter.

Business Case Development

Business case development for agile projects is not that different than it is for traditional projects. For the most part, the differences lie in a lighter level of documentation on agile projects. In addition, the business case for agile projects may include discussion about early benefits realization opportunities, which is not as typical for traditional projects.

We covered many of the concepts and calculations that feed into the project's business case in chapter 3, Value-Driven Delivery. Agile projects are business-value-driven, and so any calculations about value, such as return on investment (ROI), internal rate of return (IRR), and net present value (NPV), will be captured in the business case.

The business case describes why the sponsoring organization should undertake the project. When there are multiple projects competing for a limited supply of sponsorship funding, the organization will assess the business cases to determine which projects to undertake.

As mentioned in chapter 3, Value-Driven Delivery, the business value of a project is usually assessed in monetary terms. For projects that are undertaken for safety or regulatory compliance purposes and do not have an easily determined monetary value, we can look at the financial ramifications of not undertaking the project (such as the business being shut down, fines, lawsuits, etc.), or we can simply label the project as mandatory and not spend additional time investigating its value.

The amount of detail in an agile business case varies from project to project. For a small agile project, there may not be a distinct business case document. Instead, discussion of the business case and business benefits may be contained in the project charter or the project vision document or elevator statement. For large agile projects or those being undertaken in an organization that demands the creation of a business case document, we may see a document that includes the following sections:

» **Project overview**: A brief description of the project background and objectives
» **Anticipated costs**: How much we estimate the project to cost, including reasonable contingency funds
» **Anticipated benefits**: The benefits, monetary or otherwise, that we estimate the project to bring, such as new revenue, cost savings, better service, improved quality, compliance, improved working conditions, increased employee satisfaction, etc.
» **Business models and indexes**: Calculations of ROI, IRR, and NPV, as required by the organization
» **ROI assumptions and risks associated with the project**: The assumptions that were made when calculating the business models and indexes, such as inflation rates and customer adoption rates
» **Risks of *not* undertaking the project**: The risks (if any) that the organization faces if it chooses not to undertake the project
» **SWOT / PEST analysis**: The relevant results of SWOT or PEST analysis; SWOT (which stands for Strengths, Weaknesses, Opportunities, and Threats) and PEST (which stands for Political, Economic, Social, and Technical) analyses are graphical tools for examining different attributes of the project
» **Recommendations**: The project sponsor's recommendation for the project, such as Mandatory (regulatory compliance) or Critical (the sponsor's highest priority), or a High, Medium, or Nice-to-have project

T&T **Iteration and Release Planning**

Agile projects are divided into releases and iterations. As we've discussed at earlier points in this book, an iteration is a short development period, typically two to four weeks in duration. A release is a group of iterations that results in the completion of a valuable deliverable on the project. So a project has one or more releases, and a release contains one or more iterations, as illustrated in figure 6.25. In this diagram, we see a single project with two releases to production. The first release contains 11 iterations, and the second has 5 iterations.

Figure 6.25: Project Broken into Releases and Iterations

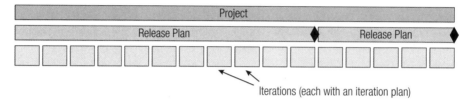

We start planning releases and iterations early in the project life cycle and revisit the planning effort multiple times as the project progresses.

Release Planning

Releases are planned around delivering useful and valuable increments of functionality to the business or customer. A release may be *date driven* ("We need something to demo at the trade show") or *functionality driven* ("Once we can capture and process customer orders, we want to go live; management reporting and account renewals can come later"). Whatever drives the release, we need to determine the functionality that can be developed and turned over or delivered for the planned release.

To put it another way, when planning a release we ask, "What proportion of the user story backlog can be delivered in the release?"

Figure 6.26: Planning a Release

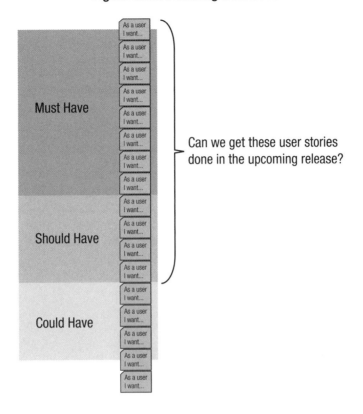

In figure 6.26, the functionality that represents all the user stories ranked as "must haves" and "should haves" in the backlog has been selected for the upcoming release. The question then becomes, "How likely is it that we will be able to complete this work by the release date?" To gauge what the team will be able to complete and when they can complete it, we initially rely on the team's estimates for the first release. Then, after the team has gone through a few iterations, we can start to look at velocity trends, as shown in figure 6.27.

Figure 6.27: Using Velocity Trends to Help Plan a Release

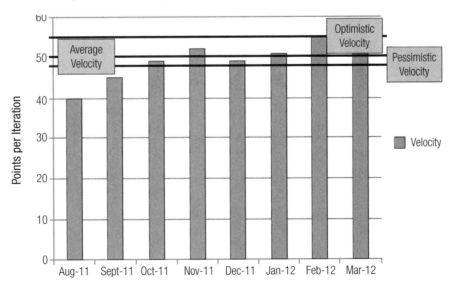

In the example in figure 6.27, the velocity started off with 40 points completed in August. In November, the project broke past the 50 points' mark, and then in February, there was a one-time occurrence of the velocity reaching 55 points. If we want to calculate best-case delivery, we could use the velocity of 55 points to make an optimistic prediction of how many story points will be delivered in every iteration going forward, but it does not look very likely that the team will be able to achieve this velocity consistently, given the velocity counts for the other months on the project. It would be safer to assume a lower monthly velocity rate for the release. Based on the data in the chart, we could use a value of 48 story points per month for the pessimistic estimate. For the most likely estimate, we calculate the average velocity, which in this case is 50 story points per month.

So if we are told the business is asking for a release in two iterations' time, we need to find out where that will take us in the user story backlog. We start by calculating 2 months x 50 points per month = 100 points' worth of functionality. We then add up the story points for the backlog items from top to bottom to find where 100 points is on the backlog, as shown in figure 6.28.

Figure 6.28: Applying Velocity Expectations to the Backlog

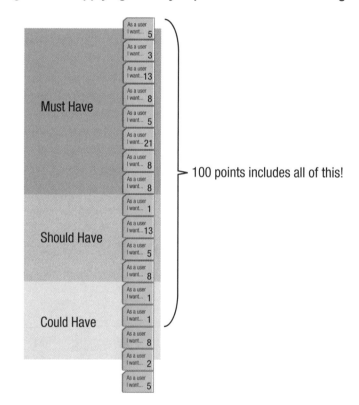

In this example, 100 points takes us all the way through the "must-have" and "should-have" functionality, as well as a couple of small "could-have" stories. So barring any unforeseen circumstances, it looks possible to deliver all the must-have and should-have stories for the release. These calculations help ensure we do not try to commit to more functionality than we can deliver within a release.

Story Maps

As discussed in chapter 3, Value-Driven Delivery, story maps can be useful ways to show release plans. Story maps allow us to lay out and group stories, first by dependencies (the "backbone" and "walking skeleton" represent the elements that we need to have on the project) and then by functionality. When using story maps to show release plans, we still need to add up the story point values within each release and check whether the plan is viable, given the team's development capacity and the amount of time designated for the release.

Figure 6.29: Story Maps Can Be Used to Show Release Plans

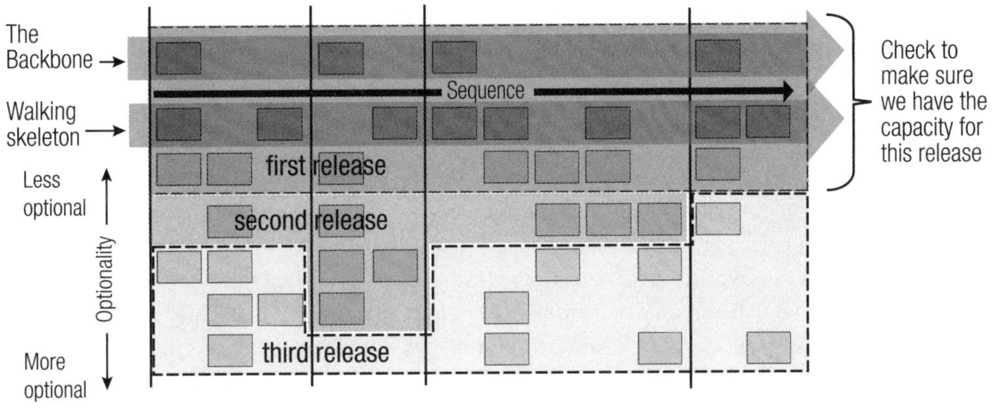

EXERCISE

Using the following information, calculate how many iterations will be needed to complete the release.

The team's velocity remains fairly stable, averaging 20 points per iteration. They have 200 points' worth of functionality left in the backlog for this release. With each iteration, they have been discovering about a 10 percent growth in work due to change requests and new functionality. The sponsors would like to know how many more iterations it will take before the release will be done.

ANSWER

If we expect to complete 20 points per iteration and we have 200 points left in our backlog, we can do the following calculation: 200 points / 20 points per iteration = 10 iterations. So at first glance, it seems like we should estimate another 10 iterations' worth of work $(200 / 20 = 10)$. However, we need to consider the 10 percent growth: $(200 \times 0.1) + 200 = 220$. We then calculate 220 points / 20 points per iteration = 11 iterations. Therefore, we expect the release to require 11 more iterations.

Iteration Planning

Iteration planning follows the same idea as release planning. In iteration planning, we ask the team to select user stories that the customer has indicated are high-priority items and that can be developed, tested, and delivered within the iteration. Going back to the previous example where the team is averaging

50 story points per month, or about 25 story points for each two-week sprint or iteration, we will use 25 story points as our iteration planning goal.

It would be easy for the ScrumMaster or project manager to select the next 25 points' worth of functionality off the top of the backlog and tell the team to get on with the iteration. However, doing so would undermine the team characteristics of self-organization and empowerment that we have worked so hard to create. So it's important for the team to discuss the goals for the next iteration with the customer or product owner. The team should then select the user stories they will commit to deliver as part of the next iteration.

We must remember that the team members are the closest to the technical details of the project and may have access to information that the project manager or ScrumMaster does not. For example, they may have some refactoring (fixing or improving previous work) scheduled for this iteration that might reduce their capacity for new work. Or conversely, the team may be confident that they can complete additional work this iteration based on some improvement initiative they have recently undertaken. So while the ScrumMaster or project manager should question any iteration projections that vary from the team's average velocity, it is important to let the team plan their own iterations. (Besides, that's what retrospectives are for, right? To ridicule the team for their poor estimating? No, not really! We will discuss the intentions behind retrospectives in chapter 8, Continuous Improvement.)

With the Scrum approach to agile projects, iteration planning involves a little more ceremony than with other approaches, so let's discuss the Scrum approach in more detail. The product owner must come prepared to the sprint (iteration) planning meeting with a freshly prioritized backlog. In the first half of the meeting, the product owner describes the backlog items they would like developed in the sprint, and the team members select a set of items that they think are achievable. The product owner has the final say on the priorities for the sprint, and the development team has the final say on the amount of work that can be accomplished in the sprint.

In the second half of the sprint planning meeting, the team breaks down the selected backlog items into their constituent parts to form the sprint backlog of action items. They then discuss how the work will be done, making local and external commitments to undertake the work within the sprint timeframe. At this stage, it is not yet important for particular people to take ownership of the tasks. Such assignments can come after the sprint planning meeting and may change throughout the sprint.

The emerging sprint backlog serves as the team's plan and commitment to deliver the selected backlog stories within the sprint. In order for the team to be confident in delivering this work, they will need to calculate their capacity and adjust it for any planned absences. Let's go back to our team of Bill, Bob, and Mary for an example. If Bob had planned to take a week off during the two-week period and we assume everyone contributes equally to the sprint, then the team's capacity would be reduced by 1/6 for this particular iteration, since 2 weeks × 3 people = 6 weeks. Now to calculate the reduced capacity of the sprint, we take our average capacity of 25 story points and subtract 1/6 of the 25 points. So 25 – 4 = approximately 21 points.

To account for individual days off, instead of weeks, you would start calculating the reduced capacity by multiplying the number of team members by the numbers of days in the sprint, and then subtract the number of days the team member is unavailable. For this example, Bob is taking 5 days off, and there are 10 days in the sprint. So we calculate 3 × 10 = 30, and then 30 – 5 = 25 days available. Therefore, the new capacity for the team would be: 25 points × (25 / 30) = approximately 21 points.

In addition to adjusting capacity during the sprint planning meeting to allow for absences, teams may determine an appropriate buffer (based on real expectations, rather than arbitrary padding) for completing unanticipated work, resolving problems, and dealing with other such issues. So if the team usually averages 25 points, it might be wise for them to commit to a reduced level that allows them a buffer for completing user stories that turn out to be larger than anticipated or handling diversions that call away resources to fix issues.

EXERCISE

Project Beta is being estimated in ideal days, assuming 8-hour days and 5-day workweeks. Each of the five people on the team averages 30 hours of availability for the project each week. How many ideal days' worth of work can they commit to deliver in their next 10-day iteration?

ANSWER

To get the answer, we do the following calculations:

5 people × 30 hours per week = 150 hours per week

150 hours per week × 2 weeks (for a 10-day iteration) = 300 hours per iteration

300 hours per iteration / 8 hours per day = 37.5 ideal developer days' worth of work

Therefore, the team should not commit to completing anything over 37.5 ideal days' worth of work.

Professional Responsibility and Ethics

Before we move on to the next chapter, let's look at how PMI's Code of Ethics and Professional Conduct (available on PMI's website: www.pmi.org) applies to adaptive planning concepts.[7] There are four main areas of this code—Responsibility, Respect, Fairness, and Honesty—and we'll cover each in turn, looking at examples of how they relate to the topics discussed in this chapter. As you read this section, think about your real-world projects and how they are impacted by these different aspects of professional responsibility and ethics.

Responsibility

» **Make decisions based on the best interests of the company**: This category includes responsibilities to report velocity shortfalls early and to help stakeholders decide what to do if it looks like some of the required functionality will not be completed on time.

Respect

- » **Maintain an attitude of mutual cooperation**: In planning, there is a careful balancing act between the product owner, who wants as much functionality as possible, the project team, who want to manage scope so they are able to successfully deliver the iteration stories on time, and the ScrumMaster or project manager, who helps coordinate the different parties. Maintaining an attitude of mutual cooperation is vital to keeping these stakeholders in check and collaborating productively. Sometimes it will be necessary for one group to compromise or make concessions in order for the needs of other groups to be satisfied. Iteration review meetings and retrospectives are good opportunities to check in with stakeholders to make sure they feel their goals are being respected and to investigate the consequences of any compromises and concessions.
- » **Negotiate in good faith**: As with other aspects of planning, negotiation is a balancing act between the parties involved. While customers or product owners, development teams, and project leaders all want the project to succeed, they often have different views on what that success looks like. During negotiations on scope and functionality, we must respect and acknowledge stakeholder requests.
- » **Deal with conflict directly**: We cannot simply ignore conflict on the project. For example, if arguments and conflict break out over estimates during a planning poker session, we need to make sure the team resolves the issue before moving on. "Parking" debates for discussion later is seldom a productive long-term strategy. Instead, it is better to let the team come to a mutually acceptable (even if not universally agreed-upon) decision on issues.
- » **Do not use your position to influence others**: If you are a team leader, ScrumMaster, or project manager, you should not use your positional power to unduly influence the team's estimates or decisions. The benefits that team empowerment bring to the project when the team does the estimating, planning, and decision-making are more valuable than getting your own way or swaying an estimate.

Fairness

- » **Do not discriminate**: We should be careful not to discriminate against team members during planning and throughout the project. For example, even when the entire team or individual team members repeatedly underestimate (or overestimate) pieces of the project, we should not hold this against them, or ridicule them. Instead, we need to help them improve their estimating skills when we discuss actual durations and costs at retrospectives.

Honesty

- » **Understand the truth**: When estimates do come out too high or too low, we need to help the team investigate why the estimates varied. We should understand that, many times, common cause variation is responsible. In other words, some things just vary, and new work is hard to estimate. However, when repeating trends emerge, we should explore the variance using objective techniques to keep the investigation from becoming personal.
- » **Be truthful in all communications**: We should openly discuss contingencies and buffers with the team and customer, rather than quietly pad estimates and feed false deadlines to the development team to create a sense of urgency. It is best to honestly explain the project facts and the role and need for contingency buffers. If we are asked to remove contingency plans, we have a professional responsibility to explain the risks and to then communicate the impacts of any cost and schedule overruns that actually occurred on the project.

Practice Exam

1. Your team committed to delivering 10 story points this iteration, but it looks like you will only complete 8. You should:

    A. Extend the iteration.
    B. Add more resources to the team.
    C. Complete 8 points, and put 2 back in the backlog.
    D. Adjust the iteration plan from 10 points down to 8.

2. Which of the following collections of planning units is most typical for agile projects?

    A. A release plan containing multiple projects, each with multiple iterations
    B. A project plan containing multiple releases, each with multiple iterations
    C. A project plan containing multiple iterations, each containing multiple releases
    D. An iteration plan containing multiple projects, each containing multiple releases

3. When converting size estimates to duration, remember to:

    A. Ignore distractions and use ideal time
    B. Divide the timebox capacity by the number of stories
    C. Factor in distractions and use available time
    D. Calculate the payback period for the estimated duration

4. The project management office is auditing your agile project and asks to see your iteration plans. They notice that only the next couple of iterations have plans. As a result, they give the project a "red flag." for having incomplete plans. The most responsible thing to do is:

    A. Explain the principles of progressive elaboration.
    B. Create detailed iteration plans for the remainder of the project.
    C. Ignore them, since they clearly have no right to be reviewing your project.
    D. Have the team create detailed plans for the rest of the project.

5. Which of the following statements correctly describes agile planning?

    A. Plan at multiple levels, and have managers create iteration plans.
    B. Use appropriate estimate ranges, and exclude diversions/outside work.
    C. Plan at multiple levels, and have team members create iteration plans.
    D. Use fixed-point estimates, and base projections on completion rates.

6. Which of the following is not a characteristic of agile estimation?

    A. Team-based
    B. Collaborative
    C. Iterative
    D. Fixed-point

7. When conducting an iteration planning meeting using a Scrum approach, which of the following statements is not true?

    A. The product owner is responsible for the backlog priorities.
    B. The team is responsible for the estimates.
    C. The team breaks down user stories into tasks.
    D. The ScrumMaster selects the topic items off the backlog.

8. You are leading a team with an average velocity of 50 points per iteration. Another team of the same size in your organization is working on a project with similar complexity. The other team's velocity is averaging 75 points per month. Your team should:

   A. Undertake affinity estimating to check their estimates
   B. Work longer hours
   C. Ignore the difference
   D. Acquire additional resources

9. Estimates should be presented as ranges to:

   A. Allow for change requests
   B. Keep the sponsors flexible
   C. Allow for scope creep
   D. Represent uncertainty in the estimates

10. Which of the following pieces of information are you least likely to find in an agile charter document?

    A. A list of who will be engaged on the project
    B. A description of how it will be undertaken
    C. An explanation as to why the project is being done
    D. A precise estimate for the project

11. An executive wants help evaluating a proposed three-year project against two proposed one-year projects. Which business case metric would be most helpful?

    A. NPV
    B. ROI
    C. MMF
    D. Velocity

12. Your team is averaging 40 story points per two-week iteration. They have 200 points' worth of functionality left in the user story backlog. How many weeks do you expect it will take until development is completed?

    A. 2.5
    B. 5
    C. 10
    D. 20

13. When using story points to estimate a project, which of the following statements is most accurate?

    A. The team owns the definition of what constitutes a story point.
    B. There should be a company-wide standard definition of a story point.
    C. The definition of a story point is refactored every iteration.
    D. Story points can be used for iteration planning but not release planning.

14. On agile projects, generally midcourse adjustments are:

    A. Not necessary
    B. The norm
    C. The exception
    D. Not required

© 2012 RMC Publications, Inc • 952.846.4484 • info@rmcproject.com • www.rmcproject.com

15. When calculating final project costs, which of the following expressions best outlines the basic concept?

    A. Time + (Rate × Other project costs)
    B. (Time × Rate) – Other project costs
    C. Time × Rate x Project duration
    D. (Time × Rate) + Other project costs

16. Affinity estimating is the process of:

    A. Averaging the over- and under-estimations.
    B. Checking that stories given the same size estimate are of equivalent magnitude.
    C. Checking that stories in the same functional areas are of equivalent magnitude.
    D. Estimating your favorite stories first.

17. The term "progressive elaboration" means:

    A. Scope always keeps growing.
    B. Plans are refined as more details emerge.
    C. Development velocity is increasing.
    D. Estimates are changed to actuals after completion.

18. You are a full-time ScrumMaster on an agile team. A team member becomes ill partway through an iteration in which the team committed to deliver 25 story points. Which action is most appropriate?

    A. Work the remaining team longer hours.
    B. Send work home to the sick team member.
    C. Start development yourself to assist the team.
    D. Deliver what you can within the sprint.

Answers

1. Answer: C
   Explanation: An iteration is timeboxed, so it must be left at its normal duration. You wouldn't change the plan for the iteration, and you typically wouldn't choose to expand the team. Instead, work that is not completed within the iteration is returned to the backlog, so the choice of completing 8 points and returning 2 points to the backlog is the correct option.

2. Answer: B
   Explanation: The correct hierarchy is that a project contains one or more releases, which in turn contain one or more iterations. Therefore, the correct choice is a project plan containing multiple releases, each with multiple iterations.

3. Answer: C
   Explanation: When converting size estimates to duration, we need to consider the availability of resources, so the choice of "Factor in distractions and use available time" is correct. If someone is only 50 percent available, a task will take twice as long as it would if the person was fully dedicated to the project, and perhaps even longer due to a loss of productivity from task switching.

4. Answer: A
   Explanation: An incomplete set of iteration plans may be a surprise to a PMO that is not familiar with agile methods. When faced with this type of situation, you should explain the benefits of agile planning and how an agile approach ties into the concepts of progressive elaboration and rolling wave planning, which are discussed in the *PMBOK® Guide.*[8] Making up plans too early is a poor use of time on an agile project and could mislead stakeholders. The choice of ignoring the request is incorrect, because it is counter to the "Respect" principle defined in PMI's Code of Ethics and Professional Conduct.[9]

5. Answer: C
   Explanation: The only correct combination is to plan at multiple levels and have team members create iteration plans. All of the other choices contain incorrect elements. Managers do not create iteration plans—teams do. Diversions or outside work are included when determining availability, and we use range estimates on agile projects, not fixed-point estimates.

6. Answer: D
   Explanation: Agile estimation is team-based, collaborative, and iterative. We do not use fixed-point estimates on our project. Instead, we estimate in a range.

7. Answer: D
   Explanation: The product owner is responsible for the backlog priorities, and the team is responsible for the estimates and breaking down the stories into tasks. The only statement that is not true is that the ScrumMaster selects the top items off the backlog.

8. Answer: C
   Explanation: Velocity is team-specific and unique to that team. In other words, a story point for one team may not have the same value as a story point for another team. Therefore, it is not appropriate to compare velocities between teams. The best choice would be to ignore the difference.

9. Answer: D
   Explanation: We present estimates as ranges to show the level of uncertainty in the estimates and to manage stakeholder expectations.

10. Answer: D
    Explanation: Due to the uncertainty and potentially higher levels of change and risk involved in agile projects, you would be least likely to see a precise cost or time estimate in an agile charter. This does not mean it's out of the question, especially if a project is working with a fixed budget, but it is the LEAST likely choice.

11. Answer: A
    Explanation: The correct choice is NPV, or net present value, because it converts multiyear returns on investment to a value in today's terms. It is the best option from the choices presented for evaluating projects with different durations.

12. Answer: C
    Explanation: This question doesn't provide information to indicate any differences in the team's availability or known project distractions, so we can do a fairly straightforward calculation to get the answer. If we average 40 points per iteration, we should get through a 200-point backlog in 5 iterations (200 / 40 = 5). Each iteration is 2 weeks long, so 5 iterations is equivalent to 10 weeks (5 × 2 = 10). The key to answering this question correctly is noticing that the question asked for the number of weeks, not the number of iterations.

13. Answer: A
    Explanation: The correct option is that the team owns the definition of the story point. Having the team define the story point creates a sense of ownership and a common understanding. In contrast, company-decreed definitions lack this sense of team ownership. The other options are incorrect because frequently changing the definition (refactoring it every iteration) makes it difficult to track velocity and check release plans. Story points, and velocity in terms of the number of points completed, are used for both iteration and release planning.

14. Answer: B
    Explanation: We expect midcourse adjustments on agile projects, so the option that states they are the norm is the correct choice.

15. Answer: D
    Explanation: Final costs are (Time × Rate for resources) + Any additional project costs.

16. Answer: B
    Explanation: Affinity estimation and triangulation check that stories assigned the same size value are of equivalent effort.

17. Answer: B
    Explanation: Progressive elaboration is the ongoing refinement of plans as more information becomes available.

18. Answer: D
    Explanation: In such a situation, we deliver what we can within the sprint. Sending work home or working the team longer are counterproductive actions in the long-term that would go against the agile principle of maintaining a sustainable pace. Starting work on development yourself would leave nobody to do the ScrumMaster role. It is better to just deliver what you can within this iteration and explain the variance.

PROBLEM DETECTION AND RESOLUTION

Chapter Seven

Q u i c k t e s t

This chapter is about identifying and solving problems. How effectively a team deals with problems has a critical impact on whether a project succeeds or fails. It is all too easy to ignore a problem for too long and continue pushing forward on a project, hoping the problem will somehow go away or resolve itself. But problems eventually stop us from working, and they often result in us having to undo work we've already done. Being hit with the need to diagnose a problem and then having to do rework to correct it can have a dramatic effect on our project schedules.

To illustrate this concept, let's look at a simple example. Assume our project is to drive 10 miles in 10 hours. (Yes, this would be a very slow, boring project, but it keeps the math simple.)

Figure 7.1: The Plan Is to Drive 10 Miles in 10 Hours

At mile 2, everything is going well. We have been traveling for 2 hours, and we have traveled 2 miles. This means our plan and our actual performance results on the project are the same.

Figure 7.2: At Mile 2, the Plan and the Actual Results Are the Same

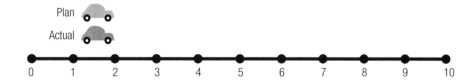

In fact, things go exactly according to plan for the first 4 hours, in which we cover 4 miles, but then we encounter a problem. With this problem in our way, completing the project according to the plan no longer looks as feasible.

Figure 7.3: At Mile 4, a Problem Is Encountered

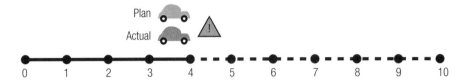

When we encounter problems on our projects, it takes time to diagnose what the issues are and to then determine what we should do about them. The time spent diagnosing the problem is time that is not spent on the execution of our project, and so we fall behind the plan. In this example, it takes us one hour to diagnose the problem.

Figure 7.4: Problem Diagnosis Takes One Hour

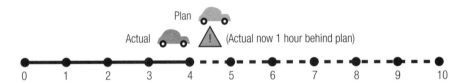

The solution to a problem often involves undoing flawed work. Perhaps we thought a direction or approach was appropriate for the project, but we have since found out it doesn't work. Now we need to backtrack and try a new approach. This is a double whammy—not only does it take time for us to remove or undo the bad work, but doing so sets us further back in the amount of work that still needs to be done on the project. So we lose time while losing what we thought was accomplished work and, as a result, fall even further behind our planned progress. In our example, let's assume it takes us two hours to undo the bad work and it also takes us two steps backwards in the completed scope on the project. Including the one hour that was spent diagnosing the problem, the total time lost on the project is now 1 + 2 + 2 = 5 hours.

Figure 7.5: Work Has to Be Undone, Taking Two Hours and Moving Two Steps Backward

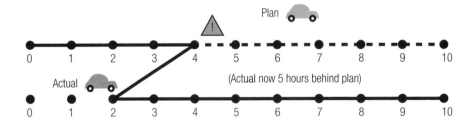

Given such an unplanned impact, pretty soon we have consumed all of our scheduled time, even if no other problems are encountered on the project. And if our budget was driven by effort, then we have used up all of our budget, too. In our example, we reach the planned project end when the project is only 50 percent complete—not a good outcome.

© 2012 RMC Publications, Inc • 952.846.4484 • info@rmcproject.com • www.rmcproject.com

Figure 7.6: The Project Should Be Finished Now but Is Only 50% Done

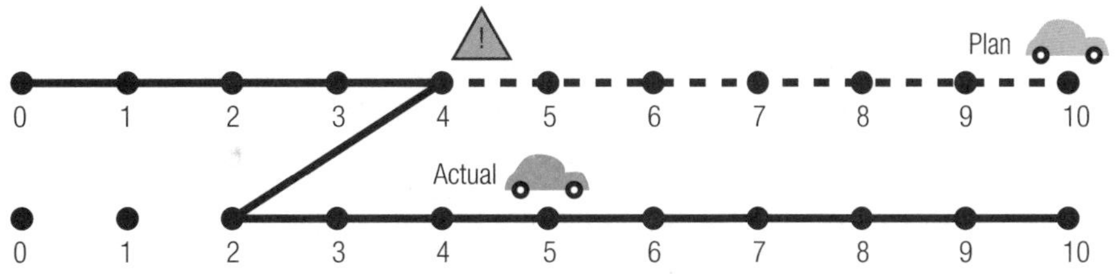

The secret to minimizing the impacts of problems is to find them as soon as possible. Detecting problems early reduces the potential for rework. We should then diagnose and solve the problems as quickly as possible so we do not consume any more unplanned time than is necessary. This may all sound like pretty basic stuff, but many projects languish in the face of problems, seemingly unaware of the double hit each day of dithering brings.

Later in this chapter, we will examine the cost of change curve, which describes the compounding impact of issues. We will also review agile tools and techniques and knowledge and skills that can be used for rapidly identifying and resolving problems.

In This Chapter

This chapter is broken into two practices: identifying problems and resolving problems. The following chart shows the tools and techniques and knowledge and skills associated with each practice. Although the names of these practices are not official terms that will appear on the exam, organizing the concepts in this way provides the context of why and how you use the T&Ts and K&Ss that you will be tested on.

Practice	Tool/Technique	Knowledge/Skill (Level)
Identifying problems	» Cycle time » Escaped defects	» Project and quality standards (Level 1) » Failure modes and alternatives (Level 3) » Variance and trend analysis (Level 3) » Control limits (Level 3)
Resolving problems	» Continuous integration » Risk-based spike » Frequent verification and validation » Test-driven development/ test-first development » Acceptance test–driven development	» Problem solving (Level 1)

Identifying Problems

The concepts we'll discuss in this section are focused on finding issues, problems, and concerns. Diagnostics like cycle time and trends can point to potential problems before they occur, while other tools like escaped defects and failure modes help identify problems that have already occurred.

Daily stand-up meetings (discussed in chapter 5, Boosting Team Performance Practices) are also important mechanisms for identifying problems. Don't forget that the third question of the daily stand-up meeting asks whether team members are experiencing any problems, blockers, or impediments to progress. The reason we ask this question is to try to surface issues or potential problems early, rather than waiting until the team comes to us with a problem, the customer complains, or we have a retrospective. When concerns are raised at daily stand-up meetings, we need to further investigate the issues and determine if there is a problem brewing.

T&T Cycle Time

Cycle time is a measure of how long it takes to get things done. Cycle time spans from when the team starts working on a piece of the project, such as a user story, until that item is finished, is accepted, and can deliver business value.

Cycle time is closely related to work in progress (WIP). During the cycle when an item has been started but not yet completed, it is considered work in progress. As we discussed in chapter 3, Value-Driven Delivery, excessive WIP is associated with a number of problems, including:

» WIP represents money invested with no return on that investment yet.
» WIP hides bottlenecks in processes, and it masks efficiency issues.
» WIP also represents risk in the form of potential rework, since there may still be changes to items until those items have been accepted. If there is a large inventory of WIP, there may in turn be a lot of scrap or expensive rework if a change is required.

It is because of these risks that agile and lean approaches aim to limit WIP. In order to do so, we must also pay close attention to cycle time, since long cycle times lead to increased amounts of WIP. So agile approaches deliberately break the project work down into small batches and emphasize the importance of finishing items and getting confirmation that they are acceptable as soon as possible. For example, projects taking a Scrum approach have small user stories, do work in two-week sprints, and encourage getting the product owner's and end user's acceptance of user stories at the end of each sprint.

By using these types of practices (which are common to all agile methods), we see a reduction in cycle time on agile projects compared to non-agile approaches. For example, on a waterfall software development project, the steps of analysis, design, code, and unit test for a piece of functionality often take months or even years. This represents a very long cycle time, which in turn results in increased levels of WIP and the associated risks and issues. With agile methods, the aim is to minimize cycle time.

To help keep the focus on minimizing cycle times, many teams write "Date Started" and "Date Done" on Kanban or task board cards, as shown in figure 7.7.

Figure 7.7: Using Task Boards to Track Cycle Time

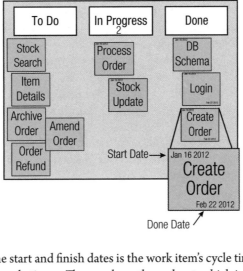

The elapsed time between the start and finish dates is the work item's cycle time. The project's cycle time is the average of these items' cycle times. Then we have throughput, which is the amount of output from a process (in other words, the amount of work the project team is able to do). The relationship of the three variables of throughput, WIP, and cycle time is indicated in the following formula:

$$\text{Cycle time} = \frac{\text{WIP}}{\text{Throughput}}$$

Knowing the team's throughput allows us to forecast future capability without specifically needing to know what the team might be asked to do. Knowing the cycle time allows us to make reliable commitments to the customer or organization about how long it will take to deliver work. WIP measures how much work we have "in the hopper" and gives us insight into issues, bottlenecks in the process, and rework-related risks.

EXERCISE: CYCLE TIME

1. Imagine a bicycle factory that produces 25 bikes per day and typically works on 100 bikes at any given time. Calculate the average length of time it takes to make a bike.

2. Improvements to the assembly process reduce the cycle time to 3 days and the WIP to 90 bikes in progress. What is the percentage of improvement in throughput?

ANSWER

1. This is a pretty basic question that we should be able to answer if we understand the definitions of WIP, throughput, and cycle time. The WIP, or the measure of work in progress, is the 100 bikes being worked on at any given time. Throughput is how many things go through the process per time interval; in this case, the throughput is 25 bikes per day. We are being asked to calculate how long it takes on average to make a bike, which is the cycle time (ha!). Since cycle time = WIP / throughput, we can calculate our cycle time as 100 / 25 = 4 days.

2. This question is trickier, because we now need to rearrange the equation to find throughput. The rearranged equation is throughput = WIP / cycle time. With our new, improved process, WIP = 90 and cycle time = 3 days, so throughput = 90 / 3 = 30 bikes per day.

    Now once we've done this calculation, we still have to find the percentage of improvement over the old throughput of 25 bikes per day. So we subtract the old throughput from the new measurement (30 – 25 = 5), and then divide the difference by the old throughput (5 / 25 = 0.2, or 20%). Therefore, increasing our throughput from 25 to 30 bikes per day is a 20 percent improvement.

So far we have just looked at cycle time for new work items, but cycle time is also useful when analyzing defects and their fixes. The cost of change graph we saw in chapter 3, Value-Driven Delivery, explains that the longer defects are left, the more expensive they are to fix.

Figure 7.8: Cost of Change

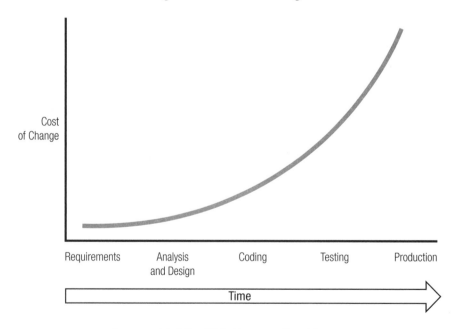

Image copyright © Scott W. Ambler, www.agilemodeling.com

There are a number of reasons for the increased expense, including:

» More work may have been built on top of the bad design, resulting in more work to be undone.
» The later it is in the development cycle, the more stakeholders are impacted by the defect and the more expensive it is to fix.

The agile techniques of pair programming, continuous integration, and test-driven development (for software projects), as well as active stakeholder participation through techniques like demonstrations and customer reviews, are all intended to find defects and change requests as quickly as possible, before the costs escalate too far up the cost of change curve.

Figure 7.9 indicates where these practices occur on the cost of change curve.

Figure 7.9: Cost of Change

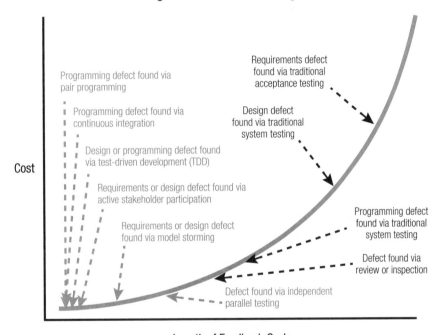

Image copyright © Scott W. Ambler, www.agilemodeling.com

So it is advantageous to catch changes and defects as quickly as possible to minimize rework and reduce costs. This is where defect cycle time comes in. Defect cycle time is the amount of time between defect injection (when the defect was accidently introduced) and defect remediation (when the defect was fixed). The length of the defect cycle time dictates how far up the cost of change graph the defect will go.

To help minimize the cost of fixes, some project teams actively track defect cycle time and have goals for rapid resolution, as indicated in figure 7.10.

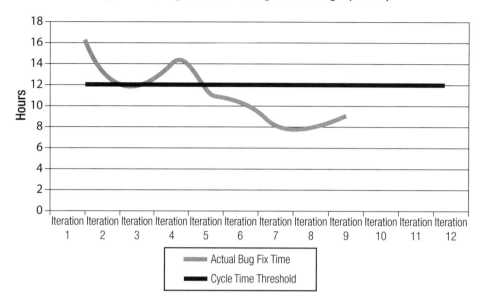

Figure 7.10: Cycle Time—Bug Fix Average (Hours)

In this graph, we can see the cycle time threshold is 12 hours. This means that, on average, the team's goal is to have all the reported defects fixed within 1.5 business days. So if a defect was found at noon on Tuesday, it should be fixed by the end of day Wednesday. In looking at the graph, we can see that for the first five iterations, the average cycle time was typically above 12 hours. In later iterations, however, the average cycle time was below the threshold, going as low as 8 hours.

By tracking the cycle time for creating new work and WIP, along with the defect cycle time, we can minimize both the potential for rework and the cost of any rework that is required on the project.

 Escaped Defects

We've been talking about investigating concerns raised during the daily stand-up meetings to discover problems early and the importance of fixing identified defects quickly, but what about defects that aren't discovered during the project's testing and validation processes and instead make it to the customer? These are called escaped defects. They are the most costly to fix and are at the top of the cost of change graph. Unfortunately, despite how hard we try to prevent them, an occasional defect will make it through all the tests and quality control processes into the final product.

By the time we learn about an escaped defect, it is obviously too late to prevent it, but we can use this information to improve our processes going forward and hopefully reduce the number of escaped defects in the future. The "escaped defects found" metric counts the number of escaped defects discovered over a period of time (days, weeks, or months). In the software development domain, for example, projects commonly track escaped defects back to the release they originated in, or escaped from. This tracking helps teams assess and improve the effectiveness of the quality assurance and quality control processes over time. The results are usually shown in a graph format, as illustrated in figure 7.11.

Figure 7.11: Number of Escaped Defects Found per Release

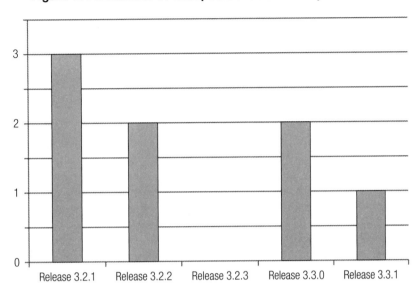

In addition to tracking the number of escaped defects per release, these graphs can be used to show trends over time, such as by month, as shown in figure 7.12.

Figure 7.12: Number of Escaped Defects Found per Month

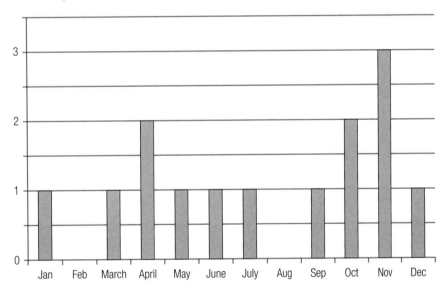

K&S
Level 1

Project and Quality Standards

Problem detection and resolution is closely related to quality management. The testing processes and other practices we put in place to find defects are part of the quality assurance and quality control efforts on our projects.

The K&S of project and quality standards refers to the agreed-upon approach the team will take to measure "fitness for purpose." In other words, what will the team do to ensure the quality and value of the product? These standards may be recorded or referenced in the project charter, or the development team may simply adopt the practices as working norms.

Quality standards and practices can include things like:

» Measuring product quality by tests passed and customer acceptance
» Automating as many tests as possible
» Making sure testing occurs as part of every iteration
» Trying to fix at least 90 percent of defects found within the next iteration
» Encouraging the quality control and quality assurance representatives to work with developers and business representatives to understand the acceptance criteria for each feature
» Only classifying defects as fixed when the business representatives, not the developers, say they are done
» Ensuring testers collaborate with the developers on defects found and walking through the steps to recreate the defect

We also need to monitor and assess the quality of our project processes using tools like defect metrics, variance and trend analysis, and root cause analysis, and take action to correct any issues we discover.

In short, project and quality metrics refer to the written or unwritten (tacit) quality and acceptance guidelines the team holds itself accountable to. These guidelines may be written as formal standards and monitored via audits, or as is more typical for small teams, they may be developed through discussion and enforced through review and retrospectives.

Failure Modes and Alternatives

The concepts we'll discuss as part of the "failure modes and alternatives" K&S come from Alistair Cockburn. These ideas relate to the human side of performance and process. They describe some truths about people that explain why, even though we know what we should be doing, we often behave differently. The five failure modes that Alistair describes in his book, *Agile Software Development: The Cooperative Game, 2nd Edition*, are:[1]

1. Making mistakes
2. Preferring to fail conservatively
3. Inventing rather than researching
4. Being creatures of habit
5. Being inconsistent

Let's take a quick look at each of these failure modes to understand the issue.

1. **Making mistakes**: It is no surprise that people make mistakes. This is one of the main reasons iterative and incremental development was created—to recognize the fact that mistakes happen and to provide mechanisms to recover and quickly overcome that fact.

2. **Preferring to fail conservatively**: When faced with uncertainty, people tend to revert back to what they know, even if they are aware that it might not be the optimal approach to take. As an example of this in an agile environment, managers may revert back to familiar (non-agile) ways of running a project if the project begins to go off track or encounters issues.

Since we are talking about people here, there are of course exceptions to this rule. Some people feel they have nothing to lose with a new approach. There are ways to move forward on a project for both mindsets—reverting to the familiar or embracing the new approach—but when people with opposing mindsets are on the same project, it can create challenges.

3. **Inventing rather than researching**: This describes a tendency that many people have (especially engineers) to invent new ways of doing things, rather than research available options and then reuse them. This tendency may be a product of education systems that reward individual thinking and scientific experimentation, combined with the intellectual satisfaction we get from solving problems. However, while it may be more fun to invent rather than research, it is also usually more costly, time-consuming, and error-prone.

4. **Being creatures of habit**: People are creatures of habit, so getting us to change how we do things is always going to be difficult. Often, even when we know there are better approaches, we do not adopt them because at some level (consciously or unconsciously), change is unappealing.

5. **Being inconsistent**: Finally, most people are very inconsistent at following a process. So the challenge is not just finding better ways of doing things, it is getting people to accept the new ways, change their own approaches, and then apply the new approaches consistently. As Karl Wiegers summarized, "We are not short on *practices*, we are short on *practice*."

So what does this mean? Are we doomed to fail? No; fortunately there are also common human traits and behaviors that help counter these common failures. These success modes can be very useful on projects. They include:[2]

1. **Being good at looking around**: This refers to people's ability to observe, review, and notice when things are not right.
2. **Being able to learn**: After seeing what's wrong, we find ways to fix it and grow our skills and knowledge along the way.
3. **Being malleable**: This is the ability to change and accept new ideas and approaches.
4. **Taking pride in work**: We are able to step outside of our job descriptions to repair or report an issue, because it is the right thing to do for the project.

Based on these success modes, Cockburn suggests some strategies for overcoming the five failure modes. These strategies are equally human, though like common sense, they often are not commonly applied. They include the following:[3]

1. **Countering with discipline and tolerance**: This strategy involves establishing a standard way of doing things and encouraging people to adopt it, while also building some capacity for tolerance and forgiveness into the approach. Then, if people diverge from the standard, we focus our energy on re-establishing the practice, providing it does not need modification.

2. **Start with something concrete and tangible**: We solve problems first in our minds and then in reality. To help people overcome resistance to a change or solution, we can create things that are concrete and tangible to represent the final solution. For example, we could create low-fidelity mock-ups that not only lay out how screens in a computer system will flow, but also invite touch and interaction by allowing stakeholders to reorder and annotate the screens. Such interaction transforms an abstract model into a tangible workflow.

3. **Copying and altering**: It is often easier to modify a working design to fit our needs than create something from nothing. "Blank page syndrome" is the paralysis that can result when we have to create a brand new solution. If we instead take the approach of altering an existing solution, we have a working framework to start from.

4. **Watching and listening**: We learn by watching others and listening to them. Something as simple as putting junior team members in line of sight and within hearing distance of more experienced team members has been found to improve the junior team members' performance, even with no other training. This approach is referred to as the "expert in earshot" recommendation.

5. **Supporting concentration and communication**: Knowledge work requires the dichotomy of both concentration and communication. In software development, for example, programmers need a sufficient amount of time to get into the quiet and productive mode known as "flow." They may spend 20 minutes getting into this state, only to have it interrupted by a minute or two of questions. However, information exchanges and conversations are essential for knowledge workers and should not be prevented. Instead, we should encourage such exchanges, since they help surface gaps in understanding and provide solutions to questions.

   The key is in managing communications wisely. As we discussed in chapter 5, Boosting Team Performance Practices, XP recommends the model known as "caves and common." Caves are quiet areas where people can retreat to perform quiet work. Common refers to the common work room where ideas are exchanged. The book *Peopleware*, by Tom Demarco and Anthony Lister, suggests establishing a "quiet work period" every day for a set period of time (e.g., 2 hours). During this quiet work period, meetings and phone calls are banned so that people can focus and get work done.

6. **Personality-matched work assignments**: We should try to match work assignments to personality types and look for mismatches. For example, people who would rather change bad code than explain what is wrong with it probably wouldn't make the best coaches. We need to play to people's personality traits (detail-oriented, social, analytical, supportive, etc.) when we assign roles.

7. **Talent**: With skilled professionals, such as knowledge workers, the difference between worst in class, average, and best in class is very large. We need to recognize the huge difference talent plays and find ways to attract and retain the best talent. This sounds like an obvious statement, yet why do so many organizations ignore it? Maybe it's because it is easier to measure the short-term impact of a 5 percent drop in salaries on the bottom line than it is to measure the unknown, longer-term (and likely much larger) impact of losing our best people.

8. **Rewards that preserve joy**: Reward structures are a tricky subject; once people start to expect the rewards, or if the rewards are ever removed, they have a huge demotivational impact. As an example, rewarding children with gifts for reading may seem like a good idea at first to get them started, but this tactic could actually backfire and lead to a child reading less once the reward system is phased out or the rewards no longer seem valuable.

   So we need to give rewards that tap into long-term, self-esteem-based motivators, such as pride-in-work, pride-in-accomplishment, and pride-in-contribution. Such rewards have long-term appeal that does not fade over time.

9. **Combining rewards**: The best reward structures combine elements to make not only a compelling package, but a truly supportive, caring work environment where personal and company objectives are aligned. No single reward system will work for everyone, so we must build many different kinds of systems.

10. **Feedback:** A little bit of feedback can replace a lot of analytical work. Agile methods "bake in" feedback throughout many of their practices. For example, XP's pair programming practice has two people working together, giving each other real-time feedback. Continuous integration provides quick feedback, and iteration reviews provide frequent feedback. The benefits of checking work before continuing with something new are universal, which is why agile methods encourage so much feedback.

EXERCISE: CATEGORIZE THE PROBLEMS

Read the scenarios in the following table, and determine which of the five common failure modes they relate to. The answer for the first scenario is provided for you as an example.

Common failure modes:

1. Making mistakes
2. Preferring to fail conservatively
3. Inventing rather than researching
4. Being creatures of habit
5. Being inconsistent

	Scenario	Failure Mode(s)
1	Tim's five-year financial forecasts did not include inflation, although including inflation is a standard company practice.	1
2	Rather than writing requirements in user-story format, Bill continued to craft detailed use-case descriptions. While these descriptions were useful, they took him four times longer to produce than the user stories created by other business analysts on the project, and they still needed to be confirmed with the business.	
3	Jim fared little better than Bill. While most of Jim's requirements were in user-story format, whenever he encountered something tricky, he reverted back to use-case formats.	
4	Pete and Kim paired on designing a new sorting algorithm that, while late, did improve reporting performance.	
5	Mary's estimates omitted any allowance for remediation work after the testing of the user interface, but she did include the allowance in her estimates for testing the reports.	
6	After the first stakeholder demo of the real-time language-translator robot that swore at the CEO, Tom switched back to playing prerecorded samples in future demos, though the team agreed it was not nearly as much fun.	

ANSWERS

	Scenario	Failure Mode(s)
1	Tim's five-year financial forecasts did not include inflation, although including inflation is a standard company practice.	Making mistakes (1)
2	Rather than writing requirements in user-story format, Bill continued to craft detailed use-case descriptions. While these descriptions were useful, they took him four times longer to produce than the user stories created by other business analysts on the project, and they still needed to be confirmed with the business.	Being creatures of habit (4)
3	Jim fared little better than Bill. While most of Jim's requirements were in user-story format, whenever he encountered something tricky, he reverted back to use-case formats.	Being creatures of habit (4) Maybe some level of preferring to fail conservatively (2) Being inconsistent (5)
4	Pete and Kim paired on designing a new sorting algorithm that, while late, did improve reporting performance.	Inventing rather than researching (3)
5	Mary's estimates omitted any allowance for remediation work after the testing of the user interface, but she did include the allowance in her estimates for testing the reports.	Making mistakes (1) Being inconsistent (5)
6	After the first stakeholder demo of the real-time-language-translator robot that swore at the CEO, Tom switched back to playing prerecorded samples in future demos, though the team agreed it was not nearly as much fun.	Preferring to fail conservatively (2) Being creatures of habit (4)

K&S Level 3 — Variance and Trend Analysis

Variance is the measure of how far apart things are (or how much things vary from each other). For example, there is variance in estimates when multiple people estimate the same thing, and there is variance between the estimates and the actual results, once work has been executed. Variance is normal and should be expected, but we do need to learn how to live within acceptable limits. And if variance fluctuates beyond the acceptable limits, we need to know how to act.

Let's look at an example of variance that is not on the exam but helps illustrate this concept. Lean software experts Mary and Tom Poppendieck tell a story about variance in pilot training.[4] Pilots were evaluated on their training flight performance, and the results were tracked and plotted.

Figure 7.13: Training Flight Performance

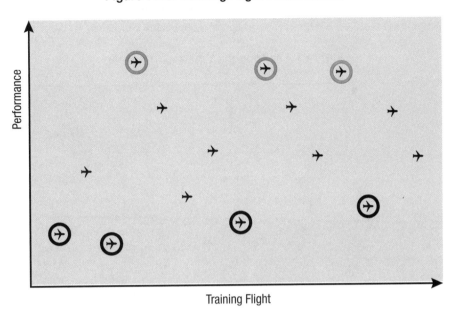

When pilots performed poorly, they were yelled at and told to improve. When pilots did well, they were congratulated and praised. The observation was that after being reprimanded, the poorly performing pilots generally improved in subsequent flights, while the top-performing pilots generally got worse in subsequent flights.

One conclusion you could draw from these results is that yelling at people is a very effective way of improving performance and that yelling should be increased, while praise and congratulations are not effective and should be stopped. This would be an incorrect conclusion, however. What was really being observed was normal variation. Some things go well, while others do not. Within any variable data set, extreme lows will probably be followed by a higher value, just as extreme highs will most likely be followed by a lower value. So what we should learn from this scenario is that processes simply vary, and we need to accept a certain degree of variance in any real-world process.

Quality expert W. Edwards Deming classifies variance into common cause variation and special cause variation. Common cause variation refers to the average day-to-day differences of doing work, and special cause variation refers to the greater degrees of variance due to special or new factors.[5]

For example, if we are given the job of driving nails into wood all day, some nails will go in straight and some will go in at a slight angle; this is common cause variation. However, if someone turns off the lights, the variance will likely be much larger, since the environment has changed (special cause variation). Deming goes on to say that there are two classic mistakes managers make:[6]

Mistake1: To react to an outcome as if it came from a special cause, when actually it came from common causes of variation.

Mistake 2: To treat an outcome as if it came from common causes of variation, when actually it came from a special cause.

An example of mistake 1 would be investigating why stories that were estimated as four days of work actually took five days to complete. An example of mistake 2 would be allowing the nailing project to continue with the lights still off or after a potential problem has been identified.

Figure 7.14: Knowing When to Intervene

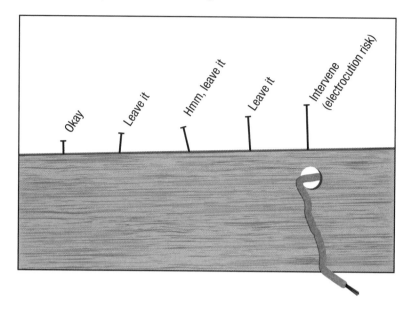

The point to understand here is that we should accept common cause variation on projects, while we should look to intervene on special cause variation. In other words, we should avoid micromanagement and instead work at removing bottlenecks and impediments. For example, asking developers why they have not coded five features this week when they completed five features last week is failing to accept common cause variation; this type of stuff just varies a bit and is not perfectly linear or predictable.

So on agile projects in particular, focusing a lot of effort on tracking conformance to a rigid plan is probably not the best use of project management time. Instead, we should look to external indicators and to the daily stand-up meeting when the team reports any issues, impediments, or blockers to their work to see if there may be special issues that need to be resolved.

EXERCISE: COMMON CAUSE OR SPECIAL CAUSE—LEAVE ALONE OR INTERVENE?

Read the following team comments and determine whether the issue being discussed is related to a common cause or special cause. The first answer is provided for you as an example.

	Comment	Common Cause or Special Cause?
1	"Our initial estimates for product testing times were on average 5 percent too high."	Common cause (if I had to guess from this limited description)
2	"I am still working on the tether for the screw top fastener. I know it should have been done yesterday, but I'll get it done today."	

	Comment	Common Cause or Special Cause?
3	"I read a press release today saying our competitor's product now does single-pass printing. Do we want to move that feature up in our backlog?"	
4	"The paint shop is running a day behind again."	
5	"Bill, our electrical safety inspector, caught malaria on vacation."	
6	"That's nothing. Helen in accounting got married in Cuba over the weekend!"	
7	"I am waiting on Ted again to finish the last of the renderings."	

ANSWER

	Comment	Common Cause or Special Cause?
1	"Our initial estimates for product testing times were on average 5 percent too high."	Common cause
2	"I am still working on the tether for the screw top fastener. I know it should have been done yesterday, but I'll get it done today."	Common cause—it sounds like a one-off task took a little longer than anticipated.
3	"I read a press release today saying our competitor's product now does single-pass printing. Do we want to move that feature up in our backlog?"	Special cause—an external change may trigger a project reprioritization.
4	"The paint shop is running a day behind again."	This is most likely common cause—hopefully it's not a big deal unless some important paint job is waiting.
5	"Bill, our electrical safety inspector, caught malaria on vacation."	This may be special cause—will the loss of the safety inspector while he recovers from malaria impede the overall project progress?
6	"That's nothing. Helen in accounting got married in Cuba over the weekend!"	Gossip/common cause—it's difficult to see how this will impact the team too much.
7	"I am waiting on Ted again to finish the last of the renderings."	This is most likely common cause—the comment does not include commentary to indicate it is a big issue.

Leading versus Lagging Measurements

Trend analysis is a particularly important aspect of measurement for project managers, because it provides insights into future issues before they have occurred. Although measurements like the amount of budget consumed, for example, are still important, such measurements are lagging metrics; in other words, they provide a view of something that has already happened. While lagging metrics that provide a perfect view of the past might be really exciting to accountants, leading metrics that provide even imperfect views into the future are really exciting to project managers. This is because leading metrics provide information about what is occurring or what may be starting to happen on the project. The early indication of a potential problem is more useful than lagging metrics, since it helps the team adapt and replan appropriately.

As an example, figures 7.15 and 7.16 present the defects, change requests, and clarifications (questions like, "How do I use the product to do X?") that were logged for a product during the month of March. For each category, the number opened, the number closed (resolved), and the ongoing tally of remaining items in that category are tracked.

Figure 7.15: Defects, Change Requests, and Clarifications Log

Observations	Mar 3	Mar 10	Mar 17	Mar 24	Mar 31
Defects Opened	5	25	30	20	10
Defects Closed	1	16	35	22	15
Defects Remaining	4	13	8	6	1
CR Opened	0	18	20	23	12
CR Closed	0	11	21	16	9
CR Remaining	0	7	6	13	16
Clarif. Opened	9	12	14	8	2
Clarif. Closed	6	14	11	9	5
Clarif. Remaining	3	1	4	3	0
Total Observations	7	21	18	22	17

CR = Change Requests
Clarif. = Clarifications

Figure 7.16: Defects, Change Requests, and Clarifications Trends

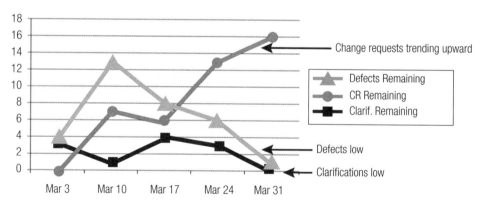

In looking at figure 7.16, we can see that the number of defects remaining spiked on March 10, but that the number has reduced since then, and that the number of clarifications bubbled along with low numbers.

However, change requests are escalating, and there is a trend emerging. For the five periods tracked, there are more change requests being opened every month than being closed.

This trend is useful not only because it tells us we are receiving change requests faster than we can process them and are increasing our WIP, but also because it indicates that we may not be spending enough time validating feature requirements before undertaking development. The metric provides insight into the project and prompts a discussion with the team about the issues and possible solutions.

Another point to keep in mind here is that the identification of trends is more important than the actual data values. So for this example, the valuable information is that we have an escalating number of changes, rather than the specific number of change requests opened in a given week.

 Control Limits

Control limits in an agile context have a fairly loose interpretation that includes tolerance levels and warning signs. Control limits help us diagnose issues before they occur, and they provide guidelines for us to operate within. Some of the agile recommendations or rules of thumb, such as teams of 12 or fewer members, could be interpreted as control limits.

One way we can use control limits is to monitor velocity to gauge how likely it is that we will be able to complete agreed-upon work by the release date. For example, if we have 600 points' worth of functionality left in the backlog and 10 months until deployment preparations begin, we should set our control limits around 60 points per month (600 / 10 = 60), which is the velocity required to meet this goal.

Figure 7.17: Velocity Control Limits

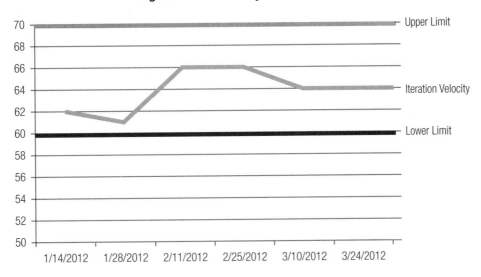

In figure 7.17, we have a lower control limit set at 60 points per iteration. If velocity dips below this limit, there is a chance the agreed-upon functionality will not be developed. Obviously, a quick dip below 60 points per month is not as bad as sustained periods; it is really the rolling average that we are most concerned with, but such graphs do provide visual indications of control and are easy to interpret.

Kanban and task boards that limit WIP are also a form of control limits on agile projects. These tools prevent too much work from being included in an activity, and they help the team control the amount of work in progress.

Resolving Problems

In the first part of this chapter, we talked about identifying problems. Now let's look at how to solve the problems once they are identified. In this section, we'll discuss agile techniques that are designed to quickly resolve problems before they get too big. Like the old saying, "A stitch in time saves nine," the problem resolution techniques used in agile methods aim to address problems before the issues progress too far up the cost of change curve.

T&T Continuous Integration

Continuous integration is a software development process. Using this technique, the team frequently integrates new and changed code into the project code repository. This practice helps minimize the integration problems that result from multiple people making incompatible changes to the same code base. Typically, the more frequently these code commits are made, the smaller the amount of code that needs to be changed to allow the new build (or version) of the software to successfully compile. Continuous integration is an example of ways agile projects address problems as early as possible. Although we'll talk about this T&T in terms of software development, the general concept can apply to other knowledge worker projects where multiple people are developing separate pieces of the project and then bringing the pieces together to create a functional, valuable product.

Figure 7.18: Continuous Integration

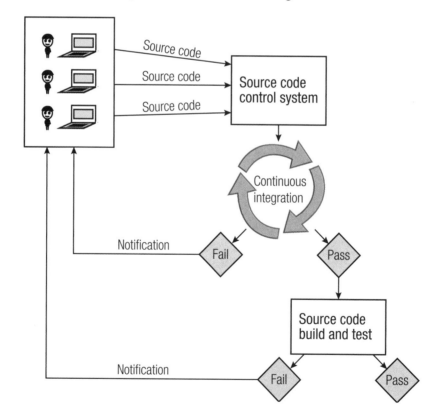

The following are the components of a continuous integration system:

» **Source code control system**: This is the software that performs version control on all the files that represent the build, or product version, being developed. Once the team has completed some changes to the source code, they will check the new version of the code into the source code control system. One commonly used source code control system is Apache™ Subversion®.

» **Build tools**: The source code will need to be compiled before tests can be run. Most integrated development environments (IDEs) such as Microsoft Visual Studio® or Eclipse™ can serve as a build tool to compile the code.[7]

» **Test tools**: As part of the build process, unit tests are run to ensure the basic functionality operates as planned. Unit test tools, such as as NUnit (for Microsoft .Net®) and JUnit (for Java), execute the small, atomic tests that are written in these tools to check the code for unanticipated changes in behavior.[8]

» **Scheduler or trigger**: Builds might be launched on a schedule (e.g., every hour) or every time a change to the source code is detected (i.e., triggered by the change). The scheduler or trigger is the component that initiates the integration process.

» **Notifications**: If a build fails, the team needs to be notified so they can correct the build as soon as possible. Notifications are usually sent via e-mail, but many of today's tools can also handle instant messaging and Twitter notifications.

For purposes of the exam, understand that continuous integration uses automated tools to start the integration process when code is checked in or at timed intervals. In addition to checking that new and changed code compiles correctly, there are automated unit tests to ensure the system still performs as intended after the new code is integrated.

Continuous integration is important for agile projects because it provides the following benefits:

» The team receives an early warning of broken (invalid), conflicting, or incompatible code.
» Integration problems are fixed as they occur, rather than as release dates approach. This moves any related changes down the cost of change curve and avoids last-minute work before releases.
» The team receives immediate feedback on the system-wide impacts of the code they are writing.
» This technique ensures frequent unit testing of code, alerting the team to issues sooner rather than later.
» If a problem is found, the code can be reverted back to the last known bug-free state for testing, demo, or release purposes.

The disadvantages or costs of using continuous integration are:

» The setup time required to establish a build server machine and configure the continuous integration software; this is typically done as an iteration 0 activity (before the development work begins on the project)
» The cost of procuring a machine to act as the build server, as this is usually a dedicated machine
» The time required to build a suite of automated, comprehensive tests that run when code is checked in

Despite the costs, continuous integration is established as a standard good practice for software development projects, and most multi-person teams use the approach. The benefits of this technology over older practices, such as the "daily build and smoke test," are significant; with continuous integration, far more tests are run per day, and less time passes before a problem is identified. This T&T is a prime example of how we can shorten the time between defect injection, defect detection, and the subsequent resolution of the defect.

T&T Risk-Based Spike

A risk-based spike is a short proof of concept exercise that the team undertakes to investigate an issue. As an example, imagine we are building a container-based algae production unit to capture carbon dioxide (CO_2) emissions. This production unit calls for underwater lighting using cheaply available parts. In this scenario, we might undertake a spike to test waterproofing options for fluorescent tubing. By testing various options in short, small-scale experiments, we can reduce the project risk associated with a key component of the project's success (developing cost-effective underwater lighting) early and at the lowest cost.

This approach of doing short experiments to investigate risky portions of the project is at the heart of risk-based spikes. If the proof-of-concept exercise is successful, then we can eliminate that risk, and the overall risk profile of the project can be reduced.

Figure 7.19: Algae Project Risks

Risk Name	Jan			Feb			Mar			Apr		
	Impact	Prob.	Severity	Impact	Prob.	Severity	Impact	Prob.	Severity	Impact	Prob.	Severity
Cost-effective underwater lighting	3	2	6	3	0	0	3	0	0	3	0	0
Exhaust gas heat recovery insulation	2	2	4	2	2	4	2	1	2	2	0	0
Biomass harvesting and preservation	2	2	4	2	2	4	2	1	2	2	1	2
Algae cross contamination	3	1	3	3	1	3	3	1	3	3	1	3

Figure 7.20: Algae Project Risk Profile

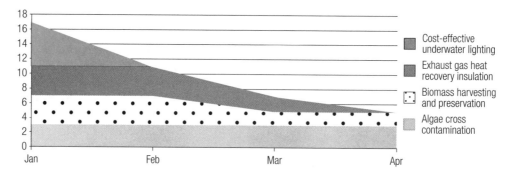

In figure 7.20, we can see that the risk-based spike undertaken to trial "underwater lighting" in January worked, because this risk was then eliminated. Also during February, additional risk response strategies were put in place to help address other risks; as a result, the risks associated with "exhaust gas heat recovery insulation" and "biomass harvesting and preservation" were reduced, and the "exhaust gas heat recovery insulation" risk was eventually eliminated.

If a proof-of-concept exercise is not successful, however, we can try a different approach. If none of the approaches we try are successful, we reach a condition known as "fast failure." Although it sounds bad, fast failure can in some ways be a good outcome; rather than continuing on a project that would have eventually failed, the remaining funds and resources from the project can now be directed to other projects awaiting resources.

Figure 7.21: Fast Failure

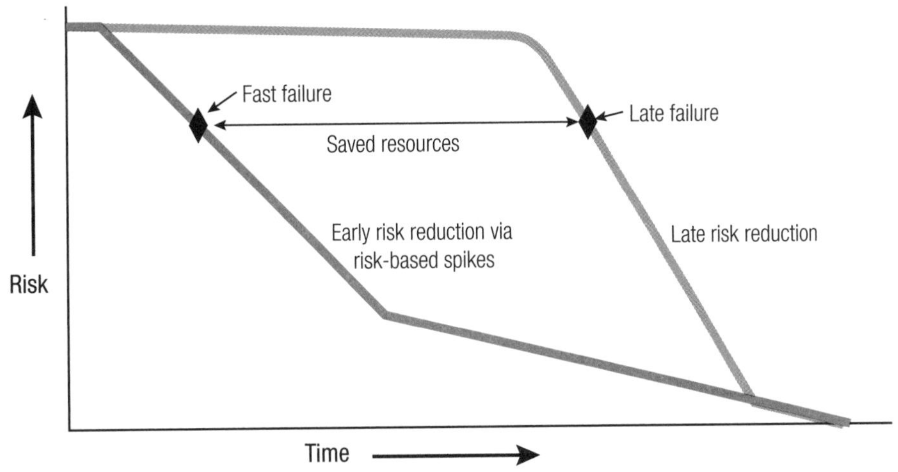

Research and development companies with a business model that relies upon new product development recognize that a certain percentage of their projects will not be successful. They generally operate with the philosophy that if something was easy, other companies would have done it by now, and instead they look for the breakthrough new approach. In these environments, fast failures greatly reduce the amount of sunk costs in projects that aren't viable and allow the company to try more approaches each year, increasing the odds of finding a revolutionary new product.

Risk-based spikes are often used on software projects to test unfamiliar or new technologies early in the project before proceeding too far with development. For example, imagine the team's analysis of a medium-priority feature raised the question of "Can we interface with the old legacy system from a mobile device?" The team may investigate this question through a risk-based spike before they continue too far down the path of analyzing, designing, and developing this feature.

EXERCISE

Think about how each of the following risks might be investigated through a risk-based spike, and describe what short proof-of-concept exercise you would undertake to explore the risk.

1. We are not certain whether the remote data center can validate new credit card applications in the two-subsecond response time needed to ensure a reasonable customer experience.

2. We do not know if project Alpha has solid management support, and we have concerns about getting approval for buying the development and production machines when it comes time to do so.

[ ]

3. Project Beta will require working with Ted in the database group again, and the last time we had to do that, there were major arguments about approach and approvals.

[ ]

ANSWER

1. This is a classic technical risk that can be investigated by a small-scale test. We need to do some performance benchmark tests for various times of the day and under various activity loads and then measure the response times to see if the two-subsecond response time is achievable.

2. People often associate risk-based spikes with technical work, but there is nothing stopping us from also using this approach for business and human resource risks. So for this scenario, if we are not sure whether there is management support for project Alpha, let's try getting approval to order those development and production machines in the first iteration of the project and surface the issue sooner rather than later.

3. This is another nontechnical risk that we can again use a risk-based spike to address. How about scheduling some work with Ted as early as possible in the project to see if we can find a way to improve the relationship and get things to go more smoothly this time? If the approach fails, then at least we know about the issue before his work is on the project's critical path, when problems could jeopardize the success of the project. Exploring the issue early gives us time to help resolve it within the project or escalate it to others outside of the project who can address it.

T&T Frequent Verification and Validation

The theme of frequent verification and validation is practiced at many levels on agile projects. It is an effective antidote, both to the fact that making mistakes is part of being human and to the mismatch of expectations that arises when we listen to someone's description of an end goal and interpret their description slightly differently than they intended. With frequent verification and validation, we are checking to make sure things are working and progressing as they should, and we are looking for any mismatches in expectations. In doing so, we enable the project to rapidly converge on the real solution, even when this solution changes from the originally stated requirements.

Figure 7.22 is a variation on a common Extreme Programming graphic that is typically used to show the frequent planning and feedback loops. However, this graphic also works well to illustrate how frequent verification and validation is undertaken on agile projects.

Figure 7.22: Frequent Verification and Validation on Agile Projects

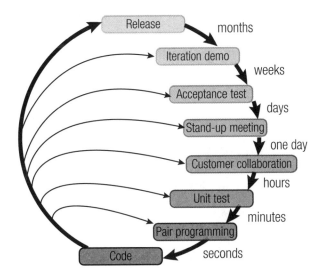

In this diagram, we can see how the software practice of pair programming offers very short (lasting a few seconds) cycles of verification and validation. If two people are pairing and one person spots an error or a misunderstanding of the desired intent, the issue is addressed almost immediately since the two developers discuss the code as they are writing it.

At the next level, we see that unit tests are run every few minutes by developers to verify that the code is achieving the desired outcome and to validate whether the existing functionality still works. Customer collaboration (the next level) should also occur frequently. This collaboration provides feedback on whether designs are correct and objectives are being met. Through daily stand-up meetings, we can validate who is working on what, and when things should be done and ready to integrate. Then every couple of weeks, we perform product demonstrations and iteration reviews to verify that we are building the right product and to validate the correctness of the solution thus far. So as figure 7.21 illustrates, we have cycles within cycles that are all concerned with frequent verification and validation on the project.

Because agile methods accept that building new and sometimes intangible products will have communication challenges, there are multiple levels of deliberate checks and confirmation activities to make sure we catch issues as soon as possible. Agile software projects automate as many of these tests as possible, which removes the human element from their execution. Automation also allows the tests to be run more frequently at lower costs. Again, like the other problem resolution T&Ts we'll discuss in this section, the idea behind frequent verification and validation is all about finding issues as soon as possible and keeping them low on the cost of change curve.

T&T | Test-Driven Development (TDD) / Test-First Development (TFD)

Test-driven development (TDD) and test-first development (TFD) are also techniques from the software development industry. TDD and TFD encourage bringing a different mindset to development, and they employ short test and feedback cycles. There are differences between TDD and TFD, but for purposes of the exam, you simply need to understand at a high level the behaviors these techniques foster and why they are beneficial. For that reason, we will examine these techniques together under the single heading of test-driven development, or TDD.

The philosophy behind TDD is that tests should be written before the code is written. In other words, developers should first think about how the functionality should be tested and then write tests in a unit testing language (like NUnit or JUnit) before they actually begin developing the code. Initially the tests will fail, since developers have not yet written the code to deliver the required functionality.

So with TDD, developers begin a cycle of writing code and running the tests until the code passes all the tests. Then if necessary, they clean up the design to make it easier to understand and maintain without changing the code's behavior. This last process is called "refactoring."

Figure 7.23: Test-Driven Development

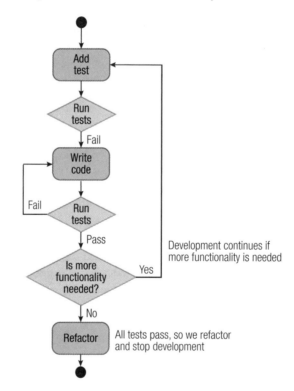

Red, Green, Refactor / Red, Green, Clean

As we discussed earlier in this chapter, developers usually use continuous integration tools to run builds. These tools notify developers whether the code passed or failed by communicating a green or red status. The process of writing a test that initially fails, adding code until the test passes, and then refactoring the code is known as "Red, Green, Refactor" or sometimes "Red, Green, Clean."

The following are some key benefits of closely linking code to tests in this way:

» By focusing on the tests first, we must think about how the functionality will be used by the customer. This puts us in the mindset of being concerned with the outcome before the implementation, which studies have found leads to better designs and higher levels of client satisfaction.
» Writing the tests before the code ensures that we have at least some tests in place. Better test coverage of the code enhances systems quality and allows the development team and customer to be more confident in the code.
» Early and frequent testing helps us catch defects early in the development cycle, which prevents the defects from becoming widespread and costly to fix. Eliminating defects early in the development cycle while the code is still fresh in the developers' minds, rather than later in the project, also reduces the amount of time spent finding the cause of the defects.
» The approach of writing systems in small, tested units leads to a more modular, flexible, and extendable system.

There are also disadvantages or costs to this approach, including:

» The unit tests are usually written by the same developer who will implement the code; therefore, we will likely see the same misinterpretations of requirements in both the test and the code.
» Some types of functionality, such as user interfaces, are difficult or time consuming to reliably test via unit tests.
» The tests themselves also need to be maintained, and as the project grows and changes, the sustainment load for test scripts goes up.
» As people see higher numbers of passing tests, they may get a false sense of security about the code quality.

T&T Acceptance Test–Driven Development (ATDD)

The technique of acceptance test–driven development (ATDD) moves the testing focus from the code to the business requirement. As with TDD, the tests are created before work starts on the code, and these tests represent how the functionality is expected to behave at an acceptance test level.

Typically we capture these tests when we pull the user story from the backlog and discuss its desired behavior with the business representatives. The acceptance tests may be captured in a functional test framework, such as "FIT" (Framework for Integrated Testing) or "FitNesse."[9] The overall process goes through the four stages of discuss, distill, develop, and demo, as illustrated in figure 7.24.

Figure 7.24: Acceptance Test–Driven Development (ATDD) Cycle

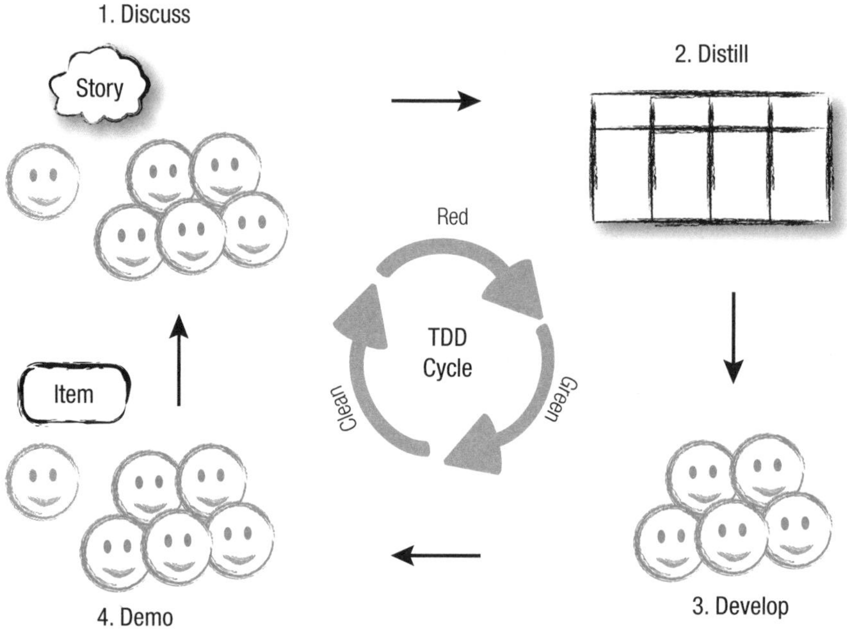

1. Discuss
Story

2. Distill

Red

TDD Cycle

Clean

Green

4. Demo

3. Develop

Item

ATDD model developed by Elisabeth Hendrickson, Grigori Melnick, Brian Marick, and Jim Shore, based on a model by Jim Shore. Copyright © 2012 Quality Tree Software, Inc. Licensed Creative Commons Attribution.

Let's look at these four stages in a little more detail:

1. **Discuss** the requirements: During the planning meeting, we ask the product owner or customer questions that are designed to gather acceptance criteria.
2. **Distill** tests in a framework-friendly format: In this next phase, we get the tests ready to be entered into our acceptance test tool. This usually involves structuring the tests in a table format.
3. **Develop** the code and hook up the tests: During development, the tests are hooked up to the code and the acceptance tests are run. Initially the tests fail because they cannot find the necessary code. Once the code is written and the tests are hooked to it, the tests validate the code. They may again fail, so the process of writing code and testing continues until the code passes the tests.
4. **Demo**: The team does exploratory testing using the automated acceptance testing scripts, and demos the software.

When we combine the tasks of defining acceptance criteria and discussing requirements, we are forced to come to concrete agreement about the exact behavior the software should exhibit. In a way, this approach enforces the discussion of the "definition of done" at a very granular level for each requirement.

 For all of these techniques—TFD, TDD, and ATDD—the main point you need to understand for the exam is that it is a good practice for the development team to engage in thinking about how the system (or product, if we expand this concept to nonsoftware development projects) will be tested before they start developing the product. Another key point to keep in mind for the exam is that creating tests before developing the product means we end up with tests for the majority of the development work, which in turn means the product will be better tested.

EXERCISE: TECHNICAL TERM FISHING

Review the following list of terms and circle any that are NOT associated with agile verification and validation:

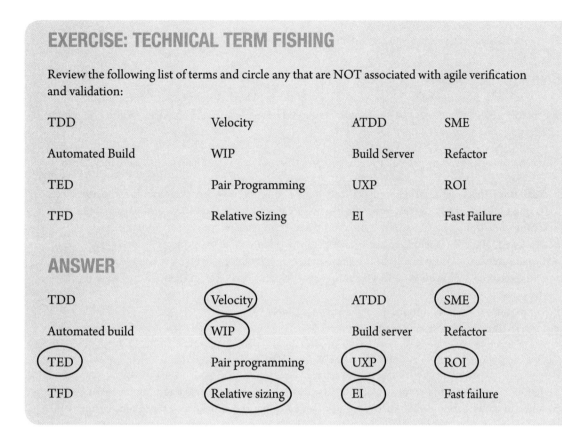

TDD	Velocity	ATDD	SME
Automated Build	WIP	Build Server	Refactor
TED	Pair Programming	UXP	ROI
TFD	Relative Sizing	EI	Fast Failure

ANSWER

TDD	(Velocity)	ATDD	(SME)
Automated build	(WIP)	Build server	Refactor
(TED)	Pair programming	(UXP)	(ROI)
TFD	(Relative sizing)	(EI)	Fast failure

K&S Level 1 — Problem Solving

The last activity we'll discuss in this chapter is problem solving. Although we should take steps to find indications of problems early and then take action to avoid problems before they occur, it is inevitable that our projects will still encounter problems. Therefore, we need to understand ways to solve them.

Agile methods encourage engaging the team in identifying, diagnosing, and solving problems. So rather than it being the domain of the project manager or external sleuths and "fixers" to look for and correct problems, it is very much a whole-team activity. The next chapter, Continuous Improvement, will discuss the retrospective process, but we'll examine the problem-solving component of retrospectives now.

There are three steps involved in team-based problem solving, as indicated in figure 7.25.

Figure 7.25: Problem-Solving Steps

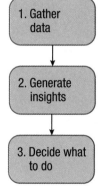

1. Gather data
2. Generate insights
3. Decide what to do

Let's discuss each of these steps in more detail.

Step 1: Gather Data

Data-gathering activities help create a shared view of the problem. Without data, the team is simply speculating on what changes and improvements should be made. In gathering data, we are collecting and integrating the pieces of the puzzle to solve.

There are several team-based facilitation techniques that can be used to help gather data, including:

» **Timeline**: This technique helps participants think about the project from a time-based perspective.
» **Triple nickels**: With this technique, the top five ideas are elaborated by five groups, five times.
» **Color code dots**: This is a group-based affinity clustering technique.
» **Mad, sad, glad**: This technique explores the emotive elements of the project.
» **Locate strengths**: With this technique, the participants look for what went well.
» **Satisfaction histogram**: With this technique, participants review what their feelings were throughout the project.
» **Team radar**: This is a multidisciplined assessment tool.
» **Like to like**: This is a strengths diagnostic tool.

Let's look at the first two techniques (timeline and triple nickels) in more detail.

Timeline   The team can use the timeline technique to diagnose the origin and progression of a single problem or a number of problems. To start, the facilitator draws a timeline for the review period, which can be an iteration or the timeline of the problem. The facilitator then asks team members to recall good, problematic, and significant events that occurred during the timeline.

Working individually at first, team members write events on colored sticky notes. The color of the notes indicates how the team members categorize the event (as good, problematic, or significant). When everyone has a collection of notes, they are invited to place them on the timeline and review what other people have posted.

By asking team members to recall the timeline, we get better insight into the events and what contributed to the issues. As a result, we may get clues about how to avoid similar problems in the future. The spatial representation of cause and effect that this technique provides and the opportunity to see other people's interpretations of events help us recall additional details and build on the inputs of others.

After the cards are posted, the team discusses the timeline from left to right, adding new cards as required. They also record below the timeline their feelings about the events and draw a trend line to indicate the team feelings (see figure 7.26). Expressing their emotional response can help surface additional information that might be useful in generating insights (step 2 of the team-based problem-solving process).

Figure 7.26: Timeline Exercise

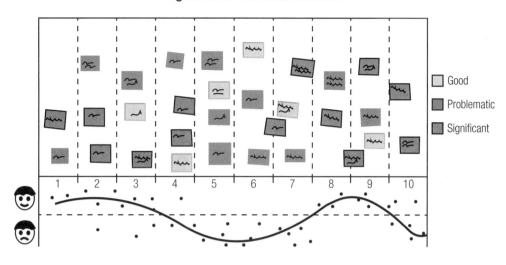

Triple Nickels   Triple nickels is a data-gathering exercise in which participants spend five minutes gathering data on at least five ideas related to a specified topic. The team is divided into groups of five (or if the entire group is less than seven people, the exercise is done as one group), and the groups conduct five rounds of expansion. (This technique gets its name from a shooting competition that engages five targets from five yards in five seconds.)

This exercise asks people to work individually at first and think of at least five issues that occurred during an iteration. The team members then record the issues on sticky notes or cards. After the first five minutes are up, everyone passes their cards to the person on their right. They then spend five minutes building on the ideas on the cards they have just received. This process repeats five times so everyone gets to contribute their own ideas and has an opportunity to think about and add to the ideas of the other group members. The goal of this technique is to create an environment where participants have time to do both personal reflection and to expand on other people's ideas.

Figure 7.27: Triple Nickels

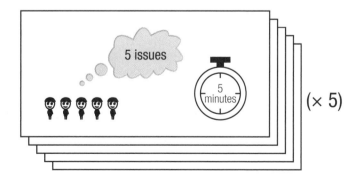

Step 2: Generate Insights

Now let's look at the second step in the problem-solving process—generating insights. This step involves collaborative exercises that are aimed at analyzing the data gathered in the previous step and making sense out of it. The activities done in this step help the team interpret and understand the implications of the issues before they move on to solving them.

Activities to help the team generate insights include:

» Brainstorming
» Five whys
» Fishbone
» Prioritize with dots
» Identify themes

Let's look at the first three techniques (brainstorming, five whys, and fishbone) in more detail.

Brainstorming   Brainstorming exercises aim to generate a large number of ideas that are then filtered into a select list of ideas to move forward in the process. The high volume of ideas generated during such exercises helps counter the common issue that the best ideas are rarely offered first. Teams can take different approaches to brainstorming, including:

» **Free-for-all**: Everyone calls out ideas.
» **Round-robin**: People pass a token around the group. When a team member receives the token, he or she has to suggest an idea and then passes the token to the next person.
» **Quiet time**: Everyone gets five to seven minutes to work individually and think of ideas themselves, and then they are gathered together.

Once the ideas have been generated, they are filtered based on criteria that is also generated by the team. For example, if the team was brainstorming ideas about problems related to the availability of business representatives, the team may decide to add filters for items they are "able to influence" and items they are "unable to influence." They then review each idea in reference to the filters and decide whether to include or exclude the idea for the next step in the problem-solving process, deciding what to do.

Five Whys   This aim of this exercise is to discover the cause-and-effect relationships underlying a particular problem and get to the root cause of the problem. The technique originates from Toyota and is routinely used in lean techniques.

When using the five whys exercise in a team setting, people work in pairs or small groups. Within their groups, they ask "Why?" five times to move beyond the automatic, habitual answers and to get to the root cause of the problem. Here is an example:

Question 1: Why did we get that system crash in the iteration demo?
  Answer 1: We tried to access sales data for a store with no sales.

Question 2: Why does accessing a store with no sales cause a problem?
  Answer 2: The fetch routine returns a null value that is not handled by the system.

Question 3: Why don't we catch null values and display a more meaningful error message?
  Answer 3: We do catch them where we know about them, but this was the first time we had seen it for sales.

Question 4: Why aren't all query returns coded to handle nulls?
  Answer 4: I don't know; it has never been a priority.

Question 5: Why is it not a priority, as it seems like it's really a weak link in the system?
  Answer 5: Agreed. We should add it to the module walkthrough checklist.

Here's another example—though this one should not apply to you!

Question 1: Why did you fail the PMI-ACP exam?
  Answer 1: I don't know. I guess I mustn't have answered enough questions on the exam correctly.

Question 2: Why did you not answer enough questions correctly?
  Answer 2: Every question has four answers to choose from, and you actually have to know what they are asking about.

Question 3: Why did you not know what they were asking about?
  Answer 3: Well, I have been kind of doing agile for a while and thought that would be enough without really studying.

Question 4: What exam areas did you not study for or have experience in?
  Answer 4: Well I know Scrum, but the XP, lean, and Kanban stuff was all Greek to me.

Question 5: Why did you not read up on these topics and go through the sample questions in this book?
  Answer 5: Because I underestimated the breadth of the exam, and thought I could bluff my way through.

Fishbone   A fishbone diagram is a visual tool that often accompanies the five whys exercise. It is a way to display the root cause analysis of problems. With this technique, the team identifies factors that are causing or affecting the problem situation and looks for the likely causes.

The process starts with drawing an empty fishbone diagram and writing the problem at the "head." The next step is to identify the categories of contributing factors, which are then also written on the diagram. The categories can be related to the questions in the five whys exercise, or they can be related to a set of commonly used categories, such as:

» People, procedure, policies, place
» Systems, suppliers, skills, surroundings

Another option is for the team to choose whatever categories make sense for the problem. The facilitator of the exercise asks the team members "What are the [fill in category name] factors contributing to the problem?" The answers are then filled in as "bones" on the categories.

Figure 7.28: Fishbone Diagram

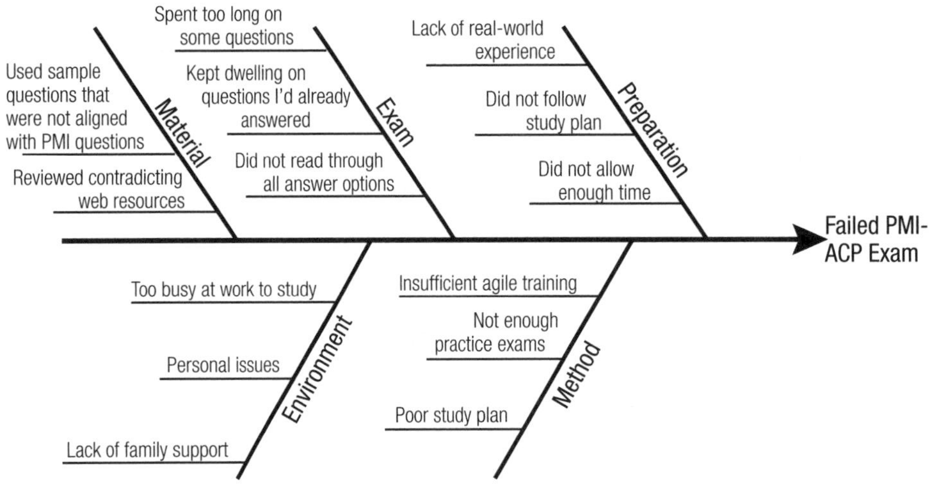

In the example in figure 7.28, this fishbone diagram investigates the factors that could contribute to the problem of failing the PMI-ACP exam. (This is, of course, a fictitious example, because it is not going to happen to you, right?)

Step 3: Decide What to Do

The last step in the problem-solving process is deciding what to do about the problem. The team-based techniques that are used in this step involve experiments to validate approaches and measurable goals to track progress and problem resolution. They help build a clear set of actions for solving the problem.

The techniques commonly used in this process include:

» Short subjects
» SMART goals
» Retrospective planning game
» Circle of questions

Let's look at the first two of these techniques (short subjects and SMART goals) in more detail.

Short Subjects   This activity helps the team agree on problem-resolution actions. The team is presented with flip charts or whiteboards with categories written on them, and the team then agrees on which ideas to pursue. The categories may include:

» What Went Well, Do Differently Next Time
» Keep, Drop, Add
» Start Doing, Stop Doing, Do More Of, Do Less Of

Figure 7.29 shows an example of a short subjects session that was held for a software project. This session used the categories of Start Doing, Stop Doing, Do More Of, and Do Less Of.

Figure 7.29: Short Subjects Problem-Solving Technique

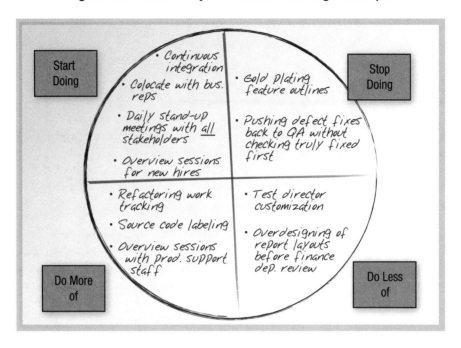

SMART Goals   This activity helps the team create goals that are **S**pecific, **M**easurable, **A**ttainable, **R**elevant, and **T**imely (SMART). Goals with these characteristics are more likely to be successfully achieved. At the beginning of the SMART goals exercise, the facilitator lists the SMART characteristics on a flip chart or whiteboard and then contrasts a non-SMART goal, such as *"We need to do more testing,"* with a SMART version of the goal, such as *"Each module must have and pass a unit test, functional test, and system test before iteration end."*

Figure 7.30: SMART Goals Problem-Solving Technique

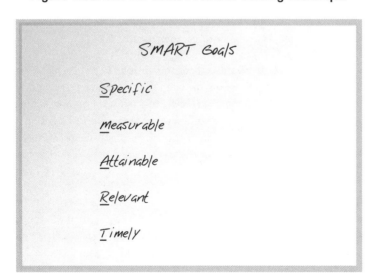

Once everyone understands the characteristics of SMART goals, smaller groups are formed to transform problem-solving actions into SMART goals. The team then reviews each goal. They discuss whether the goals are indeed SMART goals and make refinements where necessary. The process of ensuring the goals have SMART characteristics also confirms people's understanding of what will happen and helps them form mental models of what will be done to complete the goals and resolve the problems.

Why Such a Focus on Engaging the Team?

Before we move on to the professional responsibility and ethics discussion for this chapter, I'd like to take some time to address a key concept—why it's so important to engage the team in problem detection and resolution. When attempting to solve project problems, organizations too often overlook the best source of solutions—the project team. The team usually has the best practical solutions even when they may not be the best theoretical solutions.

A story from one of my projects might help illustrate this idea. While managing a government project during an IT vendor change, we needed to quickly build rapport with the business users of the system and with the subject matter experts (SMEs) in order to maintain the previous team's development pace. The problem we faced was how to get to know the business folks better and connect the team members and the SMEs. Instead of contriving some project social event and trying to get buy-in from the business and the team, I presented the problem to the team in a planning meeting.

After some back and forth, a team member suggested that since quite a few of the business people went 10-pin bowling, perhaps we should arrange a bowling social event. Other team members concurred, and we brainstormed ideas for mixing up the teams (so it was not us versus them). We ran the event. It went really well and led to other activities, all of which greatly contributed to a strong relationship between stakeholders and to a successful project.

As the project manager, I could have chosen to consult the PMO, human resources department, or social psychology experts to determine the optimal team-building event, but then I would have had to "sell" the event to the team. There are many benefits to involving the team in solving problems. Gaining the team's buy-in from the start is one of them.

Let's look now at the different benefits of team engagement:

1. **By asking the team for a solution, we inherit consensus for the proposal**: In the previous example, the fact that the solution came from the team and not from me meant I did not have to sell it to the team—it already had their support. It is easier to guide a suboptimal solution that has good support to a successful outcome than it is to build support for an optimal solution and make sure it is successfully executed. If challenges arise and people subconsciously ask "Whose bright idea was this?" they have to answer, "Oh yeah, it was ours," and they are more likely to continue working on the solution.

2. **Engaging the team gives us access to a broader knowledge of the facts**: Team members are closer to the details and bring additional insights to a problem and the potential solutions. For example, I did not know that the business folks liked to bowl. This information was collective knowledge; one team member, Chris, knew three users bowled, and Julia, another team member, knew that two SMEs did as well. So together we found a new piece of useful information. Asking the group for ideas taps the collective knowledge of the team.

3. **Solutions are practical**: Anyone who has worked hard to craft a solution only to be told "That will not work here because . . ." will know how frustrating and disheartening these words are. Team-sourced solutions have been vetted for practicality and, because they are created internally, they also include solutions for implementation issues.

4. **When consulted, people work hard to generate good ideas**: The simple act of asking for suggestions engages team members beyond the role of "coder," "tester," or "engineer." People appreciate having their input valued, so when they are asked for their ideas, they generally work hard to create innovative and effective solutions.

   Treating workers as interchangeable resources is a poor model inherited from the command-and-control methods of the industrial revolution. Leading companies such as Toyota and 3M recognize that their best ideas come from inside their companies, and that they need to make use of this intellect. It is partly due to these methods that these companies innovate better, have higher quality products, and have better labor relations.

5. **Asking for help shows confidence, not weakness**: Asking for ideas and solutions to problems is not a sign of incompetence or an inability to manage. Just because we ask for input does not mean we are stupid. Instead, it demonstrates that we value the opinions of others and are thoughtful. In essence, asking for help demonstrates how all problems should be tackled, as described in the next benefit.

6. **Seeking others' ideas models desired behavior**: Part of the role of a leader is to model desired behavior. In other words, we need to behave as we wish others to behave. If we stay silent, make decisions with incomplete awareness of the facts, and do not ask for help when we need it, what message are we sending to the team? Whether we realize it or not, the message is obvious to team members that we expect them to behave the same way and work in isolation. Time and money spent on team-building activities is wasted if we take a management-in-a-vacuum approach.

   In contrast, when we demonstrate good problem-solving techniques, team members are encouraged to solve their problems in this way, too. Teams that can effectively solve problems and build support for solutions are the real powerhouse of successful projects. As leaders, we need to make sure we are supporting and mirroring these best practices.

Beyond the benefits we get from engaging the team in problem solving, there are a few other points to consider about using this approach, including cautions to keep in mind. Let's discuss these next.

Usage and Cautions

People do not want to be treated as work drones. Instead, if we ask them to think, they will amaze us with innovative, practical solutions that have great backing from the people who need to implement the solutions. In the previous discussion, I used a trivial example of a team-building activity because it was quick to explain, but this approach of team engagement works best on complex, embedded process problems that would take days to outline to an expert. The team has the first-hand knowledge of the problem and, more importantly, what types of actions are practical to solve it.

Of course, involving the team is not a silver-bullet or cure-all approach. Here are some points that we need to keep in mind:

» **Solve real problems**: We should use the team to help solve real problems only, not make decisions like which brand of printer toner to buy. Remember that we are always setting an example and modeling behavior for our team. If people go too far and consult their team members for every little decision (such as what color dialogue box they should create), no work will get done. Engaging the team in solving a problem is a tool to use when you are stuck and the problem is important.

» **Poor team cohesion**: If the team is fragmented and has opposing groups, then resentment that the other group is "fixing their problems" will undermine the process. We need to get the team members aligned with each other for team problem solving to be most effective.

» **Team and project changes**: If a significant portion of the team changes over a long period, we need to recanvas the team to make sure they are still on board with the approach to the problem resolution. Exercising the bright ideas of others is nearly as bad as not being consulted, so we need to check whether people still agree that it is a good policy. Likewise, if the project changes significantly, we need to perform a checkpoint in light of these new facts and get the team to review the approach.

» **Follow-through**: Once you ask for solutions, make sure you follow through on executing them. It is pretty demoralizing to be asked to work on a solution and then see that solution wither. It is fine to go back to the team with implementation problems that need to be solved, but we shouldn't waste people's time by asking for their input if we are simply going to ignore it.

In summary, your team is best suited for coming up with solutions to your project problems. And not only do team members provide the best solutions; including them in the problem-solving process will improve their performance on the project as well. People relish being included and appreciate opportunities to help solve problems. So take advantage of all these benefits—unleash the team's problem-solving power on your projects.

Professional Responsibility and Ethics

Before we move on to the next chapter, let's look at how PMI's Code of Ethics and Professional Conduct (available on PMI's website: www.pmi.org) applies to problem detection and resolution concepts.[10] There are four main areas of this code—Responsibility, Respect, Fairness, and Honesty—and we'll cover each in turn, looking at examples of how they relate to the topics discussed in this chapter. As you read this section, think about your real-world projects and how they are impacted by these different aspects of professional responsibility and ethics.

Responsibility

» **Make decisions based on the best interests of the company**: We must deal with project problems early; delaying taking action is not in the best interest of the company, as it forces changes up the ever-steepening cost-of-change curve. If we give in to temptations to "hang on and see if things get better," we are not acting responsibly or serving our stakeholders' needs. Instead, we need to address issues as they arise. Early resolutions are typically faster and better than the costly failures that result when problems simmer for too long.

» **Protect proprietary information**: If in investigating a problem, we find that issues or errors lie with external vendors, we need to be careful that we communicate this information only to the concerned parties and that we are respecting agreements related to proprietary information and confidentiality.

» **Report unethical behavior and violations**: If the problems team members complain about concern rudeness, disrespect, harassment, or prejudice to staff, then we must communicate these issues to the human resources department and any other appropriate group. It is not sufficient to only try and fix them within the project.

Respect

» **Maintain an attitude of mutual cooperation**: Problem solving should focus on finding and fixing the issues, not pointing fingers or assigning blame. Taking a team approach to identifying and solving problems is not possible when people are busy blaming each other.

» **Respect cultural differences**: We should recognize that people from some cultures may feel less comfortable reporting or discussing problems in the presence of their managers. Therefore, we should provide mechanisms to allow for safe contribution and anonymous reporting of problems.

» **Deal with conflict directly**: Problems that relate to team conflict should be dealt with immediately. The response of "Save it for the retrospective" is not appropriate. Conflict can be extremely stressful and should be dealt with promptly and with privacy.

» **Do not use your position to influence others**: We need to facilitate, not dictate; we should let team members solve project problems. In doing so, not only do we get better solutions, but we achieve better buy-in for those solutions.

Fairness

» **Look for and disclose conflicts of interest**: Maybe we have found the problem, and it is us! If the team has problems with the project manager, ScrumMaster, or team lead, we should offer the assistance of third-party facilitators and be ready to listen to the concerns.

Honesty

» **Understand the truth**: When diagnosing problems, we should try to understand why people are acting the way they are. What motivates their behavior? Sometimes people behave in unexpected ways because their environment of rules, rewards, and reprimands has been shifted away from a healthy balance. Problem identification should get to the heart of why things are happening to determine what the real fix needs to be.

» **Be truthful in all communications**: People don't like receiving bad news now, but they like receiving worse news later even less. It can be difficult at first to report on bad news and problems, but early reporting is the best thing to do. By reporting problems early, we have a better chance of fixing them. And then once the problems are resolved, we'll be able to report better news in the future.

Practice Exam

1. Which activity does not actively reduce a problem's position on the cost of change curve?

    A. Pair programming
    B. Test-driven development
    C. Velocity
    D. Acceptance test–driven development

2. Your team has identified a number of problems during a retrospective session and you now want to help understand and fix the issues. The sequence of activities you should undertake is:

    A. Generate insights, gather data, decide what to do
    B. Gather data, generate insights, decide what to do
    C. Decide what to do, gather data, generate insights
    D. Decide what to do, generate insights, gather data

3. The term used for describing errors that are missed by quality assurance and control processes and that make it into production is:

    A. Cost of change
    B. Undocumented features
    C. Escaped defects
    D. Change requests

4. Trends in project data are useful since they can offer insights and are what type of indicator?

    A. Lagging metrics
    B. Leading metrics
    C. Lead times
    D. Little's Law

5. The concept of control limits can be described as:

    A. Visual controls that show acceptable ranges
    B. Change control procedures to help manage flow
    C. Budget processes that help teams estimate better
    D. Exception reporting techniques with escalation paths

6. In software development, the process of frequently integrating new and changed code is known as:

    A. Integrating continuously
    B. Continuous integration
    C. Integration control
    D. Constant integrations

7. The shorthand summary of test-driven development activities is:

    A. Red, Green, Yellow
    B. Red, Green, Refactor
    C. Green, Red, Clean
    D. Green, Red, Refactor

8. On agile projects, the term "cycle time" usually refers to:

   A. The average duration of an iteration
   B. Time taken for work from start to finish
   C. The time for SMEs to review the product
   D. Time between releases of a product

9. A short period of proof-of-concept work is known as:

   A. Risk stops
   B. Spikes of iteration
   C. Risk-based spike
   D. Test-first design

10. Which of the following is not a form of frequent verification and validation?

    A. Pair programming
    B. Unit testing
    C. Iteration demos
    D. Iteration planning

11. You are managing an agile project and measure small amounts of variance in task durations. You should:

    A. Undertake root-cause analysis to eliminate it
    B. Engage the team in diagnosing the problem
    C. Diagnose the issue as part of your ScrumMaster role
    D. Accept some variance as inevitable

12. You are a team member on a software development project and have been asked to follow a test-driven development process. The sequence of activities you would undertake is:

    A. Write code, write test, refactor
    B. Write test, refactor, write code
    C. Write test, write code, refactor
    D. Write code, refactor, write test

13. When solving problems in a team setting, goals for problem resolution should be SMART. The characteristics of SMART goals are:

    A. Simple, Marketable, Attainable, Risk Tolerant, Timely
    B. Simple, Malleable, Attainable, Relevant, Testable
    C. Specific, Measurable, Attributable, Relevant, Testable
    D. Specific, Measurable, Attainable, Relevant, Timely

14. The purpose of continuous integration is to:

    A. Always have a version of the software ready for release
    B. Shorten lengthy compile times
    C. Facilitate the practice of pair programming
    D. Find code issues as soon as possible

15. Fast failure is the term used to describe:

    A. Finding fatal design flaws early
    B. Developing without proper testing
    C. The last step of the ATDD process
    D. An element of continuous integration

16. On a timeline graph used in the gathering data phase for team-based problem-solving, the line underneath the X-axis usually represents:

    A. Team velocity at the time
    B. Team satisfaction/feelings
    C. Team risk rankings at the time
    D. Team hours of work

17. When diagnosing problems, we ask "why" five times:

    A. To get to the root cause of an issue
    B. Because asking six times would be ridiculous
    C. Because people unconsciously deceive themselves about problems three or four times
    D. To fully gather data around the issue

18. You are a team lead helping your team decide what to do about some problems identified in a retrospective. What are some of the techniques you can use?

    A. Smart Subjects, Short Goals, Retrospective Planning Game
    B. Smart Subjects, Retrospective Poker Game, Smart Goals
    C. Short Subjects, Smart Goals, Retrospective Planning Game
    D. Retrospective Poker Game, Short Subjects, Circle of Questions

Answers

1. Answer: C
   Explanation: The only item in this list not concerned with finding problems early is velocity. All the other activities help reduce the costs of changes.

2. Answer: B
   Explanation: The sequence of activities for problem solving is gather data, generate insights, and then decide what to do.

3. Answer: C
   Explanation: Escaped defects are errors that are missed by the quality assurance and control processes and make it into production.

4. Answer: B
   Explanation: Trends are leading metrics, since they allow us to extrapolate from the series and determine what might happen in the future if the trend continues unchecked.

5. Answer: A
   Explanation: Control limits are visual controls that show acceptable ranges. They do not help manage flow, improve estimates, or escalate issues.

6. Answer: B
   Explanation: The process of frequently integrating new and changed code is known as continuous integration. The other choices here are either madeup or are not widely used terms.

7. Answer: B
   Explanation: The shorthand summary of test-driven development is Red, Green, Refactor or Red, Green, Clean, in that order. This summary refers to the stages of first writing tests that will fail (generating a Red status), then writing code until it passes the tests (generating a Green status), and finally refactoring or cleaning up the code.

8. Answer: B
   Explanation: Cycle time is the period of time from the start to the finish of work.

9. Answer: C
   Explanation: A short period of proof-of-concept work is known as a risk-based spike.

10. Answer: D
    Explanation: Iteration planning is not a way of verifying or validating a product. Instead, it is concerned with planning, scheduling, and capacity management.

11. Answer: D
    Explanation: The question states that the variance amounts are small. Since some amount of variance is inevitable, we should simply accept it. It would be inappropriate to undertake root-cause analysis or other forms of investigation for this common cause variation.

12. Answer: C
    Explanation: The correct sequence is to write a test (which should fail initially), write code until it passes the tests, and then refactor the design to clean things up before moving on to the next item.

13. **Answer:** D

   Explanation: SMART stands for Specific, Measurable, Attainable, Relevant, Timely.

14. **Answer:** D

   Explanation: The purpose of continuous integration is to find code issues as soon as possible. The other options are not related to continuous integration.

15. **Answer:** A

   Explanation: Fast failure is the term used when a project hits an unsolvable roadblock early in its lifecycle.

16. **Answer:** B

   Explanation: The timeline graph usually shows team satisfaction/feelings below the line to help the team recall how they felt and promote the recollection of additional data.

17. **Answer:** A

   Explanation: When diagnosing problems, we ask "why" five times to get to the root cause of an issue.

18. **Answer:** C

   Explanation: Techniques for deciding what to do about problems include Short Subjects, Smart Goals, and Retrospective Planning Game. "Short Goals" and "Retrospective Poker Game" are not valid techniques.

CONTINUOUS IMPROVEMENT

Chapter Eight

Quicktest

This last chapter is about continuous improvement on agile projects. We'll build on the problem-solving aspect of retrospectives that we discussed in chapter 7, Problem Detection and Resolution. We'll also cover additional practices that agile methods use to identify and make improvements *during* the project, rather than afterwards.

In This Chapter

This chapter will discuss the continuous improvement tools and techniques and knowledge and skills that the exam will test you on. The following chart provides a breakdown of those T&Ts and K&Ss:

Practice	Tool/Technique	Knowledge/Skill (Level)
Continuous improvement practices	» Retrospectives » Process tailoring	» Knowledge sharing (Level 1) » Principles of systems thinking (Level 3) » Process analysis (Level 2) » Applying new agile practices (Level 3) » PMI's Code of Ethics (Level 2) » Continuous improvement processes (Level 2) » Self-assessment (Level 2)

Continuous Improvement Practices

Most traditional projects capture the majority of their lessons learned at the end of the project. The intent behind capturing these lessons is to allow the organization to apply them to future projects with a similar business or technical domain, or to projects that have similar team dynamics.

This approach, frankly, is too little, too late. We need to apply the benefits of learning as we go—on our current project, and as soon as possible. The immediate application of lessons learned is especially critical for quickly changing projects and for projects with high degrees of uncertainty and risk, where staying the course could be fatal to the project if circumstances change.

So agile projects schedule continuous improvement activities into the plan as part of the methodology. The agile approach to lessons learned is deliberate and frequent, and it helps ensure that the team regularly considers adaptation and improvement to the point where it becomes habitual and part of their normal way of working.

In the life cycle view shown in figure 8.1, we can see that the "Learn" step, which involves inspecting, adapting, and improving, happens as part of every iteration.

Figure 8.1: Capturing Lessons Learned While They Are Still Actionable

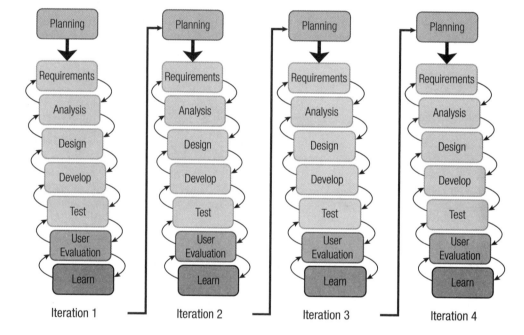

Now let's look at the T&Ts and K&Ss that are part of this "Learn" step, beginning with retrospectives.

T&T Retrospectives

Retrospectives, which are common to all agile methods, are the primary learning, reflection, and readjustment events on agile projects. A retrospective is a special meeting that takes place after each iteration, in which the team members gather to inspect and improve their methods and teamwork.

Since retrospectives happen during the project, the lessons and improvements that result from them are applicable and pertinent to upcoming work; after all, the upcoming work will have the same business domain, technical domain, and team dynamics as the iteration being assessed. In other words, the retrospective offers immediate value to the current project, rather than just documenting good advice in the hopes that a project with similar domains or dynamics will come along.

I started out my career as a project manager using traditional project management methods. When I would read other project managers' lessons learned reports, I would be dismissive of the risks and problems they encountered. I would tell myself that I would never be so foolish as to fall into those traps or make such basic mistakes, so those problems wouldn't befall my projects. As a result, I never really took the lessons learned as seriously as I could have.

Now, however, when my team identifies issues, those issues are very real and applicable. This is our project, and this is my team reporting these problems right now, so I'd better help them create some solutions or get ready to experience the ongoing impacts. Reviewing lessons learned throughout the project makes the issues and lessons very real and pressing. Like getting bad news sooner, this is actually a good thing, even if the advantages can be hard to see at the time.

Retrospectives offer a number of benefits for teams, including the following types of improvements:

- » **Improved productivity**: By applying lessons learned and reducing rework, the team can get more productive work done.
- » **Improved capability**: Retrospectives provide a venue for spreading scarce knowledge, and as the number of people who have the scarce knowledge increases, so does the number of people who can perform tasks associated with the knowledge.
- » **Improved quality**: We can improve quality on our projects by finding the circumstances that led to defects and removing the causes.
- » **Improved capacity**: Retrospectives focus on finding process efficiency improvements, which can improve the team's capacity to do work.

So what do we have to do to get these benefits? The retrospective process goes through the following five steps (also illustrated in figure 8.2):[1]

1. Set the stage
2. Gather data
3. Generate insights
4. Decide what to do
5. Close the retrospective

Figure 8.2: The Retrospective Process

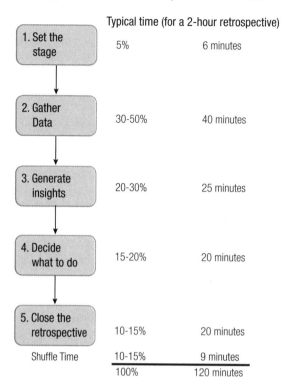

These steps operate in an ongoing cycle that is synchronized with the iterations, as shown in figure 8.3.

Figure 8.3: Retrospectives and Iterations Feed into Each Other

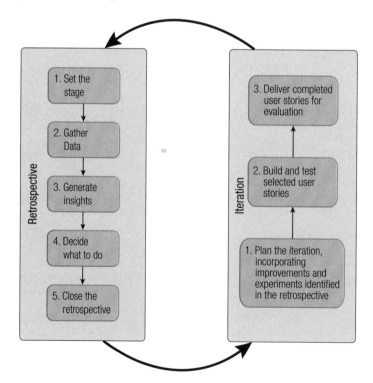

In this image, we see how the retrospective steps (shown on the left-hand side of the diagram) feed into the subsequent iteration's activities of executing the resulting improvements and experiments. Of course, the subsequent iteration will also build and deliver a product and generate its own opportunity for review and adaptation, so the cycle continues.

Let's discuss the retrospective steps in more detail.

Step 1: Set the Stage

At the start of the retrospective, we need to set the stage to help people focus on the task at hand of reflecting on how things went. We also prepare the participants for the next steps in the retrospective of gathering data and generating insights. In setting the stage, we aim to create an atmosphere where people feel comfortable speaking about things that may not have gone so well on the project.

One technique often used to get people to participate is to to get them started speaking early in the retrospective process. The theory behind this approach is that if they do not speak soon after the retrospective begins, then an understanding that it is okay not to speak is being established. A sense that silence is acceptable is counterproductive, as the whole point of the retrospective is to get people talking about how things went and what we want to do in the future. Therefore, we can start people talking early by asking for introductions the first time a session is held. We can also ask participants to outline what they hope to get from the retrospective, or say one or two words that describe how they felt about the iteration and our progress. The goal is to get people used to speaking in the group setting early in the process and then encourage them to continue contributing throughout the meeting.

The next part of setting the stage is to outline the retrospective's approach and topics for discussion. Providing such an outline establishes a clear purpose and agenda and prevents people from regarding this as "another aimless meeting." We also need to establish some team values and working agreements about how to run the retrospective. These are team-owned agreements about what is acceptable (e.g., talking about problem areas) and what is not acceptable (e.g., personal criticism or unsubstantiated complaints).

The final element of setting the stage is to get people into the right mood for contributing information and ideas. Participants may be feeling uneasy about bringing up problematic issues, for fear of conflict. They might feel that criticisms about the process may reflect poorly on them, their peers, or management. However, the real goal of the retrospective is simply to find ways to improve. The fact that we've made mistakes before is of little consequence if we can move on and not make those mistakes again. Yet getting people to understand and believe this concept is easier said than done, so we need to gauge the participants' willingness to share and speak openly during the retrospective and try to increase their comfort level.

Activities to help set the stage include:

» Check-in
» Focus on/focus off
» ESVP
» Working agreements

Let's take a brief look at each of these activities.

Check-In   We use this exercise to help people put aside their concerns and focus on the retrospective. In a round-robin format, we ask people to summarize in one or two words what they hope to get from the retrospective, the main thing on their mind, or how they are feeling about the retrospective.

Focus On / Focus Off   We use this activity to establish a mindset for productive communication. The whiteboard in figure 8.4 summarizes the emphasis for the retrospective meeting.[2]

Figure 8.4: Focus On/Focus Off Activity

In the focus on/focus off exercise, we refer participants to the whiteboard and ask them to discuss what the terms (i.e., inquiry, dialogue, conversation, understanding, advocacy, debate, argument, and defending) mean to them, inviting them to provide examples. Then we ask people if they are willing to stay in the left "Focus On" column. If there is disagreement, we should speak to the problems of moving into the right-hand column and try for consensus again.

ESVP   This is a group exercise in which participants anonymously associate themselves with one of the following identities and record their choice on a slip of paper:

» **Explorers**: Explorers are eager to discover new ideas and insights, and they want to learn everything they can.
» **Shoppers**: Shoppers will look over all available information and will happily go home with one useful new idea.
» **Vacationers**: Vacationers aren't interested in the work of the retrospective, but they are happy to be away from their regular job.
» **Prisoners**: People who classify themselves as prisoners feel like they are being forced to attend the retrospective and would rather be doing something else.

The anonymous results are collected and tallied for the group to see, as shown in figure 8.5, so we can gauge the participants' level of energy and commitment.[3]

Figure 8.5: ESVP Exercise

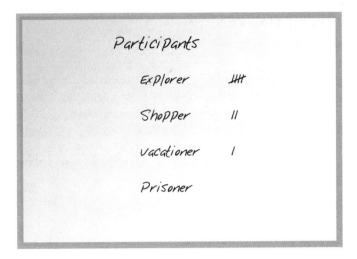

After the results have been tallied, we should conspicuously tear up and discard the slips of paper so no one worries about their answers being traced back to them via handwriting analysis. Then we ask the participants how they feel about the scores and what those scores mean for the retrospective.

Working Agreements For this activity, we have the participants form small groups and give them different topics to work on. We ask the small groups to define and explain the working agreements they would like to see in place for the retrospective. Then with the entire group, we spend time clarifying and refining ideas, building a single master list to work from.

EXERCISE: SET THE STAGE

Test your understanding. What do you think the goals of the "set the stage" step in the retrospective process are?

ANSWER

In setting the stage, we aim to:

» Explain why we are doing the retrospective
» Get people talking so they are comfortable contributing throughout the retrospective
» Outline the approach and topics of the retrospective
» Establish ground rules
» Check safety levels; in other words, determine if people feel comfortable enough to contribute to the review

Now let's move on to the next steps in the retrospective process. Steps 2 through 4—gather data, generate insights, and decide what to do—were also discussed in chapter 7, Problem Detection and Resolution, as the steps that make up the problem-solving process.

Step 2: Gather Data

In the gathering data phase, we create a shared picture of what happened during the iteration (or release or project, depending on the focus of the retrospective). Without a common vision for what occurred, the team will simply be speculating on what changes or improvements to make and may actually be addressing different issues or concerns without realizing it.

As we discussed in chapter 7, Problem Detection and Resolution, there are several team-based activities that can be used to gather data, including:

» Timeline
» Triple nickels
» Color code dots
» Mad, sad, glad
» Locate strengths
» Satisfaction histogram
» Team radar
» Like to like

When we are finished with this step in the process, we should have a comprehensive collection of observations, facts, and findings, all of which have a shared understanding by the team.

Step 3: Generate Insights

This stage gives the team time to evaluate the data that was gathered in the previous step and derive meaningful insights from it. The goal of the generating insights stage is to help team members understand the implications of their findings and discussions.

As we discussed in chapter 7, Problem Detection and Resolution, there are several team-based activities to help the team generate insights, including:

» Brainstorming
» Five whys
» Fishbone
» Prioritize with dots
» Identify themes

Step 4: Decide What to Do

The activities involved in the "decide what to do" step move the team from thinking about the iteration they just completed into thinking about the next iteration, including what they will change and how they will behave differently. In this step, the team identifies the highest-priority action items, creates detailed plans for experiments, and sets measurable goals to achieve the desired results.

As with the previous two steps, decision-making activities were discussed in chapter 7, Problem Detection and Resolution. There are several activities that can be used to help the team decide on an action plan, including:

» Short subjects
» SMART goals
» Retrospective planning game
» Circle of questions

Step 5: Close the Retrospective

The final step is closing the retrospective. We provide the team members opportunities to reflect on what happened during the retrospective and to express appreciation to each other. Activities that summarize what the team decided to keep and what to change, what we are thankful for, and where we can make the best use of our time going forward, help round out the retrospective and reinforce its value to the project.

There are several team-based activities that can be used in this final stage, including:

» Plus/Delta
» Helped, Hindered, Hypothesis
» Return on Time Invested (ROTI)
» Appreciations

To illustrate the types of activities that can be undertaken to help close a retrospective, we will examine the first two in more detail (Plus/Delta and Helped, Hindered, Hypothesis) and just briefly touch on the last two exercises.

Plus/Delta   In this exercise, we capture and validate the team's ideas for what we should do more of (things that are going well) and what we should change (things that are not going well) on a whiteboard or flip chart, similar to the example shown in figure 8.6.[4]

Figure 8.6: Plus/Delta Activity

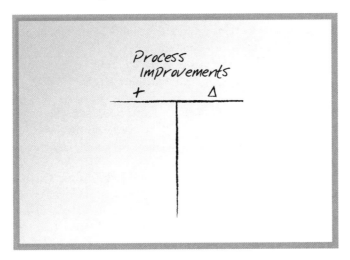

Helped, Hindered, Hypothesis   This exercise helps generate feedback on the retrospective process itself and produces ideas for improvement. To run this session, we first prepare three flip charts, one titled "Helped," one titled "Hindered," and the last with the title of "Hypothesis." We explain to the team that we are looking to improve the retrospective process and would like feedback on what they think helped, what was a hindrance, and any ideas for improvement (hypotheses) for retrospectives going forward. Participants then write ideas on sticky notes and post the notes on the appropriate flip chart.

Return on Time Invested (ROTI)   This is another exercise to generate feedback on the retrospective process. This exercise focuses on whether people believe their time was well spent.

Appreciations   During this exercise, team members have a chance to express appreciation to other team members for their help, contributions, problem-solving efforts, etc.

So those are the five steps of the retrospective process. In summary, these important agile workshops enable the team to take the impediments and problems reported at daily stand-up meetings, along with items identified after reflection and observation, and do something to improve the situation while the lessons and actions are still relevant to the project.

K&S Level 1   Knowledge Sharing

Knowledge sharing is a key component of agile methods. This should come as no surprise, since agile methods are designed for knowledge worker environments. (As a quick recap, a knowledge worker project is characterized by subject matter experts collaborating to create or enhance a product or service; see chapter 2, Agile Framework, for more on the concept of knowledge worker projects.) Given that information and knowledge is the basic commodity of agile projects, it is only right that we emphasise how to share it.

Knowledge sharing happens at many levels, in both obvious and subtle ways. Product demonstrations are an example of an obvious method. The main purpose of such demonstrations is not to show off the product, since the team knows very well what works and does not work; instead, demos are done because they are high-ceremony ways to share knowledge through the following kind of dialogue:

Team to customer: Here is what we think you asked for and what we have been able to build. Please tell us if we are on the right track.

Customer to team: I like these bits, and this is okay, but you got this piece wrong. Oh, and that reminds me—we really need something over here to do X.

An example of a less obvious way to share information is team co-location. This practice is not done to save space or ease management overhead; instead, it is done to leverage the sharing of tacit (unwritten) knowledge that occurs in face-to-face environments and through osmotic communication.

Just about every agile practice is structured for maximum knowledge sharing. On software projects, for example, developers are a tech savvy bunch, so why aren't the daily stand-up meetings done via e-mail or some other form of technology? The answer is simple. It's because the real goal of the stand-up meeting is to share information within the team, not just generate lists of work done, work planned, and any issues that have arisen. This same concept applies to most agile practices; when we examine how they are structured through the lens of maximizing knowledge transfer, all the peculiarities suddenly make sense. For example, think about XP's core practices. To some extent, the majority of these practices have a knowledge transfer component, as indicated in figure 8.7.

Figure 8.7: The Knowledge Transfer Aspect of XP's Core Practices

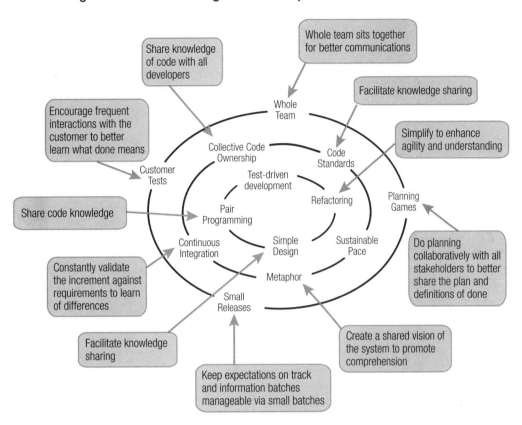

Retrospectives are also knowledge transfer vehicles. Another way agile methods emphasize knowledge sharing is by using simple tools like cards on a wall to plan and schedule a project. These simple approaches include more team members and require less skill and training and fewer tools than do software programs like Primavera or Microsoft Project®.[5] Simple tools also help build a common understanding of the plan.

So if we understand that knowledge sharing is a good thing, why is it sometimes difficult to achieve and sustain? In the book *Knowledge Management in Theory and Practice*, Kimiz Dalkir identifies that "individuals are most commonly rewarded for what they know, not what they share."[6] This reward system actually discourages knowledge sharing. To promote the idea of sharing knowledge, the organizational culture should instead encourage and reward the discovery, innovation, and transfer of information.

Measuring Up to Encourage Desired Behavior

Robert Austin, author of *Measuring and Managing Performance in Organizations*, extended the idea of the Hawthorne Effect, which we discussed in chapter 4, Stakeholder Engagement. According to Austin, "You get what you measure, in fact you get only what you measure, nothing else. So you tend to lose the things that you can't measure, like knowledge sharing, insight, collaboration and creativity."[7] This indeed is a quandary and a potential problem, but luckily people have found ways to measure and reward knowledge sharing so we don't lose its benefits. The following story illustrates this concept.

Nucor Steel has been one of the most successful steel companies in the United States from the 1980s through the present day. Where other companies have folded in the face of fierce foreign competition and poor labor relations, Nucor has remained competitive and profitable and has maintained good worker relations. They attribute a lot of this success to their "pay for performance" scheme, which is based on team productivity.

At Nucor, unlike companies that use traditional productivity-based bonus schemes, if you are a steel plant manager, you do not get paid based on how well your plant does, but on how well all the steel plants perform. At the next level down, department managers do not get a bonus based on the performance of their department, but on the performance of all the departments. This approach continues all the way through the organization, including team leads who get paid based on the productivity of all teams, not just their own, and individuals who get paid based on their team's performance, rather than their own.

This approach results in knowledge sharing. For example, if a plant manager creates an enhancement to a process or discovers a money-saving idea, they are incented to share the idea with other plants. Likewise, teams that streamline processes are rewarded for sharing their ideas with other teams, and team members who can help out their teammates are also rewarded.

The approach described in this example is called "measuring up," which refers to measuring something at one level above the normal span of control (e.g., the team level, rather than the individual level) to encourage cooperation and knowledge sharing. It happens on agile projects, even though it does not get much publicity. Mary Poppendieck, a lean method expert, advises "Instead of making sure that people are measured within their span of control, it is more effective to measure people one level above their span of control. This is the best way to encourage teamwork, collaboration, and global, rather than local optimization."[8]

We see examples of measuring up in the way we track velocity. We could quite easily trace velocity to individual team members and determine who is the most productive, but this approach would likely encourage negative behaviors and a lack of cooperation. So instead we measure velocity at a team level; as a result, team members are motivated to help each other. The same concept applies to knowledge sharing. For knowledge sharing to occur, we need to base our tracking and rewards on team accomplishments, so there are no benefits to hoarding information or being the guru of subject X.

This is why many of the agile techniques, such as common code ownership and pair programming, promote knowledge sharing; we want knowledge shared throughout the team, not just residing in one person. Agile methods' prolific use of large graphs and information radiators, personas, and wireframes all support the concept of information sharing, too.

So the mindset and approach is "Let us show you what we know, and then you can tell us if we are right or wrong." This is a great way to surface and resolve misunderstandings, but it can be an alien approach to organizations that are more reserved and cautious in their communications. The mindset is not about boasting or showing off, however. It is about managing risks, confirming that the way we are doing things is appropriate and valuable, and focusing on knowledge transfer. These are all key components when undertaking knowledge worker projects, which transform information, rather than concrete and steel.

EXERCISE: KNOWLEDGE SHARING

Test yourself! Summarize the key points about knowledge sharing. Write down why it is a valued practice and how it can be achieved on co-located and on geographically dispersed projects.

ANSWER

The main point you need to understand can be stated very simply—knowledge sharing is good. In addition, you should know that agile methods have a lot of knowledge-sharing events, including retrospectives, demos, and planning meetings. They also have a lot of knowledge-sharing practices, such as pair programming and physical co-location of the team, which allows for the osmotic communication of knowledge. If team members are geographically separated, technology like instant messaging and VoIP tools can be used to allow information sharing activities to continue, despite the physical distance.

T&T | Process Tailoring

When we tailor processes on agile projects, we amend the methodology to better fit the project environment we are using it in. Some methodologies are quite tailoring-friendly. For example, in his book on Kanban, David Anderson notes:[9]

> *Kanban is giving permission . . . to create a tailored process optimized to a specific context . . . You have permission to try Kanban. You have permission to modify your process. You have permission to be different. Your situation is unique and you deserve to develop a unique process definition tailored and optimized to your domain, your value stream, the risks that you manage, the skills of your team, and the demands of your customers.*

In contrast, methods like Scrum are less keen on tailoring. Instead, the Scrum methodology makes recommendations about how to transform the enterprise into an agile environment that will better support a Scrum approach, since changing the methodology could potentially damage or pollute Scrum with nonstandard practices to suit the environment.

Clearly there are benefits and risks with both extremes. When considering the question of whether process tailoring is appropriate, we should first recognize that all projects are different. They solve different problems, face different challenges, utilize different people, and operate in different organizations with different cultures and norms. The unique nature of projects is why luminaries like Jim Highsmith and

Alistair Cockburn recommend a process-per-project approach—in other words, creating processes that are situationally specific for the job at hand.

Others take a different view. Ron Jefferies asserts that "Agile isn't any damn thing." He aims to maintain an adherence to agile values and practices. His concern is that methodologies may transform the agile approach beyond recognition and then, when projects fail, those failures will be blamed on agile.

So we have two different views, both with valid points to consider. Now where does this leave us? As I see it, the balance is in risk mitigation. The risk of failure is high when people inexperienced in agile methods modify the methods. Teams that have not run through several agile projects using a by-the-book agile approach will not have firsthand experience of how the practices balance each other.

The balance and interrelationships of agile practices is complicated, as illustrated by Kent Beck's view of XP practices represented in figure 8.8.

Figure 8.8: The Balance and Interrelationships of XP Practices

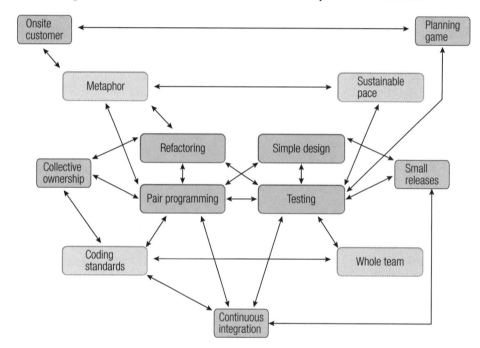

As we discussed in chapter 2, Agile Framework, removing or augmenting elements without understanding the relationship between them can lead to problems. For example, ruthless testing allows for courageous refactoring, and having frequent user conversations allows the project to have light requirements. If you remove one practice without understanding its counterbalance, you may be headed for trouble.

Personally I am very happy to tailor processes; I view agile methods as useful tools, not some sacred process that must not be touched. I look beyond the method to effective project delivery and happy sponsors, customers, and teams. Frankly, if calling it "spinach" instead of "agile" and wearing silly hats would help with the project's implementation and execution, then I would do it. However, we need to make sure we are changing things for good reasons and not just for the sake of change.

Sometimes it is tempting to avoid a practice because it is hard or is being met with resistance. This could be a sign that the practice is a poor fit for the organization, but it is equally likely that it is highlighting an underlying issue that should be resolved. For example, if a software development team is pushing back on two-week iterations because it takes three days to build and release to a test environment, we should not automatically change the iteration lengths to be three or four weeks long; instead, we should investigate why the build and release process is taking so long and improve it.

So for the exam, understand that process tailoring can be effective and productive, but that we should be aware of the risks involved in this practice. The following are the key ways to mitigate these risks:

1. **Get used to normal, out-of-the-box agile before attempting to change it**. The methods were created based on the collective wisdom of many experienced practitioners, so don't be too hasty to change them.
2. **Carefully examine the motivation to drop, amend, or append a practice**. Is the change a lazy cop-out to avoid a more fundamental problem, or will it truly address a gap or be a value-add unique to the environment?

Principles of Systems Thinking (Complex, Adaptive, Chaos)

Before we start changing agile processes, we need to understand more about the environment, or system, in which they are used. Knowledge worker projects are characterized by the level of complexity around requirements, as well as the complexity of the technology used on the projects. The combination of these complexities gives us the project landscape illustrated in figure 8.9.

Figure 8.9: Different Levels of Complexity on Projects

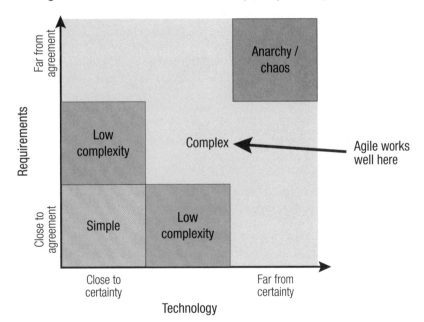

We see projects range from simple (lower left) up to those categorized as anarchy or chaos (upper right). An agile approach works really well for projects in the middle ground. These projects are complex and have uncertainty around both requirements and the technical approach. Agile methods can of course be used for simple projects, too, in which the organization and the team will get the benefits of increased collaboration, communication, and visibility, but simple projects can be run just fine with traditional approaches as well. In contrast, complex projects begin to struggle when they are merged with traditional methods.

Agile is no silver bullet or panacea, however. If there is no clear agreement on what we are supposed to be building or what approach and tools we are using to build it, then our project is in a state of chaos. In this case, neither agile nor any other approach can assure success.

We have to keep in mind this system-level understanding of the environment in which agile projects are operating when we think about modifying the methods.

 ## Process Analysis

Process analysis is closely related to process tailoring and the principles of systems thinking. When we perform process analysis, we are reviewing and diagnosing issues with agile methods or, more likely, our home-grown add-ons and replacements to agile methods. This analysis may then lead to a decision to tailor the process.

Alistair Cockburn provides the following list of methodology anti-patterns (or bad things about methodologies) to watch out for:[10]

1. **One size for all projects**: It is not possible to create the optimal methodology for all types of projects, all technologies, and all team sizes. Therefore, be wary of claims of a one-size-fits-all approach.

2. **Intolerant**: A methodology is like a straightjacket in that it is a set of conventions and policies people agree to adhere to and use. The size and shape of the straightjacket should be chosen by the team and should not be made any tighter than necessary, so people have a little wiggle room in their actions.

3. **Heavy**: There is a common but incorrect belief that the heavier a methodology is in artifacts and practices, the safer it is. However, adding weight to a methodology is not likely to improve the team's chance of delivering the project successfully. Instead, it diverts the team's time from the real goal of the project.

4. **Embellished**: All methods tend to get embellished. We add in things that we think we "ought to" or "should" be doing, but we need to look out for these words as signals for potentially expensive, error-prone additions. Get the people directly affected by the process to review the methodology, and watch their faces closely for indications of what they know they won't do but are afraid to admit they won't do; these items are the embellishments.

5. **Untried**: Many methodologies are untried. They are proposals created from nothing and are full-blown "shoulds" in action. For example, how often have you heard statements like, "Well, this really looks like it should work"? Instead of creating complex theoretical methodologies, it is better to reuse, adjust, tune, and create just what is needed. See what actually works on projects and use that, not something untried that we believe "should work."

6. **Used once**: A methodology that is used once is a little better than one that is untried, but it is still no recipe for success. The reality is that different projects likely need different approaches, and just because an approach worked under one set of circumstances does not guarantee it will work under another.

If the previous items are the things to watch out for with a methodology, what are the success signs that we might be doing something right? Because so many projects fail to create high-quality products that satisfy stakeholders and are delivered on time while also keeping the leadership and the team happy, we are doing well with our approach if meets the following criteria:

1. **The project got shipped**: The product went out the door.
2. **The leadership remained intact**: They didn't get fired for what they were doing (or not doing).
3. **The people on the project would work the same way again**: They found the approach to be effective and enjoyable.

Cockburn also lists seven principles that are recurring attributes of methodologies that tend to meet these success criteria:[11]

1. **Interactive, face-to-face communication is the cheapest and fastest channel for exchanging information**: Make face-to-face communication the default communication approach, and structure the workplace and the project events or ceremonies to leverage this approach.

2. **Excess methodology weight is costly**: Written documentation is slow to produce and takes time away from completing the project, so minimize such documentation to a barely sufficient level.

3. **Larger teams need heavier methodologies**: As team sizes grow, osmotic communication and tacit knowledge become harder to maintain, so more knowledge needs to be committed to documentation.

4. **Greater ceremony is appropriate for projects with greater criticality**: As the penalty for errors in a product escalates, so too should the ceremony and care taken in developing the product. For example, failure in developing a video game wastes users' leisure time and may result in poor game sales. Failure in developing a word processor wastes business time. As the criticality of a product increases through the levels of affecting essential funds to affecting people's lives (e.g., life-saving medical equipment), the rigor associated with the project should also increase.

5. **Increasing feedback and communication reduces the need for intermediate deliverables**: We can either write a long document to demonstrate that we understand customer requirements (an intermediate deliverable that takes a lot of time away from actually building the product), or we can build something that shows we understand the requirements (and that is actually part of building the product and moves the development work of the project along).

6. **Discipline, skills, and understanding counter process, formality, and documentation**: Jim Highsmith cautions us, "Don't confuse documentation for knowledge," since knowledge can be tacit (unwritten). We should also recognize that "Process is not discipline." Discipline is choosing to do something a certain way, while process is just following some instructions. And finally, "Don't confuse formality with skill." In terms of formality and skill, one does not relate to the other. We should be looking for smart people who can undertake exploratory work and apply their skills and understanding, rather than those who follow process and formality to create documentation.

7. **Efficiency is expendable in nonbottleneck activities**: Following the Theory of Constraints concepts, unless we are improving the constraint in our system, our improvements will provide no benefit for the project's total output. For example, improving our requirements-gathering or analysis activities will not benefit the project if the bottleneck for the process is coding or testing. Unless the coding or testing processes are improved, the project as a whole will not see any increases in efficiency. So we need to look carefully for the constraints and make our improvements there.

EXERCISE: SUMMARIZE THE PROCESS ANALYSIS KEY POINTS

See how many of the anti-patterns (items to watch out for), success criteria, and guiding recommendations you can remember by listing them in the following table.

Anti-Patterns	Success Criteria	Guiding Recommendations

ANSWER

Anti-Patterns	Success Criteria	Guiding Recommendations
One size for all projects	The project got shipped	Face-to-face communications
Intolerant	The leadership remained intact	Excess methodology weight is costly
Heavy	The team would use it again	Larger teams need heavier methodologies
Embellished		More ceremony for more critical projects
Untried		Increasing feedback and communications reduces the need for intermediate deliverables
Used once		Discipline, skills, and understanding over process, formality, and documentation
		Efficiency is expendable in nonbottleneck activities

Applying New Agile Practices

There are times on our projects when we need to look to new and emerging practices to augment our own processes. At these times, we should keep in mind the recommendations of using approaches that have been tested and used on projects in which the product was shipped, the leadership stayed intact, and the teams would use the approach again. So if there is a problem on the project, such as features taking too long to work their way through the system from the time they are selected off the backlog to the point when they enter testing, we may want to look at other approaches that can help us address the issue.

By selecting existing agile practices to augment our processes, rather than trying to invent our own, we can hopefully gain the benefits of a tried approach that already has the kinks worked out of it. Doing so also follows the guideline that we research rather than invent (discussed in chapter 7, Problem Detection and Resolution), which generally saves us time. However, when choosing a new practice, we should be careful to check that the environment for which it was designed or found to be successful is not considerably different from our own, since practices are situationally specific.

Going back to our example of wanting to streamline features through the development process, we could employ techniques from Kanban to help address the problem. By limiting the WIP on the project and tracking the cycle time, we could get faster throughput and a more predictable cycle time.

I equate adopting new practices to taking a new drug; you should not do it unless you have to, and then only after doing some research. When thinking about applying new practices, consider the following:

1. **Is there a natural solution?** Can the problem be fixed by addressing the root cause? Is the answer really to adopt a new approach, or is it to stop doing the thing that is giving rise to the problem?

2. **Investigate yourself**: Check the validity of the claims, look for some case studies, and follow up with people on the project if possible. Did the new approach really have the benefits that are being claimed, or is someone just trying to make a name for themselves and omitting mention of undesirable side effects?

3. **Try small doses**: Try the new practice for just one or two iterations at first. See if it works before committing the entire team or organization to the new approach. If the practice does work, then great; if it does not, then there is little harm done.

4. **Review the side effects**: Once the practice has been established for a while, take a good look at it during a retrospective. Are the benefits worth the inconvenience of doing it? Should we continue, stop, or try something else?

The following practices are popular and are often considered for inclusion by agile teams, but at the time of writing this book, they have not "crossed the chasm" to mainstream agile adoption:

1. **Behavior-driven development**: This is an outside-in, pull-based, multiple-stakeholder approach to testing.

2. **Lean start-up**: This is a low-cost, path-finding approach to solutions that employs regular review and pivot points.

3. **Real options**: This is a calculation-based approach to decision theory for evaluating decision timing and options.

 As agile methods continue to expand and evolve, so too will the practices considered "normal," or part of the standard. The PMI-ACP exam content outline will be reviewed annually, and it will be updated when techniques gain popular acceptance.[12] (So it is good that you are taking your exam soon, rather than in a few years from now, since the content might be even broader then!)

 ## PMI's Code of Ethics and Professional Conduct

We have reviewed how elements of PMI's Code of Ethics and Professional Conduct may come into play for the T&Ts and K&Ss we've discussed in previous chapters.[13] Now let's touch on a few other important aspects of the Code, including what it means for potential PMI-ACP credential holders (you).

First of all, did you realize that PMI's Code of Ethics and Professional Conduct is not only for PMI members? It also applies to "Non-members who apply to commence a PMI certification process."[14] This means that even if you are not a PMI member, in applying to take your PMI-ACP exam, you must agree to be bound by PMI's Code of Ethics and Professional Conduct. So let's take a look at what we are agreeing to.

PMI's Code of Ethics and Professional Conduct is a document that outlines four areas of professional behavior for us to conduct ourselves by. Each area of the code has a set of aspirational standards and a set of mandatory standards. The aspirational standards describe the ideals PMI is asking practitioners to strive for, or aspire to. The mandatory standards are behaviors PMI expects all practitioners to follow. The structure is shown in figure 8.10. In this partially expanded mind map of the Code, we can see the aspirational components of the Responsibility section.[15]

Figure 8.10: The Structure of PMI's Code of Ethics and Professional Conduct

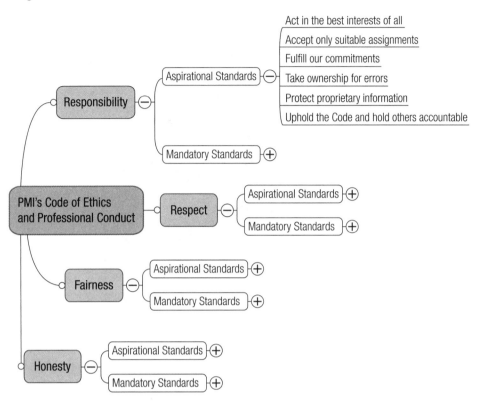

The other aspect of the Code to be aware of is the disciplinary and ethics compliance process. If someone believes you are in violation of the mandatory standards, they are supposed to report you, and if you encounter another PMI member in violation of the standards, you are supposed to report them.[16] The PMI Ethics Committee will then investigate any such reports.

 PMI provides the full version of the Code of Ethics and Professional Conduct on its website (www.pmi.org).[17] You should read it and be familiar with it. However, you will not be heavily tested on the Code, as you will likely see only one or two questions about it on the exam. The main goal of including PMI's Code of Ethics and Professional Conduct in the exam content outline is to bring candidates' attention to the Code and let them know it exists.[18] We have discussed the Code at some length in this book and encourage you to read it on PMI's website because it is good to understand what you are agreeing to when you sign up for the exam.

K&S Level 2 — Continuous Improvement Processes

Continuous improvement is the ongoing process of enhancing the project approach and the product. This process is never completed; instead, it continues throughout the project in much the same way as stakeholder communications do. Continuous improvement is something we will always do. It is more like a journey than a destination, since it is always ongoing and is part of the iterative life cycle that drives agile methods.

Continuous Process Improvement

The agile life cycle, shown in figure 8.11, employs a continuous cycle of Plan, Develop, Evaluate, and Learn.

Figure 8.11: A Continuous Cycle of Plan, Develop, Evaluate, and Learn

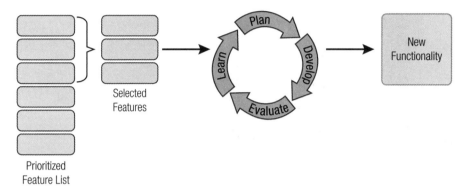

This cycle is very similar to Deming's "Plan, Do, Check, Act" cycle for problem solving and continuous improvement.[19]

Figure 8.12: Plan, Do, Check, Act Cycle

The "Develop" phase in the agile life cycle is like Deming's "Do" phase. "Evaluate" is equivalent to the "Check" phase. In the "Learn" phase, we apply the lessons from the project, in much the same way as the "Act" phase in Deming's cycle. And the "Plan, Do, Check, Act" cycle is again mirrored in agile methods with demos, reviews, and retrospectives.

Continuous improvement is also layered like an onion. In software development projects, for example, continuous improvement happens at the code level with pair programming. One person is writing code, and the other is reviewing, critiquing, and suggesting improvements. Daily stand-up meetings discuss work done and any issues or impediments on the project. These issues then become the "to-do" items for the ScrumMaster or project manager, who is responsible for removing impediments and improving the process. At a broader level, the iteration demo, review, and retrospective cycles that occur at a biweekly or monthly cadence purposely examine the process and look for improvements to make in the next iteration.

Figure 8.13: Multiple Layers of Continuous Improvement on Agile Projects

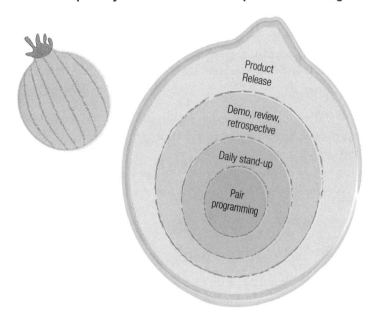

Continuous Product Improvement

Just as the team practices and processes are being refined iteratively and continuously, so too is the evolving product. Iterative and incremental development is a form of continuous improvement, with customer feedback steering us toward the final solution.

Figure 8.14: Continuous Product Improvement

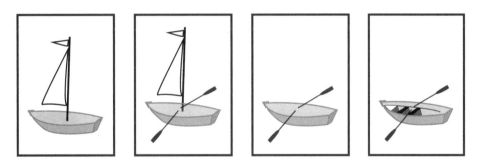

When we build small increments and get feedback, the product evolves toward the true business requirements. And sometimes the true business requirements may be quite different from the originally stated requirements, as the process of creation illuminates better options.

By this cycle of developing in small increments, reviewing, discussing how to improve, and then doing some more development and maybe enhancing a few things, the product or service is incrementally built through a process of continuous improvement.

K&S
Level 2

Self-Assessment

Assessments of how to improve are not reserved just for the process and product; they are also done on the people side of the project, which is arguably the area that offers the greatest payback. Therefore, it is standard practice for the team to reflect on how well they are doing and to look for things they can improve.

James Shore offers a self-assessment quiz and scoring model that is focused on XP practices.[20] Teams can use this model to gauge their performance. The quiz and scoring graph measures how teams perform within the following categories:

» Thinking
» Collaborating
» Releasing
» Planning
» Developing

The quiz is completed by answering questions within each category and scoring the answers on a 0–100 scale. The following table shows a few of the questions from the Planning category:[21]

Planning Questions	Yes	No	XP Practice
Do nearly all team members understand what they are building, why they're building it, and what stakeholders consider success?	25	0	Vision
Does the team have a plan for achieving success?	4	0	Release Planning
Does the team regularly seek out new information and use it to improve its plan for success?	3	0	Release Planning
Does the team's plan incorporate the expertise of business people as well as programmers, and do nearly all involved agree the plan is achievable?	4	0	The Planning Game

Once all the questions have been asked and scored, the results are plotted on a radar (spider) diagram, as shown in figure 8.15.[22]

Figure 8.15: Self-Assessment Scoring Model

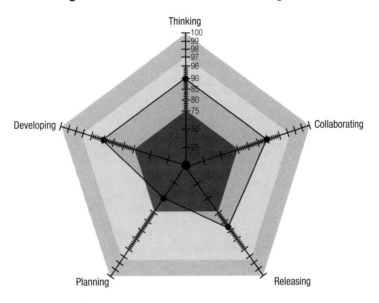

Ideally, the team is then involved in analyzing the chart to identify which areas could use improvement. The types of improvement actions that may be taken include training or adding in more working sessions with the business representatives.

Jean Tabaka also offers a model for assessing the attributes of high-performing teams. Tabaka's model investigates the following areas:[23]

1. **Self-organization**: Is the team self-organizing, rather than functioning in a command-and-control, top-down organization?
2. **Empowered to make decisions**: Is the team empowered to discuss, evaluate, and make decisions, rather than being dictated to by an outside authority?
3. **Belief in vision and success**: Do team members understand the project vision and goals, and do they truly believe that, as a team, they can solve any problem to achieve those goals?
4. **Committed team**: Are team members committed to succeed as a team, rather than being committed to individual success at any cost?
5. **Trust each other**: Does the team have the confidence to continually work on improving their ability to act without fear, anger, or bullying?
6. **Participatory decision making**: Is the team engaged in participatory decision making, rather than bending to authoritarian decision making or succumbing to decisions from others?
7. **Consensus-driven**: Are team decisions consensus-driven, rather than leader-driven? Do team members share their opinions freely and participate in the final decision?
8. **Constructive disagreement**: Is the team able to negotiate through a variety of alternatives and impacts surrounding a decision, and craft the one that provides the best outcome?

Figure 8.16: Tabaka's Self-Assessment Model for High-Performing Teams

	High Performance Teams Collaoration Criteria	Team Score	Median	Team member assessment											
				1	2	3	4	5	6	7	8	9	10	11	12
1	**Self organization** *Is the team self-organizing, rather than functioning in a command-and-control, top-down organization?*	5.0	5.0	5	5	5	5								
2	**Empowered to make decisions** *Is the team empowered to discuss, evaluate, and make decisions, rather than being dictated to by an outside authority?*	4.5	4.5	5	4	5	4								
3	**Belief in vision and success** *Do team members understand the project vision and goals, and do they truly believe that, as a team, they can solve any problem to achieve those goals?*	4.3	4.0	4	5	4	4								
4	**Committed team** *Are team members committed to succeed as a team, rather than being committed to individual success at any cost?*	4.8	5.0	5	5	4	5								
5	**Trust each other** *Does the team have the confidence to continually work on improving their ability to act without fear, anger, or bullying?*	3.5	3.5	4	4	3	3								
6	**Participatory decision making** *Is the team engaged in participatory decision making, rather than bending to authoritarian decision making or succumbing to decisions from others?*	4.5	4.5	5	4	5	4								
7	**Consensus driven** *Are team decisions consensus driven, rather than leader driven? Do team members share their opinions freely and participate in the final decision?*	2.3	2.0	3	2	2	2								
8	**Constructive disagreement** *Is the team able to negotiate through a variety of alternatives and impacts surrounding a decision, and craft the one that provides the best outcome?*	4.8	5.0	5	5	4	5								
	Total Score	4.2	4.2	4.5	4.3	4.0	4.0								

Legend: 1-Strongly disagree 3 - Neutral 5 - Strongle agree

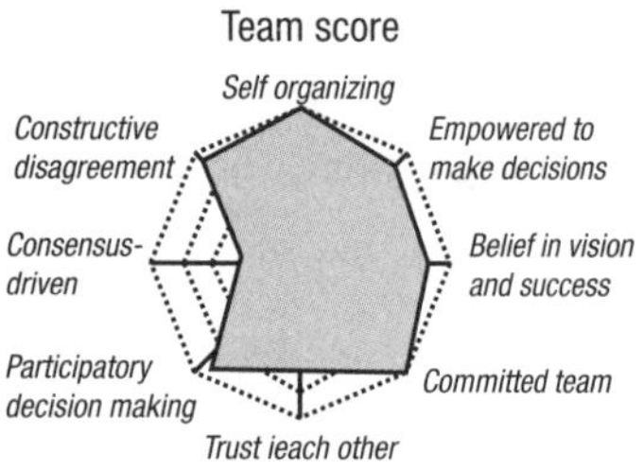

Image copyright © 2012 Edgardo Gonzalez, Projects Recovery Specialists, Ltd., www.prsl.ca

TRICKS OF THE TRADE® For the exam, you do not need to recall details of these self-assessment models. Instead, you simply need to understand what they are, when they are used, and the purpose behind them. Such tools fit into the reflect and adapt cycle; not only do we improve our product and process, but we also find ways to improve our teams.

Practice Exam

1. PMI's Code of Ethics and Professional Conduct focuses on which of the following?

   A. Service, Protection, Education, Honesty
   B. Responsibility, Respect, Fairness, Honesty
   C. Respect, Valor, Honesty, Transparency
   D. Responsibility, Transparency, Fairness, Honesty

2. When conducting a retrospective, recognized "close the retrospective" activities include:

   A. Plus/Delta; Helped, Hindered, Hypothesis; Return on Time Invested; Appreciations
   B. Plus/Minus; Helped, Hindered, Hoped; Return on Time Invested; Applause
   C. Plus/Delta; Helped, Hindered, Hoped; Return on Investment; Appreciations
   D. Plus/Minus; Helped, Hindered, Hypothesis; Return on Time Delivered; Appreciations

3. You have been asked to review a different project team's recently enhanced methodology to assess its effectiveness and desirable characteristics. The types of characteristics that you should be looking for include evidence of:

   A. A preference for face-to-face communications, significant process weight, recommendations for larger teams to use lighter methods
   B. A preference for face-to-face communications, not too much process weight, recommendations for larger teams to use lighter methods
   C. A preference for face-to-face communications, significant process weight, recommendations for larger teams to use heavier methods
   D. A preference for face-to-face communications, not too much process weight, recommendations for larger teams to use heavier methods

4. The concept of knowledge sharing on an agile project is best characterized as:

   A. Encouraged where possible and where the team shows an interest
   B. Central to many of the practices undertaken
   C. Undertaken if there is time left at the end of an iteration
   D. Undertaken principally through stand-up meetings

5. Continuous improvement is a core component of which of the following set of agile practices?

   A. Pair programming; daily stand-up meetings; WIP limits
   B. Story points; daily stand-up meetings; demos, reviews, and retrospectives
   C. Pair programming; daily stand-up meetings; demos, reviews, and retrospectives
   D. Story points; daily stand-up meetings; WIP limits

6. When considering process tailoring, it is useful to keep in mind that the network of XP practices is:

   A. Redundant
   B. Duplicated
   C. Optional
   D. Balanced

7. The recommended stages of executing a retrospective, in sequence, are:

   A. Decide what to do, set the stage, gather data, generate insights, close the retrospective
   B. Decide what to do, gather data, set the stage, generate insights, close the retrospective
   C. Set the stage, decide what to do, gather data, generate insights, close the retrospective
   D. Set the stage, gather data, generate insights, decide what to do, close the retrospective

8. You are engaging in some process analysis and have been advised to watch out for the standard anti-patterns of poor methodology practice. The types of things you should be on the lookout for are processes that display signs of being:

   A. One-of-a-kind, disciplined, heavy, embellished
   B. One-size-fits-all, disciplined, heavy, embellished
   C. One-size-fits-all, intolerant, heavy, embellished
   D. One-of-a-kind, intolerant, embellished

9. Process tailoring is best undertaken on agile projects when:

   A. There are difficulties in implementing agile practices
   B. Experienced practitioners want to address an issue
   C. The team needs new processes to keep them engaged
   D. A boost in team velocity is needed to meet the schedule

10. Your project management office (PMO) has suggested your project could benefit from some self-assessment work at the next retrospective. Which of the following benefits would they most likely be looking to achieve from a self-assessment?

    A. Improve personal and team practices
    B. Gain insights for salary performance reviews
    C. Identify personal traits for human resources counseling
    D. Assess compatibilities for pair programming assignments

11. When undertaking process analysis, what are the success criteria that characterize a useful methodology?

    A. The project got stopped, sponsorship remained intact, the team would work the same way again
    B. The project got shipped, leadership remained intact, the team would work the same way again
    C. The project got shipped, sponsorship remained intact, the team would work the same way again
    D. The project got shipped, sponsorship remained intact, the team engaged in continuous improvement

12. When adopting a new agile practice, the general recommendations are to:

    A. Develop the new approach yourself, try out the practice on local projects, inspect and review the findings early
    B. Investigate the claims yourself, try out the practice on local projects, inspect and review the findings early
    C. Investigate the claims yourself, try out the practice in small doses, inspect and review the findings early
    D. Develop the new approach yourself, try out the practice in small doses, inspect and review the findings early

13. As a manager of an agile team, when should you collect lessons learned?

    A. At the end of the project
    B. Throughout the project
    C. When projects go well
    D. When projects go poorly

14. Information exchanges in agile methods are designed to:

    A. Facilitate knowledge sharing
    B. Leverage electronic knowledge-sharing tools
    C. Maximize resource utilization
    D. Generate stable specifications

15. Your sponsor is asking about tailoring the company's newly adopted agile methodology. Your advice should be:

    A. Tailoring it will be a good way to learn the methodology
    B. Tailoring it will be a good way to ease into the initial adoption process
    C. We should tailor it first, then consider adopting it
    D. We should try it first, then consider tailoring it

Answers

1. **Answer:** B

    Explanation: PMI's Code of Ethics and Professional Conduct focuses on Responsibility, Respect, Fairness, and Honesty.[25] While the other attributes listed here are worthy, they are not the characteristics PMI is asking us to aspire to and maintain.

2. **Answer:** A

    Explanation: The recognized activities that are used to close the retrospective are Plus/Delta; Helped, Hindered, Hypothesis; Return on Time Invested; and Appreciations. The options of "Plus/Minus," "Helped, Hindered, Hoped," and "Return on Investment" are not valid retrospective closing activities.

3. **Answer:** D

    Explanation: Favorable characteristics include a preference for face-to-face communications, not too much process weight, and recommendations for larger teams to use heavier methods. The option of significant process weight is generally the opposite of the barely sufficient goal we should be striving for. However, as teams get larger, we will inevitably need to use heavier weight methodologies to compensate for the reduced face-to-face communications and the increased difficulty of maintaining tacit knowledge.

4. **Answer:** B

    Explanation: Knowledge sharing is central to many of the practices undertaken. It is true that stand-up meetings help the team members share information, but they are not the principal event for knowledge sharing. This practice is too important to be considered optional if the teams show an interest, or if there is time.

5. **Answer:** C

    Explanation: Continuous improvement is core to the practices of pair programming; daily stand-up meetings; and demos, reviews, and retrospectives. It has little to do with WIP limits or story points.

6. **Answer:** D

    Explanation: XP practices are considered to be balanced. If they were redundant, duplicated, or optional, then they would not likely be required and would not have been recommended in the first place.

7. **Answer:** D

    Explanation: The recommended stages of executing a retrospective, in sequence, are: set the stage, gather data, generate insights, decide what to do, close the retrospective. You may be tempted to think that deciding what to do comes first, but it comes after we've set the stage.

8. **Answer:** C

    Explanation: The anti-patterns we are warned to look out for are signs of the methodology being one-size-fits-all, intolerant, heavy, or embellished. If a methodology is one-of-a-kind, this might also be a warning sign, since it means the methodology has not been repeated, but it is not as concerning as a claim that the methodology is a one-size-fits-all approach. Such a claim demonstrates a lack of situational awareness. The characteristic of being disciplined is not something to be wary of, since agile methods are very disciplined; we should not mistake being disciplined for being process-heavy.

9. **Answer:** B
   Explanation: Process tailoring is not to be undertaken just for implementation issues, to entertain the team, or as a scheme to increase velocity. Velocity may improve as a result, but the question asked when it is "best" to tailor processes. The correct answer is that it is best for experienced practitioners to undertake process tailoring when there is an issue to address.

10. **Answer:** A
    Explanation: The best option provided is to improve personal and team practices. While some of the other benefits might be tangential benefits, they are certainly not the focus of self-assessment.

11. **Answer:** B
    Explanation: The success criteria indicators are: the project got shipped, leadership remained intact, and the team would work the same way again. The fact that sponsorship remained intact is interesting, but this factor is not usually dependent on the project approach. While it is commendable that the team is engaging in continuous improvement, such efforts are not considered one of the success criteria for a useful methodology.

12. **Answer:** C
    Explanation: When adopting a new agile practice, we should always investigate the claims about the practice ourselves to try and validate whether they are real. We should then try it out in small doses, so the impacts are contained if it does not work, and we should inspect and review the findings early to make sure the new approach is actually working and not causing more problems than it is solving. Trying out an approach on local projects might help us see the impacts better, but if our local projects are very large, then this could be a bad move. Likewise, developing new approaches ourselves is risky and time-consuming.

13. **Answer:** B
    Explanation: Lessons learned should be captured throughout the project when the information is still fresh and people remember the most details. This allows the lessons to be used in the remainder of the project.

14. **Answer:** A
    Explanation: Information exchanges in agile methods are designed to facilitate knowledge sharing. We deliberately do not rely on leveraging electronic tools; instead, we focus on face-to-face communications. The goal is not to increase resource utilization or generate stable specifications either.

15. **Answer:** D
    Explanation: Agile methods should be tried as-is first before considering modifications such as tailoring. We should first understand how they work before attempting to change them. If we change them first and then encounter problems, how will we know if the problems are related to tailoring the method or genuine project issues?

Conclusion

Congratulations—you have finished the book and survived! Rest assured that you now have a great exposure to all the agile "knowledge and skills" and "tools and techniques" tested on the exam. We covered some topics deeper than the exam will ask for and linked in some ideas from outside of the exam content outline. This approach will help you connect the ideas together and will allow you to rely on understanding, rather than memorization, to pass the exam. Such understanding also reinforces the concepts so you can apply what you have learned to your real-world projects. When you know the material in this book, you will be more than ready to ace the exam.

The trouble is, if this is your first time through the material, chances are that you do not really know all the material covered in this book. I know it is a terrible thing to contemplate right now since you have only just finished, but you need to go back again. Don't worry—it will be much faster this time. As you read through the book the second (and third) time, focus on the areas you struggled with. Take an iterative and incremental approach, and soon those four or five topics you dread will become one or two, and then you'll nail those, too.

A great attribute of agile is that it better fits how people think and behave. It is tolerant of mistakes and incorporates feedback and refinement into the process. So practice what you have been learning. Do a retrospective of your studies, make sure you recognize the areas in which you did well and that deserve praise, and also create a list of topics to revisit. You can also use the *PM FASTrack®* exam simulation software to help you identify where you still need improvement. Revisit topics, refine your understanding, and retest your knowledge.

And finally, good luck with the exam. If you have genuinely worked through these study materials and have the requisite training and project experience, I am confident you will pass the exam. Also, please share your thoughts and feedback—I refine, revisit, and retest, too. I would love to hear from you and can be reached at mikegriffiths@rmcproject.com.

Best regards,

Mike

> *Reminder: Purchase of this book includes access to updates regarding the PMI-ACP exam, as well as additional tips and resources. You can access this information at www.rmcproject.com/agileprep. Have this book with you when you go to the website.*

Tricks of the Trade® for Preparing for and Taking the PMI-ACP Exam

The following are tips and Tricks of the Trade® for preparing for and taking the PMI-ACP exam. Following these tips will help you stay focused on the exam. As you read through each item, think about how you have reacted to test environments in the past and make note of which tricks are particularly applicable or beneficial to you. Doing so will help you remember these points when you are ready to take the exam.

TRICKS OF THE TRADE® Before You Take the Exam

Many people fail an exam because their preparation was faulty. You can avoid that mistake. Read the following tips slowly, and honestly assess how each item applies to you.

» Know the material thoroughly, but do not approach the exam assuming it tests the memorization of facts. The exam tests knowledge, application, and analysis. You must understand how to use the concepts and processes in the real world, and how they work in combination with each other.

» The prerequisite experience in general project management and agile project management is important. If you do not have real-world experience using any of the tools and techniques tested on the exam, try to get it. If you cannot get this experience before you take the exam, make sure you can visualize how these tools and techniques would be used on real projects. This visualization will help you see the potential challenges of using the tools and techniques in the real world and help you prepare for situational questions on the exam.

» Be prepared to see ambiguous and wordy questions on the exam that might be multiple paragraphs long. Practice interpreting these types of questions.

» Decide in advance what notes you will write down when you are given a piece of scrap paper at the actual exam. You can use it as a download sheet for formulas or gaps in your agile project management knowledge.

» Deal with stress BEFORE you take the exam. There is a free tip for nervous test takers on our website, www.rmcproject.com.

» Plan and use your strategy for taking the exam. This may mean, "I will take a 10-minute break after every 50 questions because I get tired quickly," or "I will answer all the questions as quickly as possible and then take a break and review my answers."

» Expect that there will be questions you cannot answer or even understand. This happens to everyone. Be prepared so you do not get annoyed or, worse yet, doubt your abilities during the exam.

» Visit the exam site before your exam date to determine how long it will take to get there and to see what the testing room looks like. This is particularly helpful if you are a nervous test taker.

» Do not expect the exam site to be quiet. One student from an RMC class reported that a band was playing outside the testing center for three hours. Others have had someone taking an exam that required intensive typing, and thus more noise, right next to them. Many testing sites will have earplugs or headphones available.

» Do not overstudy. Getting completely comfortable with all the material in this book is just not possible. It is not worth studying for hundreds of hours. It is a waste of time and will not help you on the exam.

» Take the night off before the exam to do something relaxing and get a little extra sleep. DO NOT STUDY! You will need time to process all you have learned so you can remember it when you take the exam.

TRICKS OF THE TRADE® Taking the PMI-ACP Exam

We have gone through what you should do before you take the exam. Now what about on the big day? The following are some tips for taking—and passing—the exam.

1. You must bring your authorization letter from PMI to the test site, as well as two forms of ID with exactly the same name you entered on the exam application.

2. Make sure you are comfortable during the exam. Wear layered clothing and bring a sweater to sit on in case the chairs are uncomfortable.

3. Bring snacks! Bring lunch! You will not be able to bring snacks into the exam room, but have them accessible outside the exam room in case you get hungry. You do not need the distraction of hunger pains when taking the exam.

4. You will be given scratch paper and pencils (and possibly earplugs or headphones) and have the chance to do a 15-minute computer tutorial (if your exam is given on computer) to become familiar with the computer and its commands. Note: The testing center will require you to exchange your used scratch paper if you need more during the exam.

5. When you are given scratch paper, create your "download sheet" by writing down anything you are having trouble remembering. This will free up your mind to handle questions once the information you are concerned about is written down.

6. Some test sites provide physical calculators. At other locations, the calculators are online or on the computer and appear with every question that requires a calculation.

7. When you take the exam, you will see one question on the screen at a time. You can answer a question and/or mark it to return to it later. You will be able to move back and forth through questions during the exam.

8. The exam does not adapt to your answers. This means 120 questions are selected when your exam starts, and those 120 do not change.

9. Use deep-breathing techniques to help relax. This is particularly helpful if you are very nervous before or during the exam and when you notice yourself reading the same question two or three times. Breathing techniques can be as simple as breathing deeply five times, to provide more oxygen to your brain.

10. Smile when taking the exam. Smiling relieves stress and makes you feel more confident.

11. Use all the exam time. Do not leave early unless you have reviewed each question twice.

12. Remember your own unique test-taking quirks and how you plan to deal with them while taking the exam.

13. Control the exam; do not let it control you. How would you feel if you read the first question and had no idea of the answer? The second question? And the third question? This can happen because you are just not ready to answer questions and your level of stress is not allowing you to think. So what do you do? If you do not immediately know the answer to the question, use the "Mark for Review" function and come back to it later. This will mean your first pass through the exam will generally be quick.

14. Control your frustration and maintain focus on each question. You might very well dislike or disagree with some of the questions on this exam. You might also be surprised at how many questions you mark for review. Make sure you stay focused on the current question. If you are still thinking about question 20 when you reach question 70, there will have been 50 questions that you have not looked at closely enough.

15. First identify the actual question in the question text (it is often the last sentence), and then read the rest of the text. Note the topics discussed in the question and the descriptors (e.g., "except," "includes," "not an example of"). This should help you understand what the question is asking and reduce the need to reread questions. Determine what your answer should be, and then look at the answer options shown.

16. One of the main reasons people answer incorrectly is they do not read all four choices. Do not make the same mistake! Make sure you read the question and all four choices when you take the exam. This will help you select the BEST answer. If you find yourself forgetting to read all the options, start reading the choices backwards (choice D first, then C, etc.).

17. Quickly eliminate answers that are highly implausible. Many questions have only two plausible options and two obviously incorrect options.

18. There may be more than one "correct" answer to each question, but only one "BEST" answer. Make sure you are looking for the BEST answer.

19. Be alert to the fact that the answer to one question is sometimes given away in another question.

20. Write down things you do not understand as you take the exam. Use any extra time at the end of the exam to go back to these questions.

21. Attempts have been made to keep all choices the same length. Therefore, do not follow the old rule that the longest answer is the right one.

22. Questions will often include "distracters"—choices that distract you from the correct answer. These are plausible choices that make it appear as though some questions have two or more right answers. To many people, it seems as though there are only shades of differences between the choices. As noted earlier, make sure you look for the BEST answer for such questions.

23. Look for words like "first," "last," "next," "best," "never," "always," "except," "not," "most likely," "less likely," "primary," "initial," "most," etc. Make certain you clearly read the question and take note of these words, or you will answer the question incorrectly.

24. Watch out for choices that are true statements but do not answer the question.

25. Options that represent broad, sweeping generalizations tend to be incorrect, so be alert for "always," "never," "must," "completely," and so forth. Alternatively, choices that represent carefully qualified statements tend to be correct, so be alert for words such as "often," "sometimes," "perhaps," "may," and "generally."

26. When a question asks you to fill in a blank space, the correct answer may not be grammatically correct when inserted in the sentence.

27. You will have multiple chances to indicate that you have completed the exam. The exam will not be scored until you indicate you are ready, or your time is up. For those who pass, the computer will print out a certificate, and you will officially be certified. If you do not pass, PMI will send you information on retaking the exam. You will have to pay an additional fee to retake the exam.

28. "Rules" are meant to be broken and can change depending on the situation. This drives people crazy if they expect the exam to just test facts. You need to be able to read and understand the situations on the exam and then be able to figure out the best thing to do *in that situation*.

Use these tips as a supplement to your other exam preparation activities. If you follow them when you prepare for and take the exam, you will be able to focus on applying your knowledge and experience to answering the questions, rather than being distracted on the exam or overwhelmed by the stress of taking the test.

So good luck on the exam, and let us know when you pass by e-mailing us at agileprep@rmcproject.com!

Endnotes

Chapter 1

1. Project Management Institute, *A Guide to the Project Management Body of Knowledge (PMBOK® Guide)*, 4th ed. (Newtown Square, PA: Project Management Institute, 2008).
2. Project Management Institute, *A Guide to the Project Management Body of Knowledge (PMBOK® Guide)*, 4th ed. (Newtown Square, PA: Project Management Institute, 2008).
3. "PMI Agile Certified Practitioner (PMI-ACP)[SM]: Examination Content Outline," accessed March 14, 2012, http://www.pmi.org/en/Certification/~/media/Files/PDF/Agile/PMI_Agile_Certification_Content_Outline.ashx.
4. "PMI Agile Certified Practitioner (PMI-ACP)[SM]: Examination Content Outline," accessed March 14, 2012, http://www.pmi.org/en/Certification/~/media/Files/PDF/Agile/PMI_Agile_Certification_Content_Outline.ashx.
5. "PMI Agile Certified Practitioner (PMI-ACP)[SM]: Examination Content Outline," accessed March 14, 2012, http://www.pmi.org/en/Certification/~/media/Files/PDF/Agile/PMI_Agile_Certification_Content_Outline.ashx.
6. "PMI Agile Certified Practitioner (PMI-ACP) [SM]: Examination Content Outline," accessed March 14, 2012, http://www.pmi.org/en/Certification/~/media/Files/PDF/Agile/PMI_Agile_Certification_Content_Outline.ashx.
7. "PMI Agile Certified Practitioner (PMI-ACP)[SM]: Examination Content Outline," accessed March 14, 2012, http://www.pmi.org/en/Certification/~/media/Files/PDF/Agile/PMI_Agile_Certification_Content_Outline.ashx.
8. "Project Management Institute Code of Ethics and Professional Conduct," accessed March 2, 2012, http://www.pmi.org/~/media/PDF/Ethics/ap_pmicodeofethics.ashx.

Chapter 2

1. Project Management Institute, *A Guide to the Project Management Body of Knowledge (PMBOK® Guide)*, 4th ed. (Newtown Square, PA: Project Management Institute, 2008).
2. Mike Griffiths, "Reinventing PM for Knowledge Workers," accessed January 5, 2012, http://www.gantthead.com/content/articles/267966.cfm.
3. "Manifesto for Agile Software Development," accessed January 6, 2012, http://agilemanifesto.org.
4. "Principles behind the Agile Manifesto," accessed January 6, 2012, http://agilemanifesto.org/principles.html.
5. Jim Johnson, "The Cost of Big Requirements Up Front (BRUF)." Keynote presentation at the annual XP (eXtreme Programming) Conference. Alghero, Sardinia, May 2002.
6. David Anderson, Sanjiv Augustine, Christopher Avery, Alistair Cockburn, Mike Cohn, Doug DeCarlo, Donna Fitzgerald, et al., "Declaration of Interdependence," accessed January 6, 2012, http://pmdoi.org/.
7. "PMI Agile Certified Practitioner (PMI-ACP)[SM]: Examination Content Outline," accessed March 14, 2012, http://www.pmi.org/en/Certification/~/media/Files/PDF/Agile/PMI_Agile_Certification_Content_Outline.ashx.
8. "Project Management Institute Code of Ethics and Professional Conduct," accessed March 2, 2012, http://www.pmi.org/~/media/PDF/Ethics/ap_pmicodeofethics.ashx.

Chapter 3

1. "Manifesto for Agile Software Development," accessed October 11, 2011, http://agilemanifesto.org.
2. "Principles behind the Agile Manifesto," accessed October 11, 2011, http://agilemanifesto.org/principles.html.
3. Rita Mulcahy, *PMP® Exam Prep, Seventh Edition* with Laurie Diethelm (Minnetonka, MN: RMC Publications, 2011), 106.

4. "PMI Agile Certified Practitioner (PMI-ACP)^{SM}: Examination Content Outline," accessed March 14, 2012, http://www.pmi.org/en/Certification/~/media/Files/PDF/Agile/PMI_Agile_Certification_Content_Outline.ashx.

5. Project Management Institute, *A Guide to the Project Management Body of Knowledge (PMBOK® Guide)*, 4th ed. (Newtown Square, PA: Project Management Institute, 2008).

6. Mary Poppendieck and Tom Poppendieck, *Lean Software Development: An Agile Toolkit* (Upper Saddle River, NJ: Pearson, 2003), 3.

7. Project Management Institute, *A Guide to the Project Management Body of Knowledge (PMBOK® Guide)*, 4th ed. (Newtown Square, PA: Project Management Institute, 2008).

8. Jeff Sutherland, "Agile Contracts: Money for Nothing and Your Change for Free," dated July 12, 2010, http://jeffsutherland.com/Agile2008MoneyforNothing.pdf.

9. L. Thorup and B. Jensen, "Collaborative Agile Contracts," *Agile 2009 Conference* (2009): 195–200, http://ieeexplore.ieee.org/xpl/freeabs_all.jsp?arnumber=5261083.

10. J. Fewell, "Marriott's Agile Turnaround," *Agile 2009 Conference* (2009): 219–222, http://ieeexplore.ieee.org/xpl/freeabs_all.jsp?arnumber=5261079.

11. Poppendieck and Poppendieck, *Lean Software Development*, 3.

12. Donald G. Reinertsen, *Managing the Design Factory* (New York: Simon & Schuster, 1997), 26.

13. Reinertsen, *Managing the Design Factory*, 64.

14. Eliyahu M. Goldratt and Robert E. Fox, *The Race* (Great Barrington, MA: North River Press, 1986), 146.

15. Eliyahu M. Goldratt, *Theory of Constraints* (Great Barrington, MA: North River Press, 1990).

16. "Project Management Institute Code of Ethics and Professional Conduct," accessed March 2, 2012, http://www.pmi.org/~/media/PDF/Ethics/ap_pmicodeofethics.ashx.

Chapter 4

1. Project Management Institute, A *Guide to the Project Management Body of Knowledge (PMBOK® Guide)*, 4th ed. (Newtown Square, PA: Project Management Institute, 2008).

2. Visio and PowerPoint are trademarks of the Microsoft group of companies.

3. Bill Wake, "INVEST in Good Stories, and SMART Tasks," accessed January 27, 2012, http://xp123.com/articles/invest-in-good-stories-and-smart-tasks/.

4. James Shore and Shane Warden, The Art of Agile Development (Sebastopol, CA: O'Reilly, 2008), 156–57.

5. Alistair Cockburn, *Agile Software Development: The Cooperative Game*, 2nd ed. (Upper Saddle River, NJ: Addison-Wesley, 2007), 125.

6. Excel is a trademark of the Microsoft group of companies.

7. Word is a trademark of the Microsoft group of companies.

8. Henry Kimsey-House, Karen Kimsey-House, Phillip Sandahl, and Laura Whitworth, *Co-Active Coaching: Changing Business, Transforming Lives*, 3rd ed. (Boston: Nicholas Brealey, 2011), 33–38.

9. Speed B. Leas, *Moving Your Church Through Conflict* (Herndon, VA: Alban Institute, 1985).

10. Based on the "State of Agile Survey 2010," as stated at http://www.versionone.com/Product/Who_Needs_Tools.asp (accessed January 25, 2012).

11. Warren Bennis, *Managing People is like Herding Cats: Warren Bennis on Leadership* (Provo, UT: Executive Excellence, 1999), 189.

12. James M. Kouzes and Barry Z. Posner, *The Leadership Challenge*, 4th ed. (San Francisco: Wiley, 2007), 33.

13. Jeffrey Pinto, *Project Leadership: from Theory to Practice* (Newton Square, PA: Project Management Institute, 1998), 88.

14. Kouzes and Posner, *The Leadership Challenge*, 14.

15. Kouzes and Posner, *The Leadership Challenge*, 28.

16. "Project Management Institute Code of Ethics and Professional Conduct," accessed March 2, 2012, http://www.pmi.org/~/media/PDF/Ethics/ap_pmicodeofethics.ashx.

17. "Project Management Institute Code of Ethics and Professional Conduct," accessed March 2nd, 2012, http://www.pmi.org/~/media/PDF/Ethics/ap_pmicodeofethics.ashx.

18. "Project Management Institute Code of Ethics and Professional Conduct," accessed March 2nd, 2012, http://www.pmi.org/~/media/PDF/Ethics/ap_pmicodeofethics.ashx.

Chapter 5

1. Bruce Tuckman, "Developmental Sequences in Small Groups" *Psychological Bulletin* 63 (1965): 384–99.
2. "Situational Leadership® II Model" in *Ken Blanchard, Leading at a Higher Level, Revised and Expanded Edition: Blanchard on Leadership and Creating High Performing Organizations* (Upper Saddle River, NJ: FT Press, 2009), 77.
3. Daniel Goleman, Richard Boyatzis, and Annie McKee, "Primal Leadership: The Hidden Driver of Great Performance" *Harvard Business Review* 79, no.11 (2001): 42–51.
4. Jon R. Katzenbach and Douglas K. Smith, *The Wisdom of Teams: Creating the High-Performance Organization* (New York: HarperBusiness, 2003), 45.
5. Lyssa Adkins, Coaching Agile Teams: *A Companion for ScrumMasters, Agile Coaches, and Project Managers in Transition* (Upper Saddle River, NJ: Addison-Wesley, 2010), 26.
6. Patrick M. Lencioni, *The Five Dysfunctions of a Team: A Leadership Fable* (San Francisco: Jossey-Bass, 2002), 188–89.
7. Based on Adkins, *Coaching Agile Teams*, 79.
8. Adkins, *Coaching Agile Teams*, 84–90.
9. Adkins, *Coaching Agile Teams*, 236.
10. Cockburn, *Agile Software Development*, 110.
11. Jean Tabaka, *Collaboration Explained: Facilitation Skills for Software Project Leaders* (Upper Saddle River, NJ: Addison-Wesley, 2006), 176–79.
12. Jim Highsmith, *Agile Project Management: Creating Innovative Products*, 2nd ed. (Upper Saddle River, NJ: Addison-Wesley, 2009), 303.
13. Highsmith. *Agile Project Management*, 304.
14. "Project Management Institute Code of Ethics and Professional Conduct," accessed March 2nd, 2012, http://www.pmi.org/~/media/PDF/Ethics/ap_pmicodeofethics.ashx.

Chapter 6

1. Alfred Korzybski, "A Non-Aristotelian System and its Necessity for Rigour in Mathematics and Physics." Paper presented at the American Mathematical Society at the meeting of the American Association for the Advancement of Science, New Orleans, LA, December 28, 1931.
2. Mark Denne and Jane Cleland-Huang, *Software by Numbers: Low-Risk, High-Return Development* (Upper Saddle River, NJ: Prentice Hall, 2003).
3. Project Management Institute, *A Guide to the Project Management Body of Knowledge (PMBOK® Guide)*, 4th ed. (Newtown Square, PA: Project Management Institute, 2008), 7.
4. Laurie Williams, Gabe Brown, Adam Meltzer, and Nachiappan Nagappan, "Scrum + Engineering Practices: Experiences of Three Microsoft Teams," accessed March 6, 2012, http://collaboration.csc.ncsu.edu/laurie/Papers/ESEM11_SCRUM_Experience_CameraReady.pdf.
5. Mike Cohn, *User Stories Applied: For Agile Software Development* (Upper Saddle River, NJ: Addison-Wesley, 2004), 87.
6. Project Management Institute, *A Guide to the Project Management Body of Knowledge (PMBOK® Guide)*, 4th ed. (Newtown Square, PA: Project Management Institute, 2008).
7. "Project Management Institute Code of Ethics and Professional Conduct," accessed March 2, 2012, http://www.pmi.org/~/media/PDF/Ethics/ap_pmicodeofethics.ashx.
8. Project Management Institute, *A Guide to the Project Management Body of Knowledge (PMBOK® Guide)*, 4th ed. (Newtown Square, PA: Project Management Institute, 2008), 7, 135.
9. "Project Management Institute Code of Ethics and Professional Conduct," accessed March 2nd, 2012, http://www.pmi.org/~/media/PDF/Ethics/ap_pmicodeofethics.ashx.

Chapter 7

1. Cockburn, *Agile Software Development*, 72.
2. Cockburn, *Agile Software Development*, 91.
3. Cockburn, *Agile Software Development*, 79–91.
4. Mary Poppendieck and Tom Poppendieck, *Leading Lean Software Development: Results Are Not the Point* (Upper Saddle River, NJ: Addison-Wesley, 2009), 14–15.

5. W. Edwards Deming, *The New Economics for Industry, Government, Education*, 2nd ed. (Cambridge, MA: MIT Press, 2000), 99.

6. W. Edwards Deming, *The New Economics*, 174.

7. Visual Studio is a trademark of the Microsoft group of companies.

8. Net is a trademark of the Microsoft group of companies. Java is a registered trademark of Oracle and/or its affiliates.

9. The Framework for Integrated Testing (FIT) was developed by Ward Cunningham. For more information about FIT and FitNesse, see http://fitnesse.org and http://fit.c2.com/.

10. "Project Management Institute Code of Ethics and Professional Conduct," accessed March 2, 2012, http://www.pmi. org/~/media/PDF/Ethics/ap_pmicodeofethics.ashx.

Chapter 8

1. Esther Derby and Diana Larsen, *Agile Retrospectives: Making Good Teams Great* (Dallas, TX: Pragmatic Bookshelf, 2006), 18.

2. Derby and Larsen, *Agile Retrospectives*, 43.

3. Derby and Larsen, *Agile Retrospectives*, 46.

4. Derby and Larsen, *Agile Retrospectives*, 111.

5. Project is a trademark of the Microsoft group of companies. Primavera is a registered trademark of Oracle and/or its affiliates.

6. Kimiz Dalkir, *Knowledge Management in Theory and Practice*, 2nd ed. (Cambridge, MA: MIT Press, 2011), 169.

7. Robert D. Austin, *Measuring and Managing Performance in Organizations*, (Dorset House, 1996).

8. Mary Poppendieck, "Measure Up," *Lean Software Development* (blog), January 6, 2003, http://www.leanessays. com/2003_01_01_archive.html.

9. David J. Anderson, *Kanban: Successful Evolutionary Change for Your Technology Business* (Sequim, WA: Blue Hole Press, 2010), 17.

10. Cockburn, *Agile Software Development*, 175–79.

11. Cockburn, *Agile Software Development*, 182.

12. "PMI Agile Certified Practitioner (PMI-ACP)^{SM}: Examination Content Outline," accessed March 14, 2012, http://www. pmi.org/en/Certification/~/media/Files/PDF/Agile/PMI_Agile_Certification_Content_Outline.ashx.

13. "Project Management Institute Code of Ethics and Professional Conduct," accessed March 2, 2012, http://www.pmi. org/~/media/PDF/Ethics/ap_pmicodeofethics.ashx.

14. "Project Management Institute Code of Ethics and Professional Conduct," accessed March 2, 2012, http://www.pmi. org/~/media/PDF/Ethics/ap_pmicodeofethics.ashx, 1.

15. "Project Management Institute Code of Ethics and Professional Conduct," accessed March 2, 2012, http://www.pmi. org/~/media/PDF/Ethics/ap_pmicodeofethics.ashx, 1–5.

16. "Project Management Institute Code of Ethics and Professional Conduct," accessed March 2, 2012, http://www.pmi. org/~/media/PDF/Ethics/ap_pmicodeofethics.ashx, 2–3.

17. "Project Management Institute Code of Ethics and Professional Conduct," accessed March 2, 2012, http://www.pmi. org/~/media/PDF/Ethics/ap_pmicodeofethics.ashx.

18. "PMI Agile Certified Practitioner (PMI-ACP)^{SM}: Examination Content Outline," accessed March 14, 2012, http://www. pmi.org/en/Certification/~/media/Files/PDF/Agile/PMI_Agile_Certification_Content_Outline.ashx.

19. Paul Arveson, "The Deming Cycle," *Balanced Scorecard Institute*, accessed March 14, 2012, http://www. balancedscorecard.org/TheDemingCycle/tabid/112/Default.aspx.

20. Shore and Warden, *The Art of Agile Development*, 67.

21. Shore and Warden, *The Art of Agile Development*, 68.

22. Shore and Warden, *The Art of Agile Development*, 67.

23. Tabaka, *Collaboration Explained*, 22.

INDEX

N

Negotiation   23, 127, 144
Net present value (NPV)   63, 65, 235
Norming (team formation)   169, 189
Notifications   269
NPV   (see *Net present value*)

O

Osmotic communication   47, 187, 188, 302, 309
Outsourced vs. distributed   189

P

Padding   241
Pair programming   39, 43, 147, 255, 273, 304, 314
Parametric estimates   227
Parking lot diagram   45
Parkinson's Law   228
Participatory decision models   151, 217
Payback period   65, 66, 207
People factor   169
People vs. process   168
Performing (team formation)   169
Persona   123, 304
PEST analysis   (see *Political, economic, social, and technical analysis*)
Plan, develop, evaluate, learn cycle   314
Plan, do, check, act cycle   314
Planned value (PV)   101
Planning, adaptive   (see *Adaptive planning*)
Planning concepts   201
Planning, iteration   (See *Iteration planning*)
Planning poker   190, 214, 216
Planning, release   (See *Release planning*)
Planning, sprint   (see *Sprint planning meeting*)
Planning value   68
Plus/delta (retrospective)   301
PMI's Code of Ethics and Professional Conduct (see also *Professional responsibility and ethics*)   312
Point, story   (see *Story point*)
Political, economic, social, and technical (PEST) analysis   235
Pomodoro timer   202
Present value (see also *Net present value*)   65
Principles behind the Agile Manifesto   (see *Agile Manifesto, principles*)
Principles of systems thinking   307, 308
Prioritization   68, 74, 77, 82, 96, 129, 131, 144, 185, 201, 206
Prioritization, customer-valued   (see *Customer-valued prioritization*)
Prioritization, relative   (see *Relative prioritization and ranking*)
Prioritization schemes   74
Prioritization, value-based   (see *Value-based decomposition and prioritization*)
Prioritize with dots   280
Probability   (see *Risk probability and impact*)

Problem detection and resolution   8, 249
Problem identification   (see *Identifying problems*)
Problem resolution   (see *Resolving problems*)
Problem solving   277, 300
Problem solving, steps   277, 300
Problem solving, team   284
Process analysis   308
Process cycle efficiency   70
Process tailoring   51, 204, 305, 308
Process vs. people   (see *People vs. process*)
Procurement   (see *Agile contracting* and *Vendor management*)
Product backlog   36, 38
Product owner (Scrum team)   36
Product roadmap (see also *Story map*)   78, 131
Professional responsibility and ethics   54, 110, 159, 191, 241, 286, 312
Progress reporting   28, 98, 137, 228
Progressive elaboration   203, 209, 229
Project and quality standards   257
Project charter   (see *Charter*)
Project selection   (see *Business case development, Internal rate of return, Net present value, Payback period,* and *Return on investment*)
Project Tweet   234
Project vision   155, 158, 178, 189, 208, 235
Prototype (see also *Demonstration*)   97, 229
Prune the product tree   210, 211
Pull system   49, 50
PV   (see *Planned value*)

Q

Quality standards   (see *Project and quality standards*)
Quiet time   280
Quiet work period   260
Quiet writing   184

R

Ranking   (see *Relative prioritization and ranking*)
Rapid application development (RAD)   28
Real options   312
Red, green, refactor (Red, green, clean)   274
Refactoring   29, 43, 48, 274
Relative prioritization and ranking   77
Relative sizing   219
Release   41, 78, 131, 236
Release planning   40, 41, 204, 236
Remember the future   210
Requirements   38, 97, 123, 129, 144, 203, 209, 222, 229, 275
Requirements hierarchy   129
Requirements prioritization model   75
Resolving problems   268
Respect (XP value)   39
Retrospective   30, 131, 147, 204, 277, 294, 303, 314
Retrospective planning game   282

© 2012 RMC Publications, Inc • 952.846.4484 • info@rmcproject.com • www.rmcproject.com